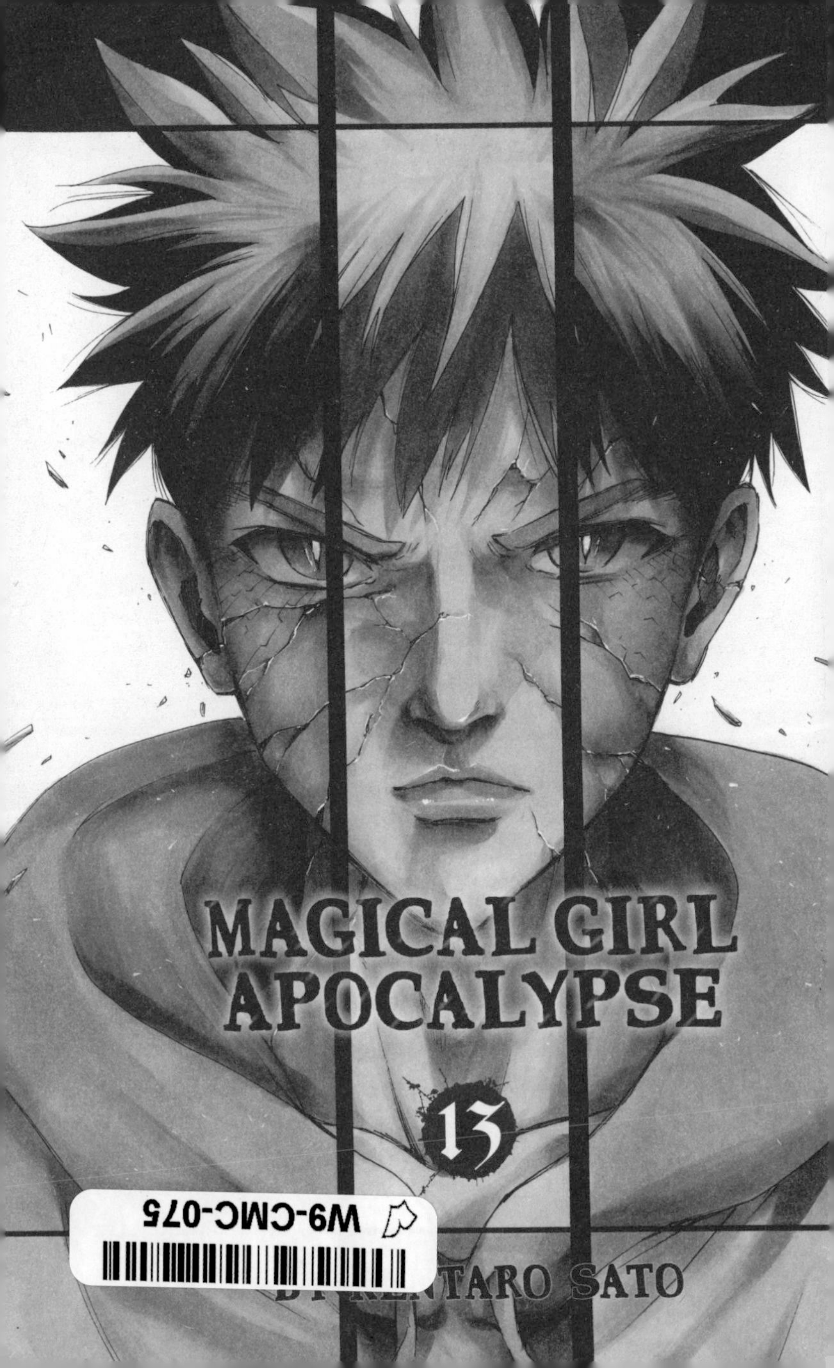
MAGICAL GIRL
APOCALYPSE
13
TARO SATO

Previously, in *Magical Girl Apocalypse...*

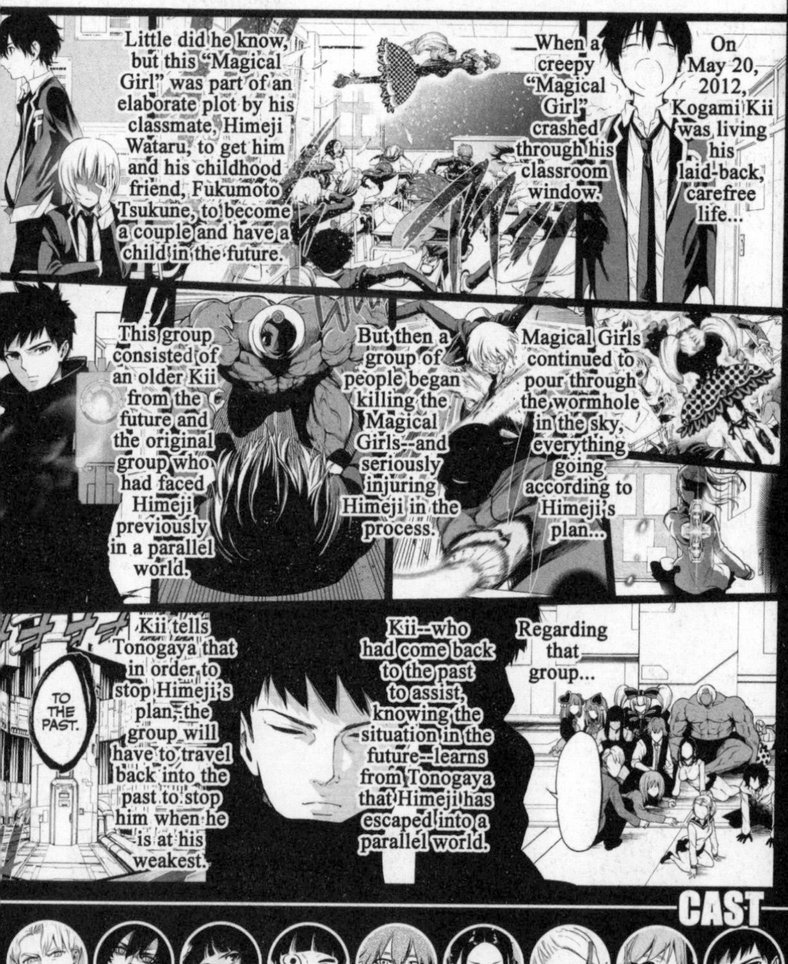
On May 20, 2012, Kogami Kii was living his laid-back, carefree life...
When a creepy "Magical Girl" crashed through his classroom window.
Little did he know, but this "Magical Girl" was part of an elaborate plot by his classmate, Himeji Wataru, to get him and his childhood friend, Fukumoto Tsukune, to become a couple and have a child in the future.
Magical Girls continued to pour through the wormhole in the sky, everything going according to Himeji's plan...
But then a group of people began killing the Magical Girls--and seriously injuring Himeji in the process.
This group consisted of an older Kii from the future and the original group who had faced Himeji previously in a parallel world.
Regarding that group...
Kii--who had come back to the past to assist, knowing the situation in the future--learns from Tonogaya that Himeji has escaped into a parallel world.
Kii tells Tonogaya that in order to stop Himeji's plan, the group will have to travel back into the past to stop him when he is at his weakest.
TO THE PAST.

CAST

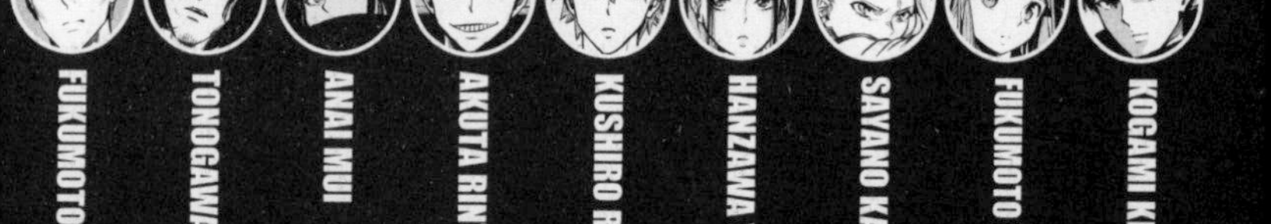

KOGAMI KII

FUKUMOTO TSUKUNE

SAYANO KAEDE

HANZAWA YORUKA

KUSHIRO REN

AKUTA RINTAROU

ANAI MUI

TONOGAWA YUUJI

FUKUMOTO SEIICHI

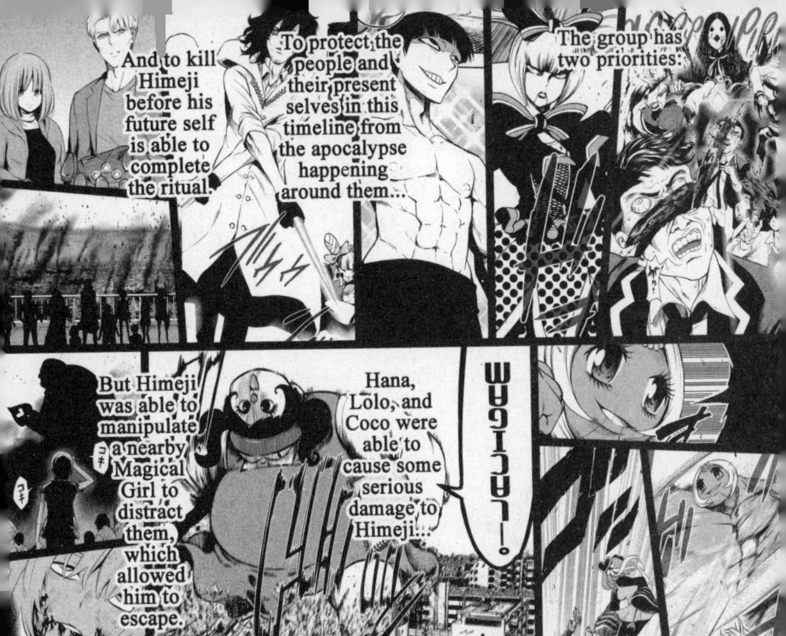
The group has two priorities:
To protect the people and their present selves in this timeline from the apocalypse happening around them...
And to kill Himeji before his future self is able to complete the ritual.
MAGICAL!
Hana, Lolo, and Coco were able to cause some serious damage to Himeji...
But Himeji was able to manipulate a nearby Magical Girl to distract them, which allowed him to escape.
Upon learning this, the future Kii speculated that Himeji would try to retreat through the wormhole and back to the future.
Tonogaya finds Himeji heading towards the wormhole, placing Kii's plans into serious jeopardy...
But then Sayano Kaede descended through the wormhole, accompanied by a strange girl in a white suit. Kaede calls the girl "Wataru" and orders her to attack Himeji...?!

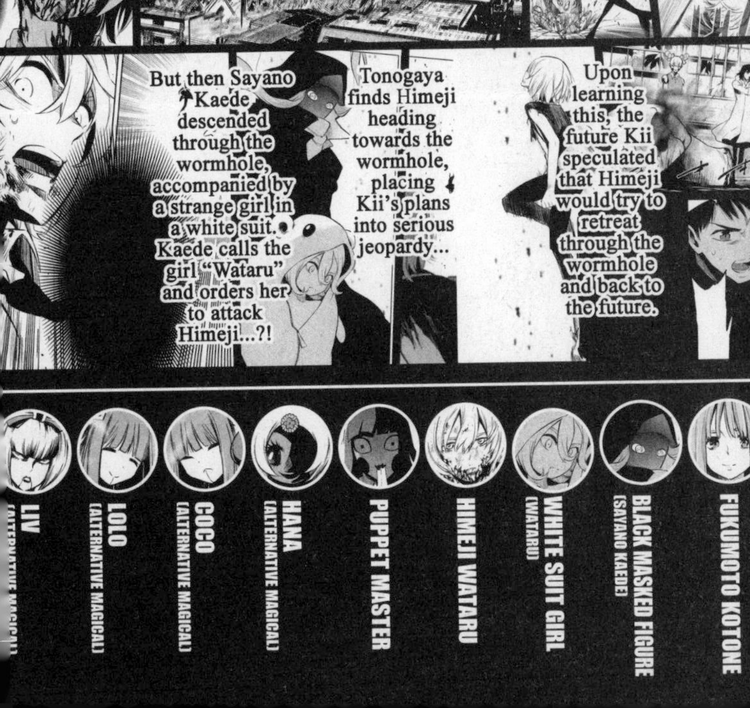
FUKUMOTO KOTONE
BLACK MASKED FIGURE [SAYANO KAEDE]
WHITE SUIT GIRL [WATARU]
HIMEJI WATARU
PUPPET MASTER
HANA [ALTERNATIVE MAGICAL]
COCO [ALTERNATIVE MAGICAL]
LOLO [ALTERNATIVE MAGICAL]
LIV

SEVEN SEAS ENTERTAINMENT PRESENTS

MAGICAL GIRL APOCALYPSE

story and art by KENTARO SATO   VOLUME 13

TRANSLATION
Wesley Bridges

ADAPTATION
Janet Houck

LETTERING AND LAYOUT
Meaghan Tucker

LOGO DESIGN
Phil Balsman

COVER DESIGN
Nicky Lim

PROOFREADER
Shanti Whitesides

ASSISTANT EDITOR
Jenn Grunigen

PRODUCTION ASSISTANT
CK Russell

PRODUCTION MANAGER
Lissa Pattillo

EDITOR-IN-CHIEF
Adam Arnold

PUBLISHER
Jason DeAngelis

MAHO SYOJYO OF THE END Volume 13
© Kentaro Sato 2016
Originally published in Japan in 2016 by Akita Publishing Co., Ltd..
English translation rights arranged with Akita Publishing Co., Ltd. through
TOHAN CORPORATION, Tokyo.

Seven Seas books may be purchased in bulk for promotional, educational, or
business use. Please contact your local bookseller or the Macmillan Corporate
and Premium Sales Department at 1-800-221-7945, extension 5442, or by
e-mail at MacmillanSpecialMarkets@macmillan.com.

Seven Seas and the Seven Seas logo are trademarks of
Seven Seas Entertainment, LLC. All rights reserved.

ISBN: 978-1-626925-92-2

Printed in Canada

First Printing: December 2017

10 9 8 7 6 5 4 3 2 1

FOLLOW US ONLINE: www.gomanga.com

READING DIRECTIONS

This book reads from *right to left*, Japanese style.
If this is your first time reading manga, you start
reading from the top right panel on each page and
take it from there. If you get lost, just follow the
numbered diagram here. It may seem backwards at
first, but you'll get the hang of it! Have fun!!

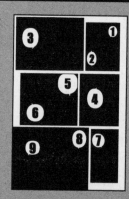

048.white W -white double-

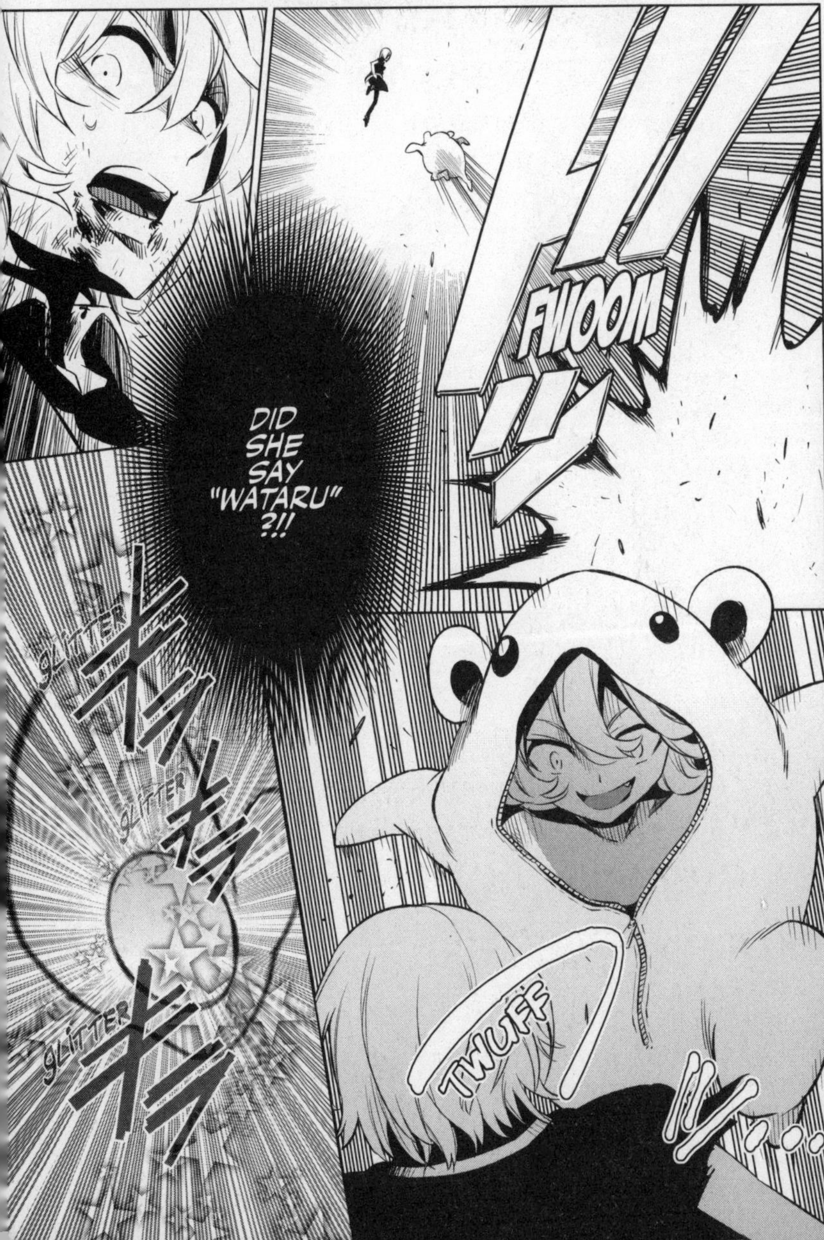
FWOOM
DID SHE SAY "WATARU"?!!
TWUFF
GLITTER
GLITTER
GLITTER

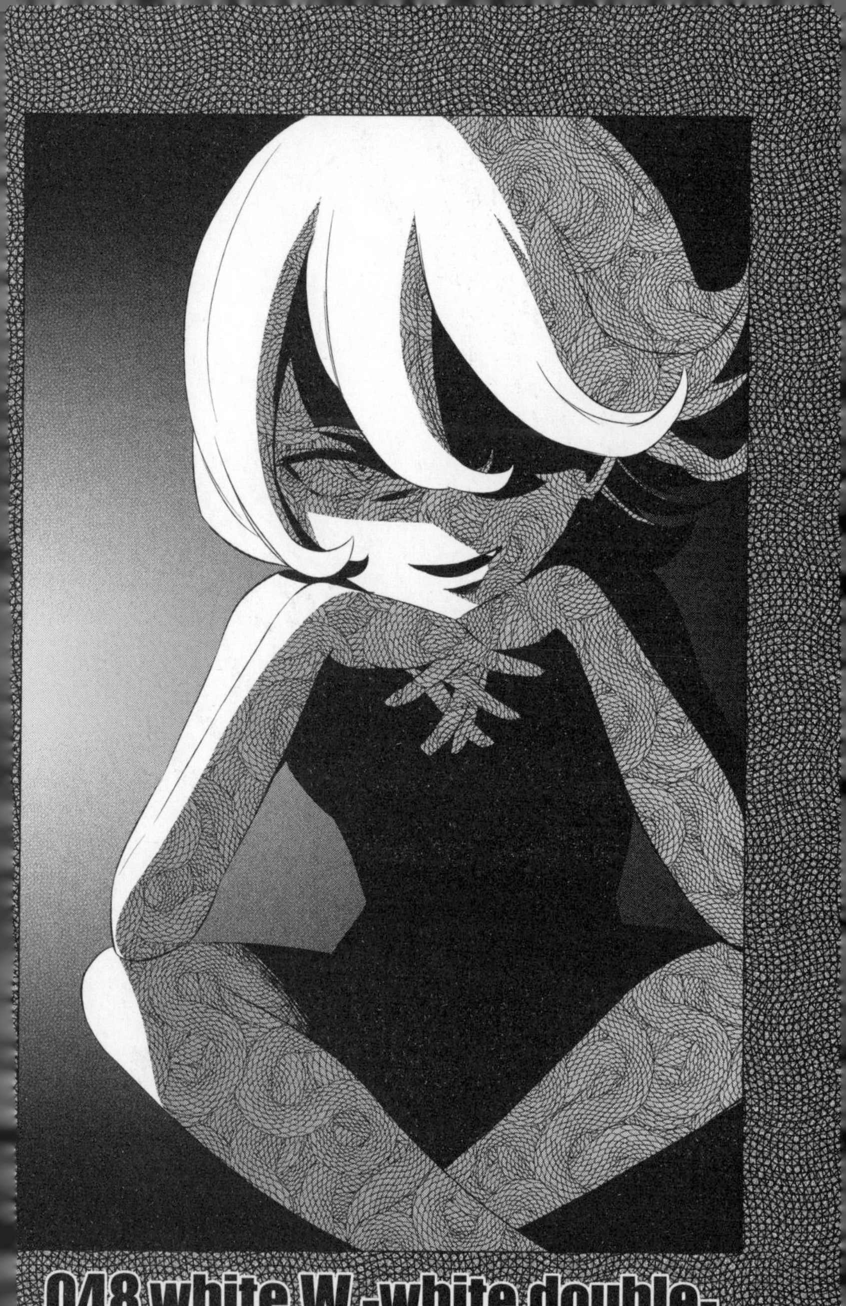

048.white W -white double-

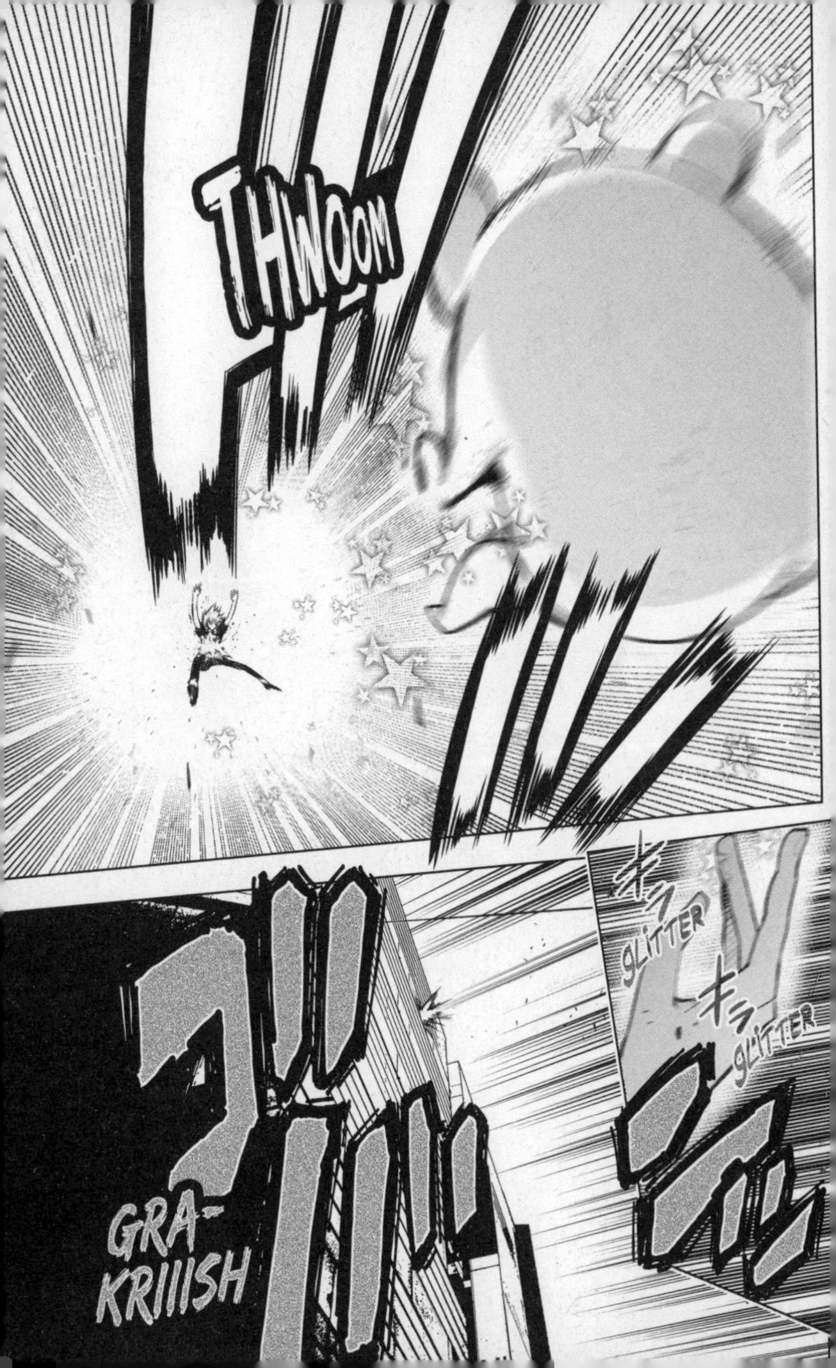
THWOOM
キラ
GLITTER
キラ
GLITTER
GRA-
KRIIISH

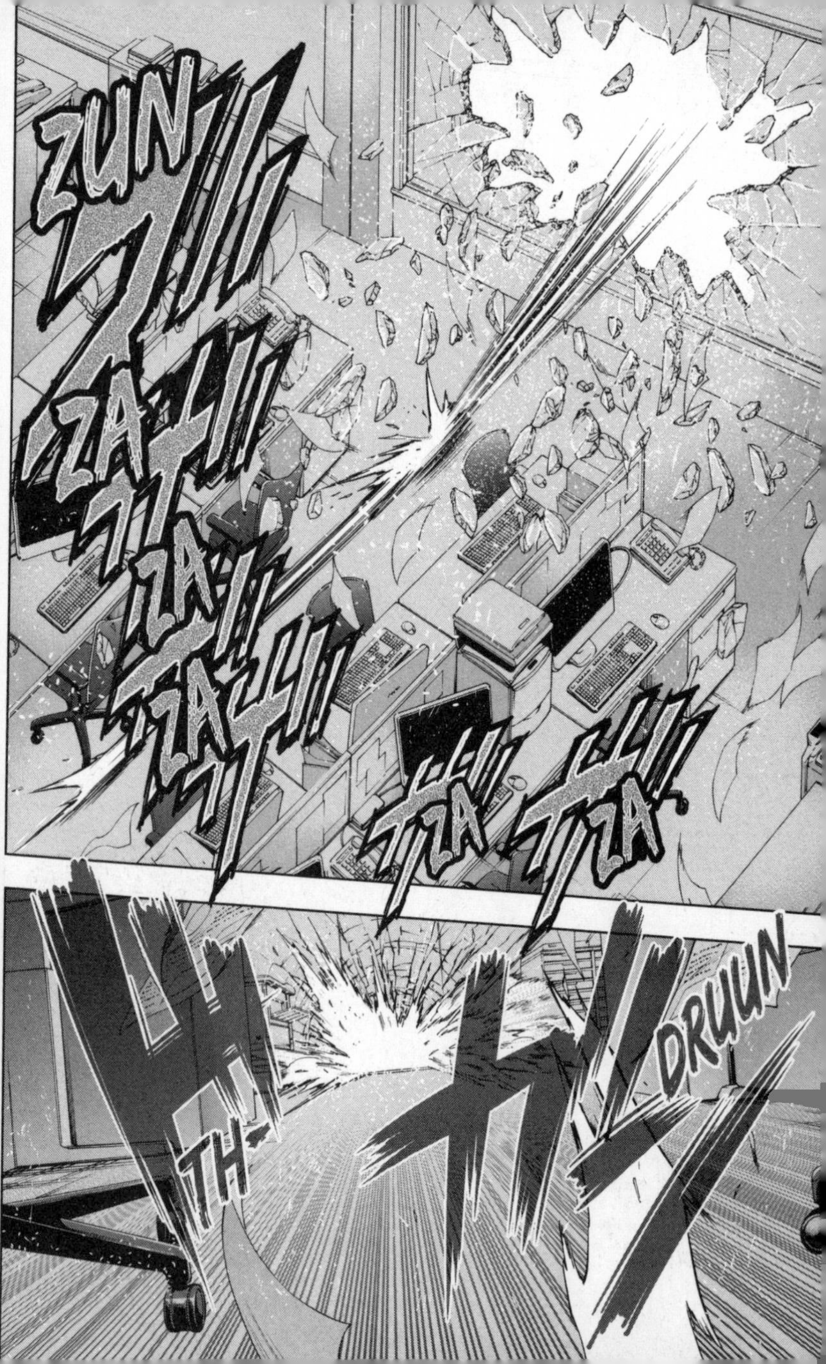
ZUN
ZA
ZA
ZA
ZA
ZA
DRUUN
TH

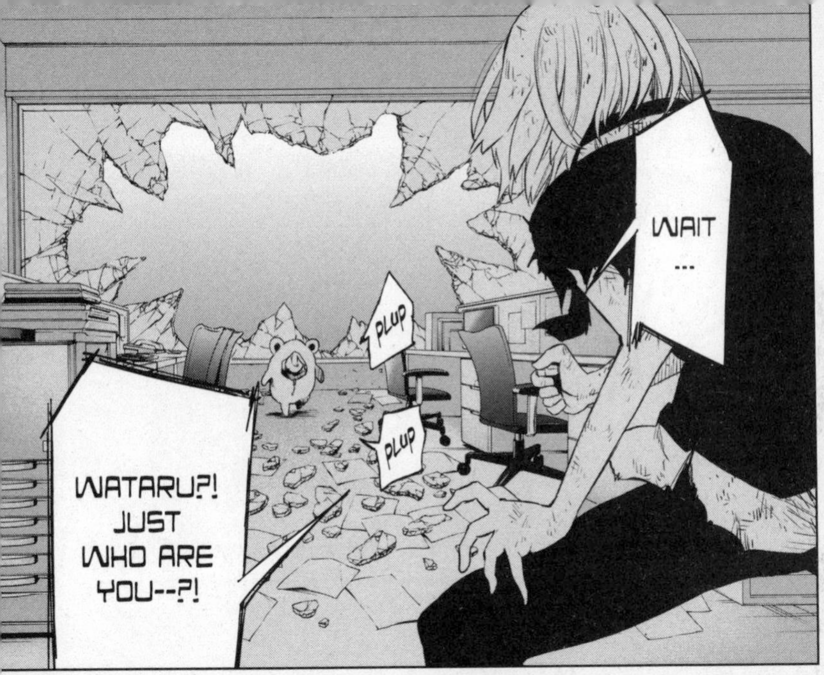
WAIT ...
PLUP
PLUP
WATARU?! JUST WHO ARE YOU--?!

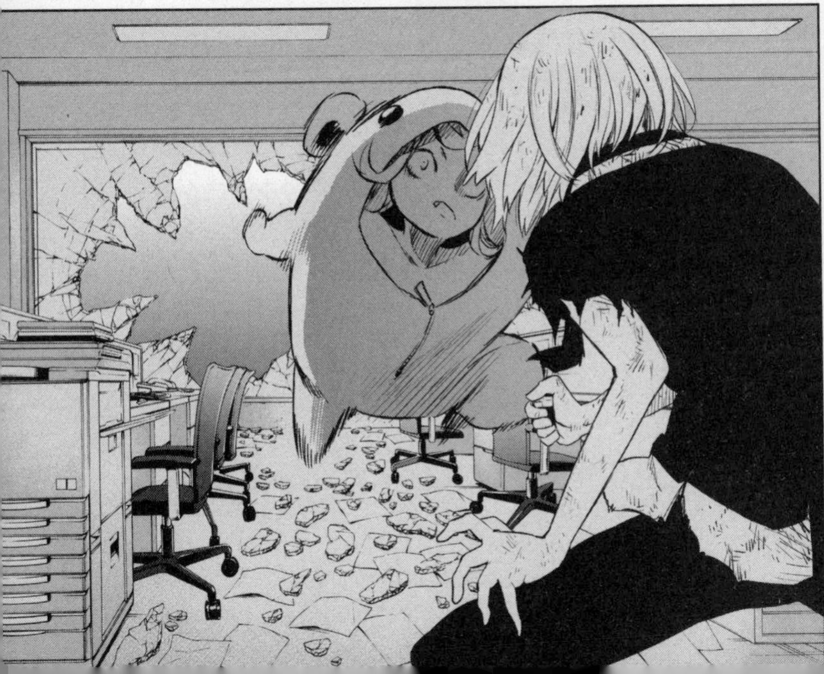

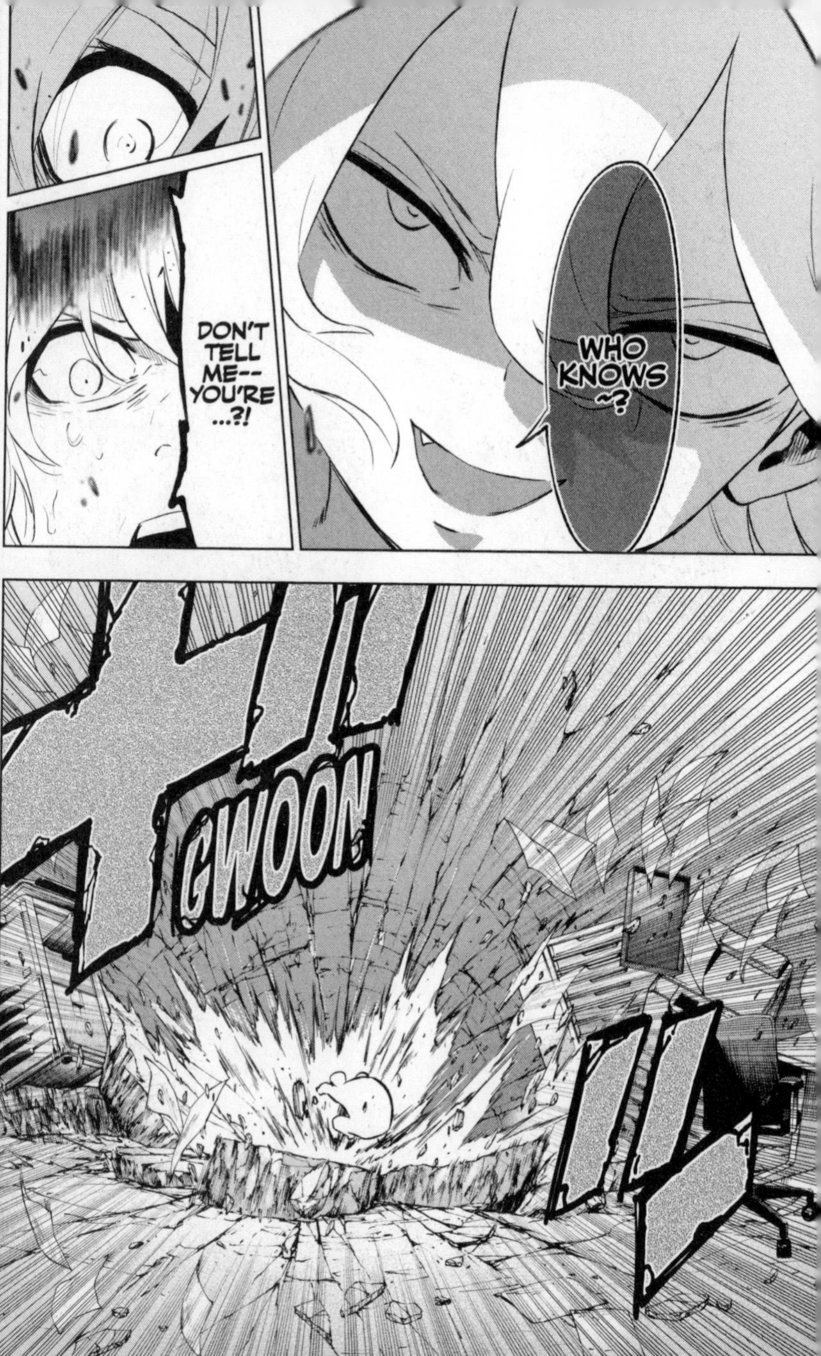
DON'T TELL ME-- YOU'RE ...?!
WHO KNOWS ~?
GWOON

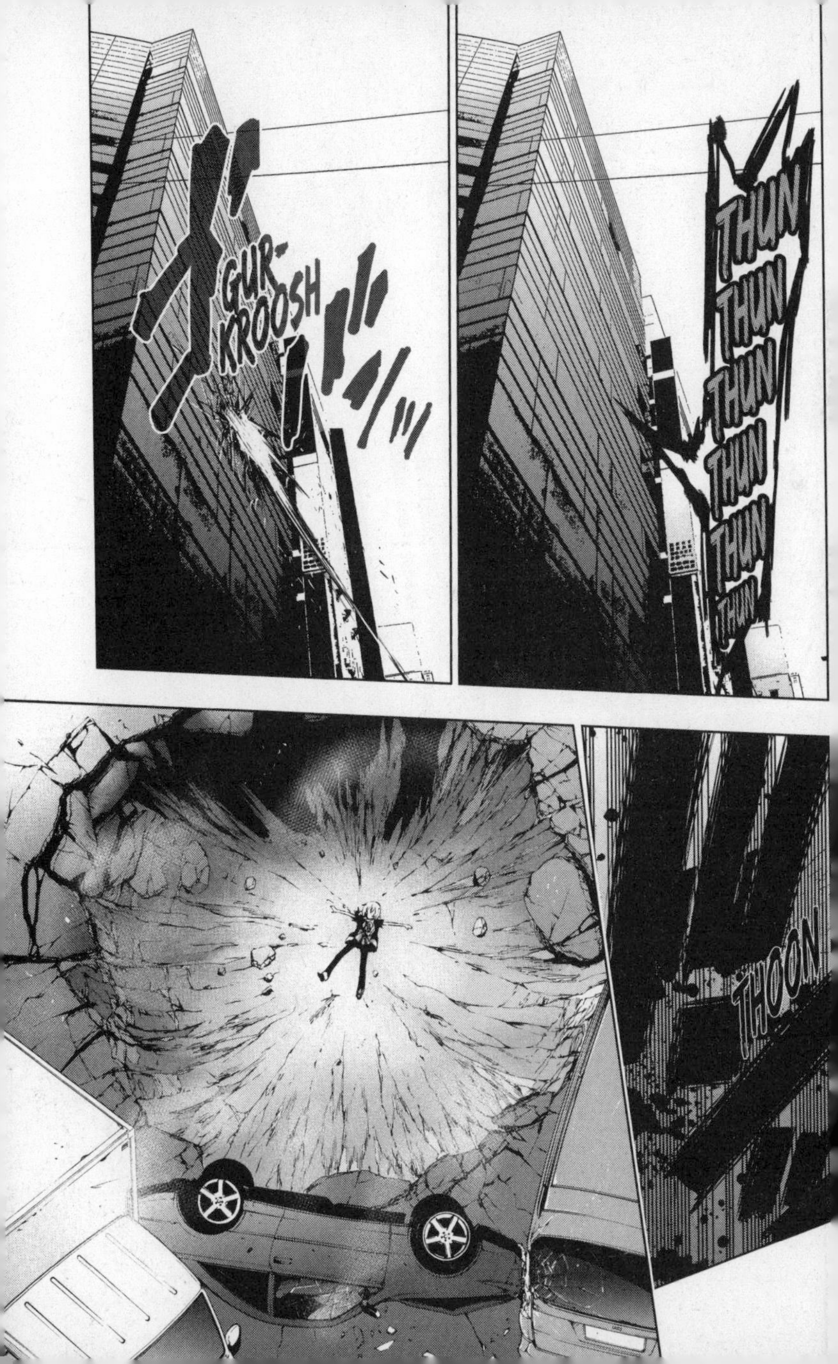
THUN THUN THUN THUN THUN THUN
GUR-KROOSH
THOON

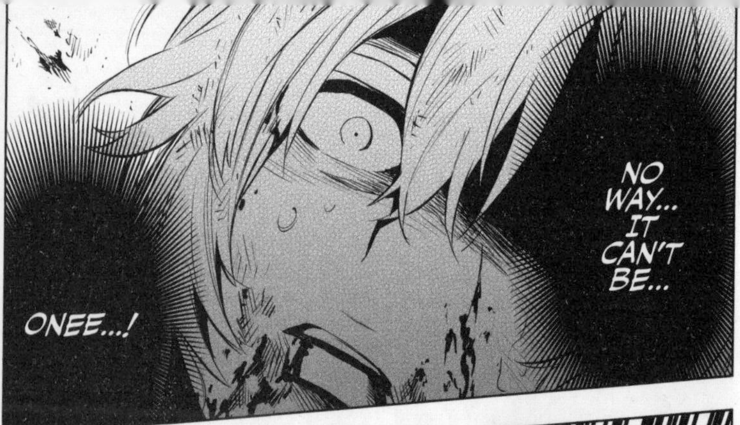
NO WAY... IT CAN'T BE...
ONEE...!
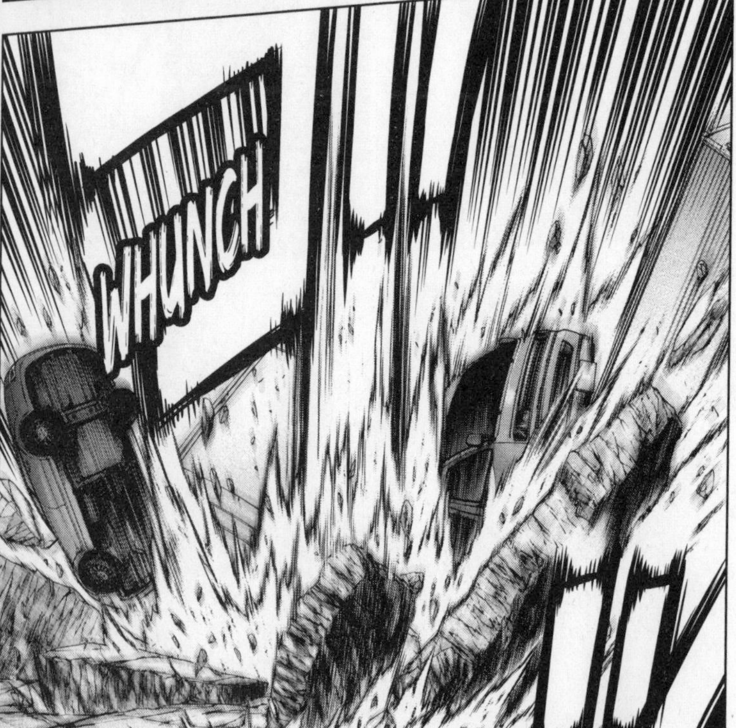
WHUNCH

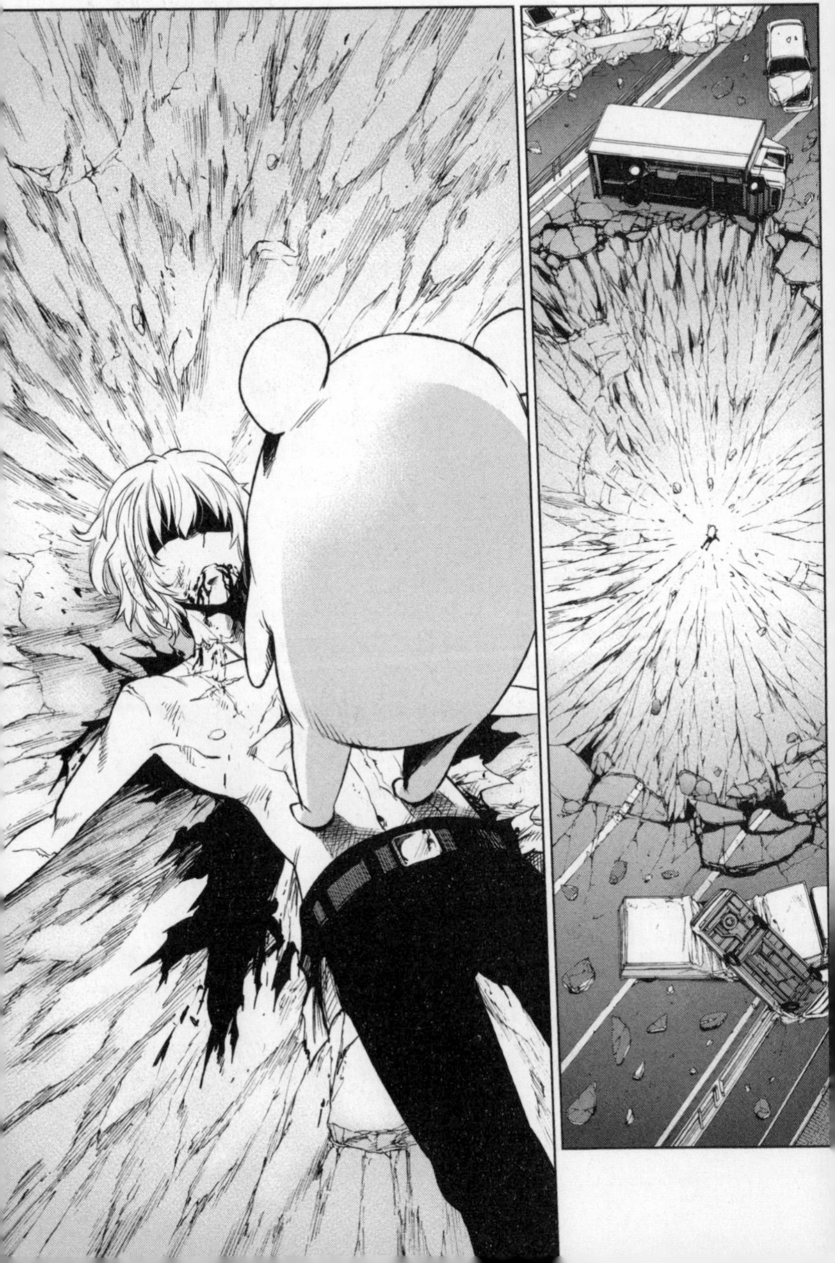

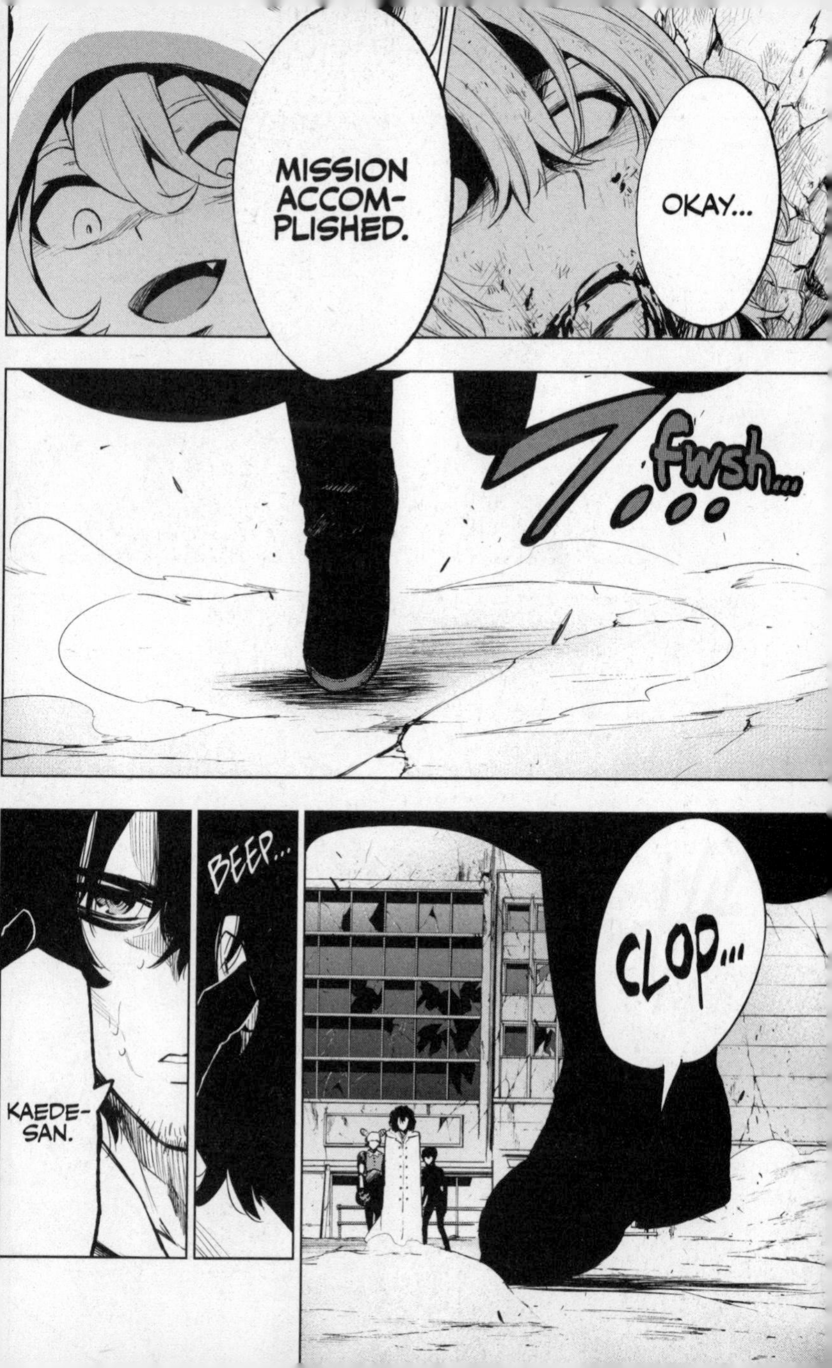
OKAY...
MISSION ACCOMPLISHED.
fwsh...
CLOP...
BEEP...
KAEDE-SAN.

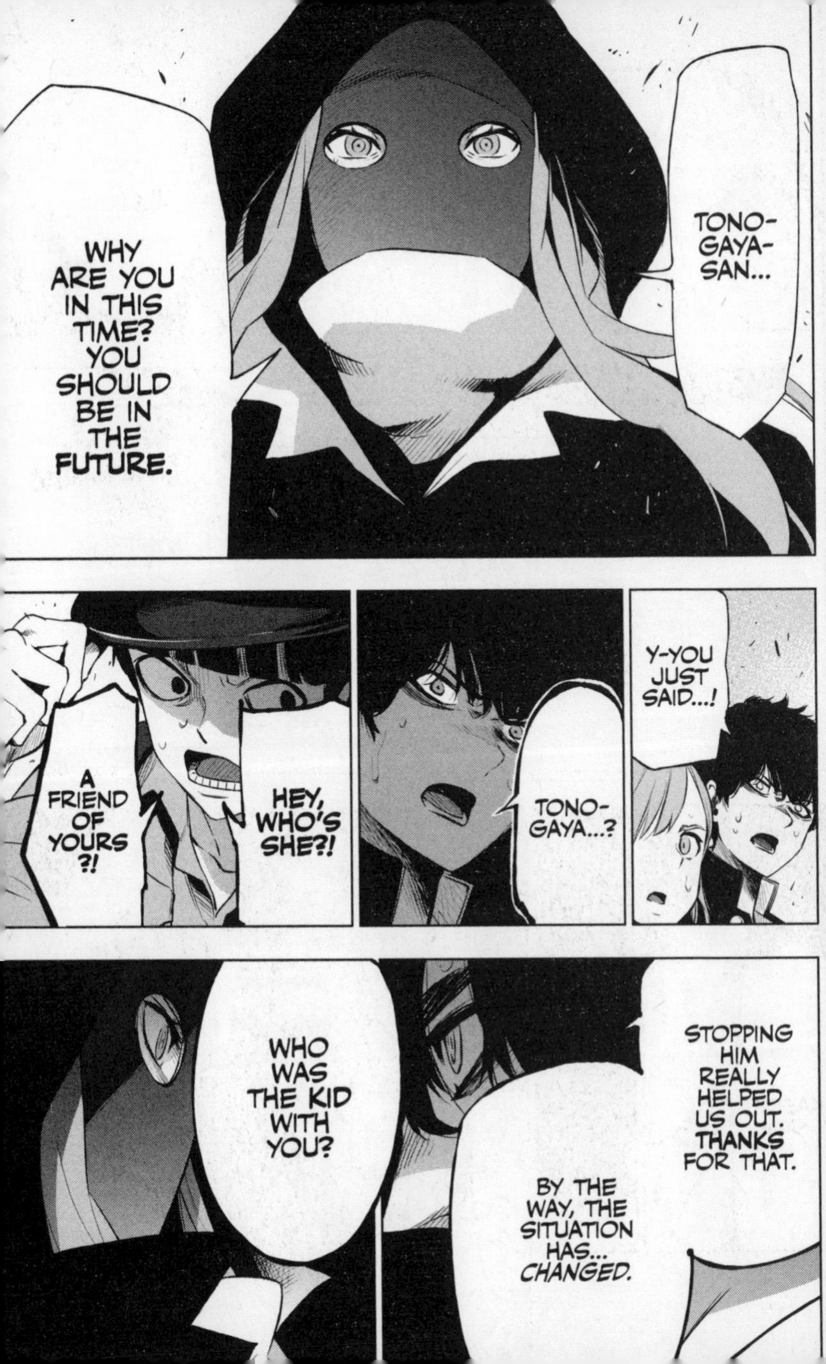
TONO-GAYA-SAN...
WHY ARE YOU IN THIS TIME? YOU SHOULD BE IN THE FUTURE.
Y-YOU JUST SAID...!
TONO-GAYA...?
HEY, WHO'S SHE?!
A FRIEND OF YOURS?!
STOPPING HIM REALLY HELPED US OUT. THANKS FOR THAT.
BY THE WAY, THE SITUATION HAS... CHANGED.
WHO WAS THE KID WITH YOU?

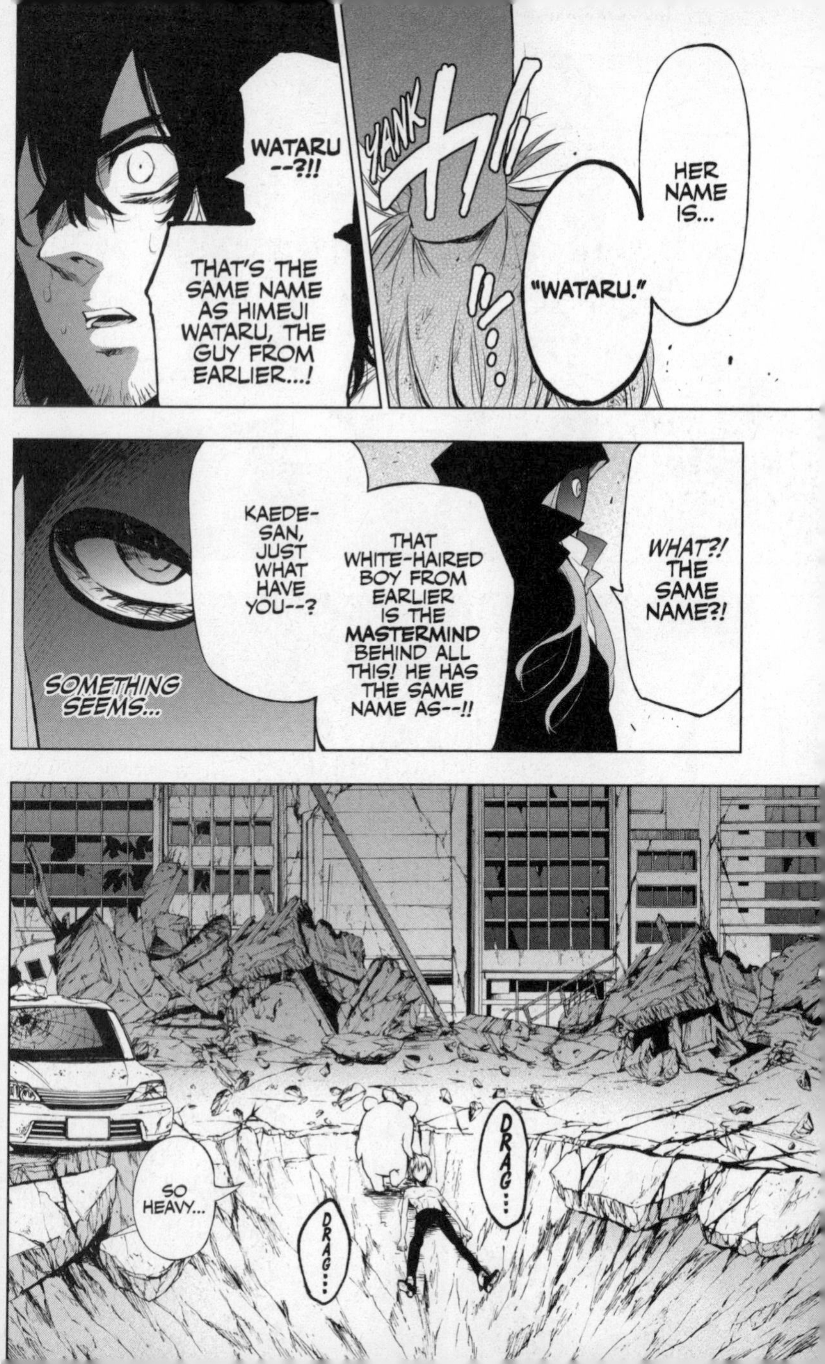
HER NAME IS...
"WATARU."
YANK
WATARU --?!!
THAT'S THE SAME NAME AS HIMEJI WATARU, THE GUY FROM EARLIER...!
WHAT?! THE SAME NAME?!
THAT WHITE-HAIRED BOY FROM EARLIER IS THE **MASTERMIND** BEHIND ALL THIS! HE HAS THE SAME NAME AS--!!
KAEDE-SAN, JUST WHAT HAVE YOU--?
SOMETHING SEEMS...
DRAG...
DRAG...
SO HEAVY...

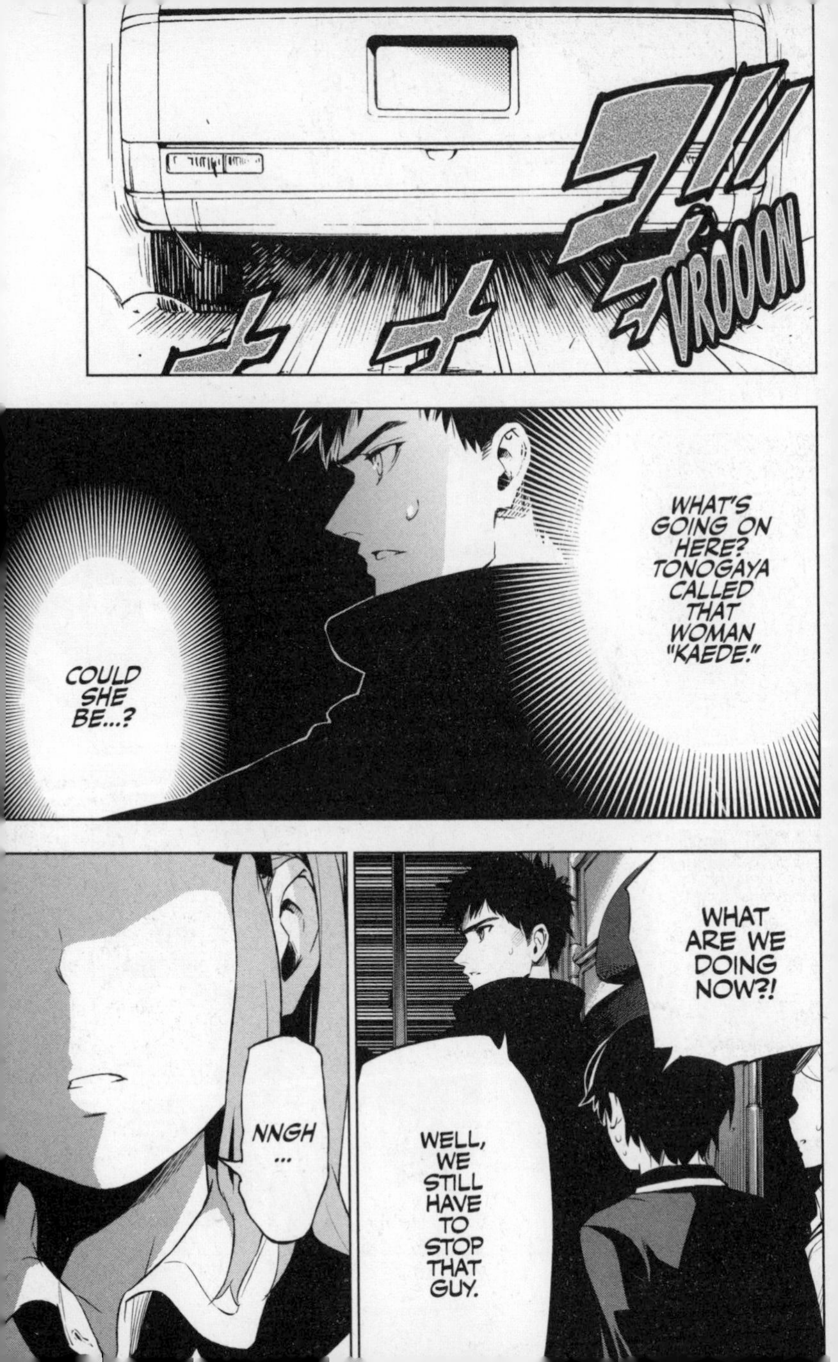
VROOON
WHAT'S GOING ON HERE? TONOGAYA CALLED THAT WOMAN "KAEDE."
COULD SHE BE...?
WHAT ARE WE DOING NOW?!
WELL, WE STILL HAVE TO STOP THAT GUY.
NNGH...

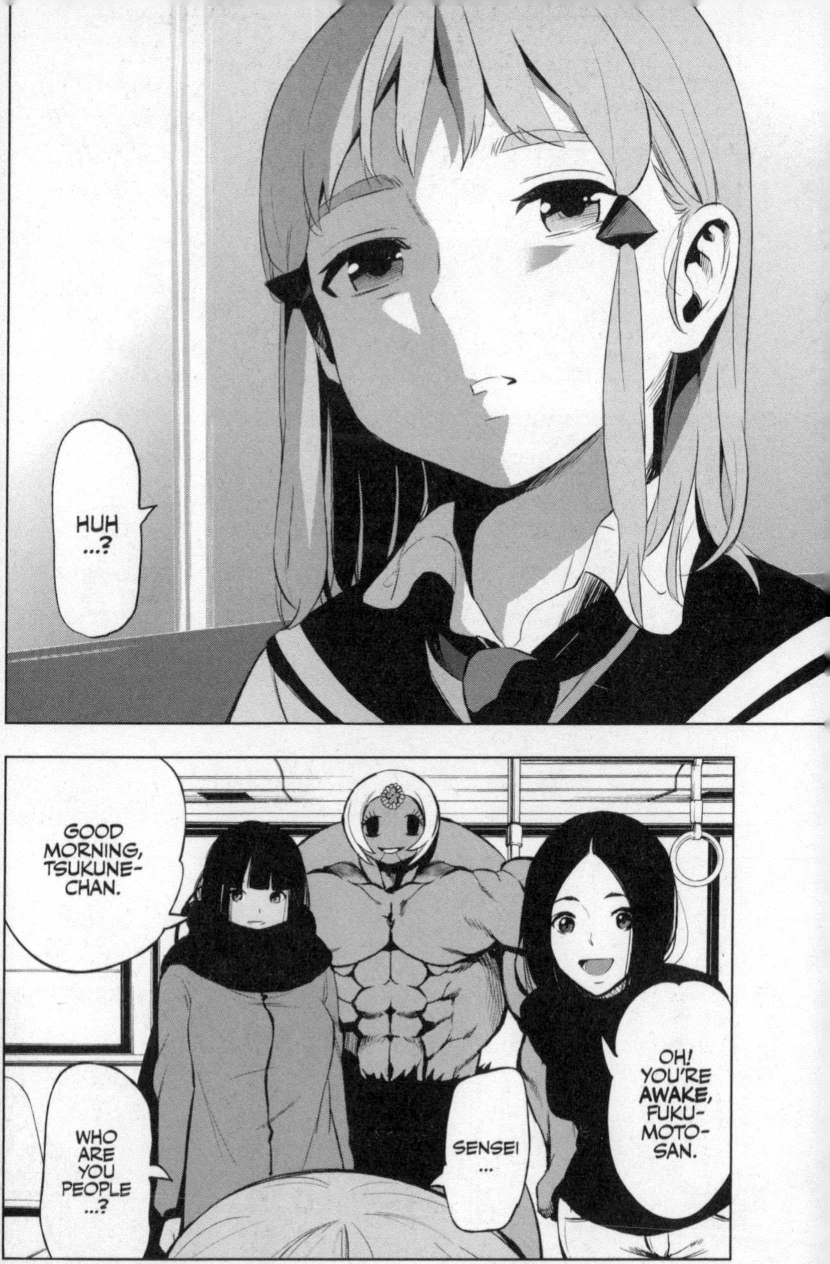
HUH ...?
OH! YOU'RE AWAKE, FUKU-MOTO-SAN.
GOOD MORNING, TSUKUNE-CHAN.
SENSEI ...
WHO ARE YOU PEOPLE ...?

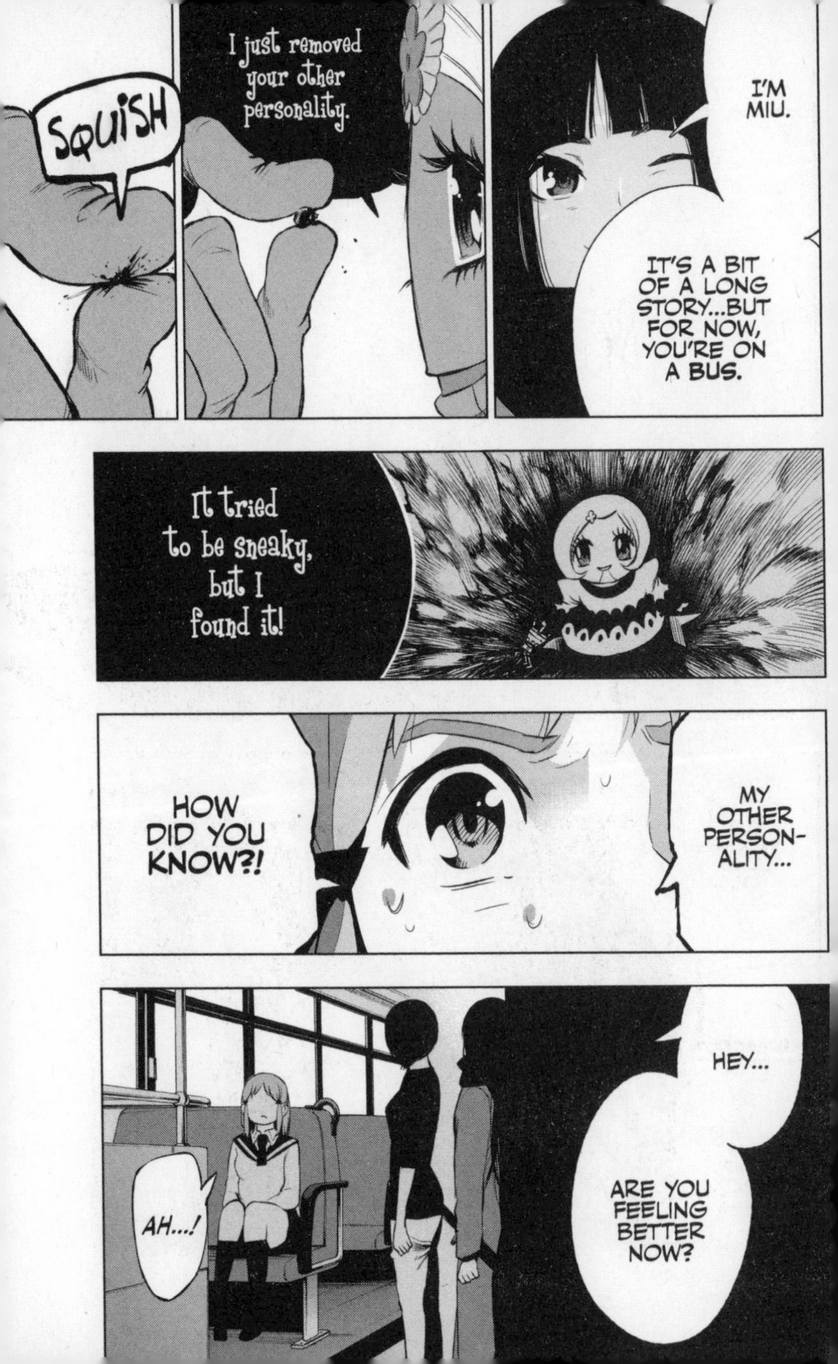
I'M MIU.
IT'S A BIT OF A LONG STORY...BUT FOR NOW, YOU'RE ON A BUS.
I just removed your other personality.
SQUISH
It tried to be sneaky, but I found it!
MY OTHER PERSON-ALITY...
HOW DID YOU KNOW?!
HEY...
ARE YOU FEELING BETTER NOW?
AH...!

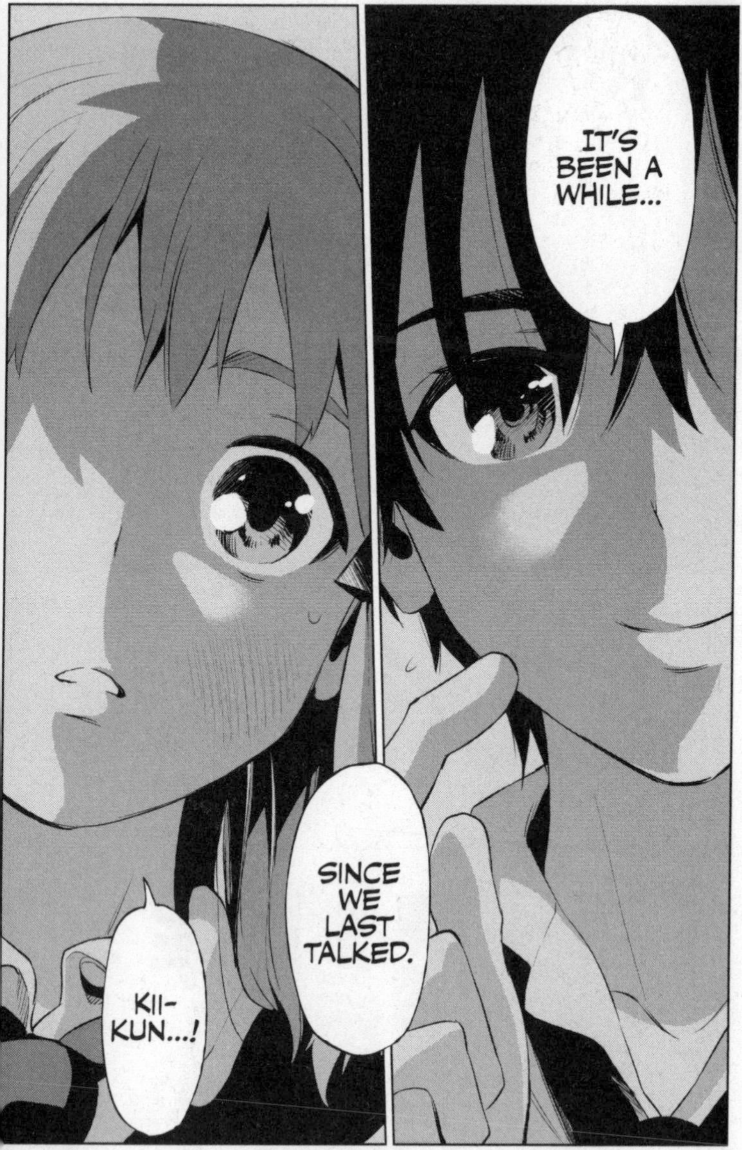
IT'S BEEN A WHILE...
SINCE WE LAST TALKED.
KII-KUN...!

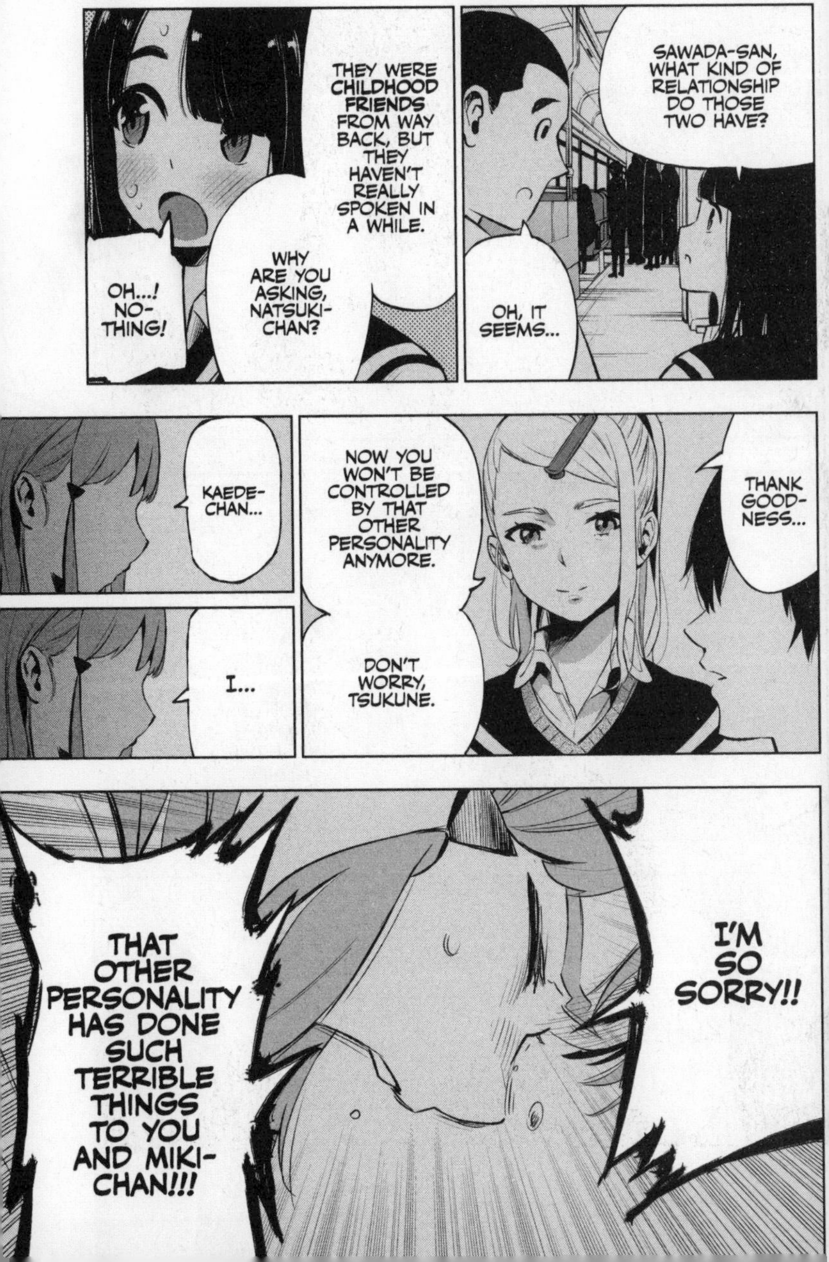
SAWADA-SAN, WHAT KIND OF RELATIONSHIP DO THOSE TWO HAVE?
OH, IT SEEMS...
THEY WERE CHILDHOOD FRIENDS FROM WAY BACK, BUT THEY HAVEN'T REALLY SPOKEN IN A WHILE.
WHY ARE YOU ASKING, NATSUKI-CHAN?
OH...! NO-THING!
THANK GOOD-NESS...
NOW YOU WON'T BE CONTROLLED BY THAT OTHER PERSONALITY ANYMORE.
DON'T WORRY, TSUKUNE.
KAEDE-CHAN...
I...
I'M SO SORRY!!
THAT OTHER PERSONALITY HAS DONE SUCH TERRIBLE THINGS TO YOU AND MIKI-CHAN!!!

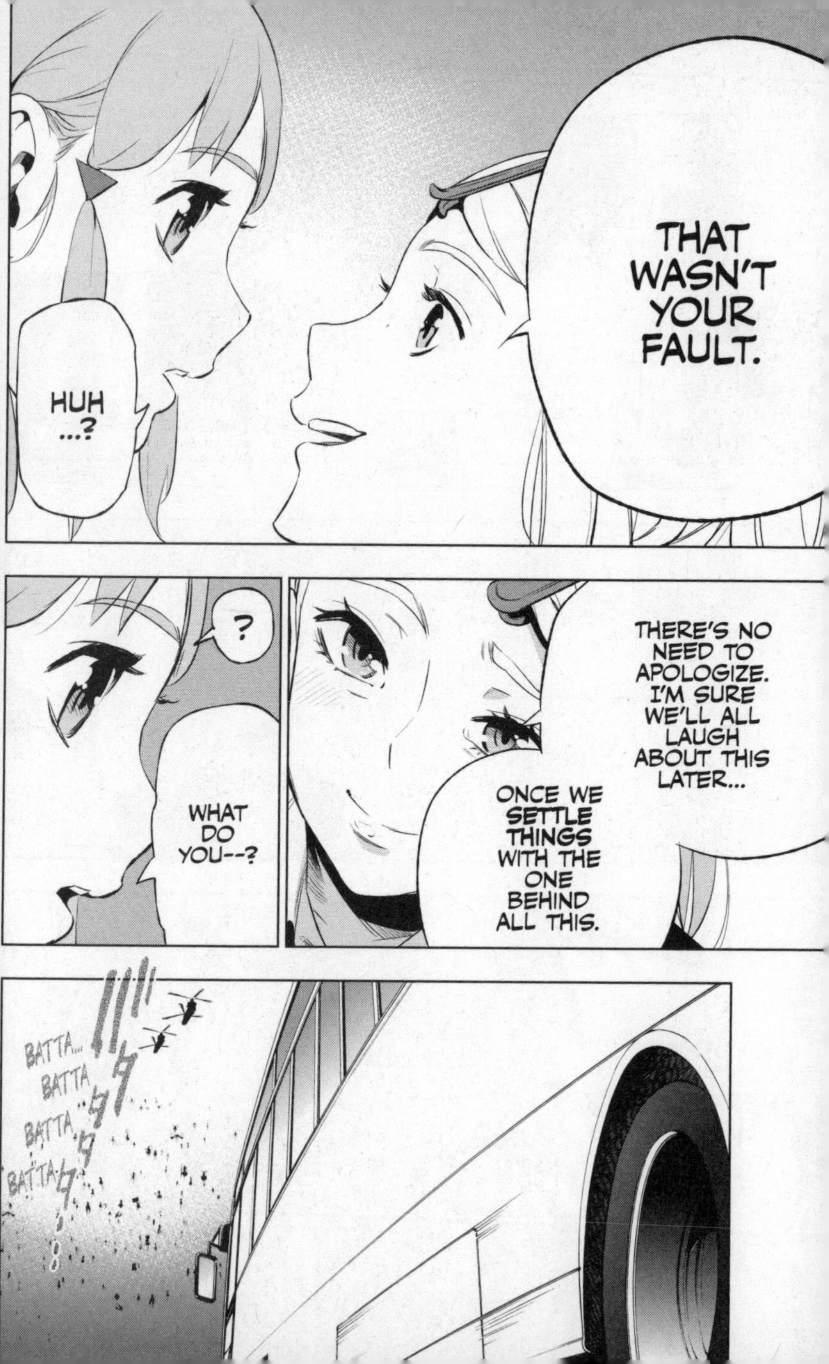
THAT WASN'T YOUR FAULT.
HUH ...?
THERE'S NO NEED TO APOLOGIZE. I'M SURE WE'LL ALL LAUGH ABOUT THIS LATER...
ONCE WE SETTLE THINGS WITH THE ONE BEHIND ALL THIS.
?
WHAT DO YOU--?
BATTA... BATTA BATTA BATTA

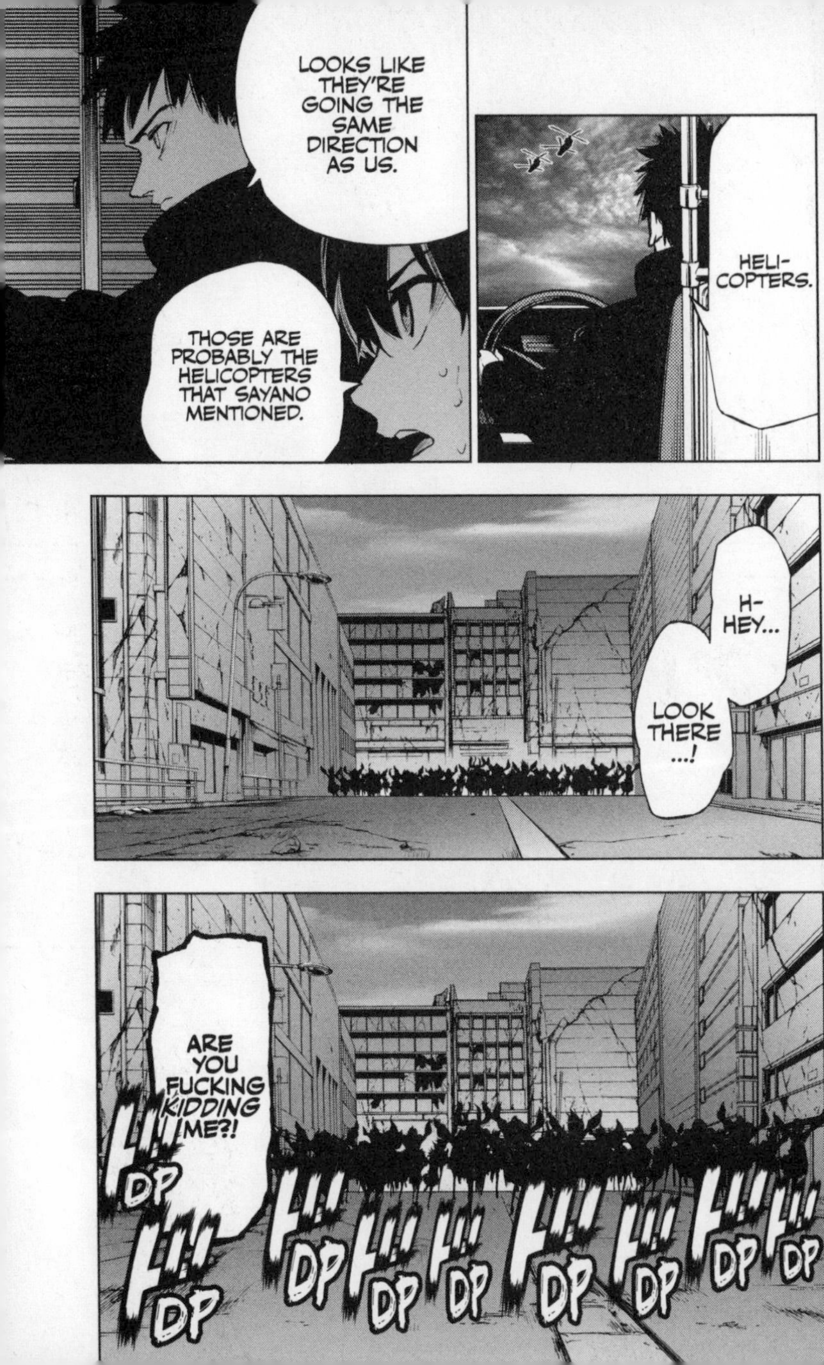
HELI-COPTERS.
LOOKS LIKE THEY'RE GOING THE SAME DIRECTION AS US.
THOSE ARE PROBABLY THE HELICOPTERS THAT SAYANO MENTIONED.
H-HEY...
LOOK THERE ...!
ARE YOU FUCKING KIDDING ME?!
DP DP DP DP DP DP DP DP DP DP

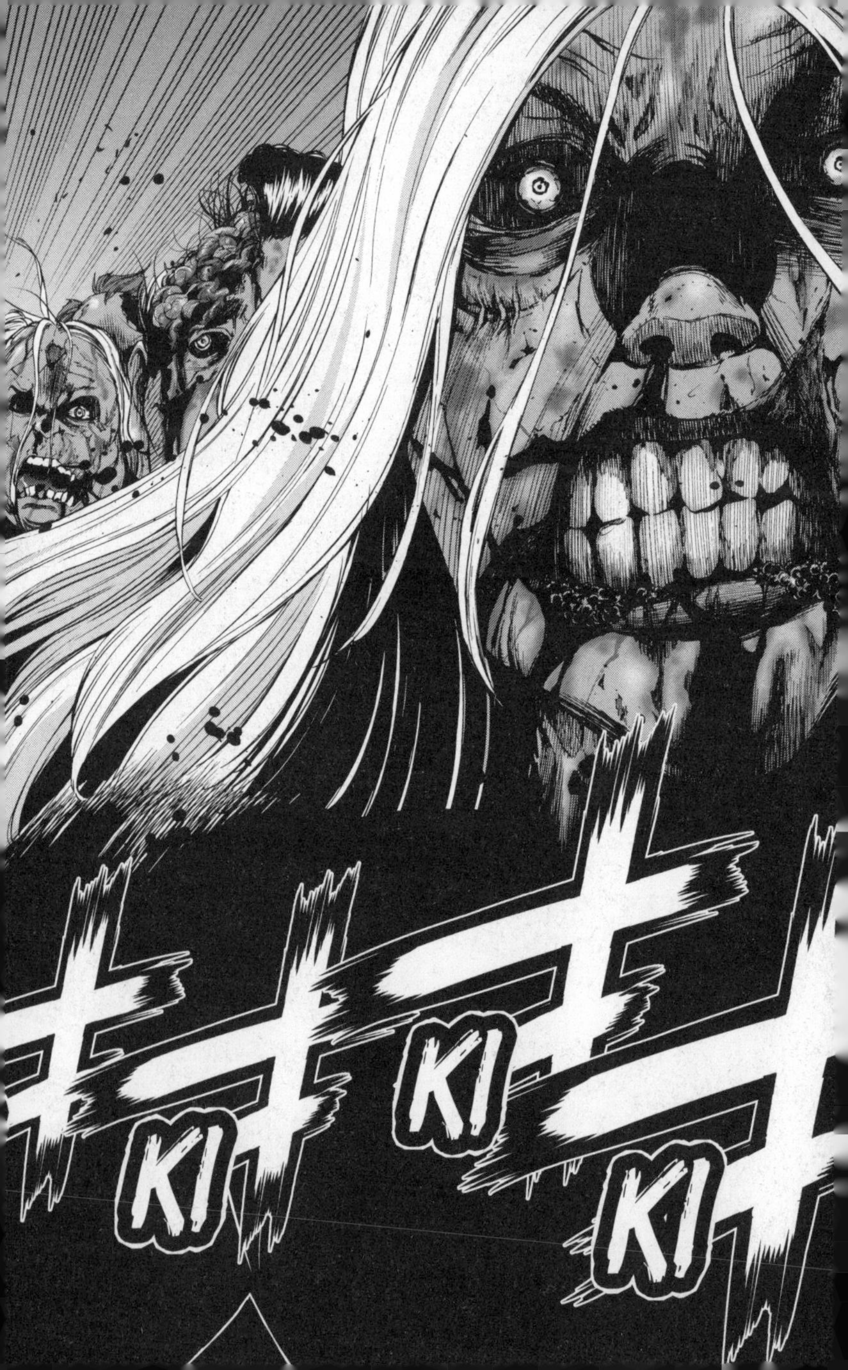
KI
KI
KI

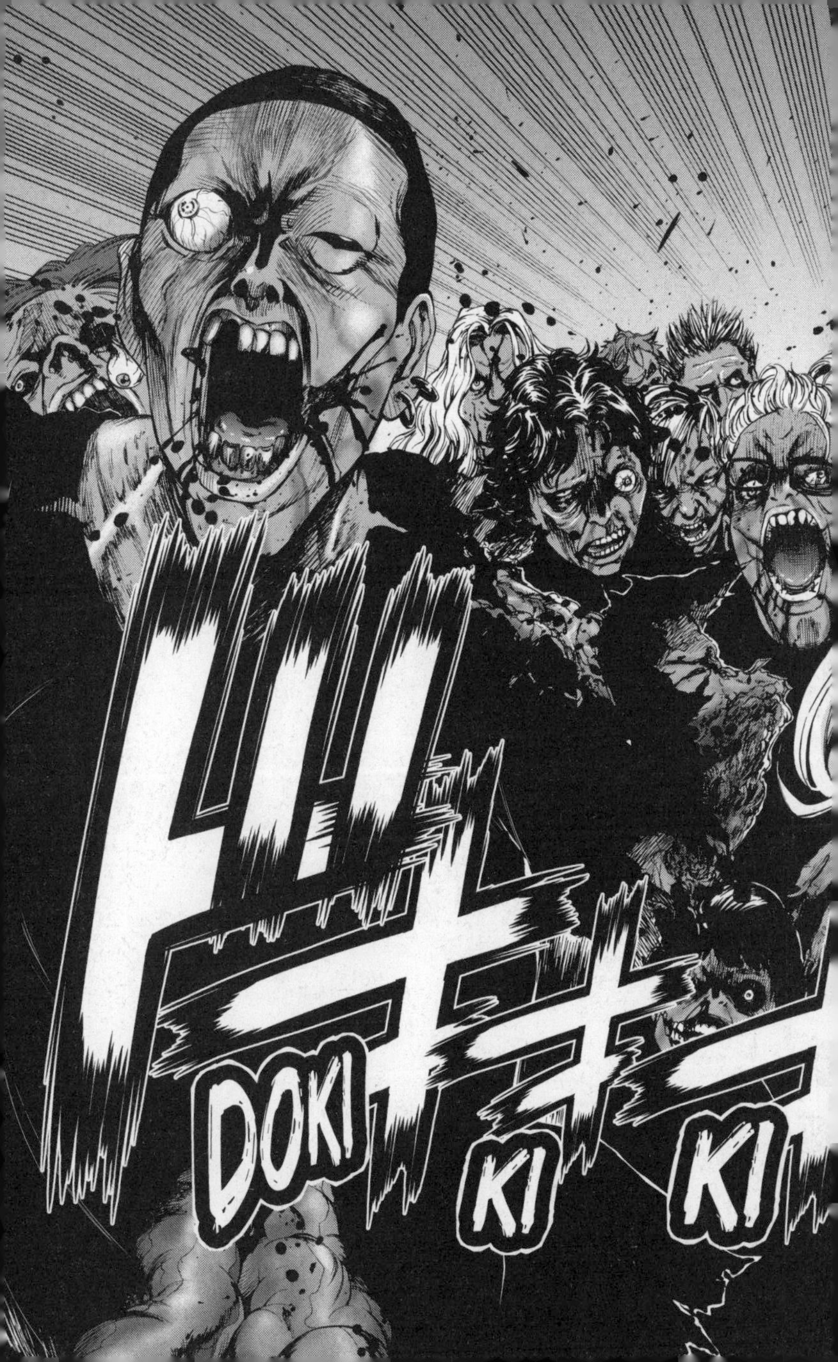
ドキ
DOKI
KI
KI

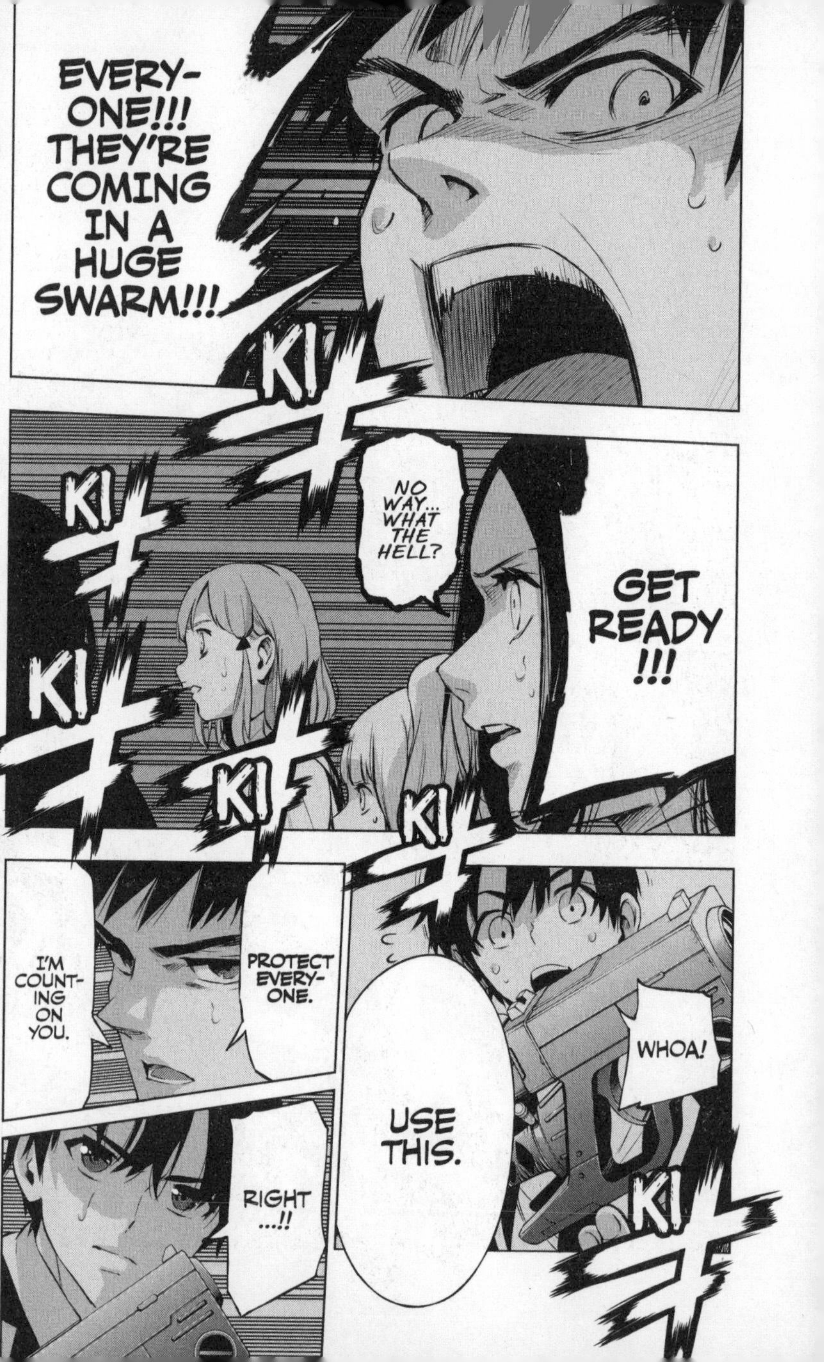
EVERY-ONE!!! THEY'RE COMING IN A HUGE SWARM!!!
KI
GET READY!!!
NO WAY... WHAT THE HELL?
KI
KI
KI
KI
KI
WHOA!
USE THIS.
KI
PROTECT EVERY-ONE.
I'M COUNT-ING ON YOU.
RIGHT...!!

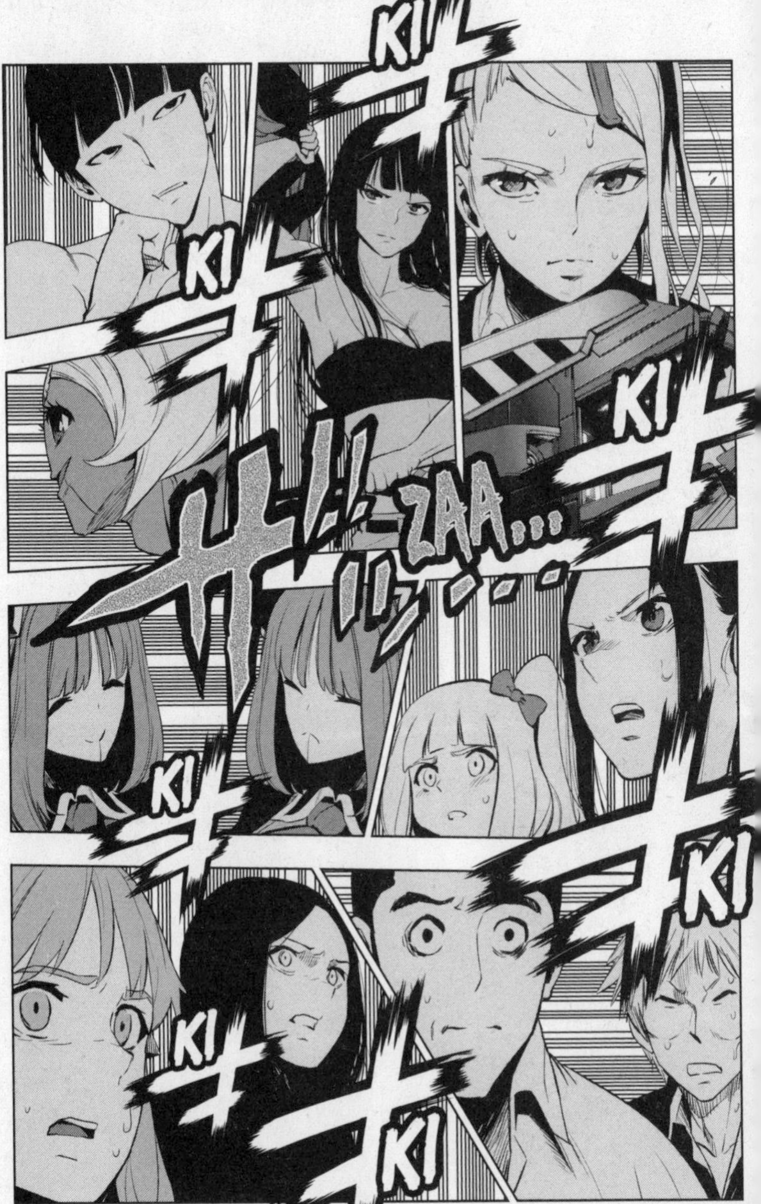
KI
KI
KI
ZAA...
KI
KI
KI
KI

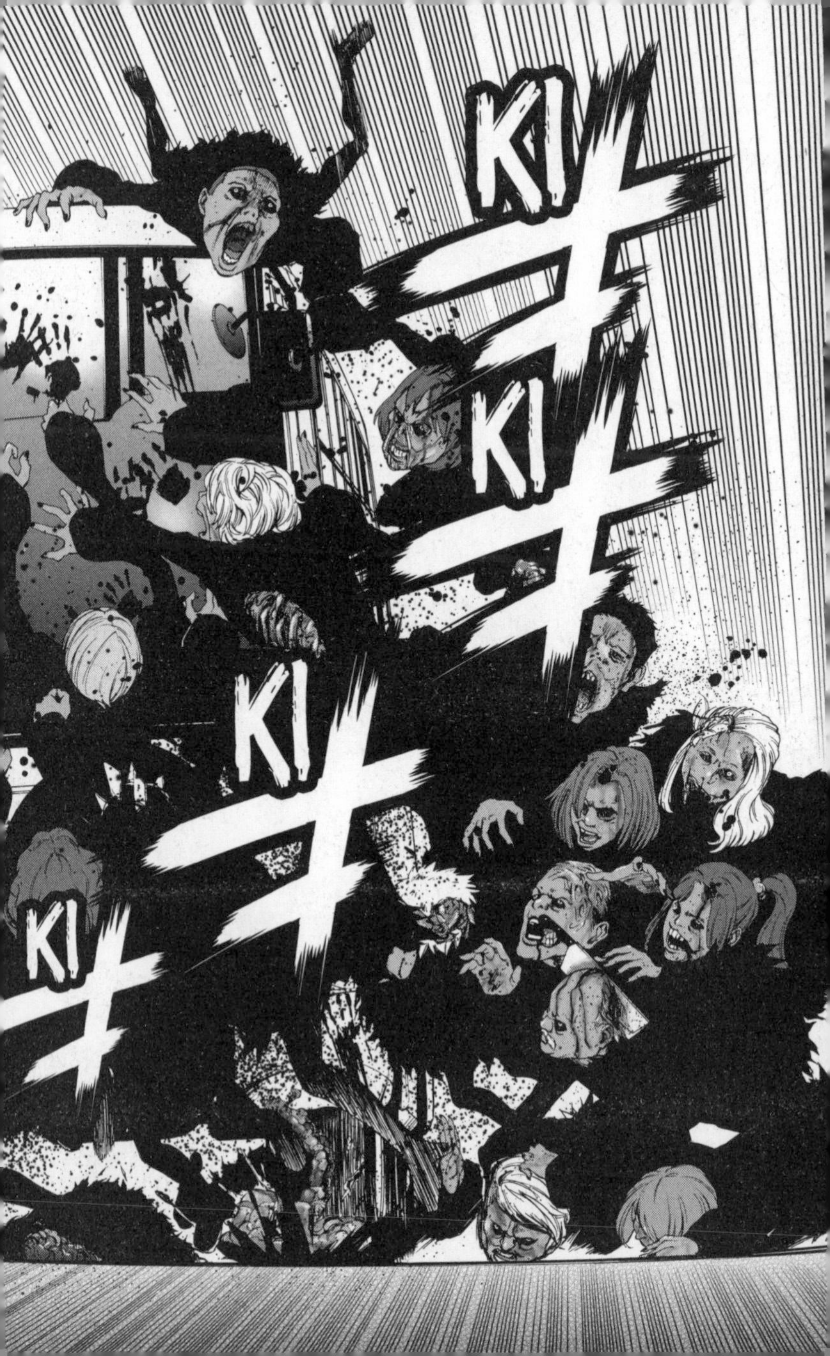
KI
KI
KI
KI

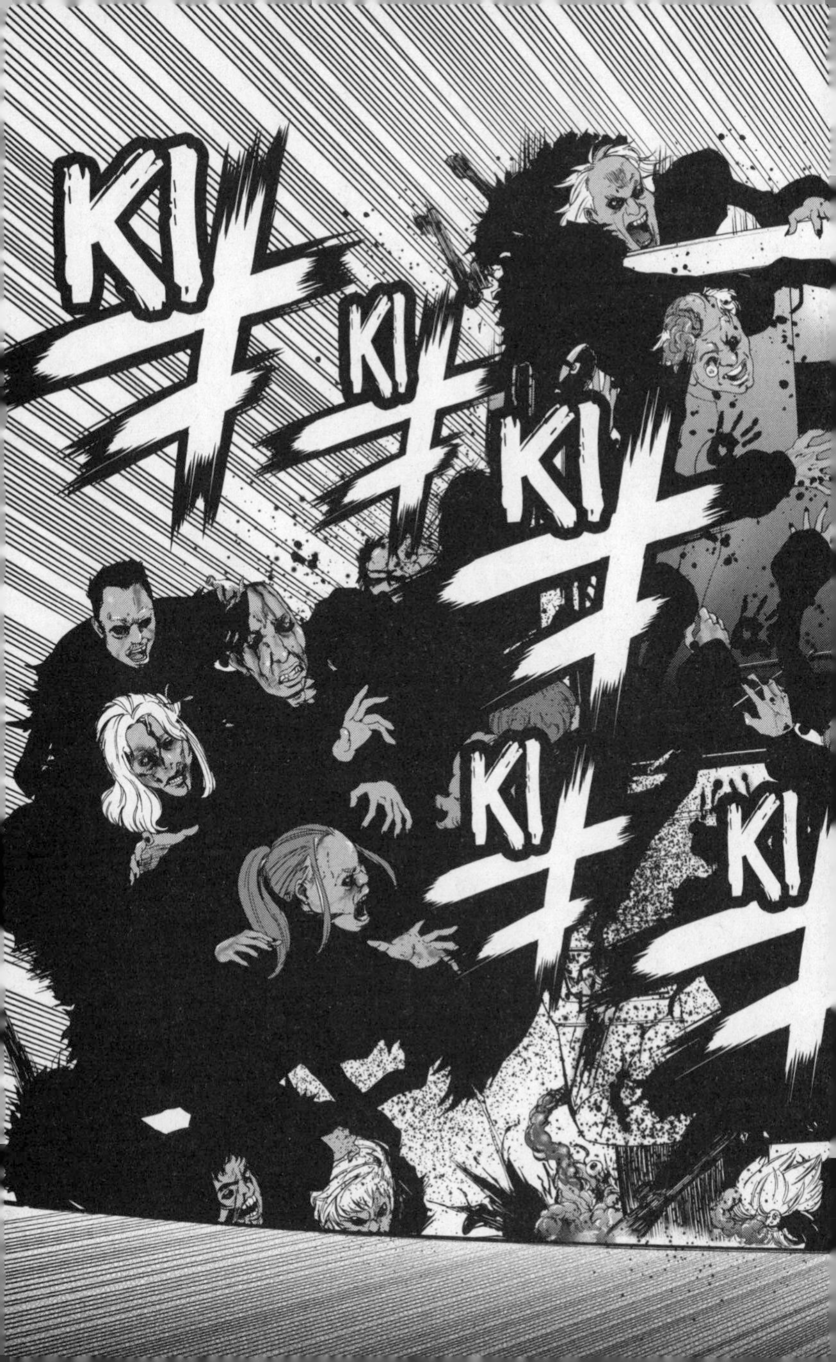
KI キ
KI キ
KI キ
KI キ
KI キ

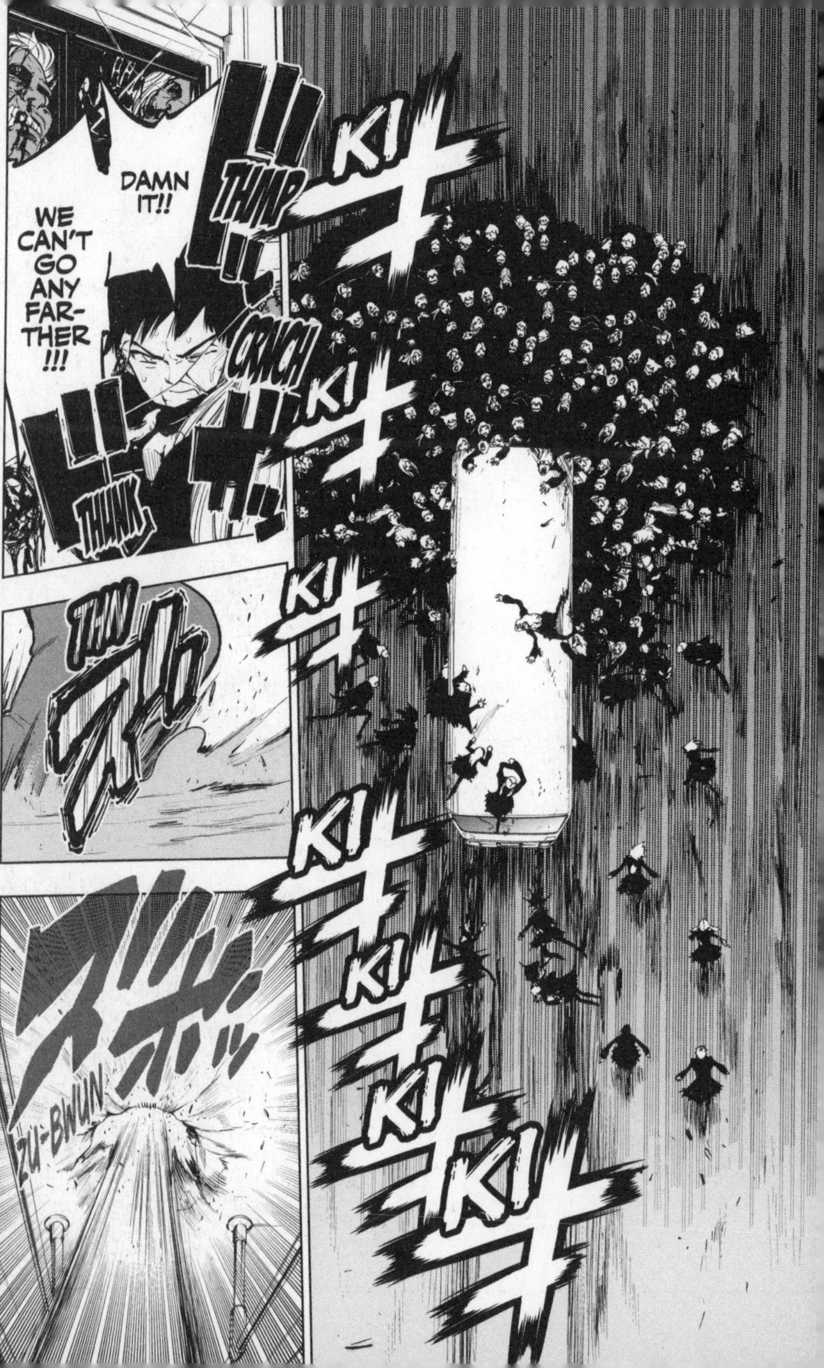
KI
KI
KI
KI
KI
KI
KI
THMP
DAMN IT!!
WE CAN'T GO ANY FAR-THER!!!
CRNCH
THUNK
THN
ZU-BWUN

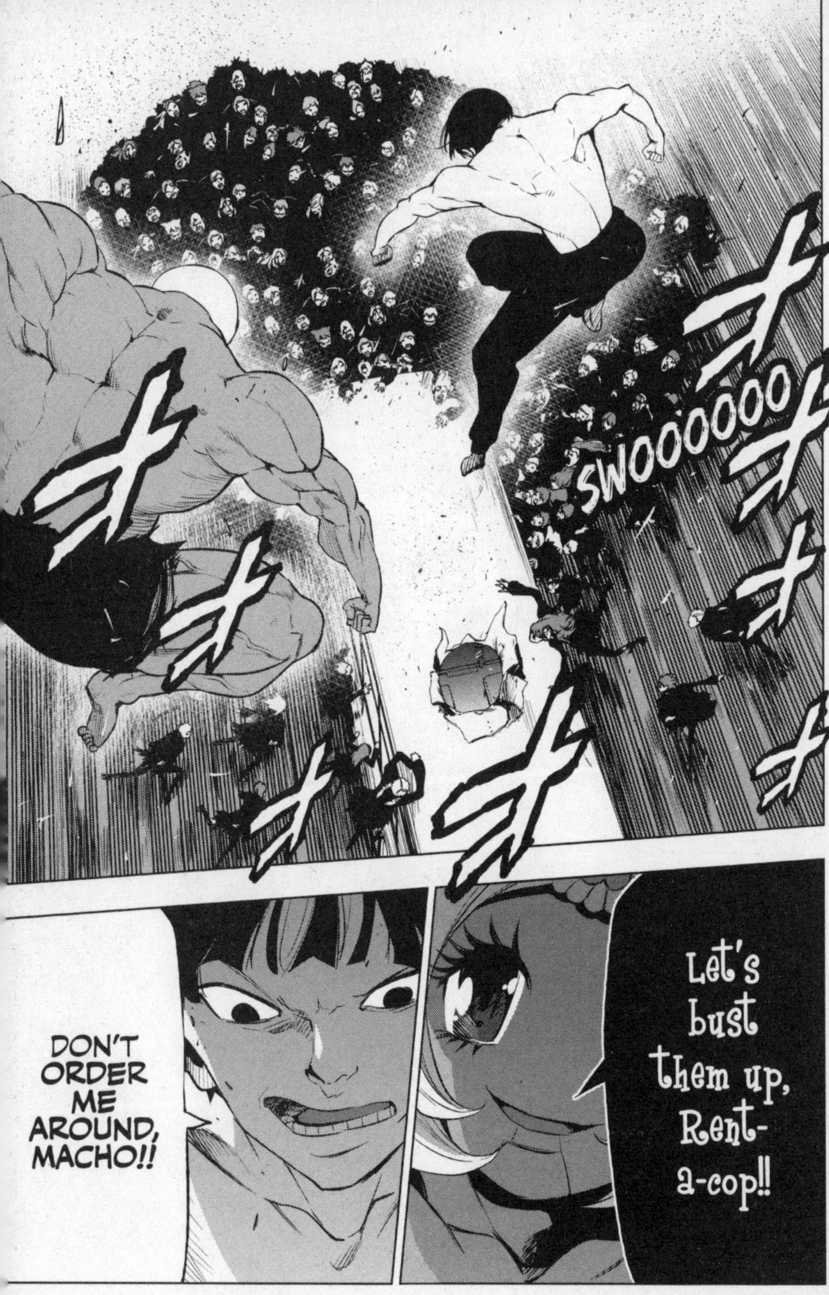
SWOOOOOO
Let's bust them up, Rent-a-cop!!
DON'T ORDER ME AROUND, MACHO!!

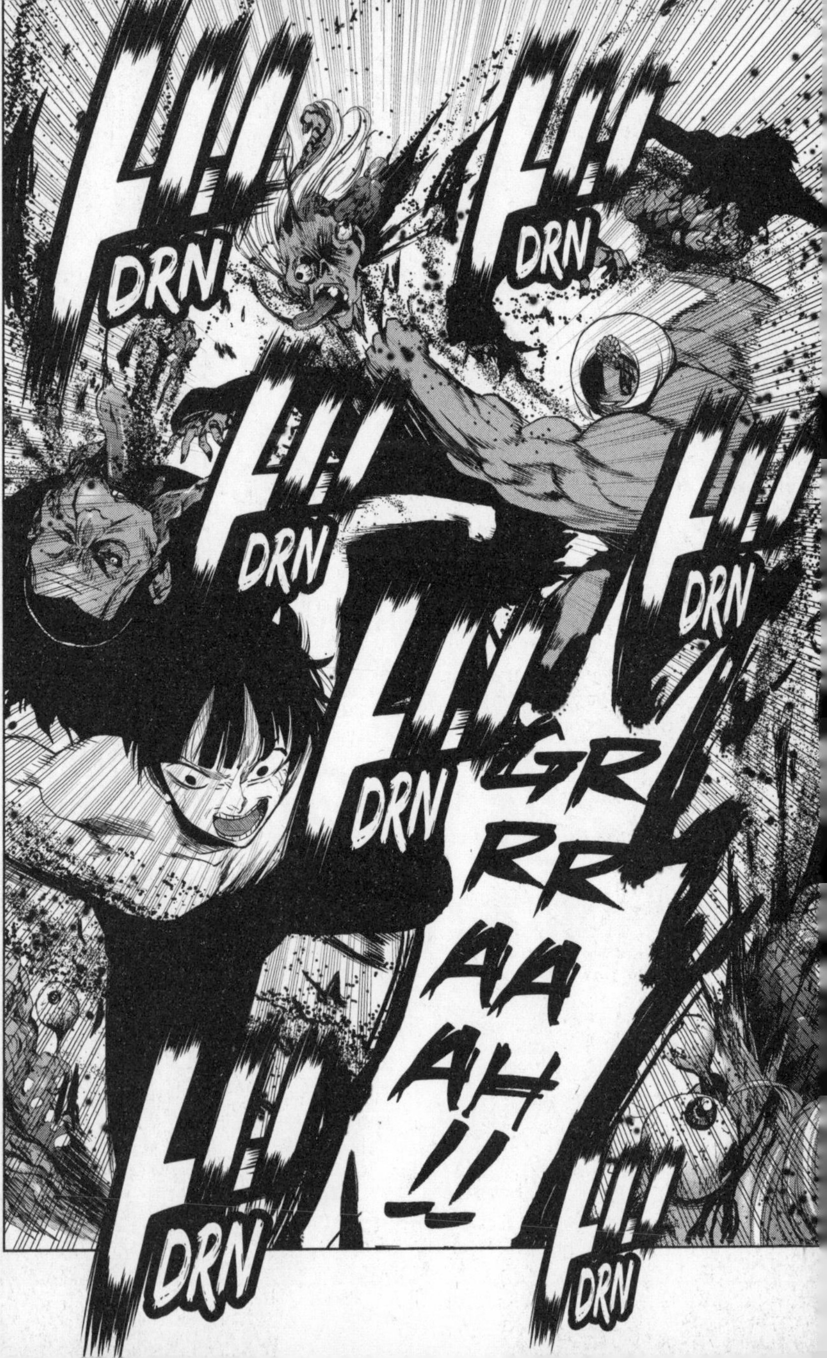
DRN
DRN
DRN
DRN
GRRRAAAH!!
DRN
DRN
DRN

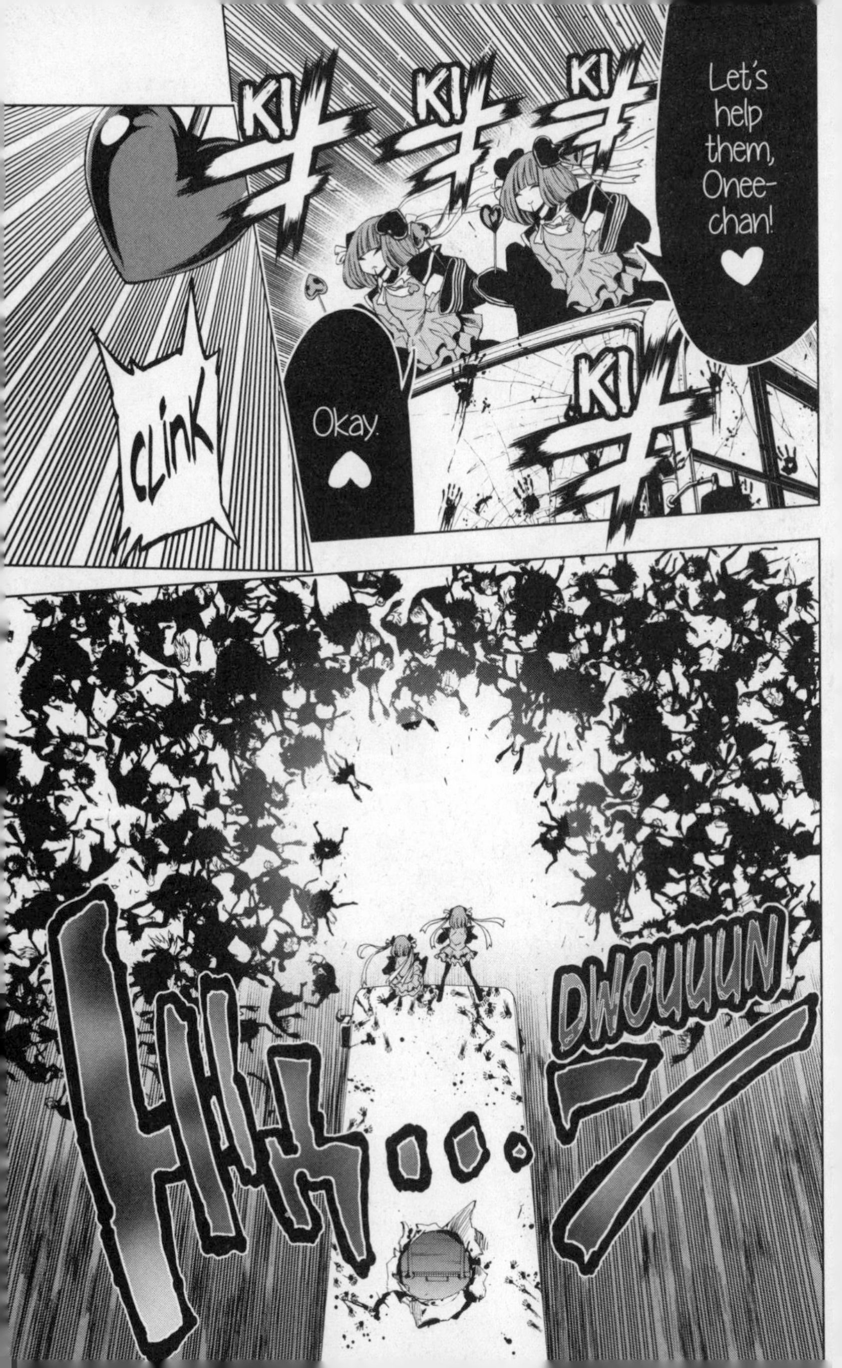
Let's help them, Onee-chan! ♥
KI KI KI
Okay. ♥
KI
CLink
DWOUUUN

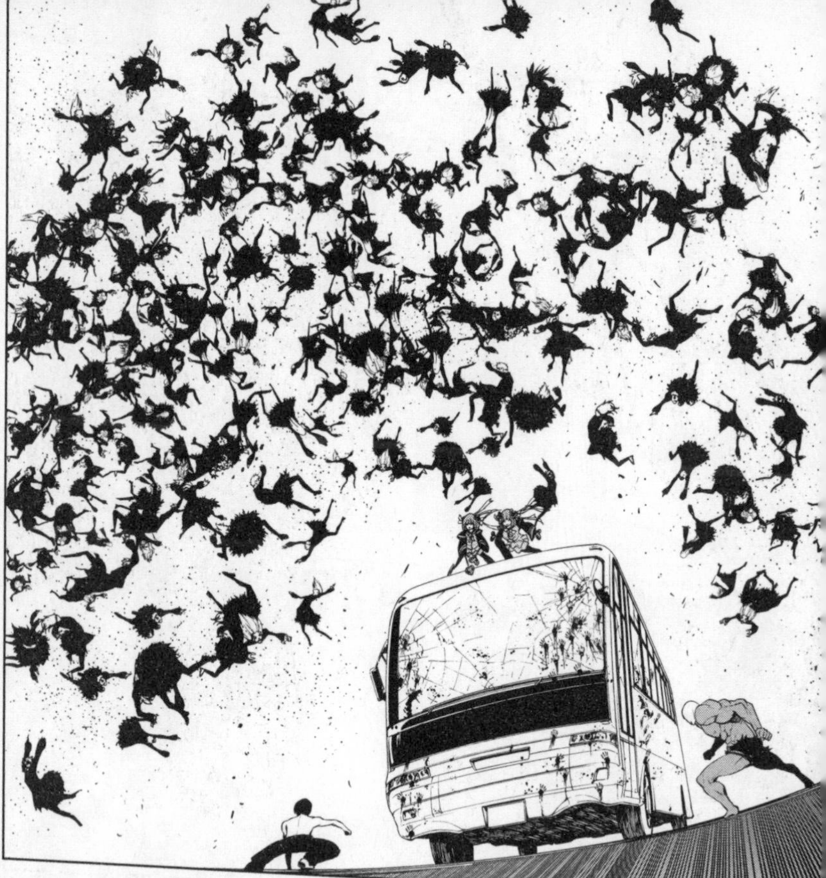

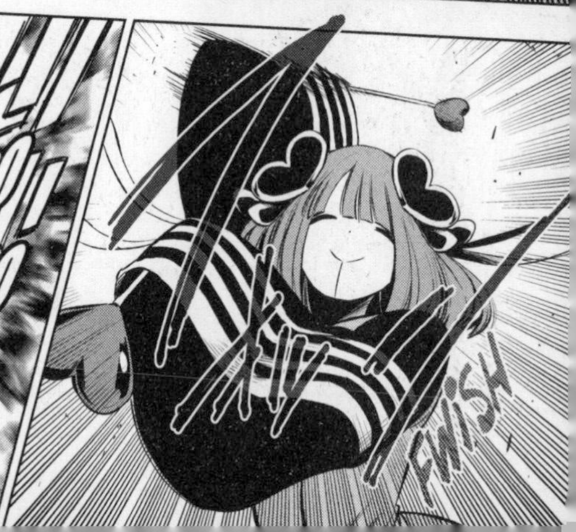
FWISH

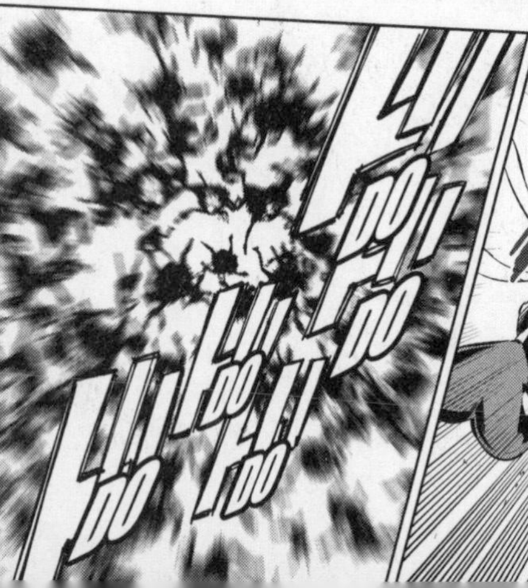
DO DO DO DO DO DO

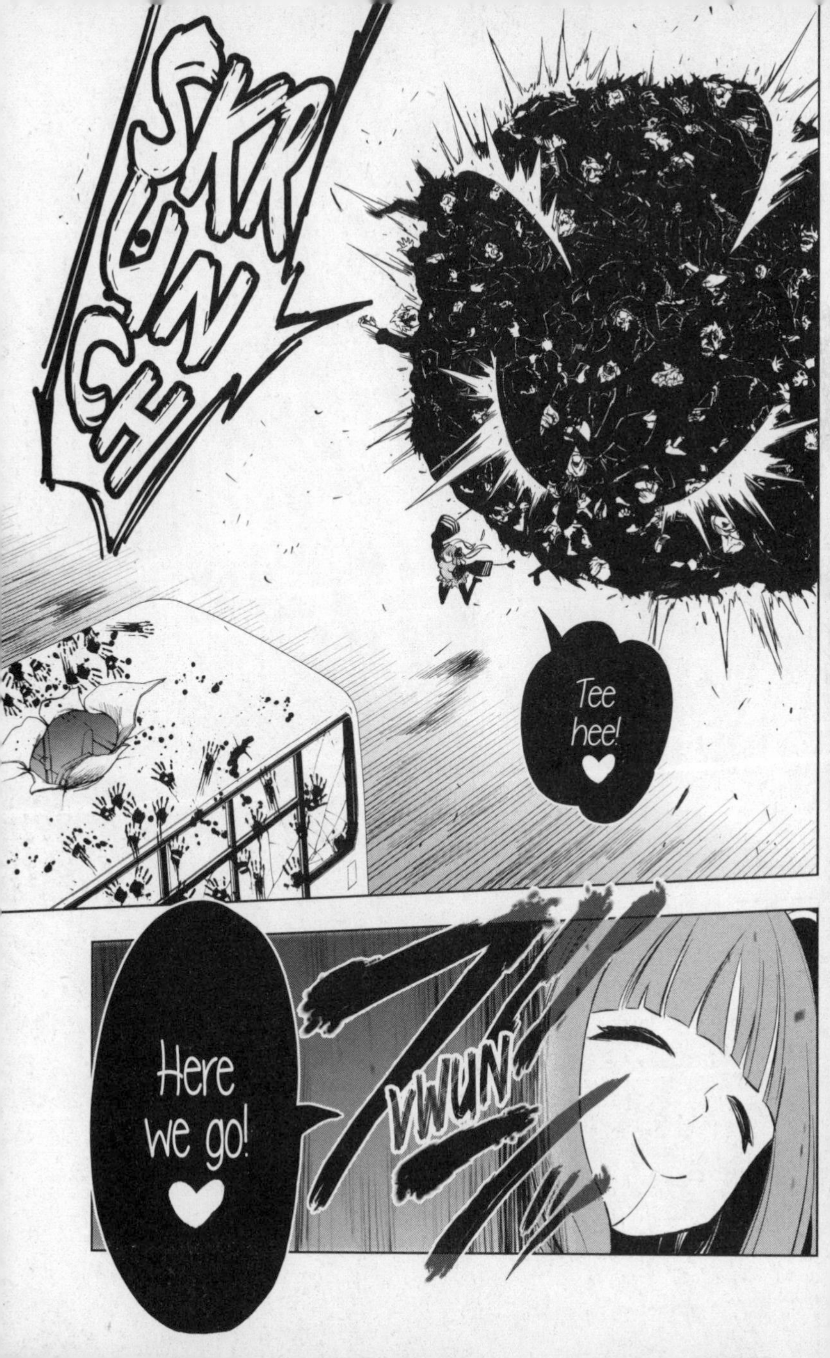
SKRUNCH
Tee hee! ♥
VWUN
Here we go! ♥

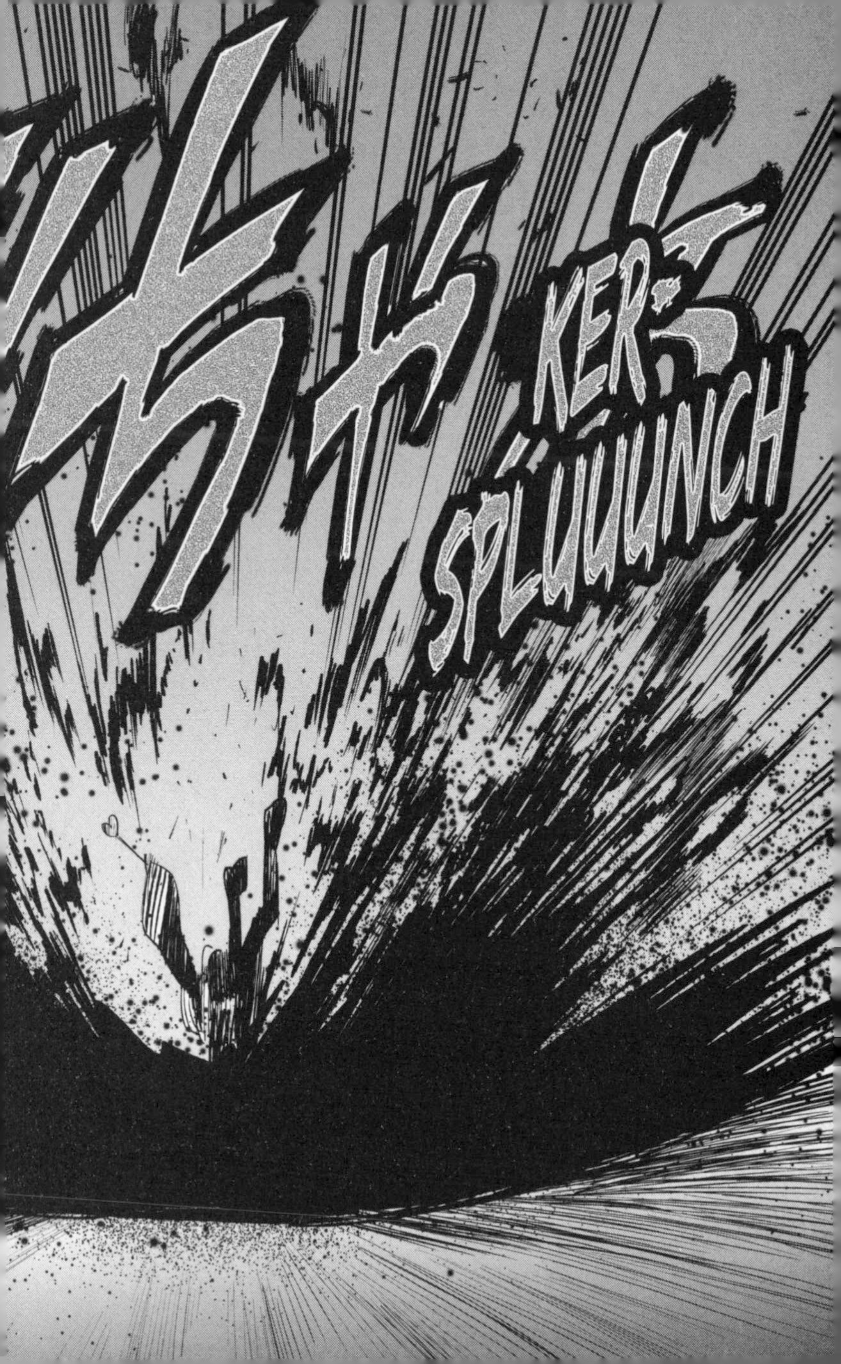
KER-SPLUUUNCH

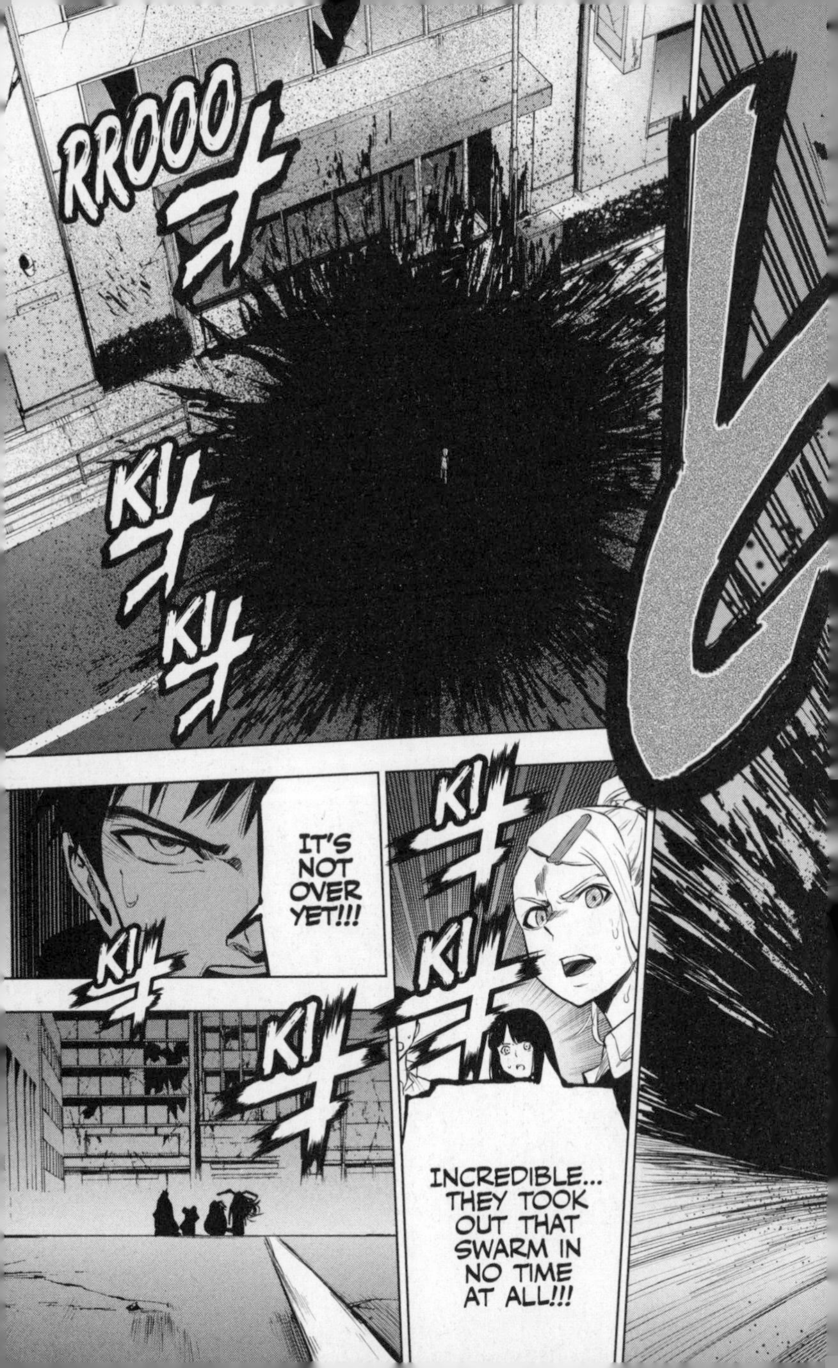
RROOO
KI
KI
KI
KI
IT'S NOT OVER YET!!!
KI
KI
INCREDIBLE... THEY TOOK OUT THAT SWARM IN NO TIME AT ALL!!!

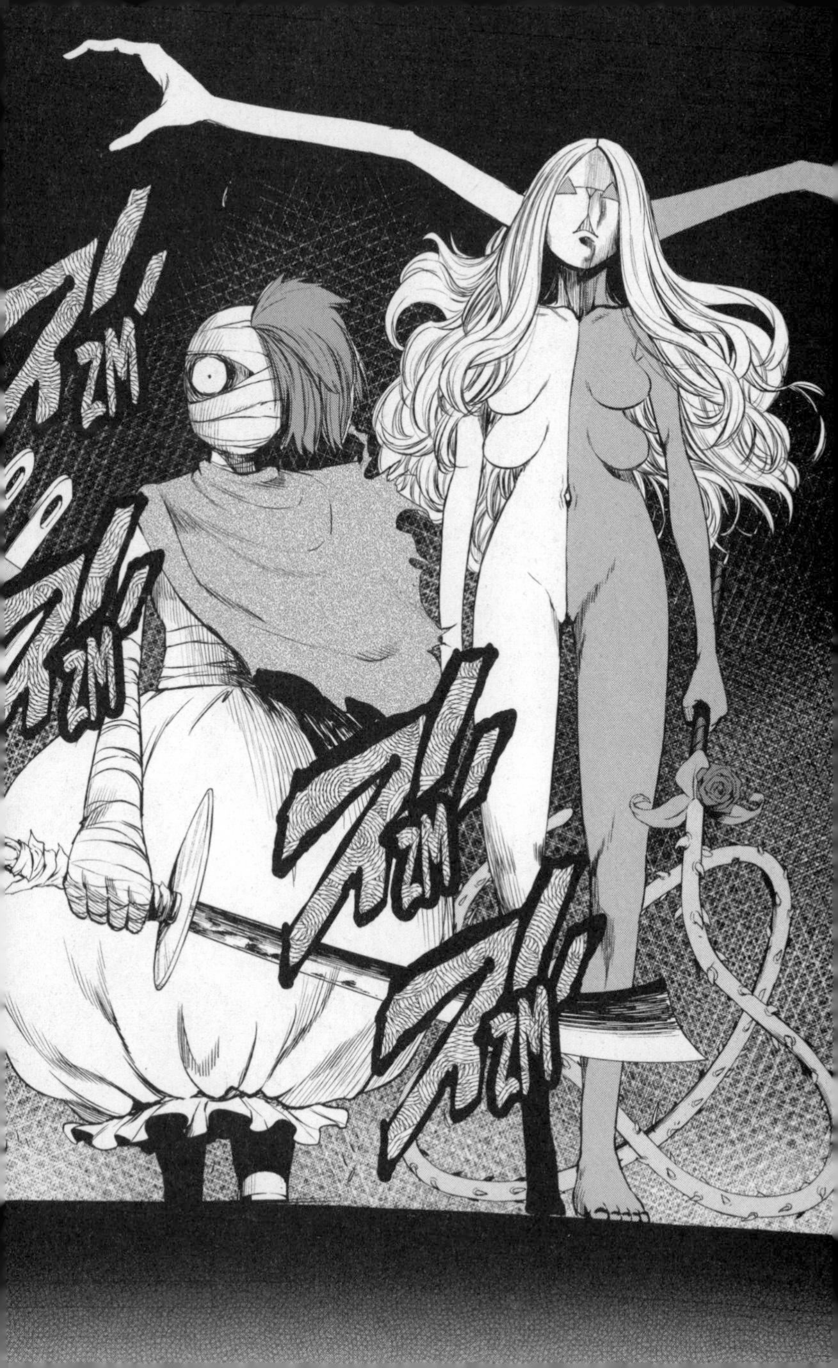
ZM
ZM
ZM
ZM

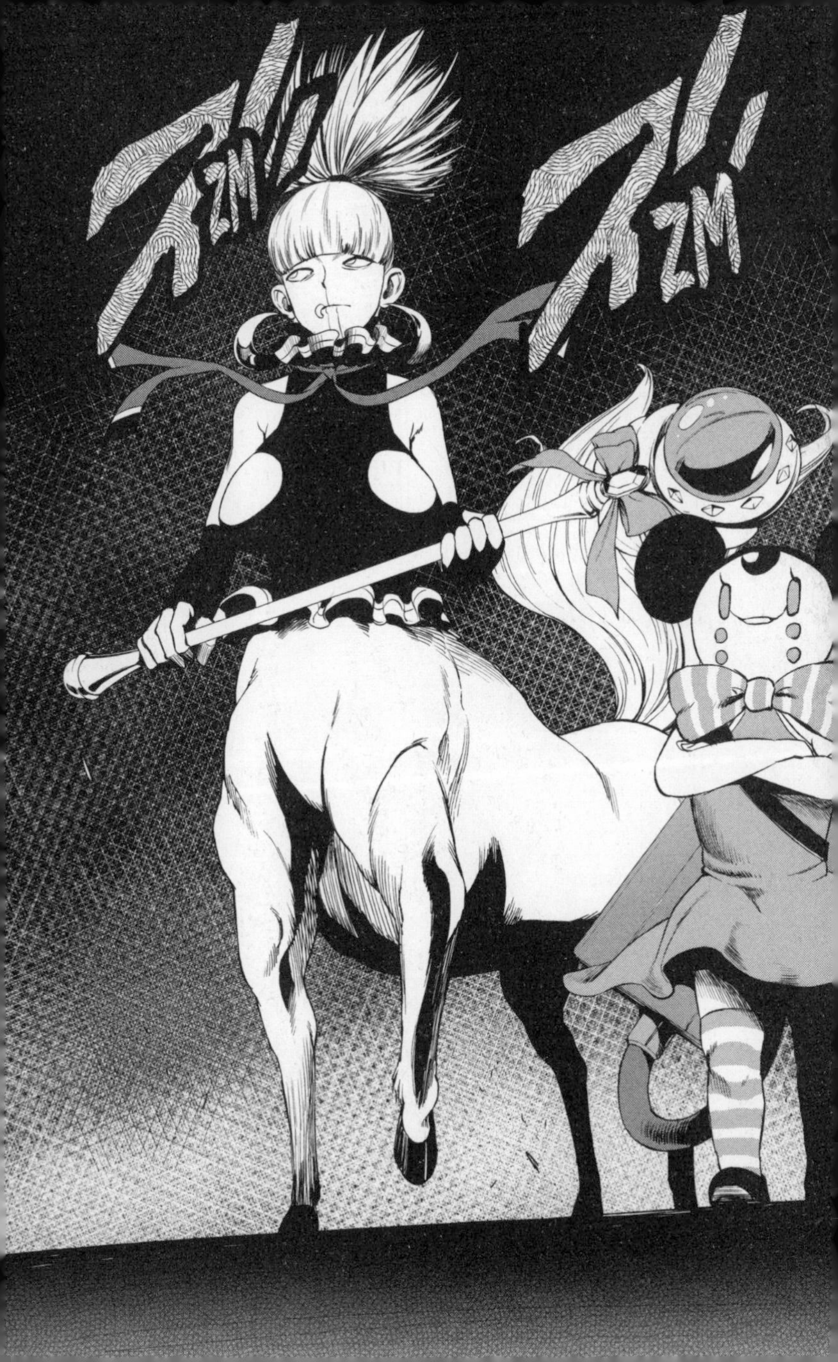
ZMM
ZM!
ZM!

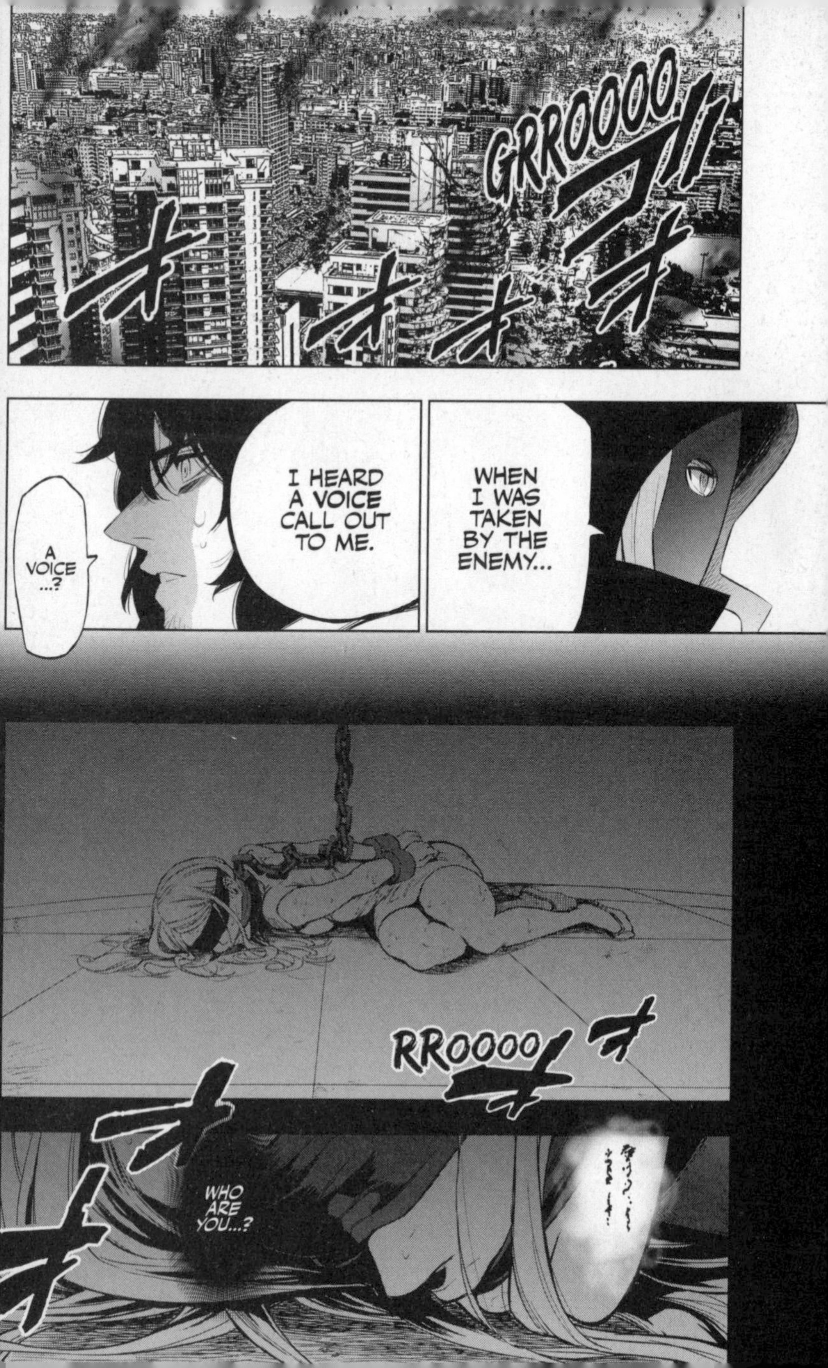
GRROOOO
WHEN I WAS TAKEN BY THE ENEMY...
I HEARD A VOICE CALL OUT TO ME.
A VOICE ...?
RROOOO
WHO ARE YOU...?

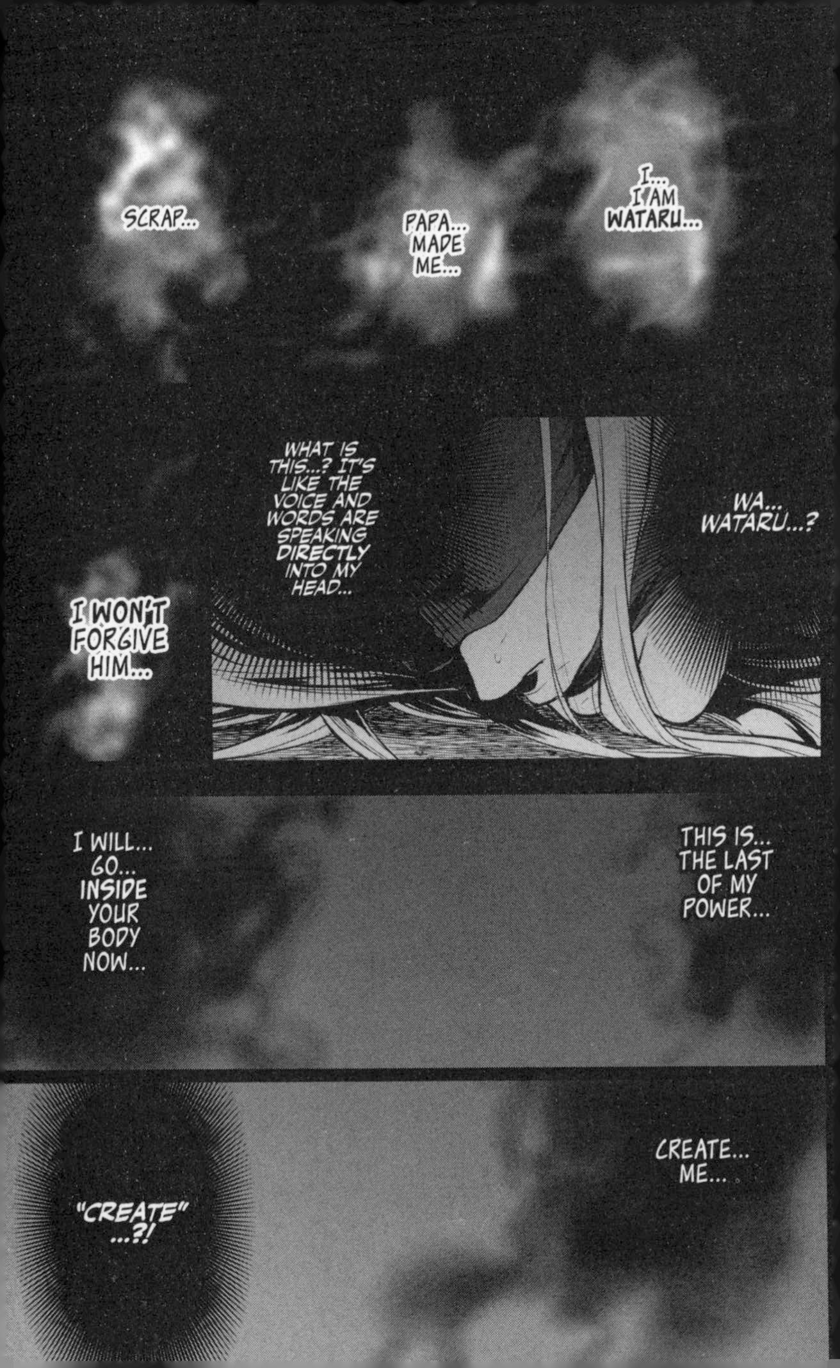
I... I AM WATARU...
PAPA... MADE ME...
SCRAP...
WA... WATARU...?
WHAT IS THIS...? IT'S LIKE THE VOICE AND WORDS ARE SPEAKING DIRECTLY INTO MY HEAD...
I WON'T FORGIVE HIM...
THIS IS... THE LAST OF MY POWER...
I WILL... GO... INSIDE YOUR BODY NOW...
CREATE... ME...
"CREATE" ...?!

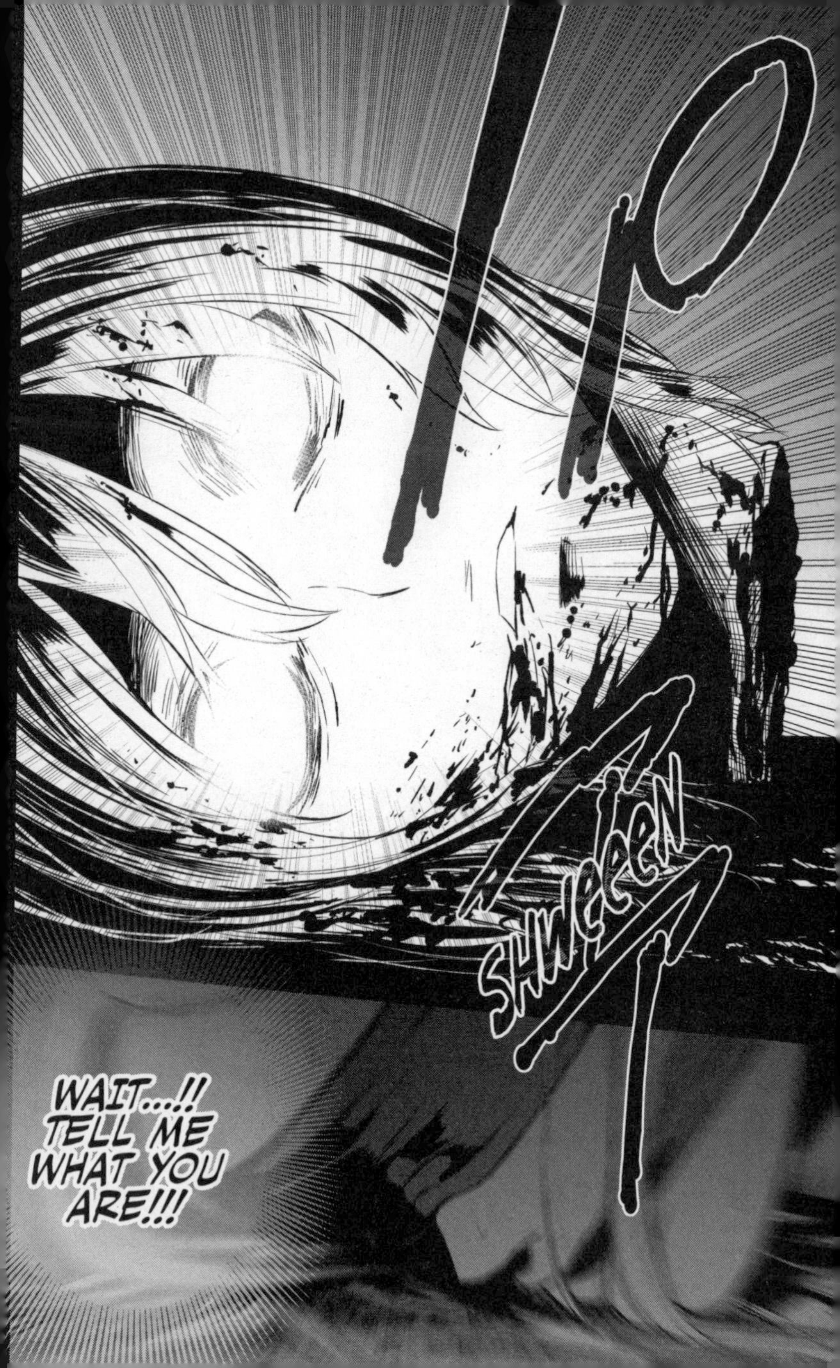
SHWEEEN
WAIT...!! TELL ME WHAT YOU ARE!!!

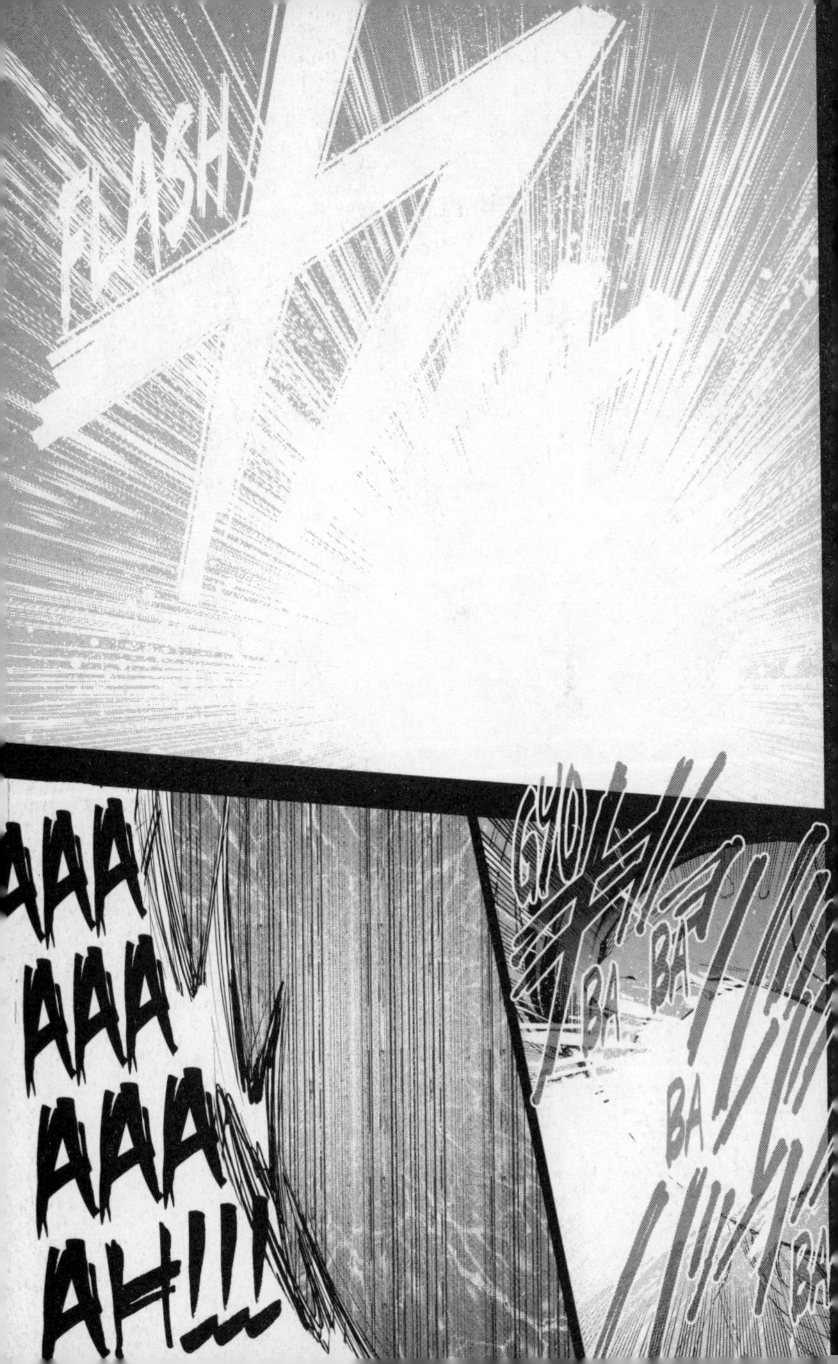
FLASH
GYO
BA BA BA BA BA
AAAAAAAAAAAH!!!

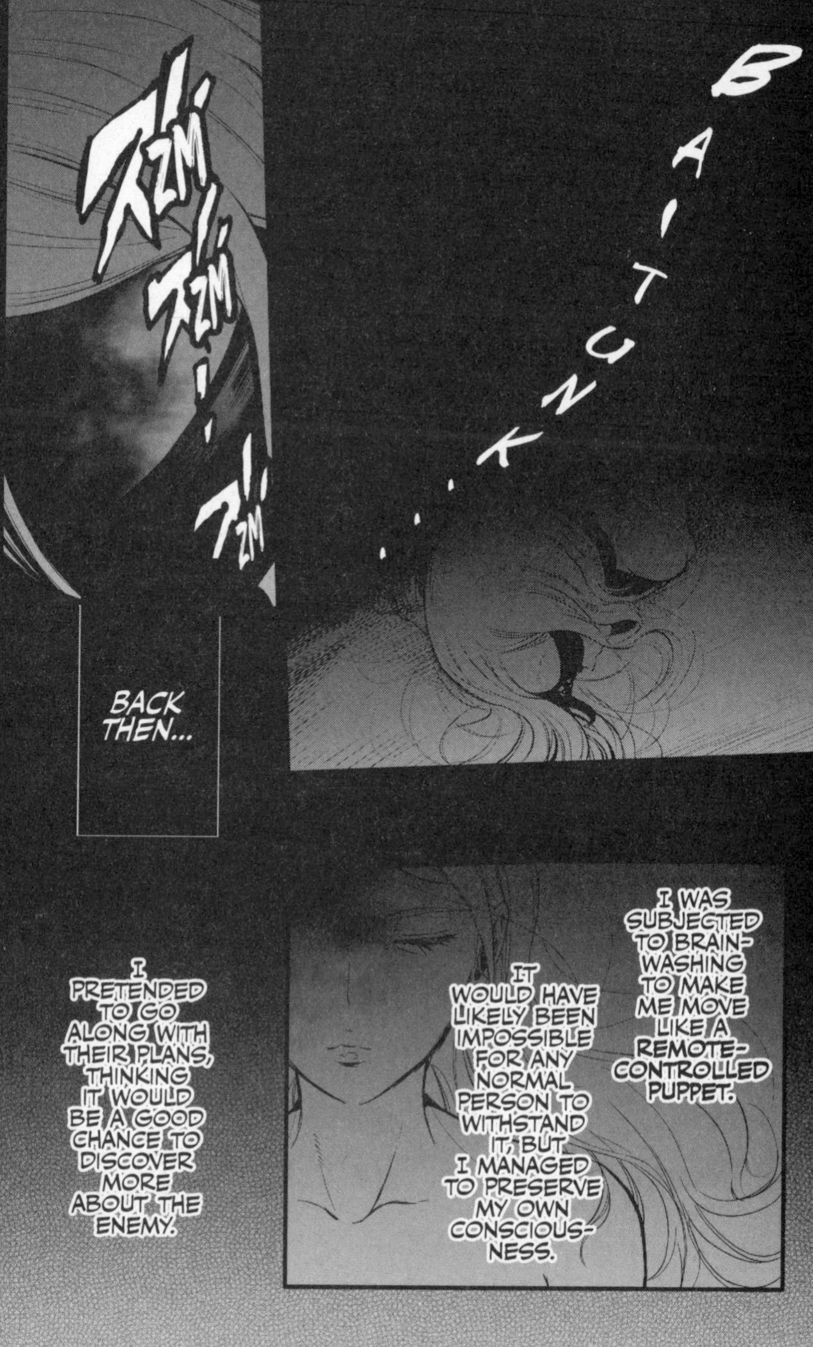
BA-TUNK...
ZZM ZZM ZZM
BACK THEN...
I WAS SUBJECTED TO BRAIN-WASHING TO MAKE ME MOVE LIKE A REMOTE-CONTROLLED PUPPET.
IT WOULD HAVE LIKELY BEEN IMPOSSIBLE FOR ANY NORMAL PERSON TO WITHSTAND IT, BUT I MANAGED TO PRESERVE MY OWN CONSCIOUS-NESS.
I PRETENDED TO GO ALONG WITH THEIR PLANS, THINKING IT WOULD BE A GOOD CHANCE TO DISCOVER MORE ABOUT THE ENEMY.

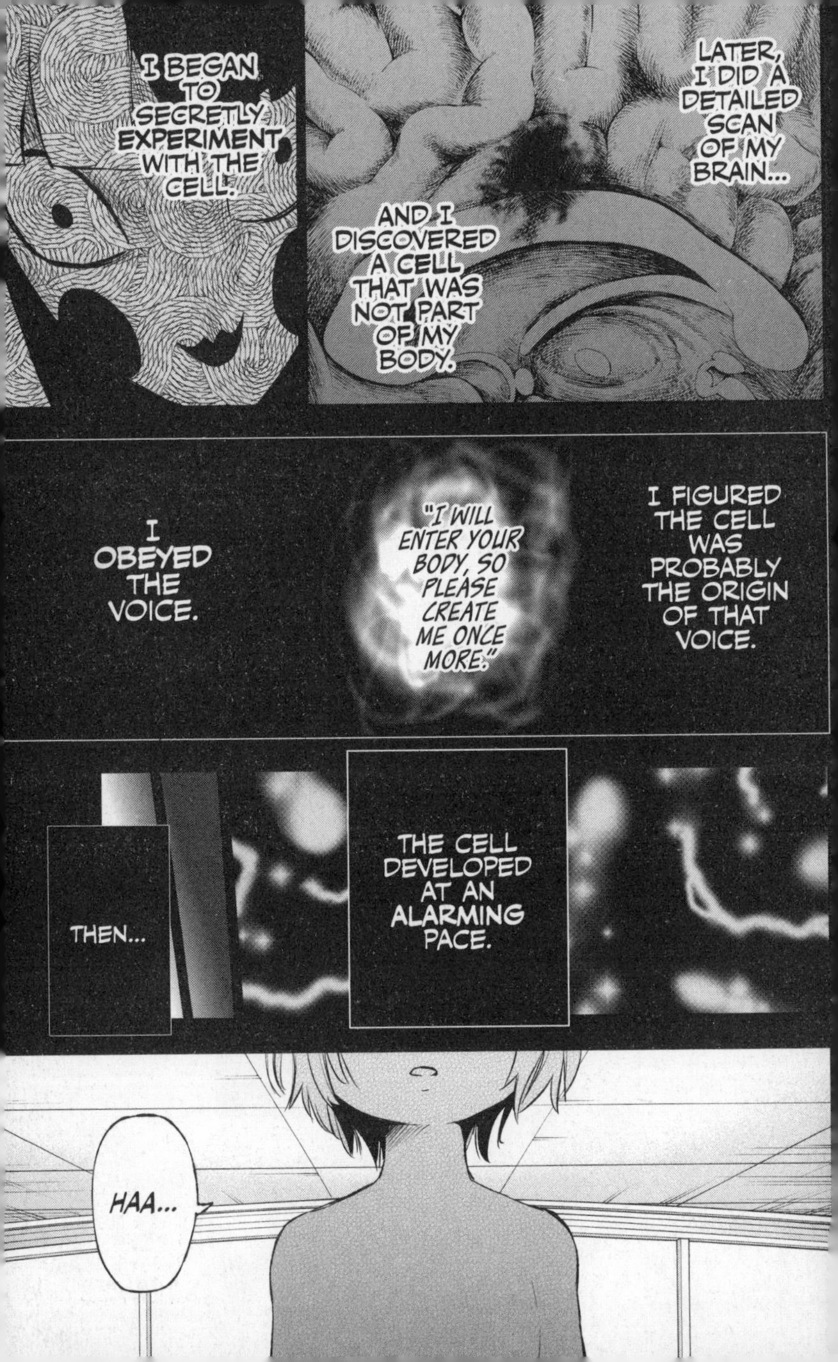
LATER, I DID A DETAILED SCAN OF MY BRAIN...
AND I DISCOVERED A CELL THAT WAS NOT PART OF MY BODY.
I BEGAN TO SECRETLY EXPERIMENT WITH THE CELL.
I FIGURED THE CELL WAS PROBABLY THE ORIGIN OF THAT VOICE.
"I WILL ENTER YOUR BODY, SO PLEASE CREATE ME ONCE MORE."
I OBEYED THE VOICE.
THE CELL DEVELOPED AT AN ALARMING PACE.
THEN...
HAA...

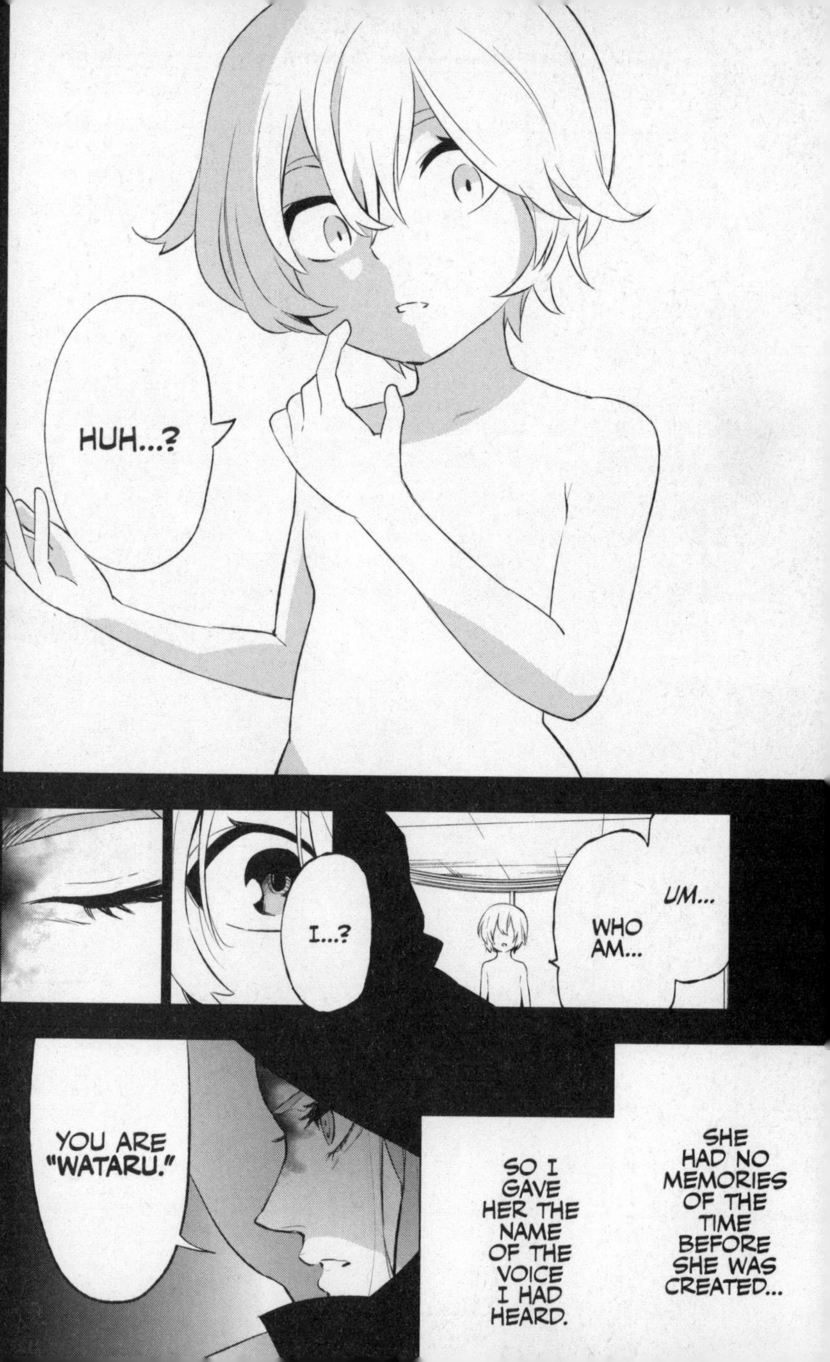
HUH...?
UM...
WHO AM...
I...?
SHE HAD NO MEMORIES OF THE TIME BEFORE SHE WAS CREATED...
SO I GAVE HER THE NAME OF THE VOICE I HAD HEARD.
YOU ARE "WATARU."

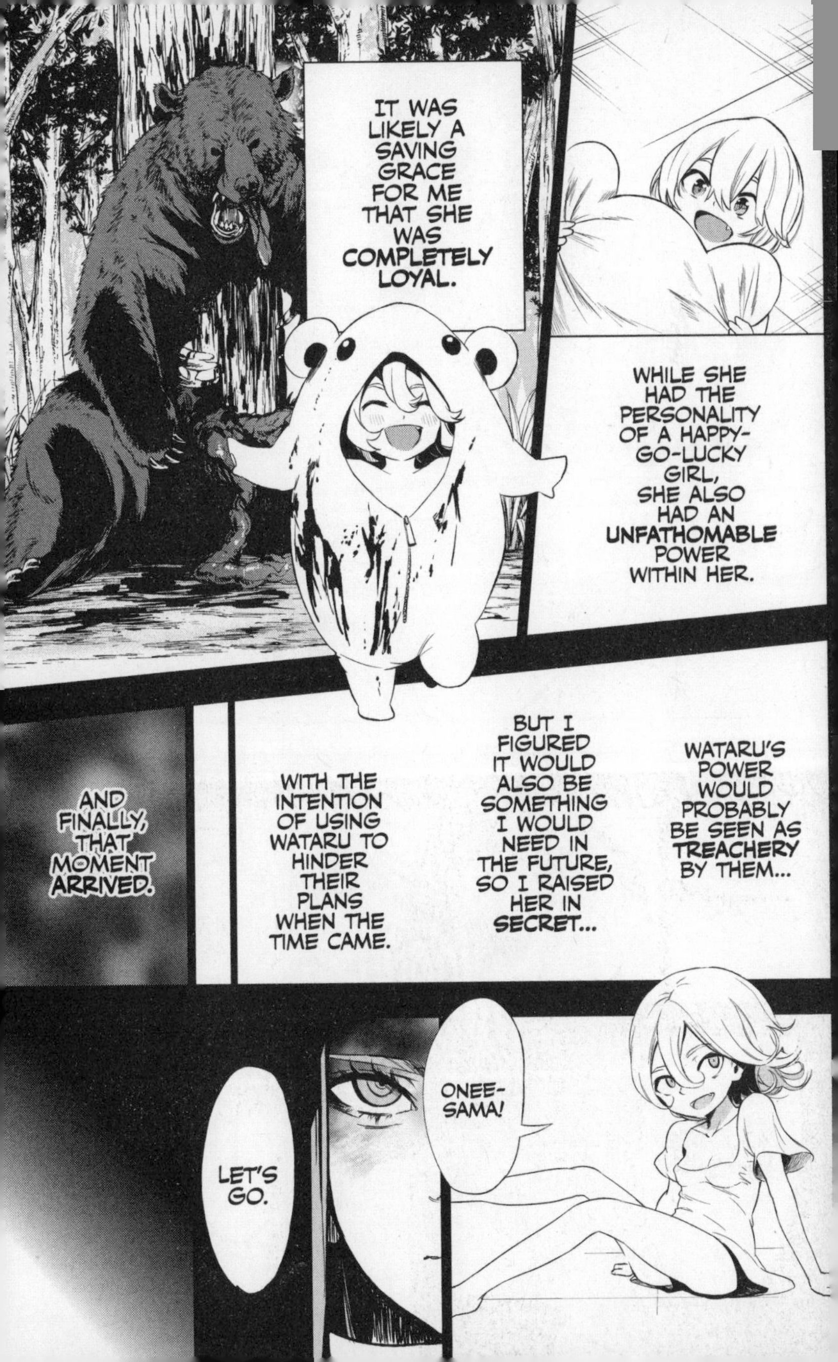
WHILE SHE HAD THE PERSONALITY OF A HAPPY-GO-LUCKY GIRL, SHE ALSO HAD AN **UNFATHOMABLE** POWER WITHIN HER.
IT WAS LIKELY A SAVING GRACE FOR ME THAT SHE WAS COMPLETELY LOYAL.
WATARU'S POWER WOULD PROBABLY BE SEEN AS **TREACHERY** BY THEM...
BUT I FIGURED IT WOULD ALSO BE SOMETHING I WOULD NEED IN THE FUTURE, SO I RAISED HER IN **SECRET**...
WITH THE INTENTION OF USING WATARU TO HINDER THEIR PLANS WHEN THE TIME CAME.
AND FINALLY, THAT MOMENT ARRIVED.
ONEE-SAMA!
LET'S GO.

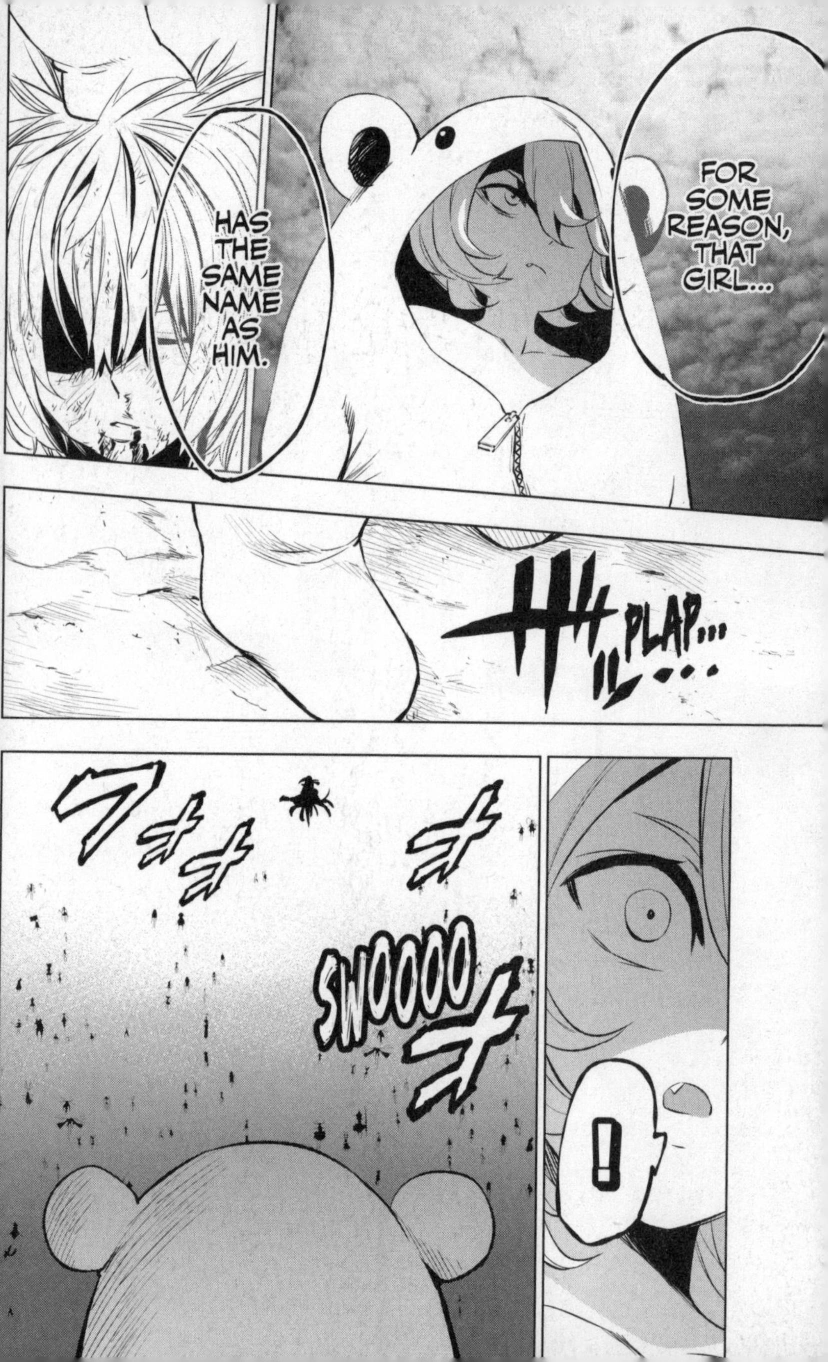

FOR SOME REASON, THAT GIRL...
HAS THE SAME NAME AS HIM.
PLAP...
!
SWOOOO

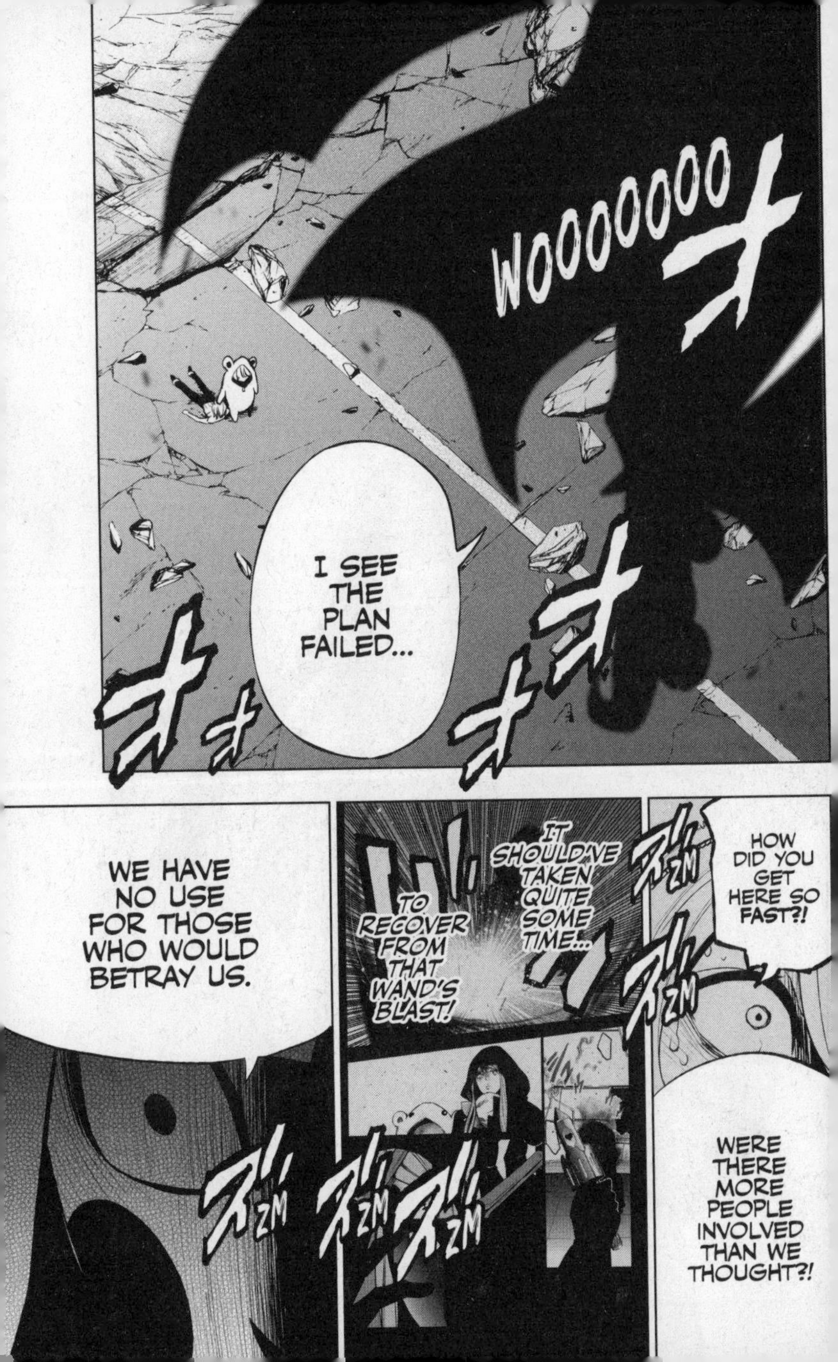
WOOOOOOO
オォォオ
I SEE THE PLAN FAILED...
HOW DID YOU GET HERE SO FAST?!
ズ ZM
ズ ZM
IT SHOULD'VE TAKEN QUITE SOME TIME...
TO RECOVER FROM THAT WAND'S BLAST!
WE HAVE NO USE FOR THOSE WHO WOULD BETRAY US.
WERE THERE MORE PEOPLE INVOLVED THAN WE THOUGHT?!
ズ ZM
ズ ZM
ズ ZM

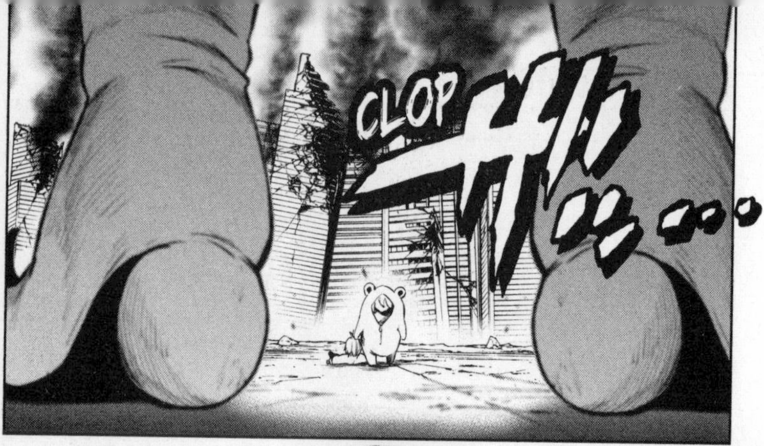
CLOP
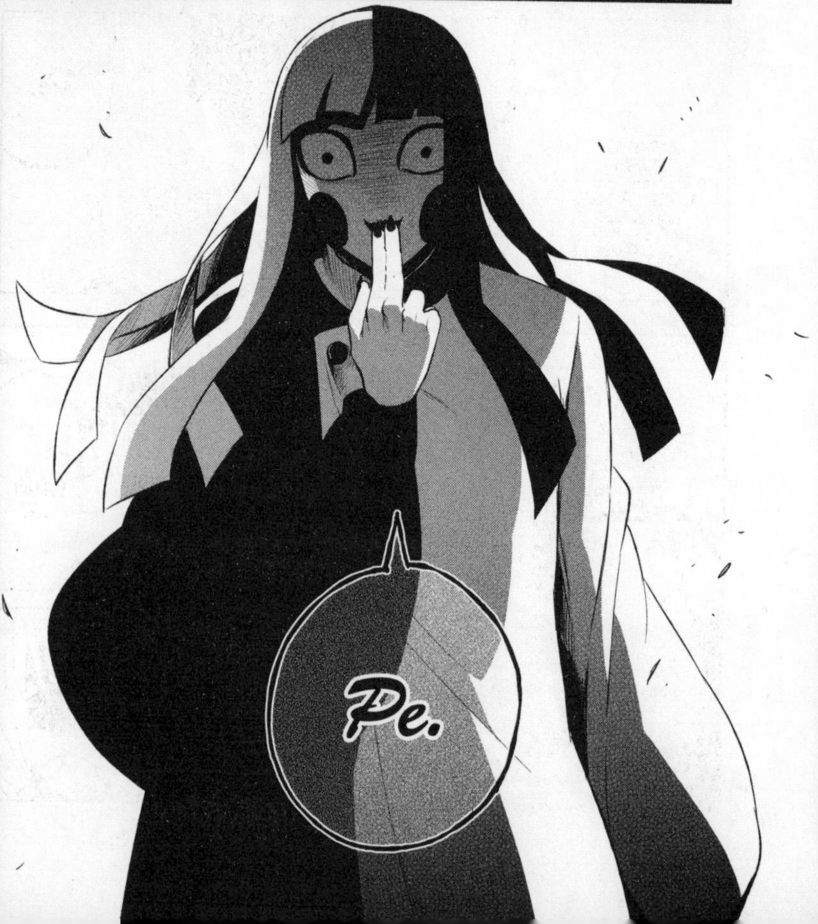
Pe.

049.to the FUTURE

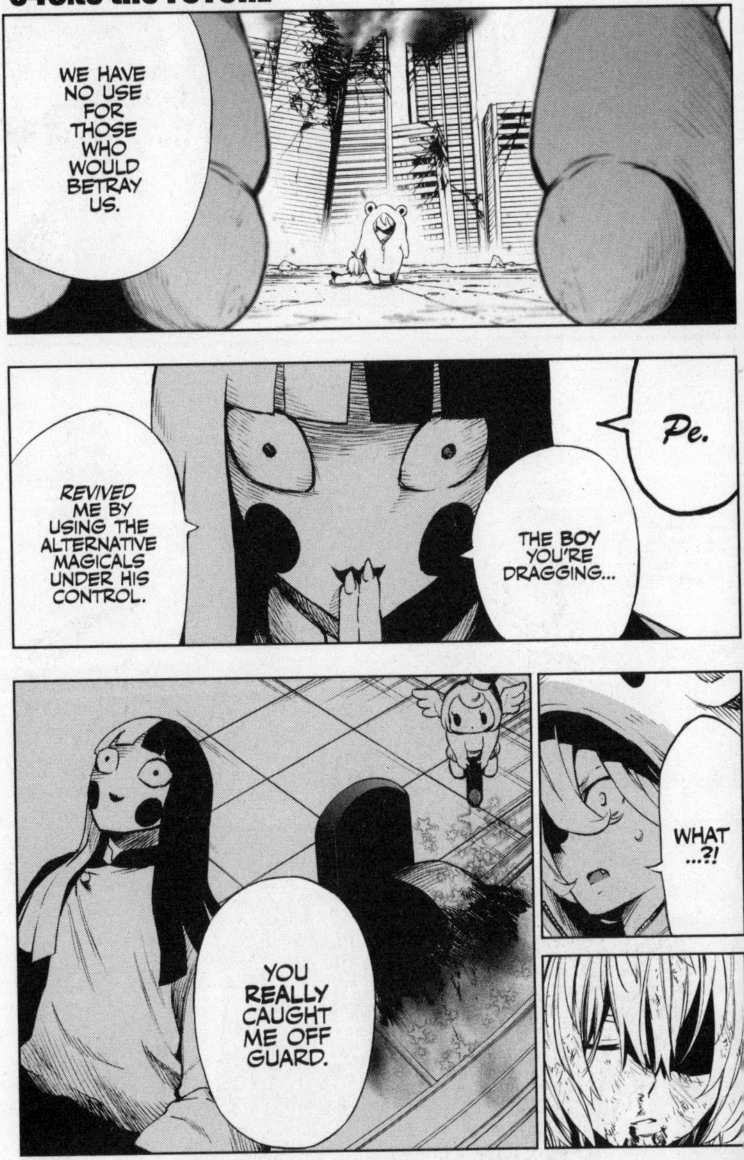
WE HAVE NO USE FOR THOSE WHO WOULD BETRAY US.
Pe.
THE BOY YOU'RE DRAGGING...
REVIVED ME BY USING THE ALTERNATIVE MAGICALS UNDER HIS CONTROL.
WHAT ...?!
YOU REALLY CAUGHT ME OFF GUARD.

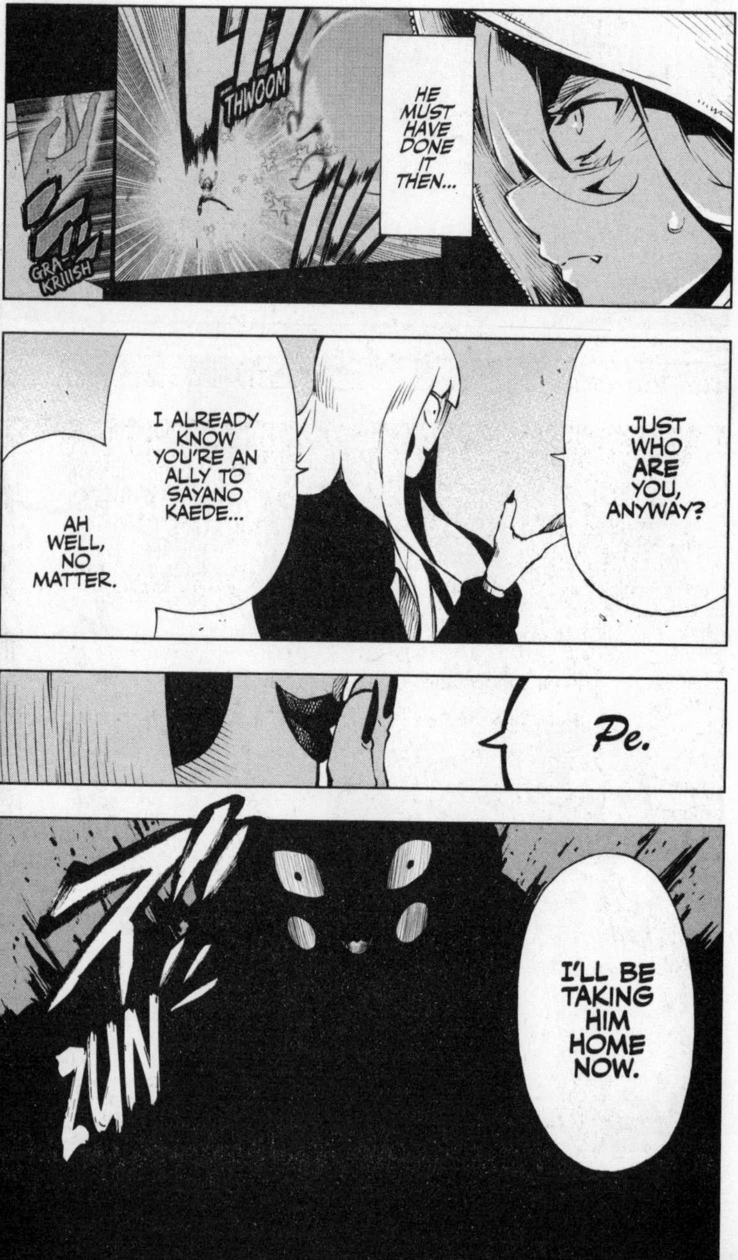
HE MUST HAVE DONE IT THEN...
THWOOM
GRA-KRIIISH
JUST WHO ARE YOU, ANYWAY?
I ALREADY KNOW YOU'RE AN ALLY TO SAYANO KAEDE...
AH WELL, NO MATTER.
Pe.
I'LL BE TAKING HIM HOME NOW.
ZUN

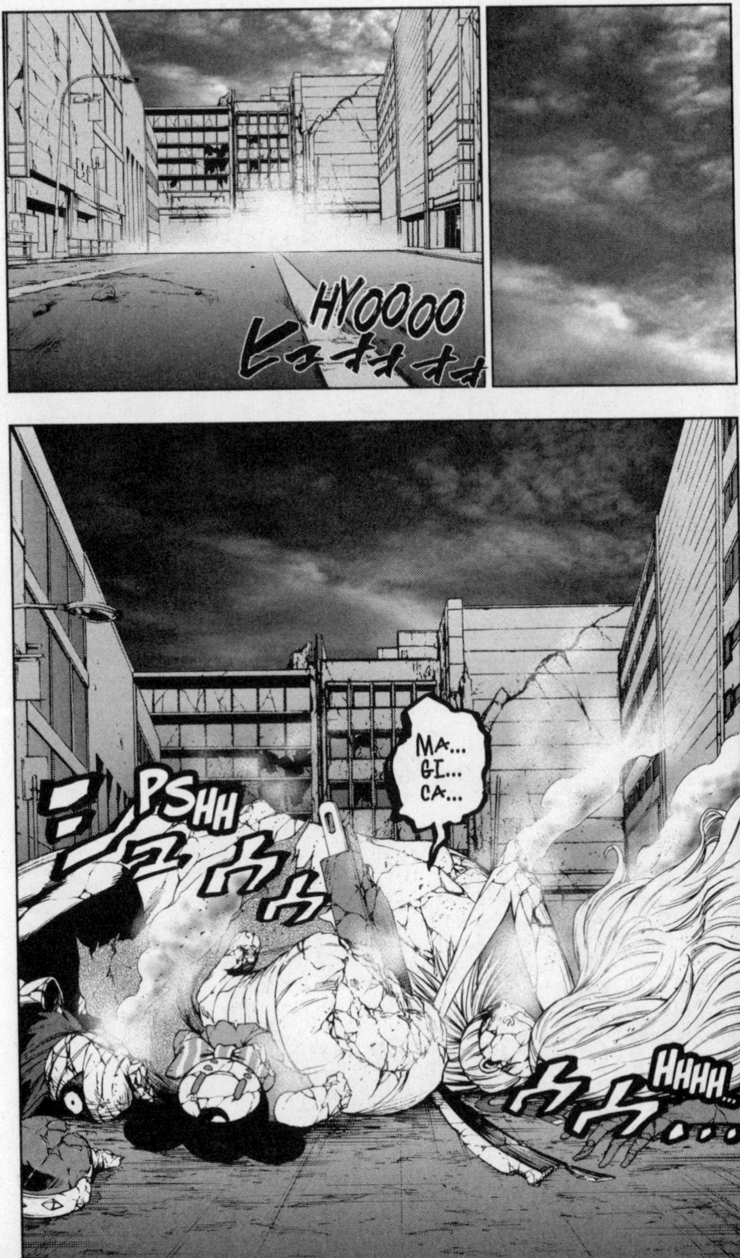
HYOOOO
ヒュオオオオ
MA... GI... CA...
PSHH
シュウウ
HHHH...
ウウ...

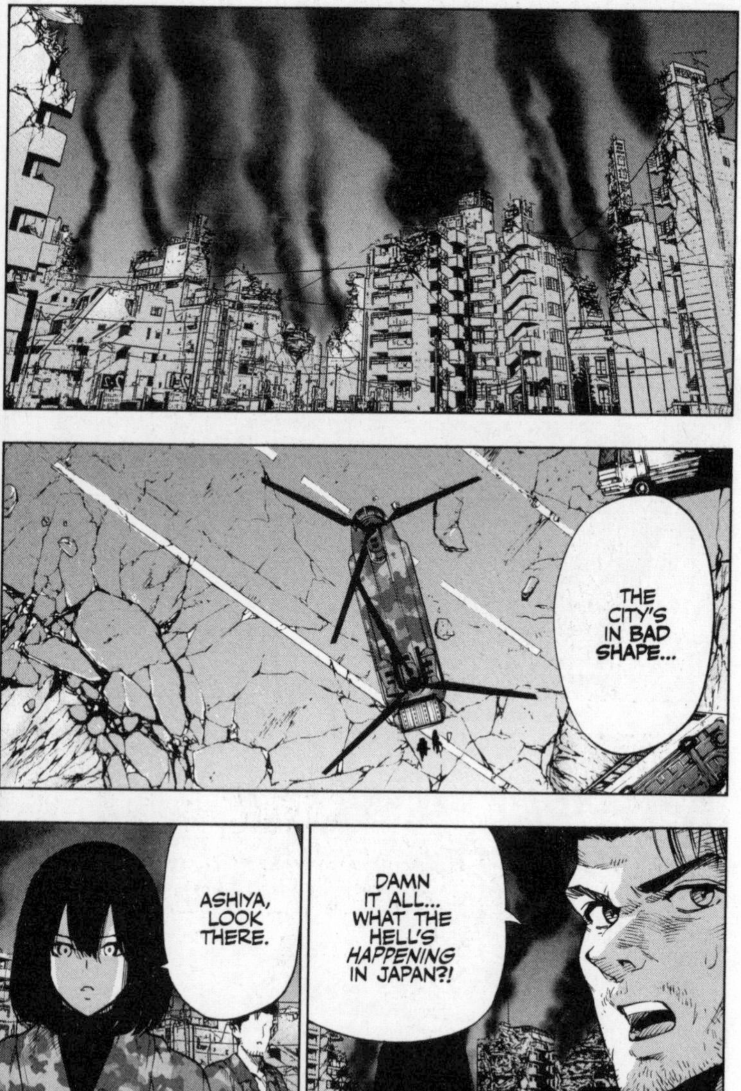
THE CITY'S IN BAD SHAPE...
DAMN IT ALL... WHAT THE HELL'S *HAPPENING* IN JAPAN?!
ASHIYA, LOOK THERE.

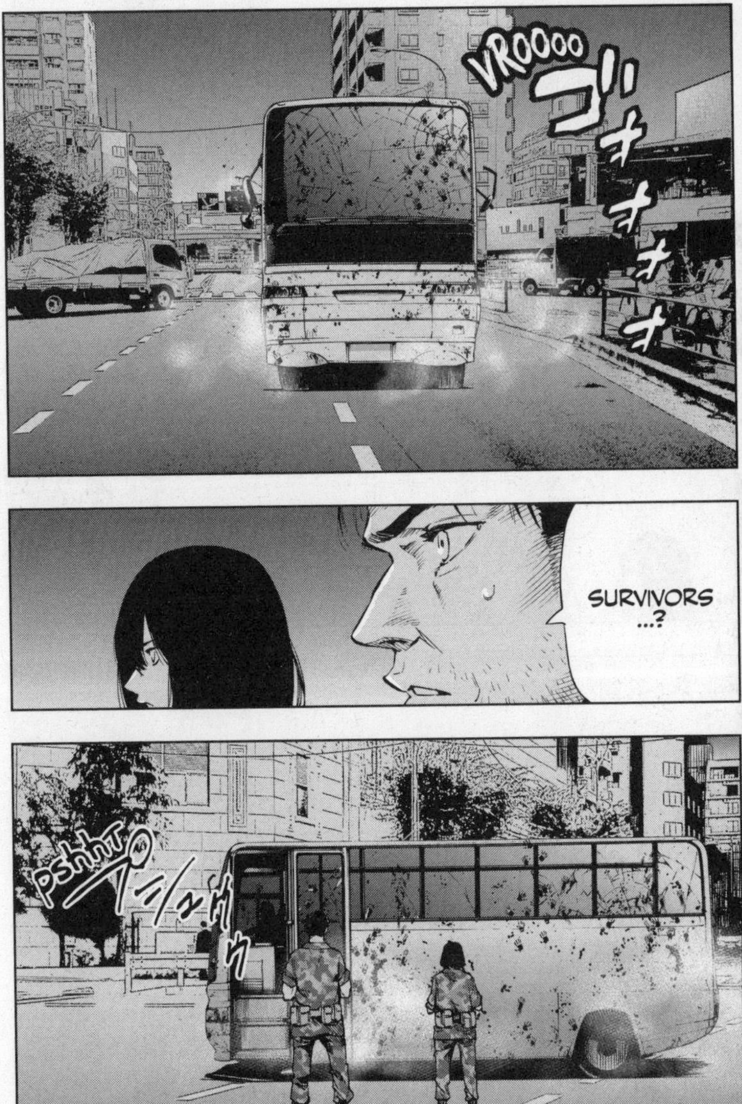
VROOOO
ゴォォォォ
SURVIVORS ...?
PSHHT
プシュゥゥ

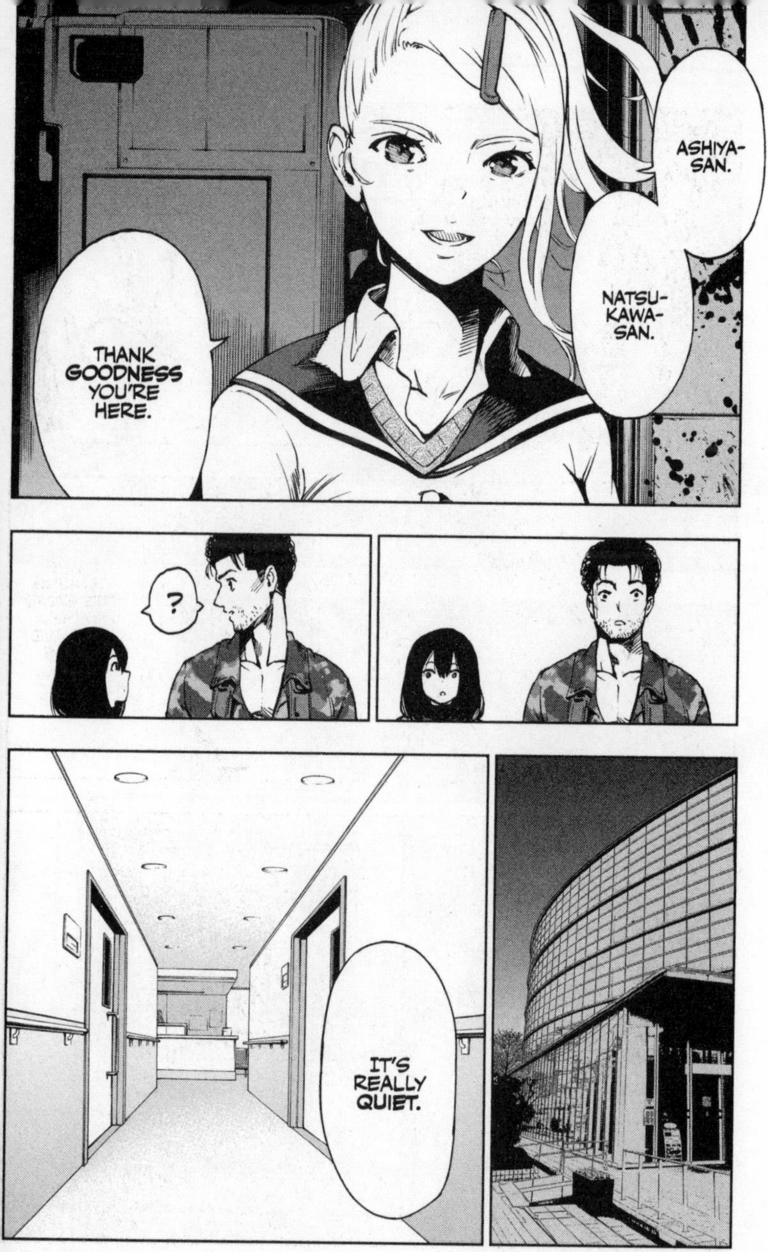
ASHIYA-SAN.
NATSU-KAWA-SAN.
THANK GOODNESS YOU'RE HERE.
?
IT'S REALLY QUIET.

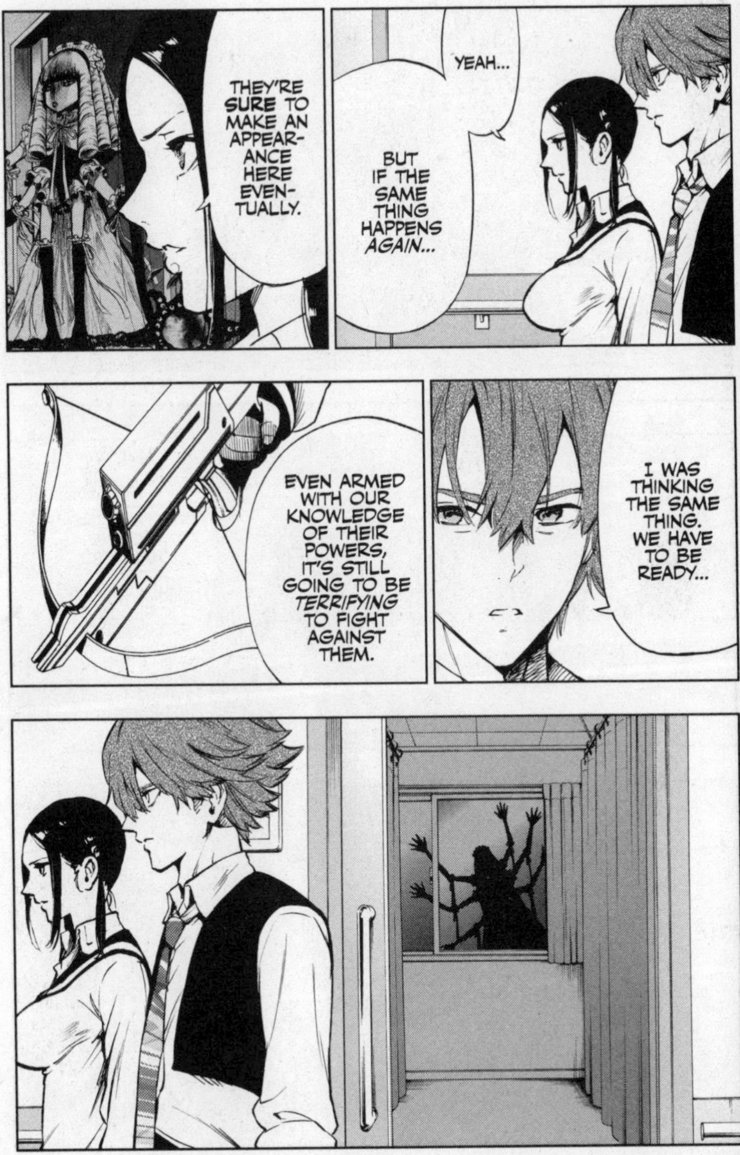
YEAH...
BUT IF THE SAME THING HAPPENS *AGAIN*...
THEY'RE **SURE** TO MAKE AN APPEARANCE HERE EVENTUALLY.
I WAS THINKING THE SAME THING. WE HAVE TO BE READY...
EVEN ARMED WITH OUR KNOWLEDGE OF THEIR POWERS, IT'S STILL GOING TO BE *TERRIFYING* TO FIGHT AGAINST THEM.

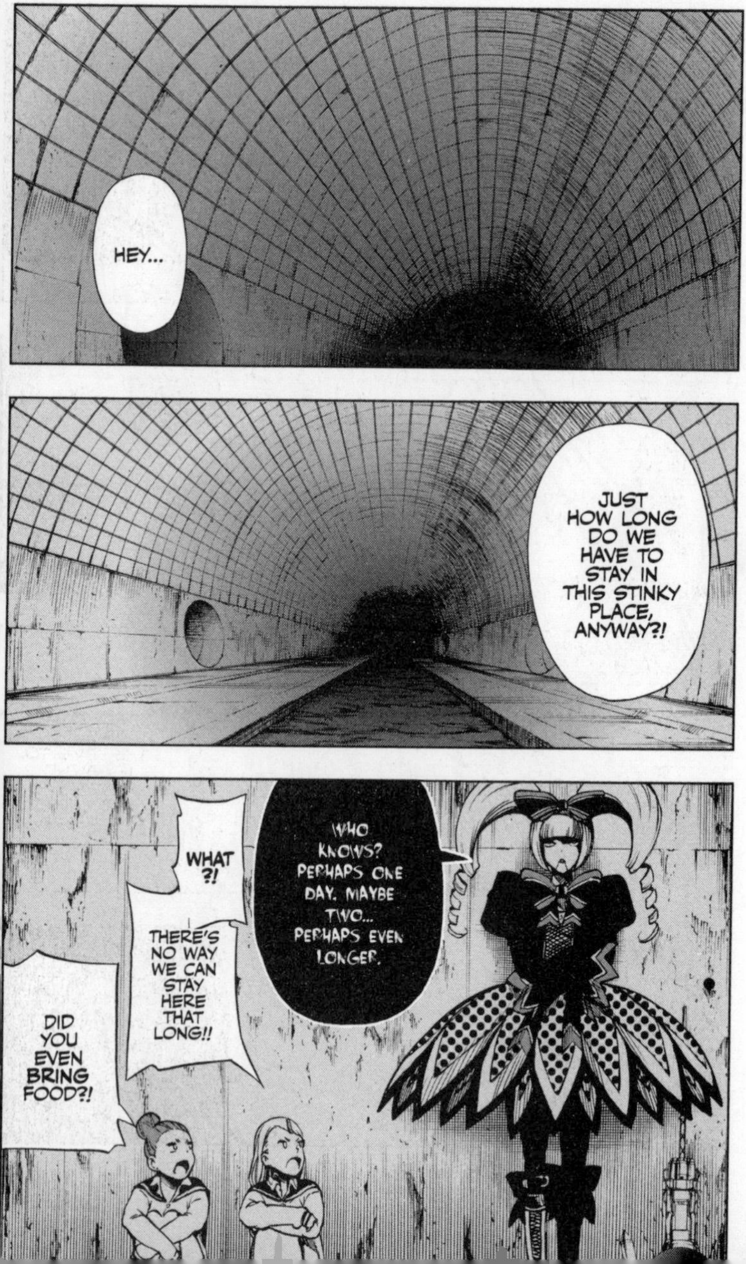
HEY...
JUST HOW LONG DO WE HAVE TO STAY IN THIS STINKY PLACE, ANYWAY?!
WHO KNOWS? PERHAPS ONE DAY. MAYBE TWO... PERHAPS EVEN LONGER.
WHAT?!
THERE'S NO WAY WE CAN STAY HERE THAT LONG!!
DID YOU EVEN BRING FOOD?!

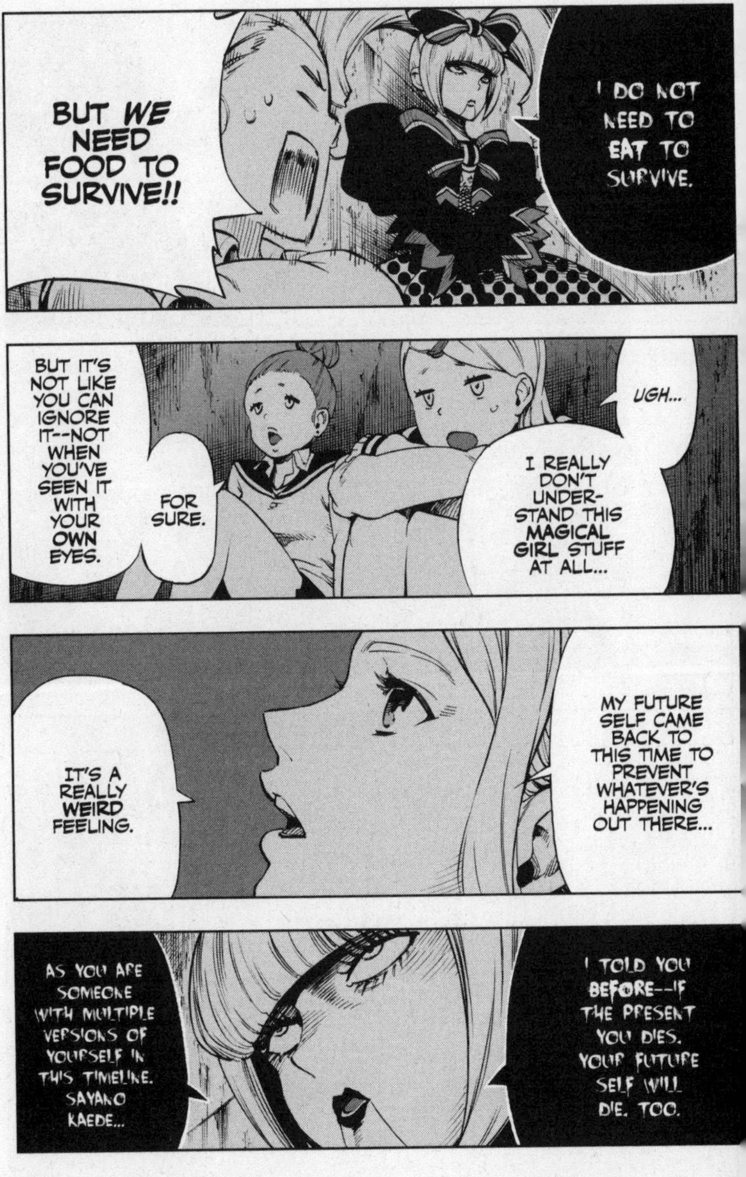
I DO NOT NEED TO EAT TO SURVIVE.
BUT WE NEED FOOD TO SURVIVE!!
UGH...
I REALLY DON'T UNDERSTAND THIS MAGICAL GIRL STUFF AT ALL...
FOR SURE.
BUT IT'S NOT LIKE YOU CAN IGNORE IT--NOT WHEN YOU'VE SEEN IT WITH YOUR OWN EYES.
MY FUTURE SELF CAME BACK TO THIS TIME TO PREVENT WHATEVER'S HAPPENING OUT THERE...
IT'S A REALLY WEIRD FEELING.
I TOLD YOU BEFORE--IF THE PRESENT YOU DIES, YOUR FUTURE SELF WILL DIE, TOO.
AS YOU ARE SOMEONE WITH MULTIPLE VERSIONS OF YOURSELF IN THIS TIMELINE, SAYAKO KAEDE...

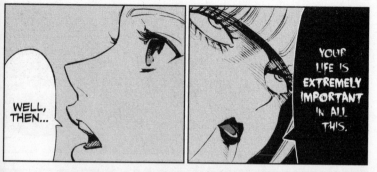

WELL, THEN...

YOUR LIFE IS **EXTREMELY IMPORTANT** IN ALL THIS.

YOU'D BETTER GIVE ME SOME-THING TO *EAT*.

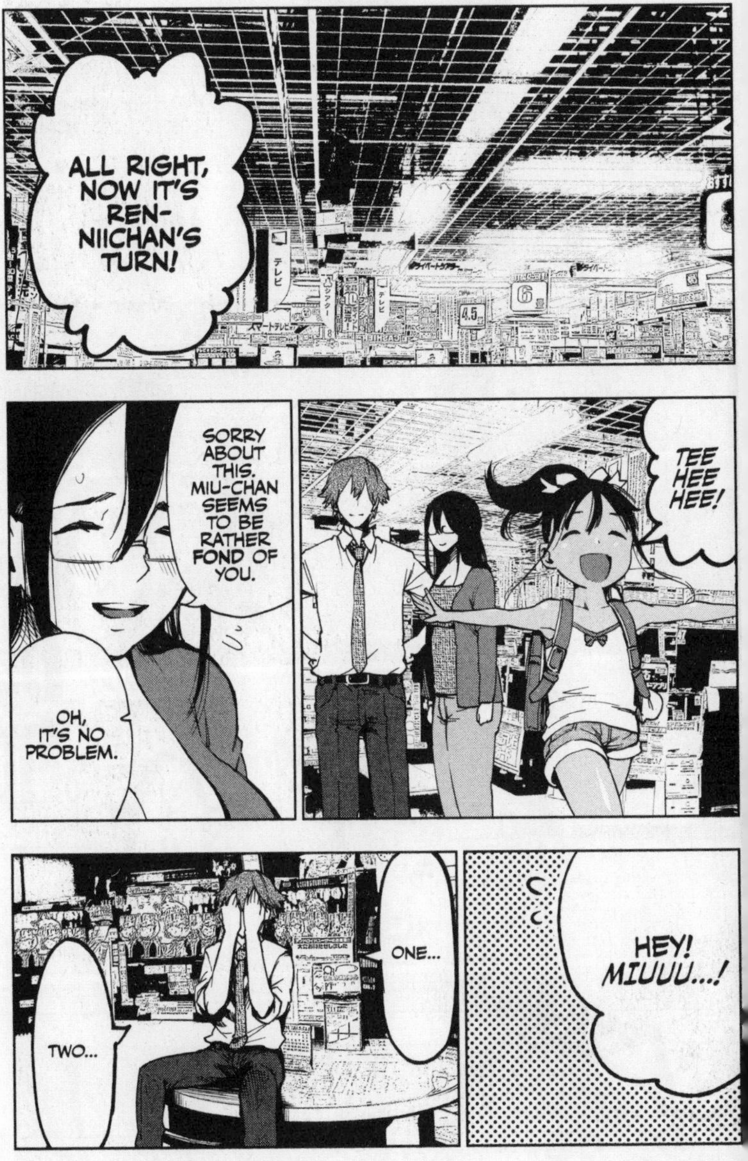
ALL RIGHT, NOW IT'S REN-NIICHAN'S TURN!
TEE HEE HEE!
SORRY ABOUT THIS. MIU-CHAN SEEMS TO BE RATHER FOND OF YOU.
OH, IT'S NO PROBLEM.
HEY! MIUUU...!
ONE...
TWO...

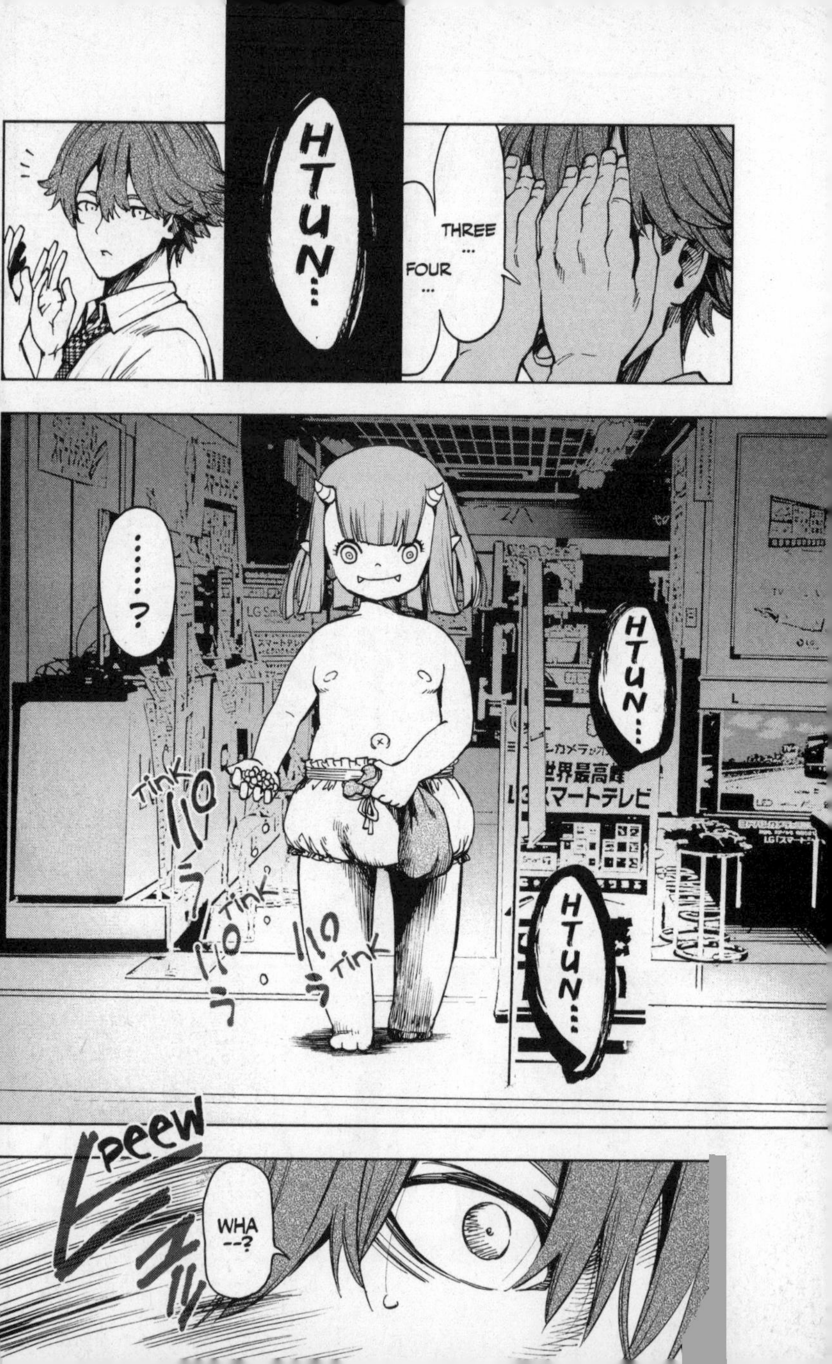
THREE... FOUR...
HTUN...
HTUN...
HTUN...
......?
Tink
Tink
Tink
世界最高峰
LGスマートテレビ
Peew
WHA--?

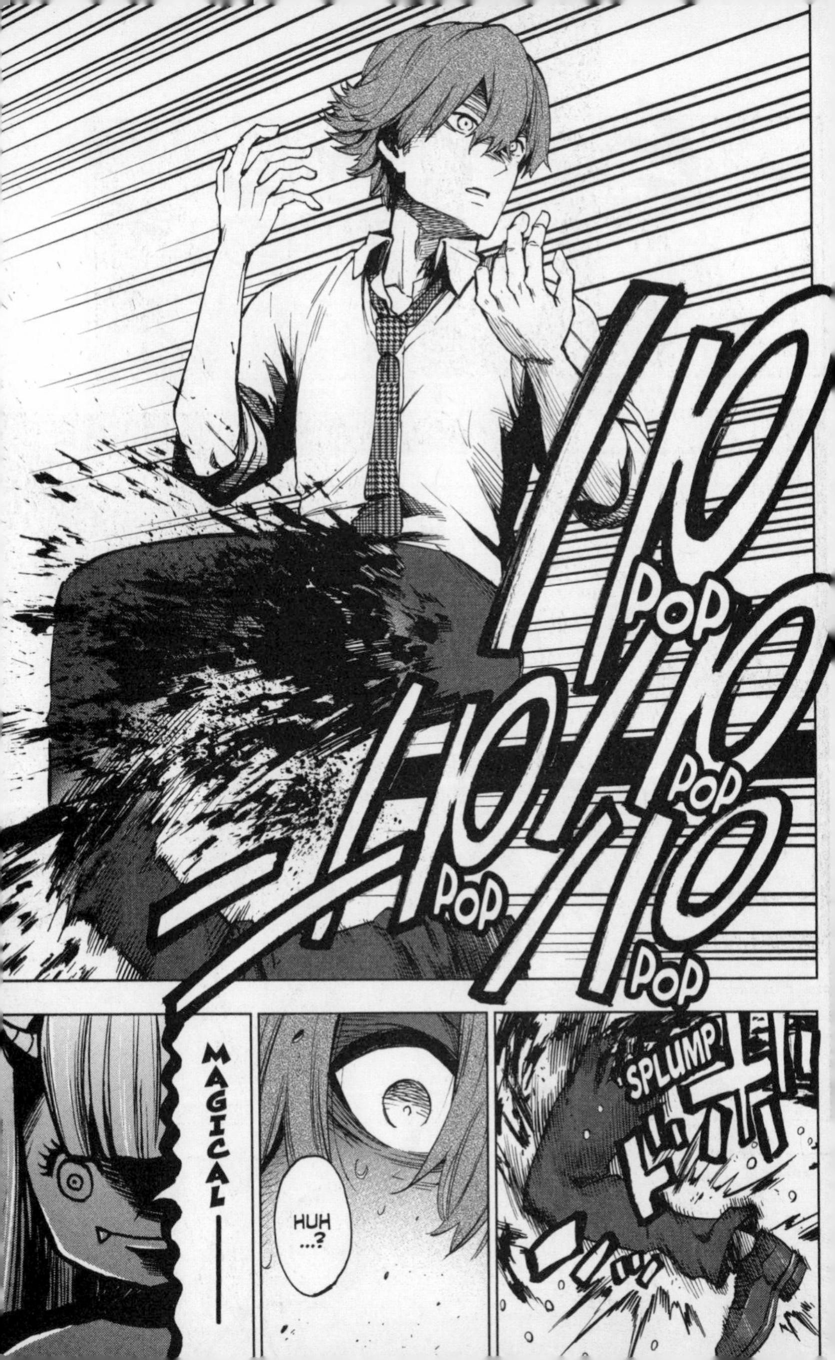
POP
POP
POP
POP
SPLUMP
HUH ...?
MAGICAL—

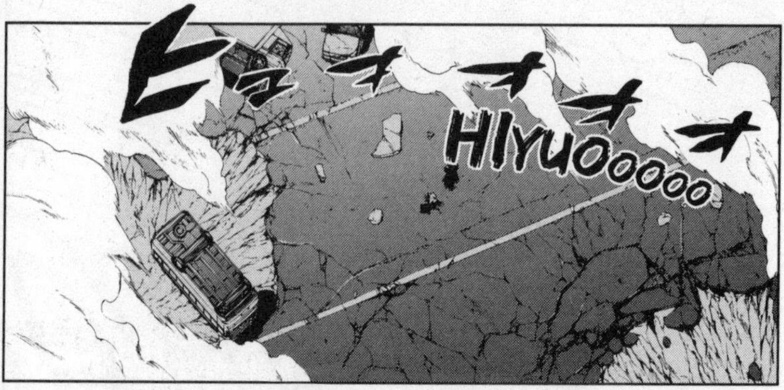
ヒュオオオオ
HIYUOOOOOO
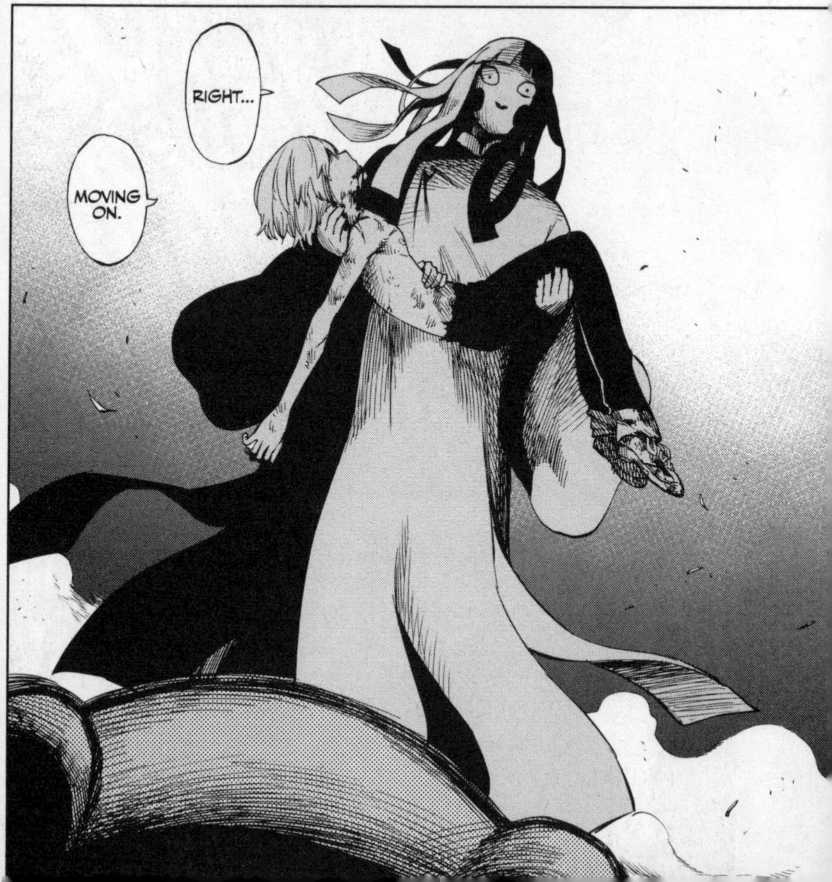
RIGHT...
MOVING ON.

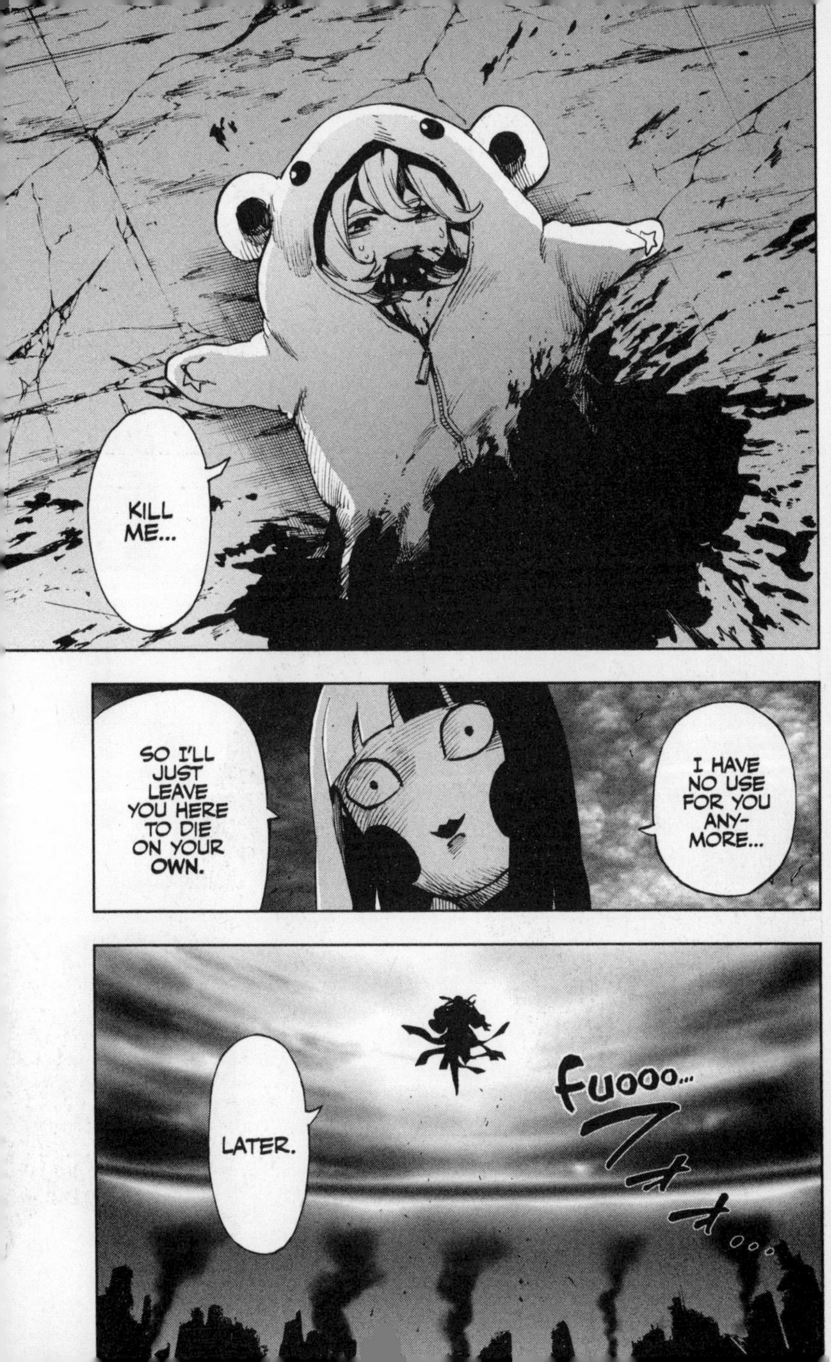
KILL ME...
I HAVE NO USE FOR YOU ANY-MORE...
SO I'LL JUST LEAVE YOU HERE TO DIE ON YOUR OWN.
fuooo...
LATER.

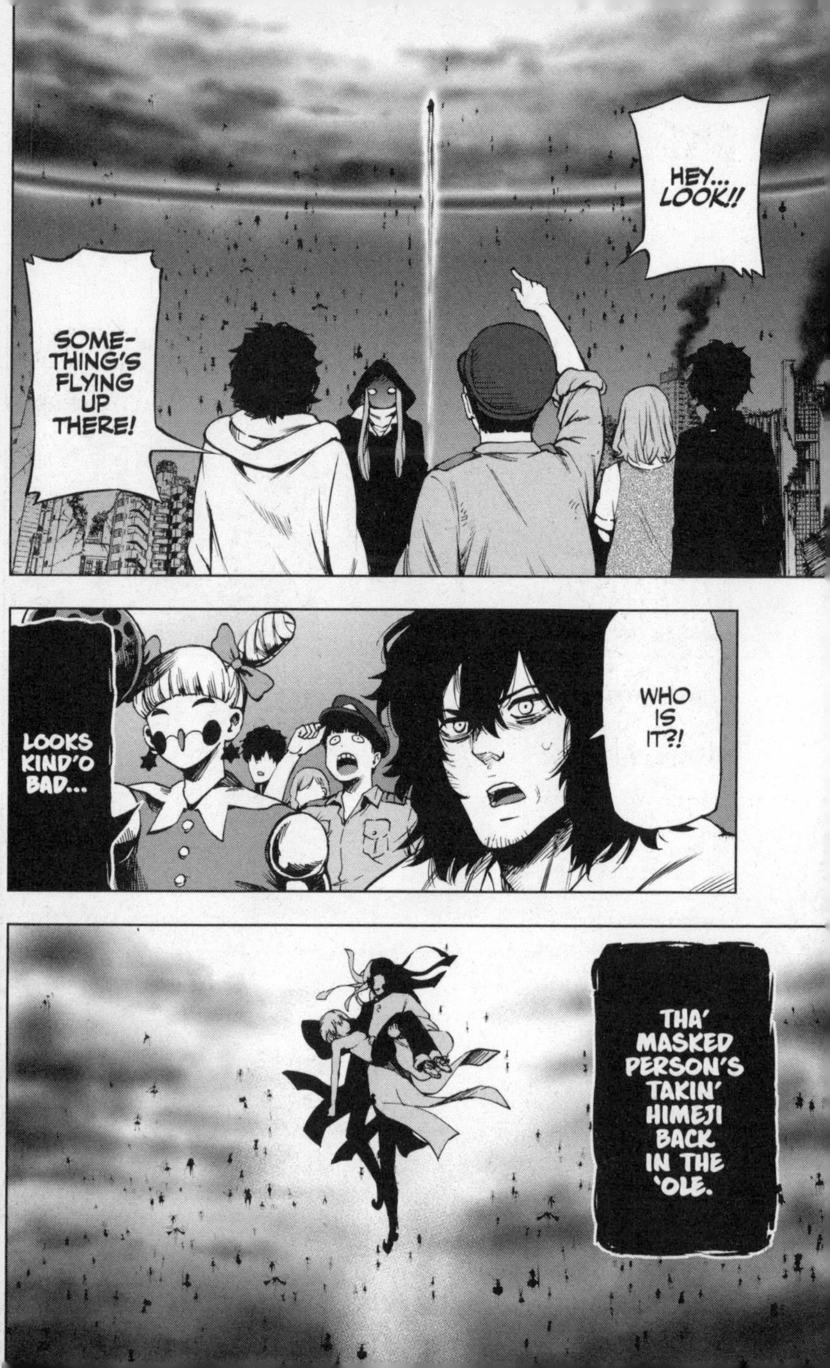
HEY... LOOK!!
SOME-THING'S FLYING UP THERE!
WHO IS IT?!
LOOKS KIND'O BAD...
THA' MASKED PERSON'S TAKIN' HIMEJI BACK IN THE 'OLE.

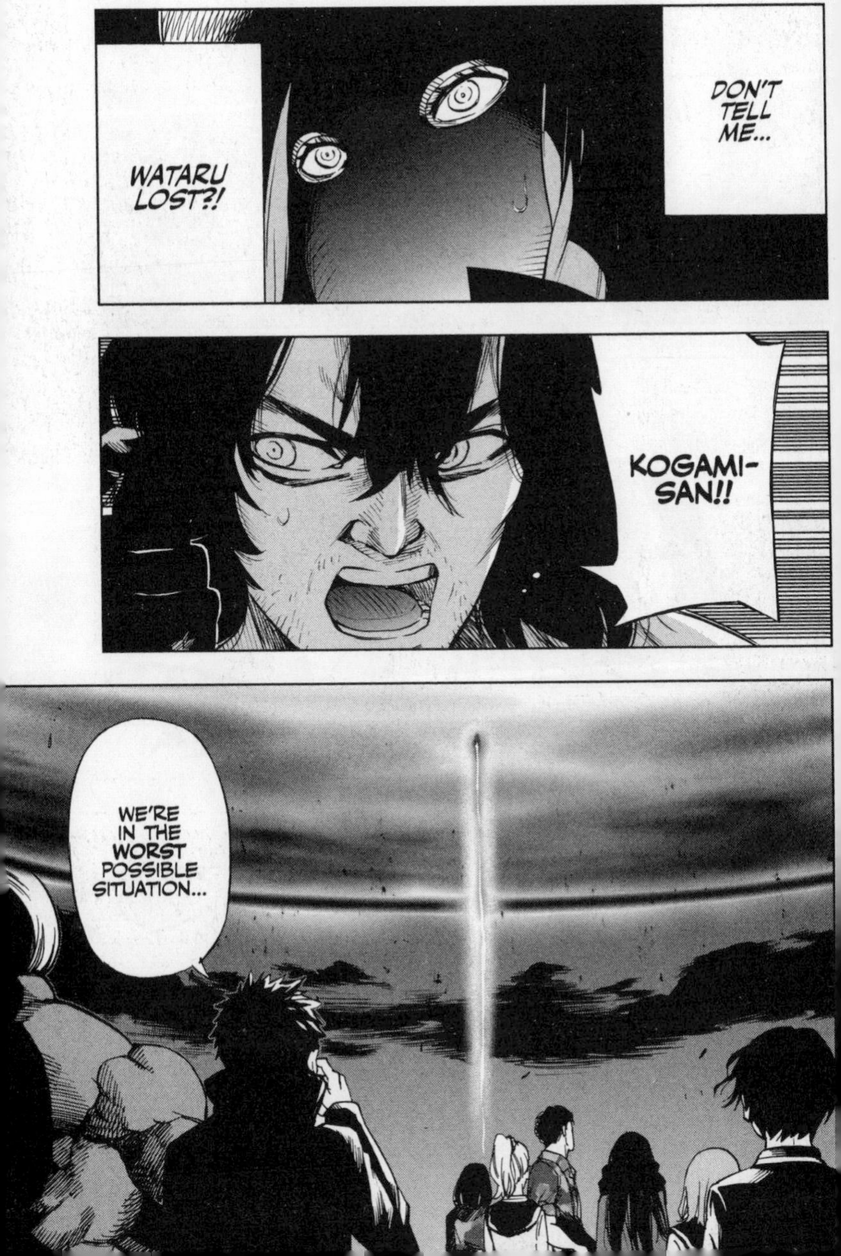
DON'T TELL ME...
WATARU LOST?!
KOGAMI-SAN!!
WE'RE IN THE WORST POSSIBLE SITUATION...

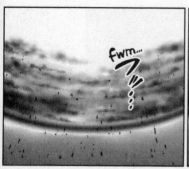

fwm...
PLEASE! WE NEED TO USE YOUR HELICOPTER TO FLY INTO THAT HOLE IN THE SKY!!
IF WE SIT AROUND, WE'RE GONNA BE TOO LATE!!
EVERYTHING...
EVERYTHING WILL COME TO AN END!!!
BUT... YOU MAY SAY THAT, BUT I...

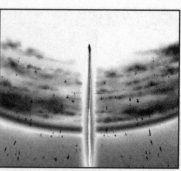

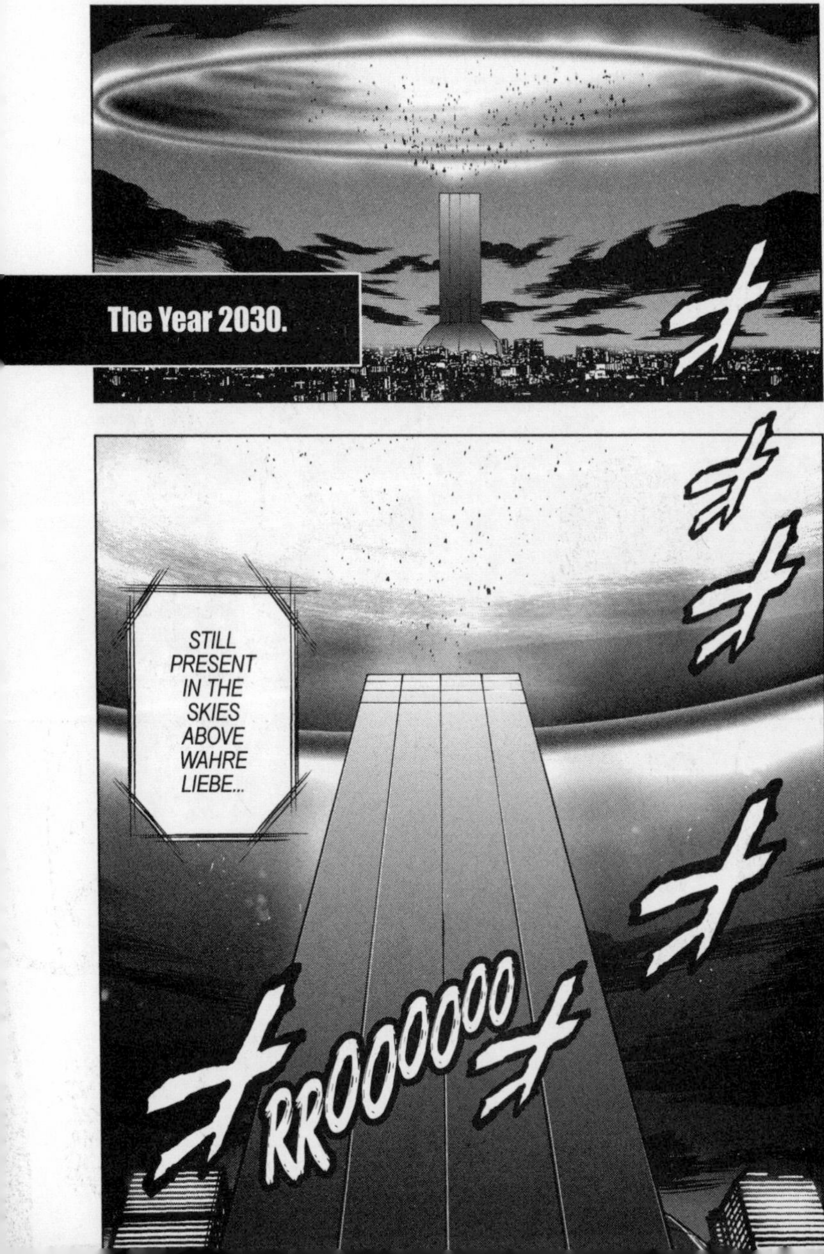
The Year 2030.
STILL PRESENT IN THE SKIES ABOVE WAHRE LIEBE...
RROOOOOO

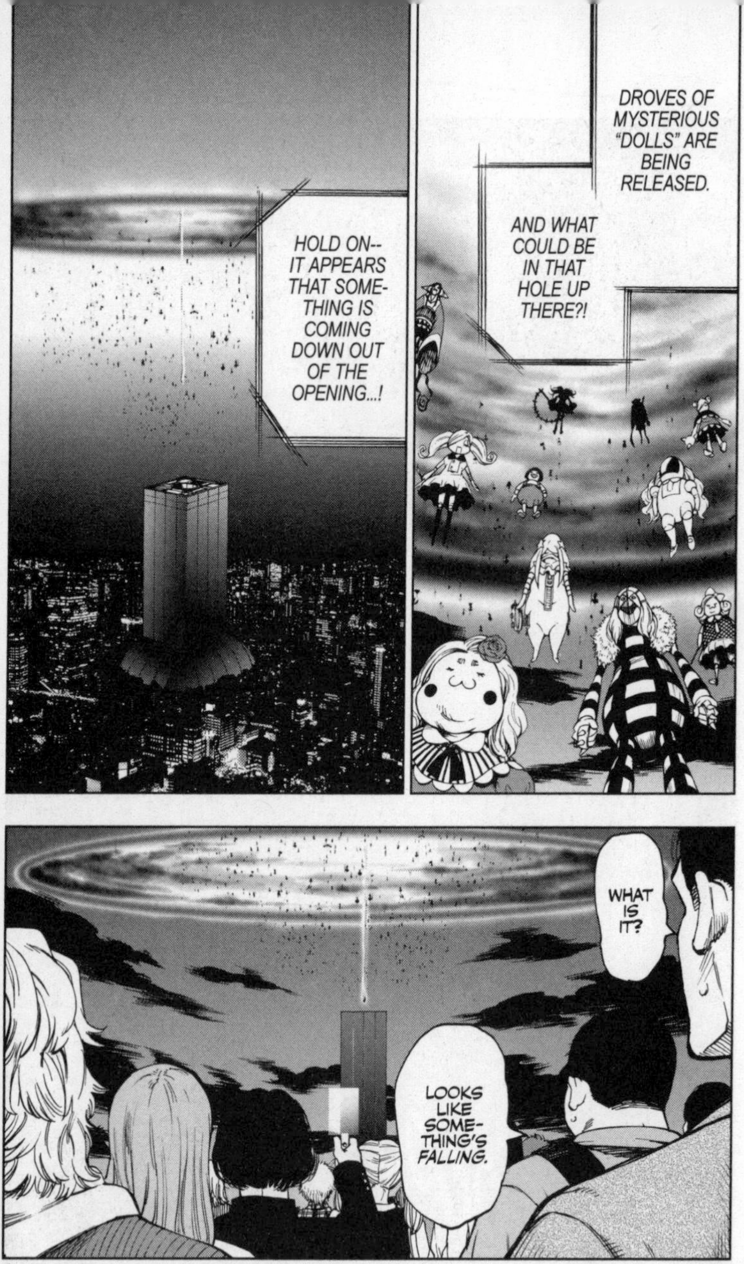
DROVES OF MYSTERIOUS "DOLLS" ARE BEING RELEASED.
AND WHAT COULD BE IN THAT HOLE UP THERE?!
HOLD ON-- IT APPEARS THAT SOME-THING IS COMING DOWN OUT OF THE OPENING...!
WHAT IS IT?
LOOKS LIKE SOME-THING'S FALLING.

....

OH GOD...

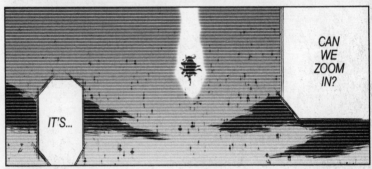

CAN WE ZOOM IN?

IT'S...

IT'S A PERSON!!

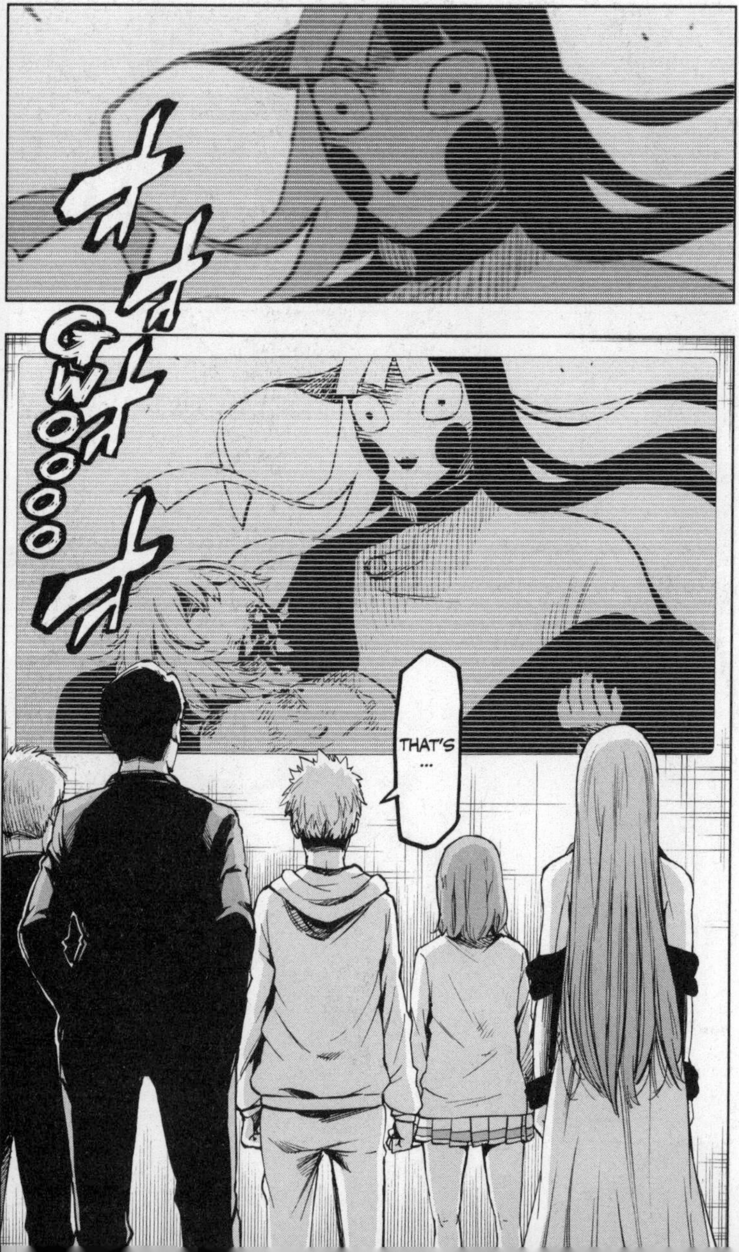
GWOOOOOO
THAT'S ...

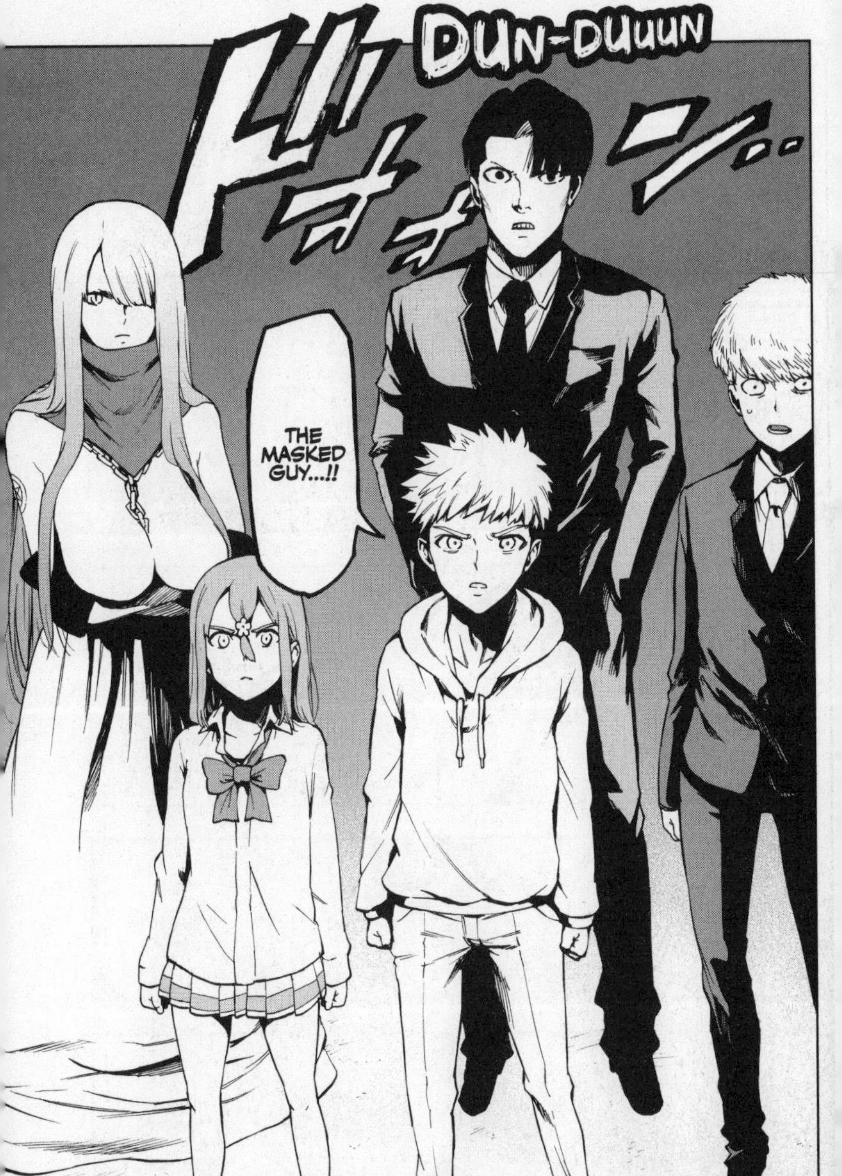
DUN-DUUUN
THE MASKED GUY...!!

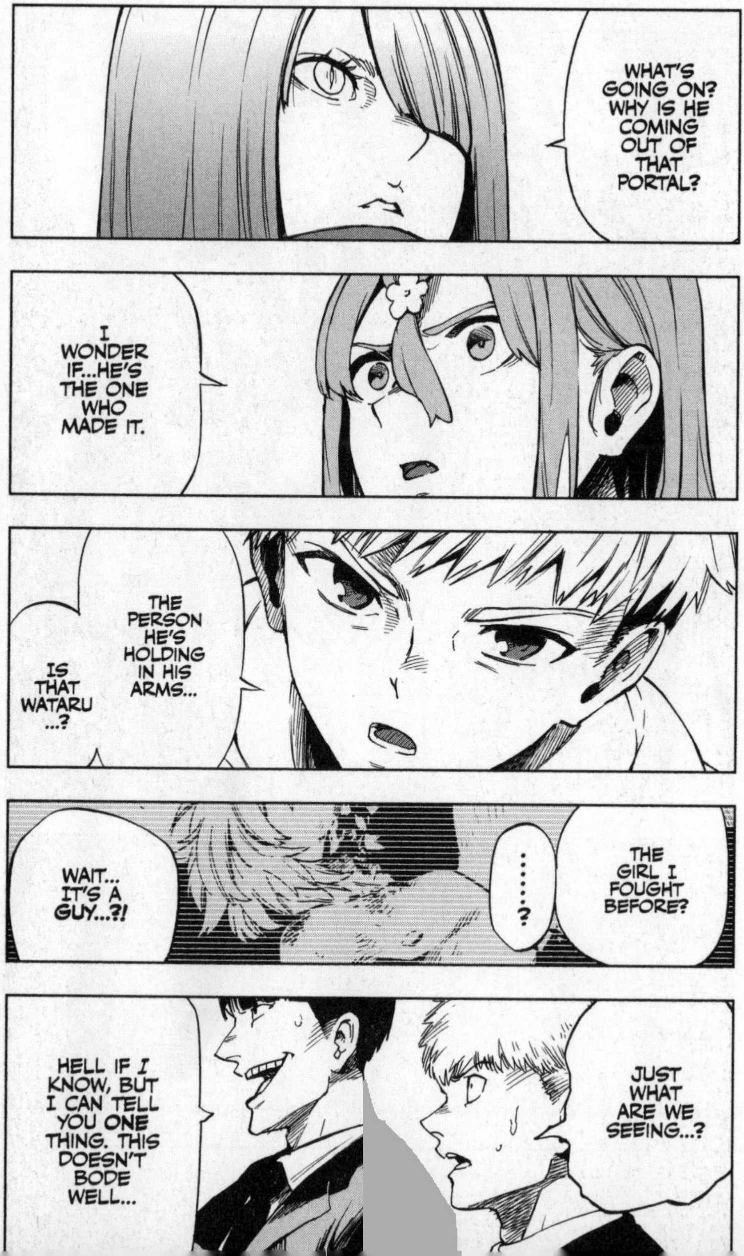
WHAT'S GOING ON? WHY IS HE COMING OUT OF THAT PORTAL?
I WONDER IF...HE'S THE ONE WHO MADE IT.
THE PERSON HE'S HOLDING IN HIS ARMS...
IS THAT WATARU ...?
THE GIRL I FOUGHT BEFORE?
......?
WAIT... IT'S A GUY...?!
JUST WHAT ARE WE SEEING...?
HELL IF I KNOW, BUT I CAN TELL YOU ONE THING. THIS DOESN'T BODE WELL...

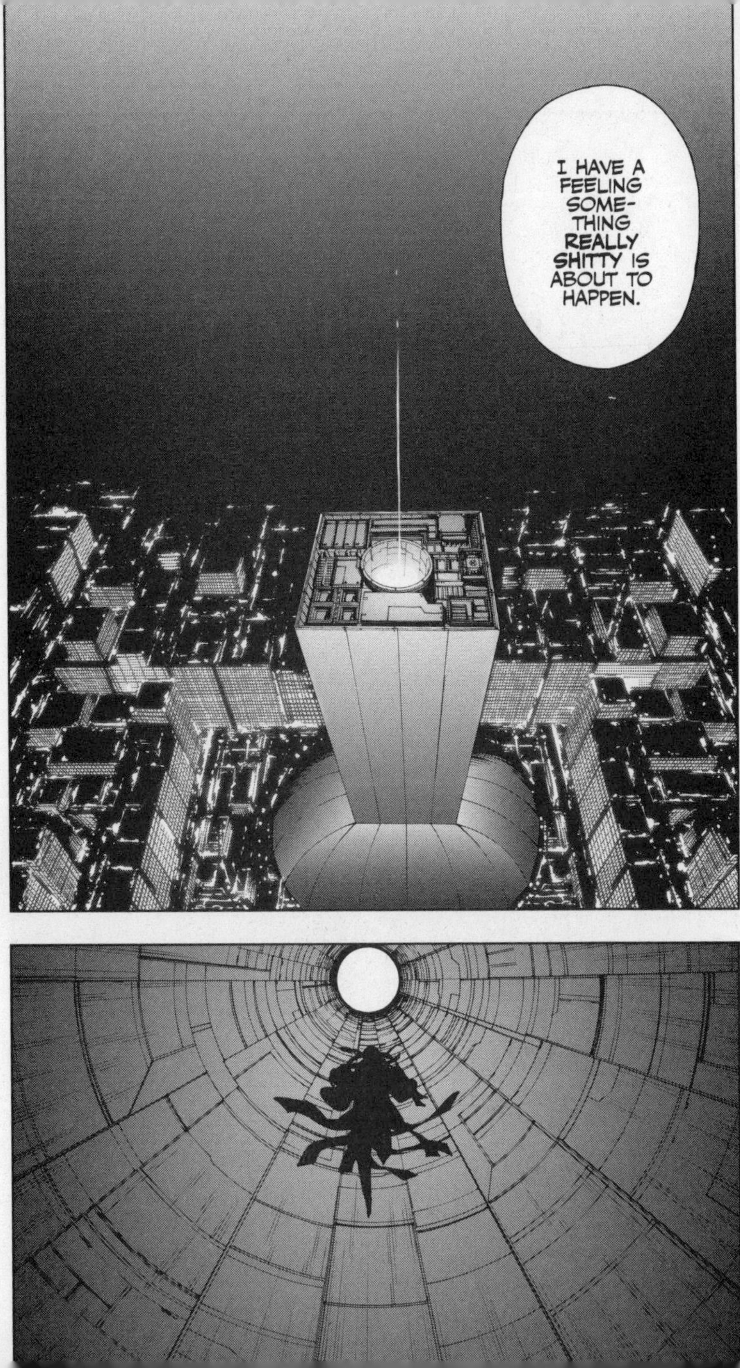
I HAVE A FEELING SOME-THING REALLY SHITTY IS ABOUT TO HAPPEN.

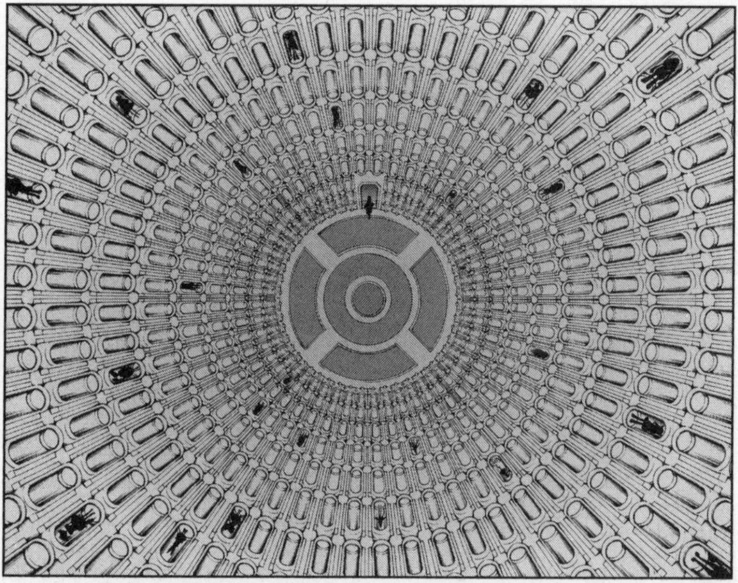
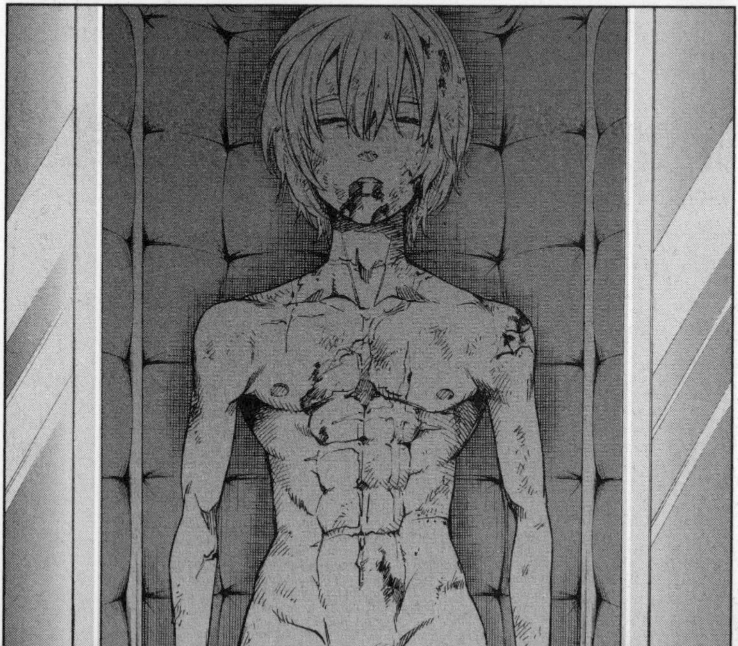

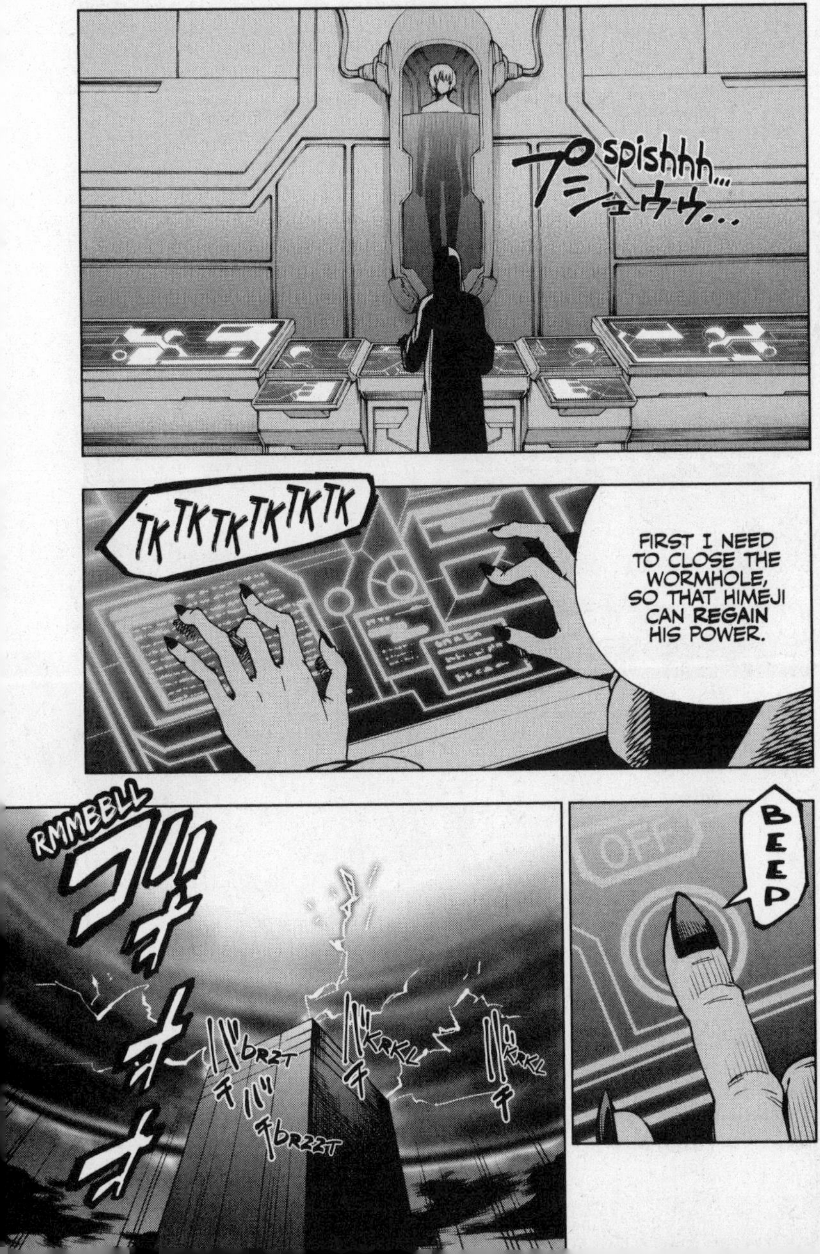
spishhh...
プシュウウ...
FIRST I NEED TO CLOSE THE WORMHOLE, SO THAT HIMEJI CAN REGAIN HIS POWER.
TKTKTKTKTKTK
BEEP
OFF
RMMBBLL
KRKL
KRKL
BRZT
BRZZT

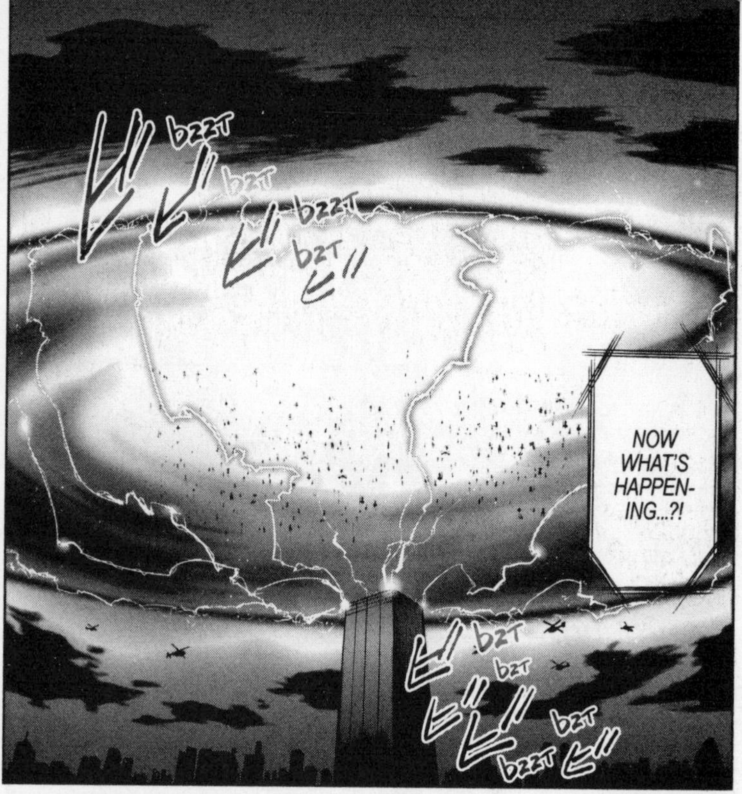
NOW WHAT'S HAPPEN-ING...?!
bzzT
bzT
bzzT
bzT
bzT
bzT
bzT
bzzT

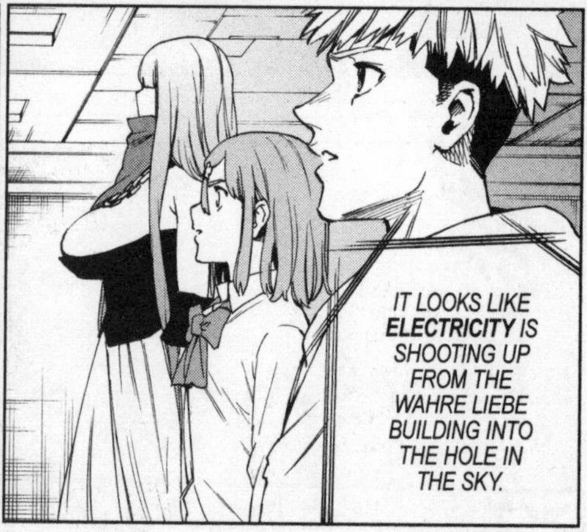
IT LOOKS LIKE **ELECTRICITY** IS SHOOTING UP FROM THE WAHRE LIEBE BUILDING INTO THE HOLE IN THE SKY.

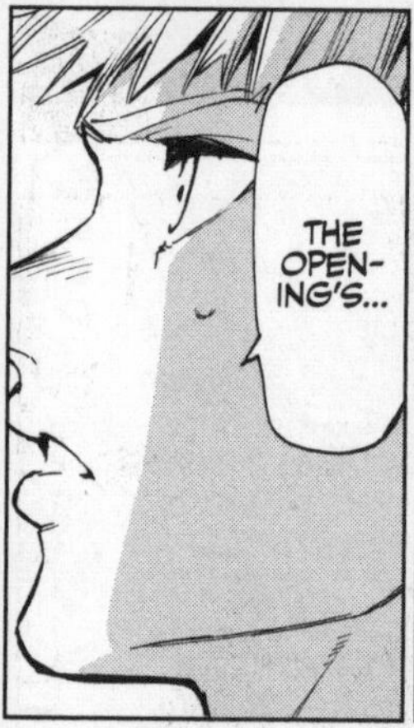
THE OPEN-ING'S...

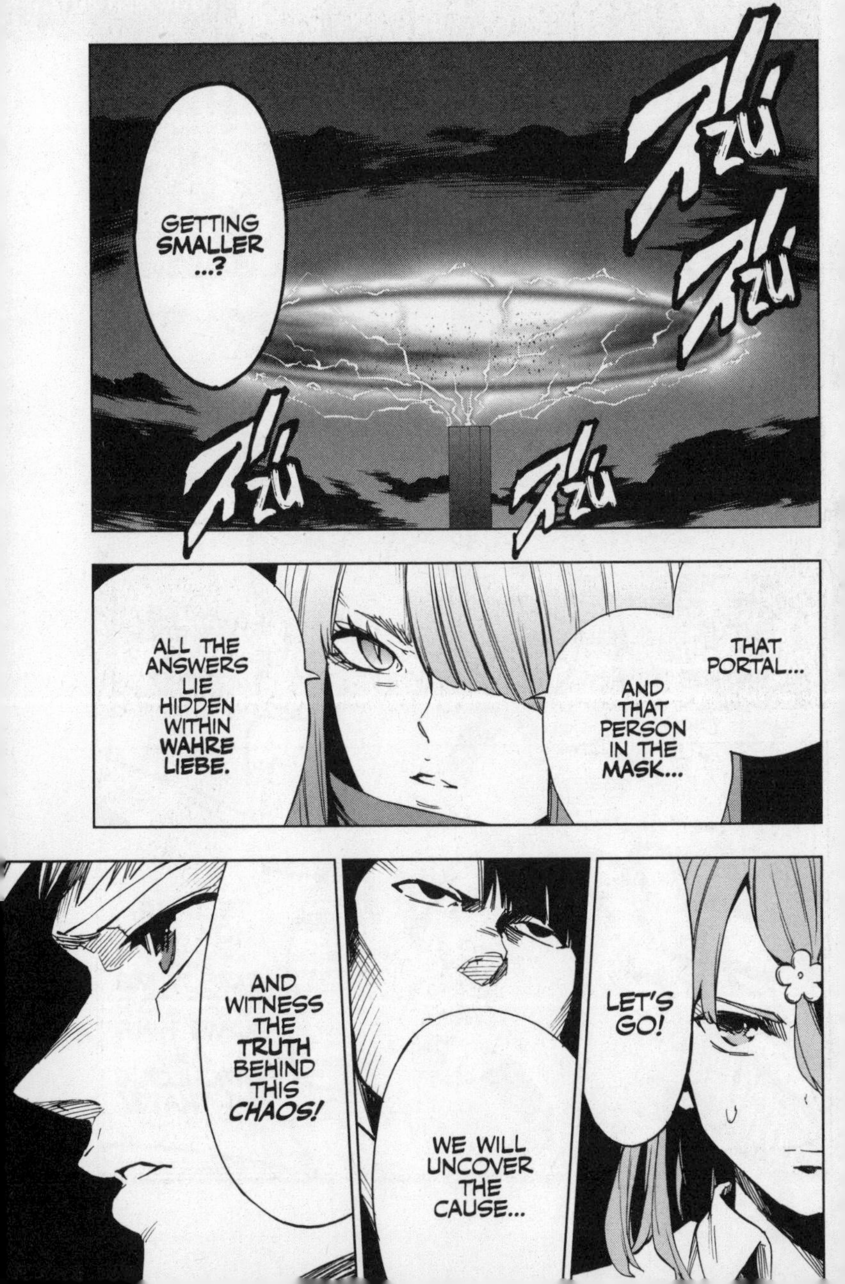
ズzu
ズzu
GETTING SMALLER ...?
ズzu
ズzu
THAT PORTAL...
AND THAT PERSON IN THE MASK...
ALL THE ANSWERS LIE HIDDEN WITHIN WAHRE LIEBE.
LET'S GO!
WE WILL UNCOVER THE CAUSE...
AND WITNESS THE TRUTH BEHIND THIS *CHAOS!*

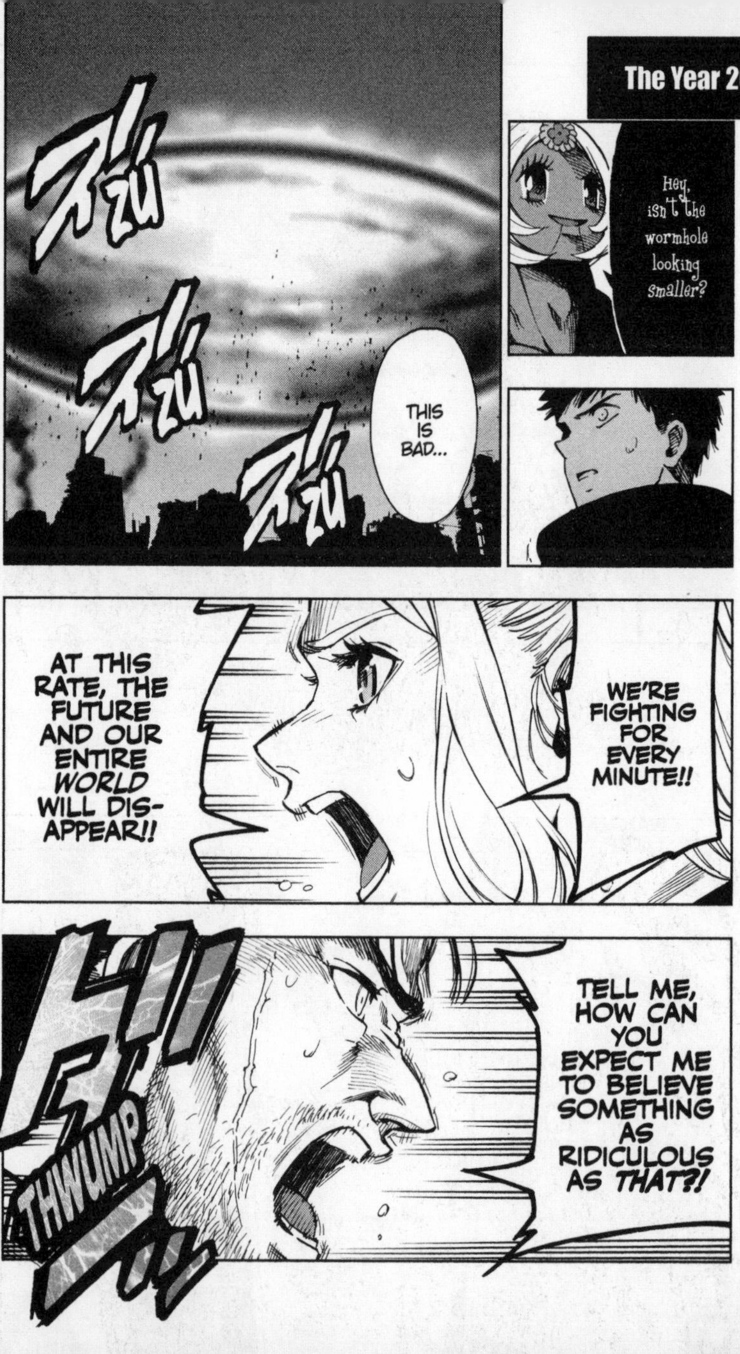

The Year 2012.
Hey, isn't the wormhole looking smaller?
zu
zu
zu
THIS IS BAD...
WE'RE FIGHTING FOR EVERY MINUTE!!
AT THIS RATE, THE FUTURE AND OUR ENTIRE *WORLD* WILL DIS-APPEAR!!
TELL ME, HOW CAN YOU EXPECT ME TO BELIEVE SOMETHING AS RIDICULOUS AS *THAT*?!
THWUMP

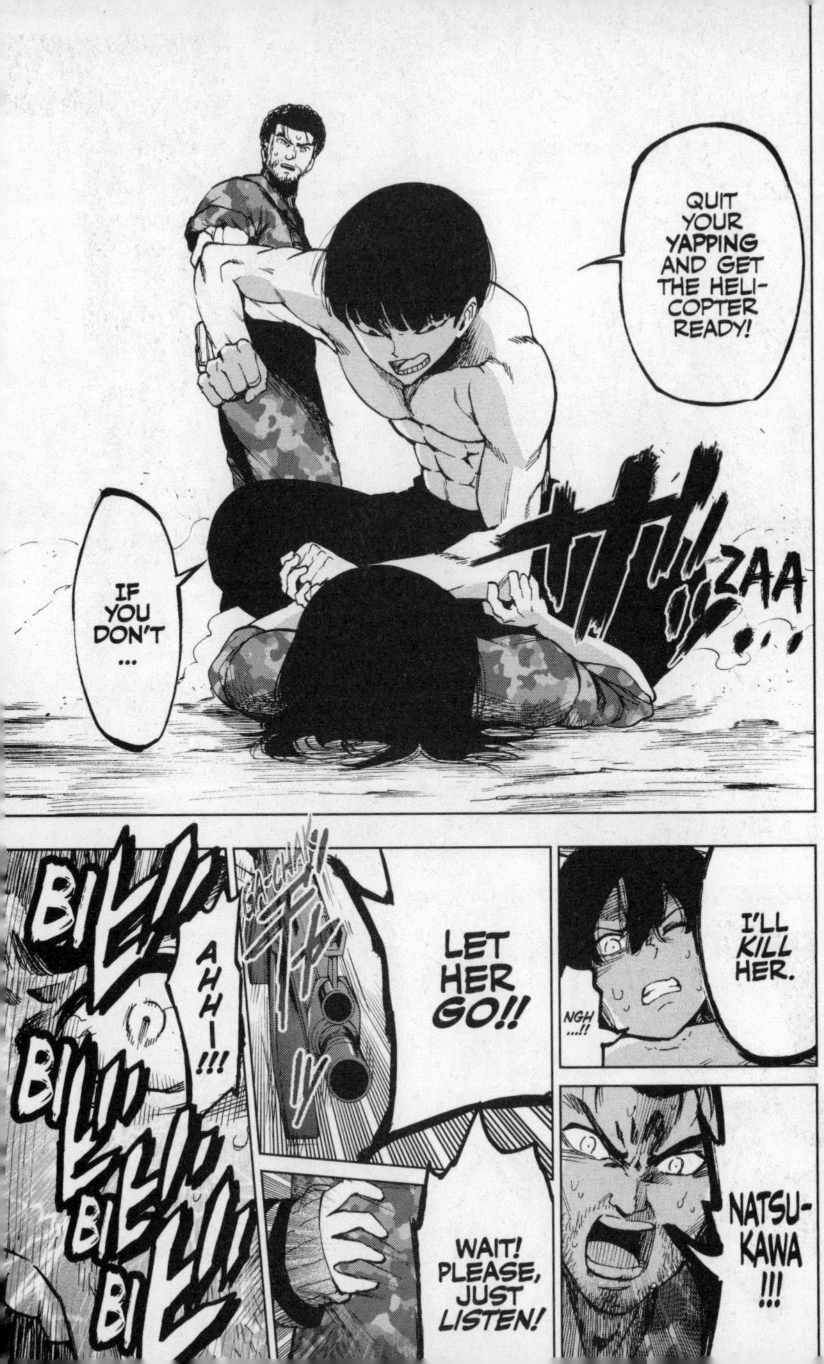
QUIT YOUR YAPPING AND GET THE HELI-COPTER READY!
ZAA...
IF YOU DON'T ...
I'LL KILL HER.
NGH ...!!
NATSU-KAWA !!!
WAIT! PLEASE, JUST LISTEN!
LET HER GO!!
AHH—!!!

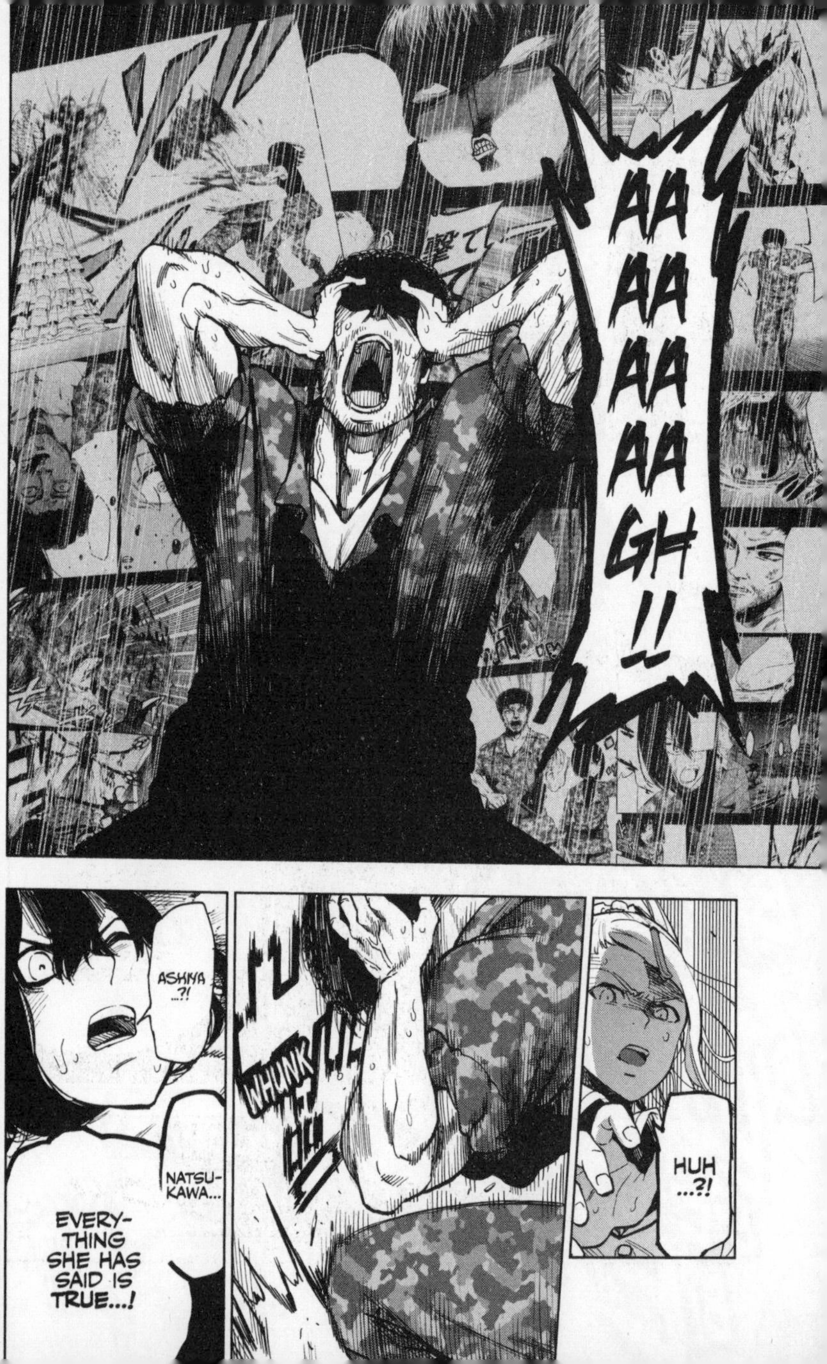
撃て
AAAAAAAAAAGH!!
HUH...?!
WHUNK
ASHIYA...?!
NATSU-KAWA...
EVERY-THING SHE HAS SAID IS TRUE...!

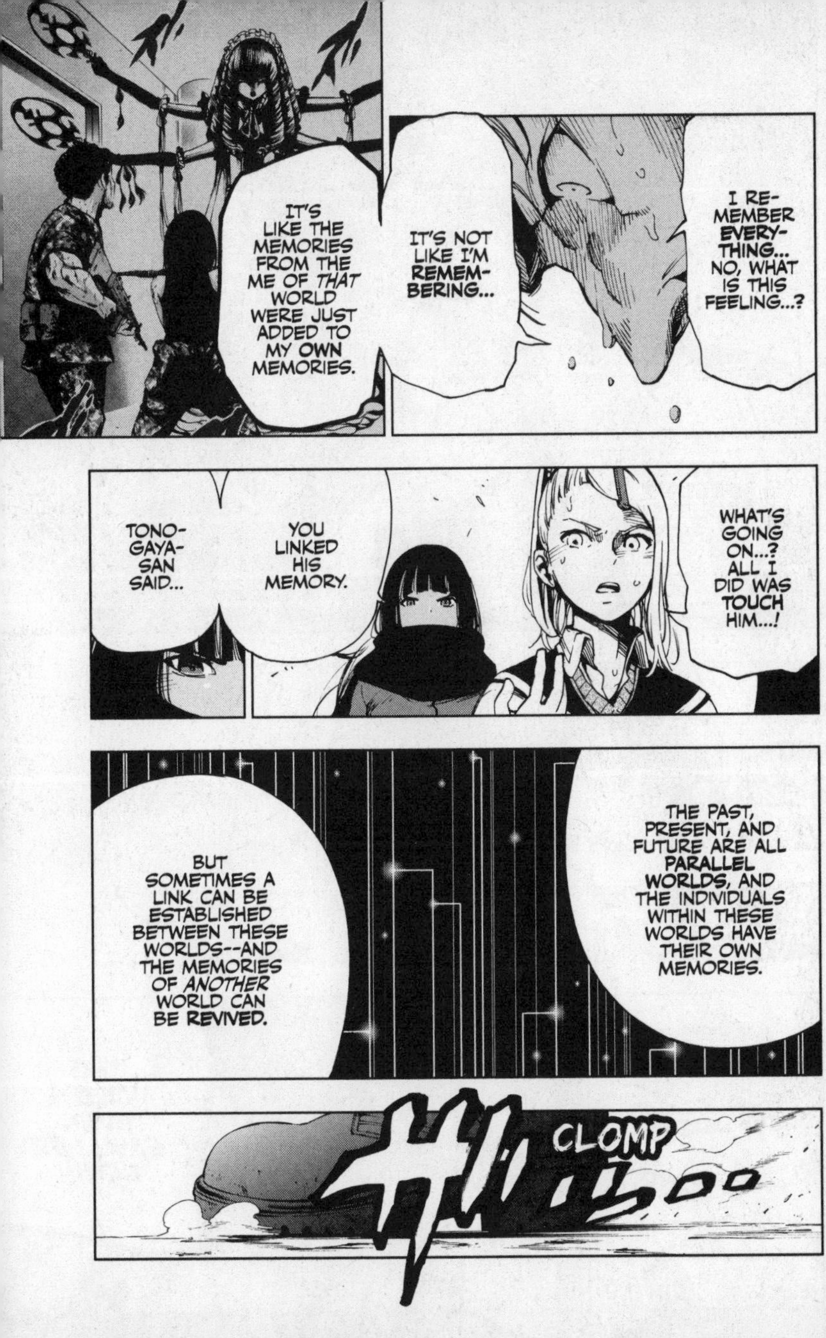
I RE-MEMBER EVERY-THING... NO, WHAT IS THIS FEELING...?
IT'S NOT LIKE I'M REMEM-BERING...
IT'S LIKE THE MEMORIES FROM THE ME OF *THAT* WORLD WERE JUST ADDED TO MY OWN MEMORIES.
WHAT'S GOING ON...? ALL I DID WAS TOUCH HIM...!
YOU LINKED HIS MEMORY.
TONO-GAYA-SAN SAID...
THE PAST, PRESENT, AND FUTURE ARE ALL PARALLEL WORLDS, AND THE INDIVIDUALS WITHIN THESE WORLDS HAVE THEIR OWN MEMORIES.
BUT SOMETIMES A LINK CAN BE ESTABLISHED BETWEEN THESE WORLDS--AND THE MEMORIES OF *ANOTHER* WORLD CAN BE REVIVED.
CLOMP

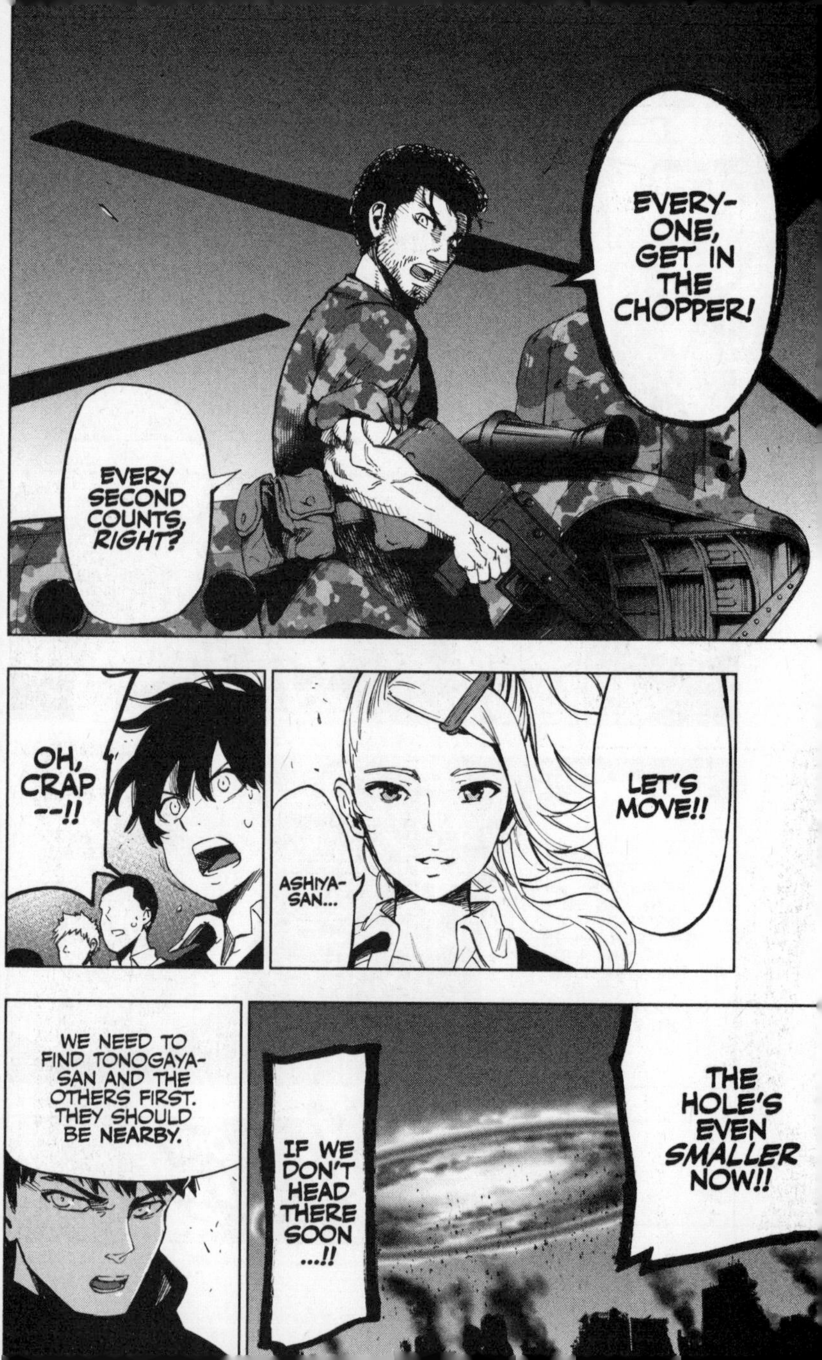
EVERYONE, GET IN THE CHOPPER!
EVERY SECOND COUNTS, *RIGHT?*
LET'S MOVE!!
ASHIYA-SAN...
OH, CRAP--!!
THE HOLE'S EVEN *SMALLER* NOW!!
IF WE DON'T HEAD THERE SOON...!!
WE NEED TO FIND TONOGAYA-SAN AND THE OTHERS FIRST. THEY SHOULD BE NEARBY.

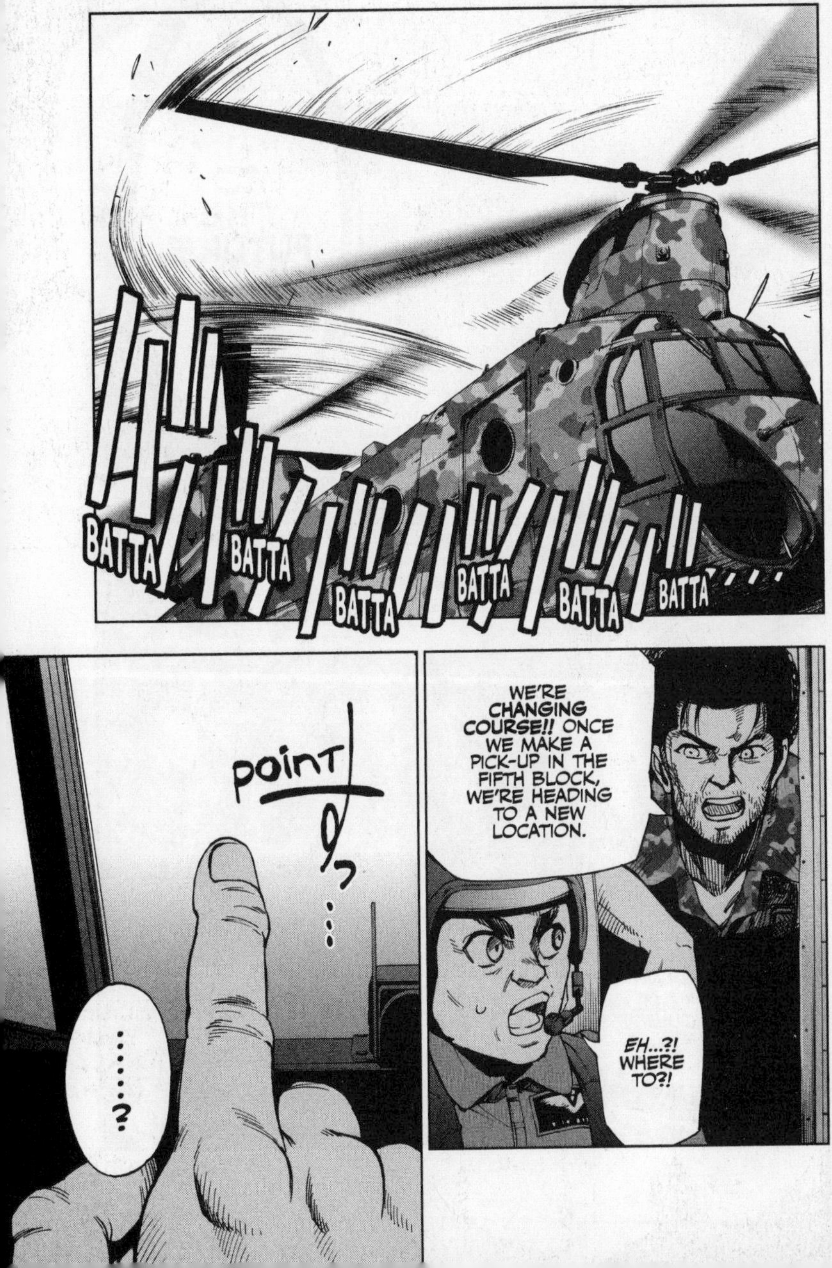
BATTA
BATTA
BATTA
BATTA
BATTA
BATTA
WE'RE CHANGING COURSE!! ONCE WE MAKE A PICK-UP IN THE FIFTH BLOCK, WE'RE HEADING TO A NEW LOCATION.
EH...?! WHERE TO?!
point
......?

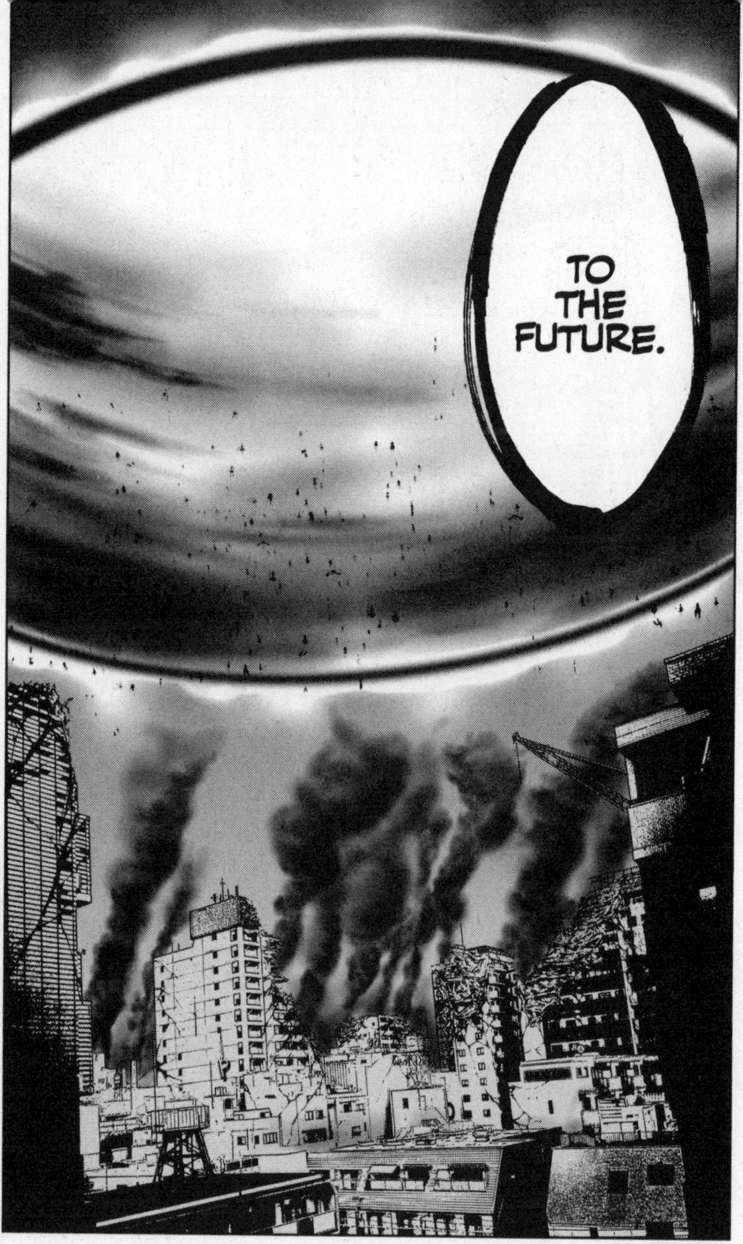
TO THE FUTURE.

HOLD ON. I'LL HEAL YOU UP.

WA- TARU...

ONEE... SAMA...

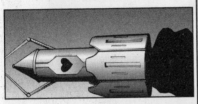

GRIIING...

BWOOON

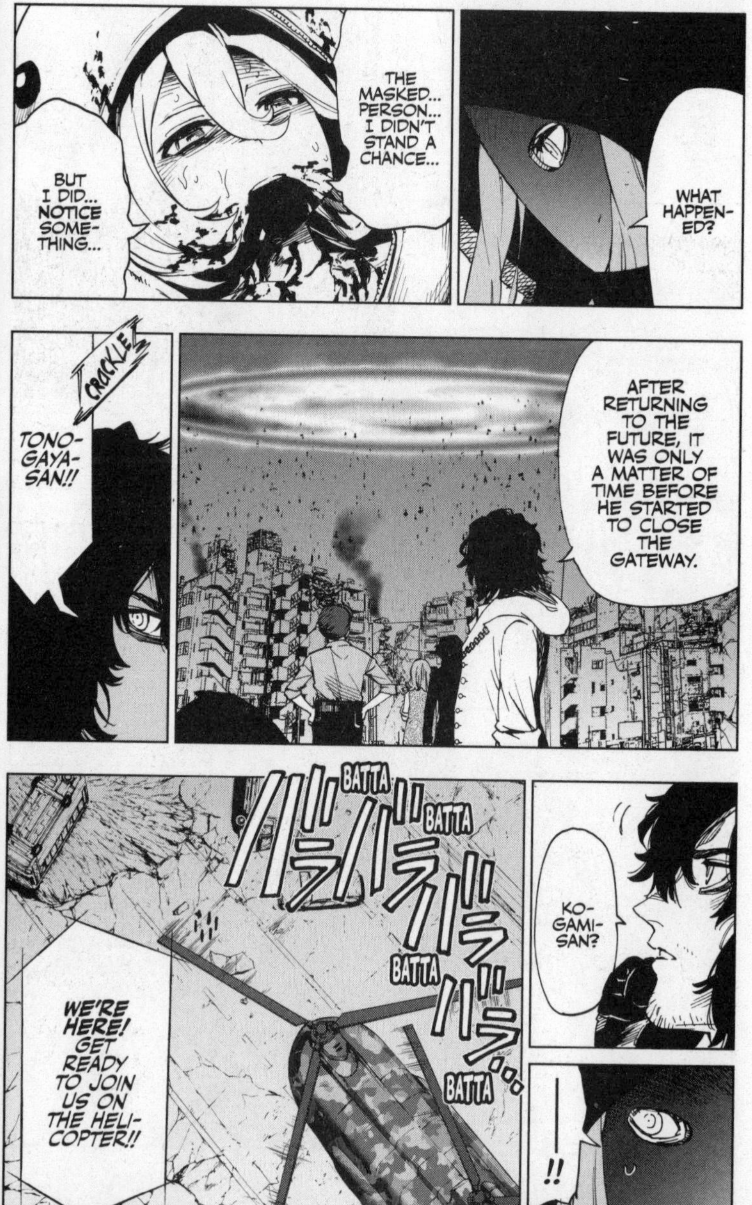
WHAT HAPPENED?
THE MASKED... PERSON... I DIDN'T STAND A CHANCE...
BUT I DID... NOTICE SOMETHING...
AFTER RETURNING TO THE FUTURE, IT WAS ONLY A MATTER OF TIME BEFORE HE STARTED TO CLOSE THE GATEWAY.
CRACKLE
TONOGAYA-SAN!!
KOGAMI-SAN?
——!!
BATTA
BATTA
BATTA
BATTA
WE'RE HERE! GET READY TO JOIN US ON THE HELICOPTER!!

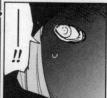

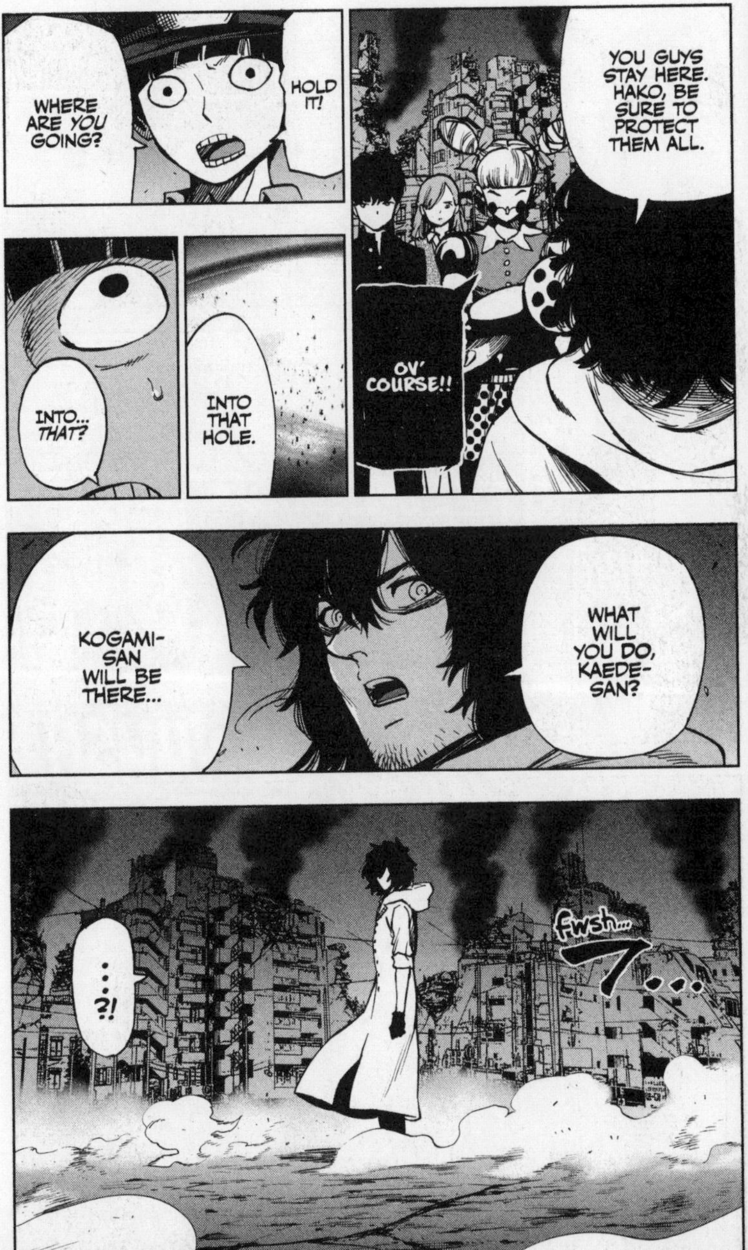
YOU GUYS STAY HERE. HAKO, BE SURE TO PROTECT THEM ALL.
OV' COURSE!!
HOLD IT!
WHERE ARE *YOU* GOING?
INTO THAT HOLE.
INTO... *THAT?*
WHAT WILL YOU DO, KAEDE-SAN?
KOGAMI-SAN WILL BE THERE...
fwsh...
...?!

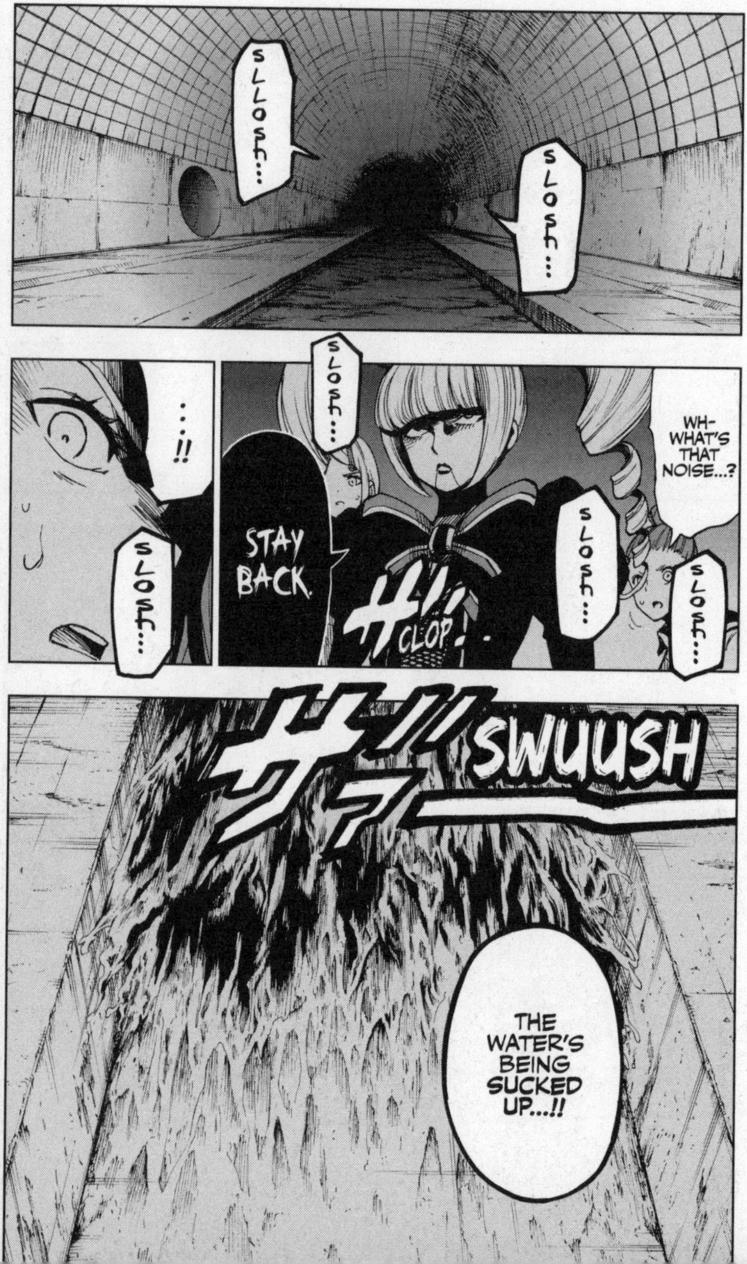
SLOSH...
SLLOSH...
WH- WHAT'S THAT NOISE...?
SLOSH...
SLOSH...
SLOSH...
STAY BACK.
CLOP
...!!
SLOSH...
SWUUSH
THE WATER'S BEING SUCKED UP...!!

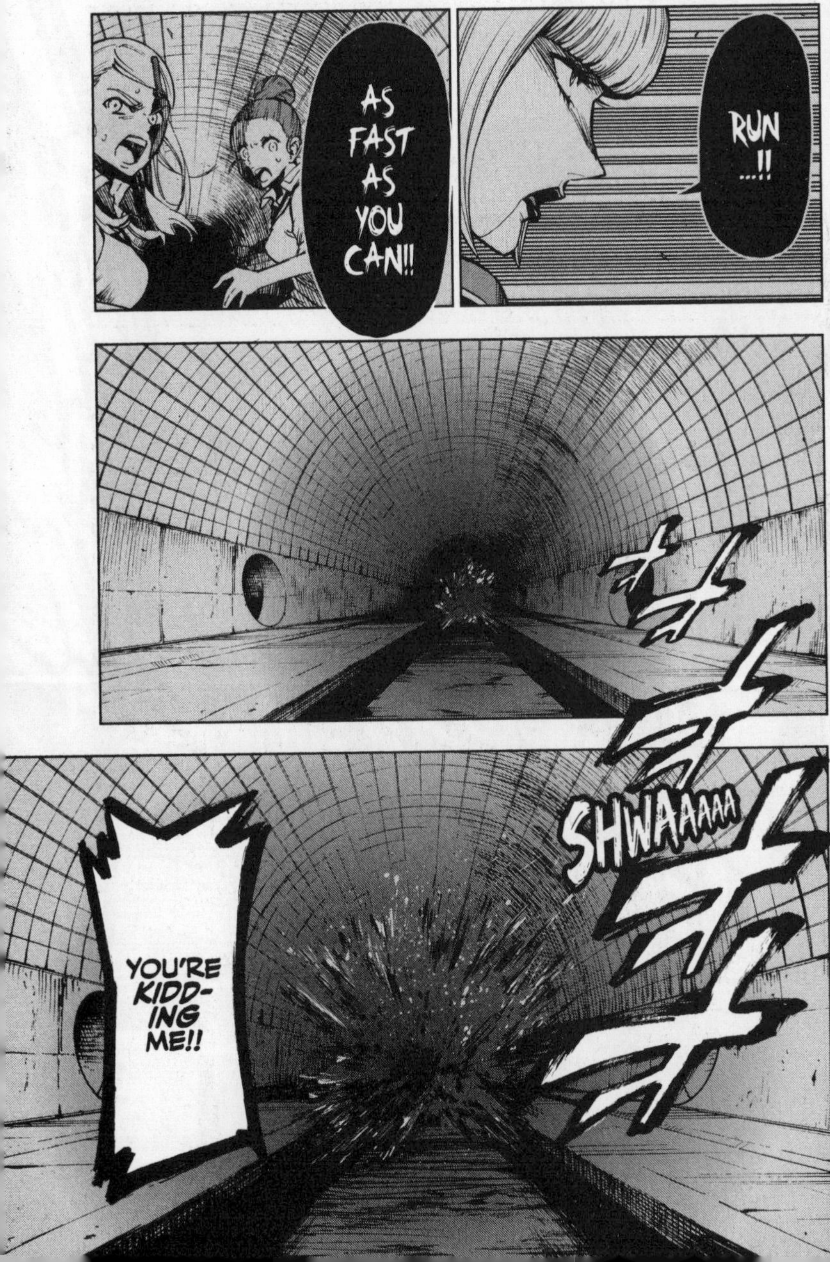
RUN ...!!
AS FAST AS YOU CAN!!
SHWAAAAA
YOU'RE KIDD-ING ME!!

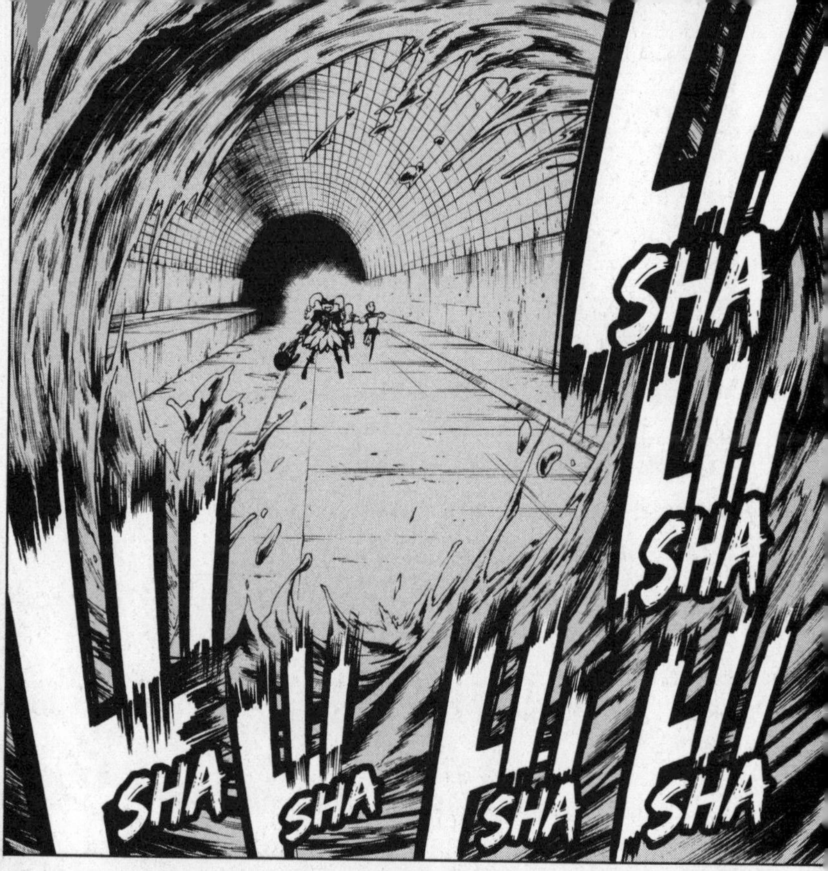
SHA
SHA
SHA
SHA
SHA
SHA
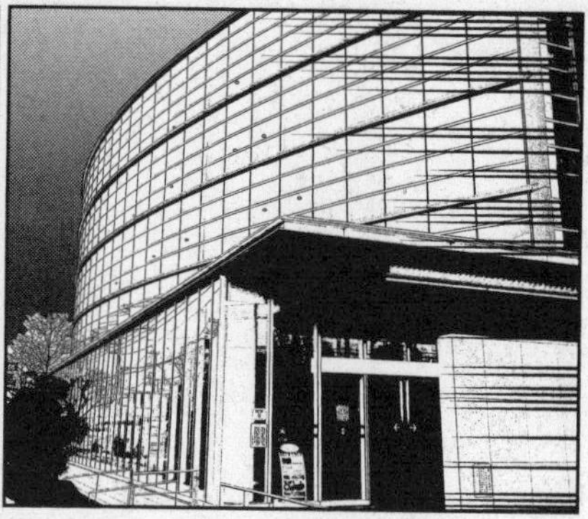
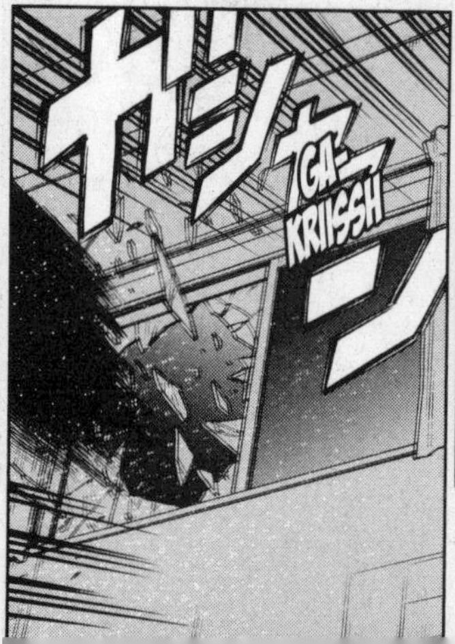
GA-KRIISSH

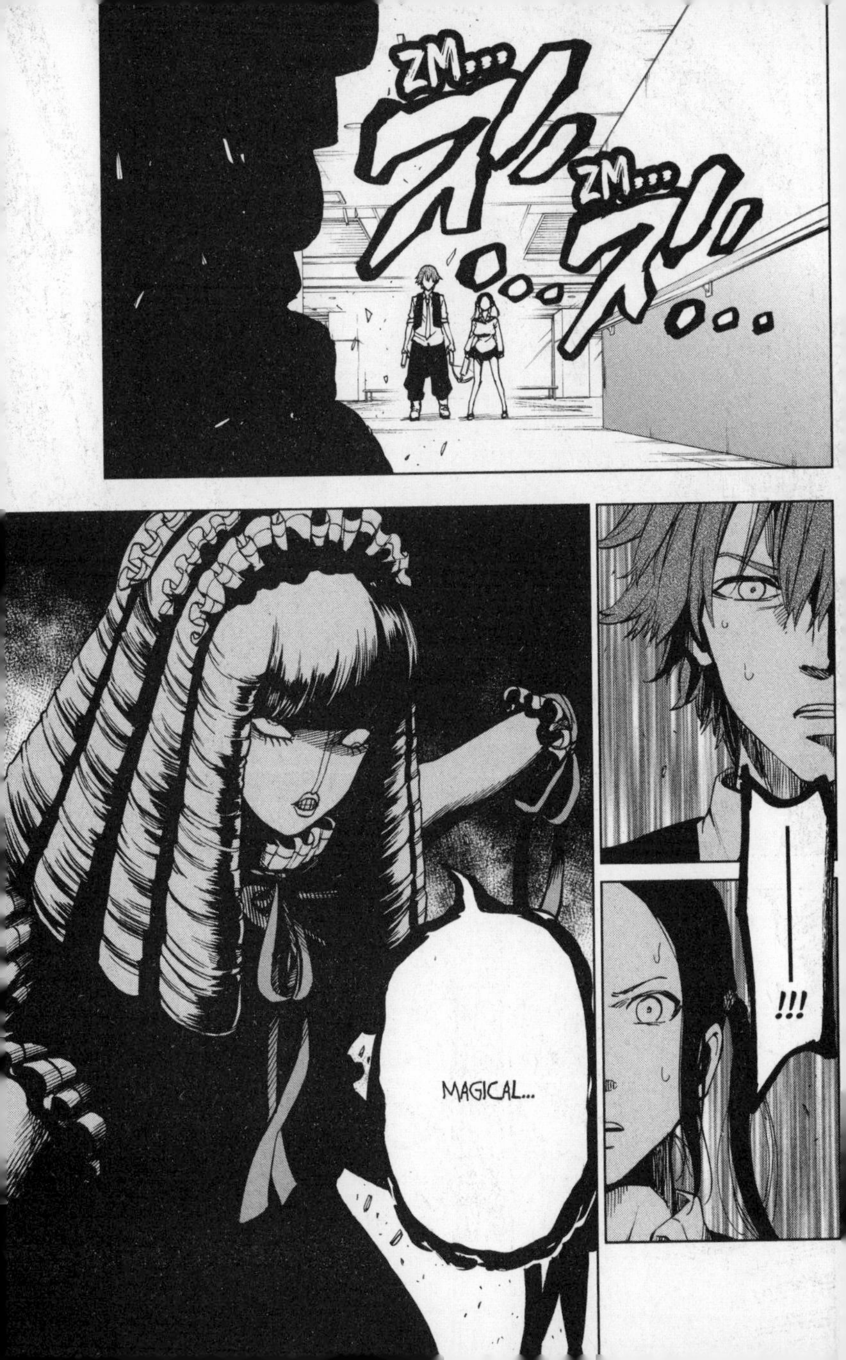
ZM...
ZM...
!!!
MAGICAL...

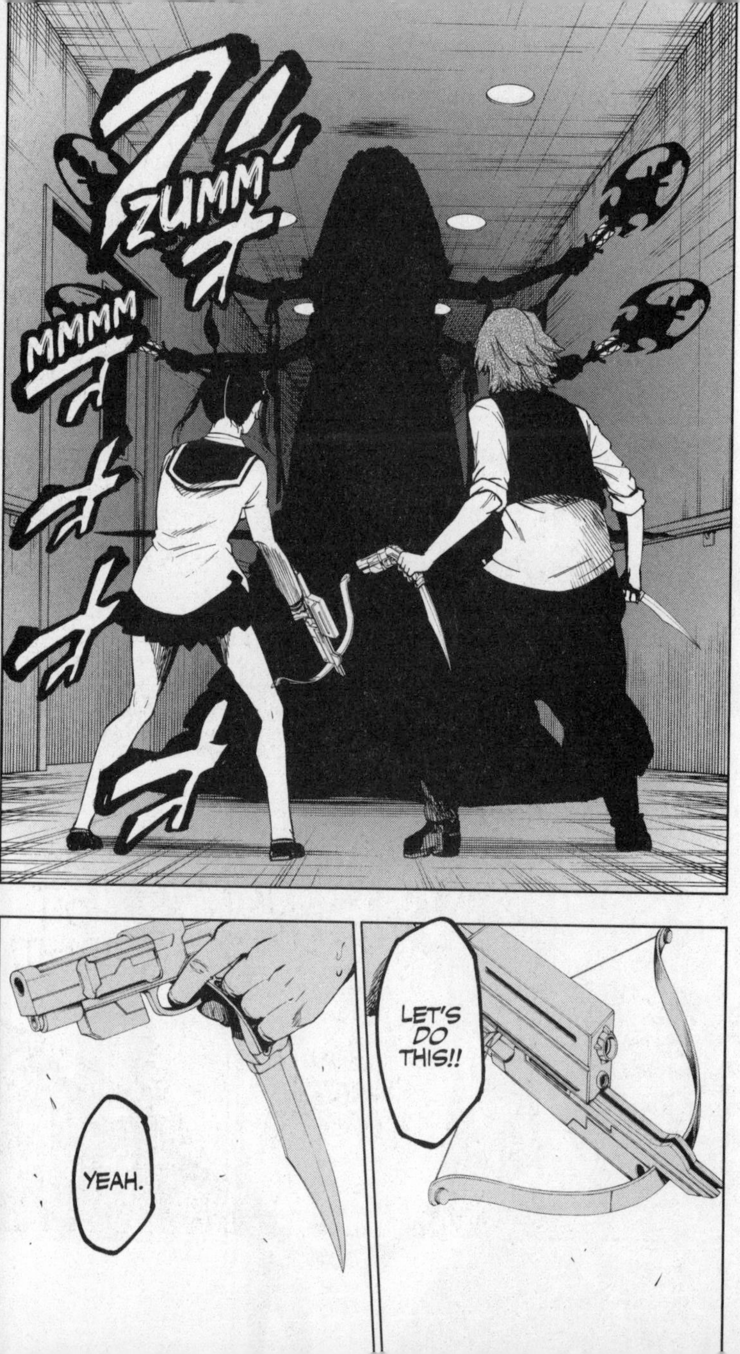
ZUMM
MMMM
LET'S DO THIS!!
YEAH.

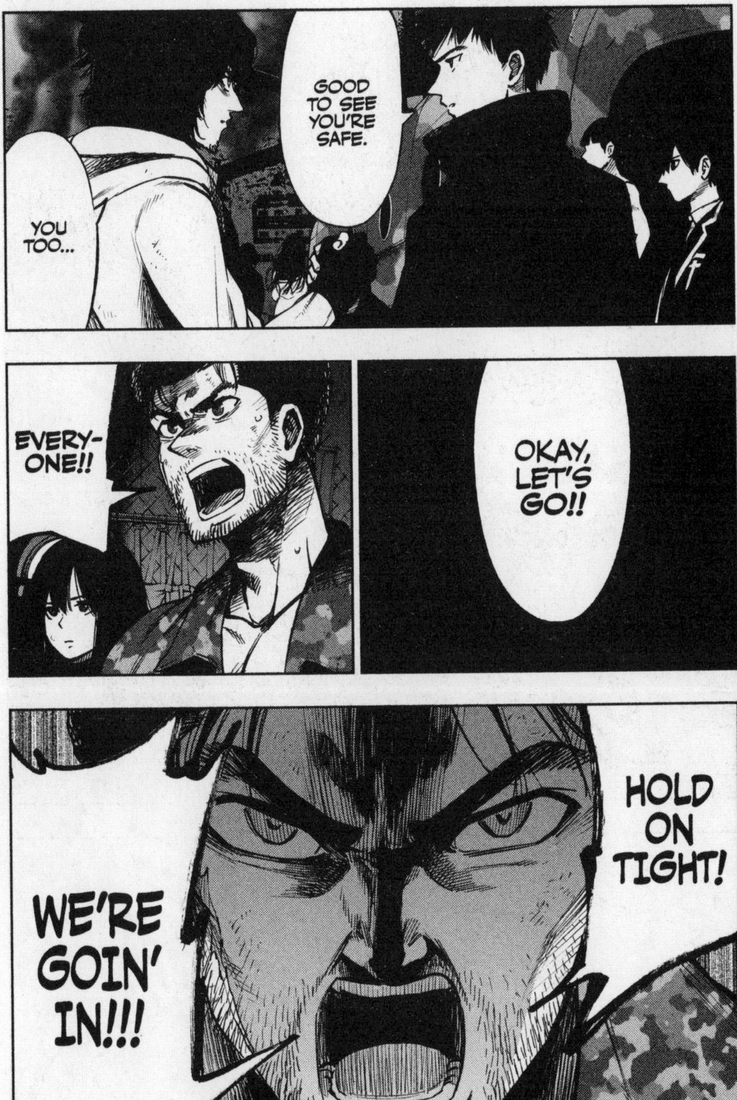
GOOD TO SEE YOU'RE SAFE.
YOU TOO...
OKAY, LET'S GO!!
EVERY-ONE!!
HOLD ON TIGHT!
WE'RE GOIN' IN!!!

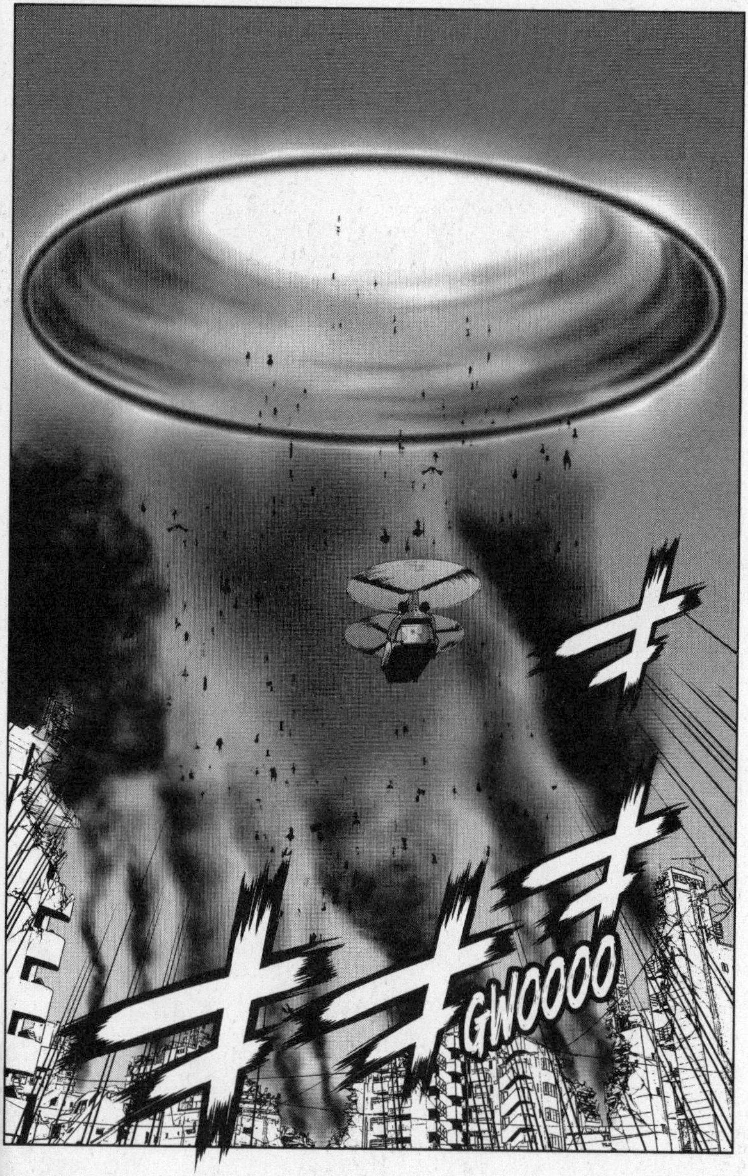
GWOOOO

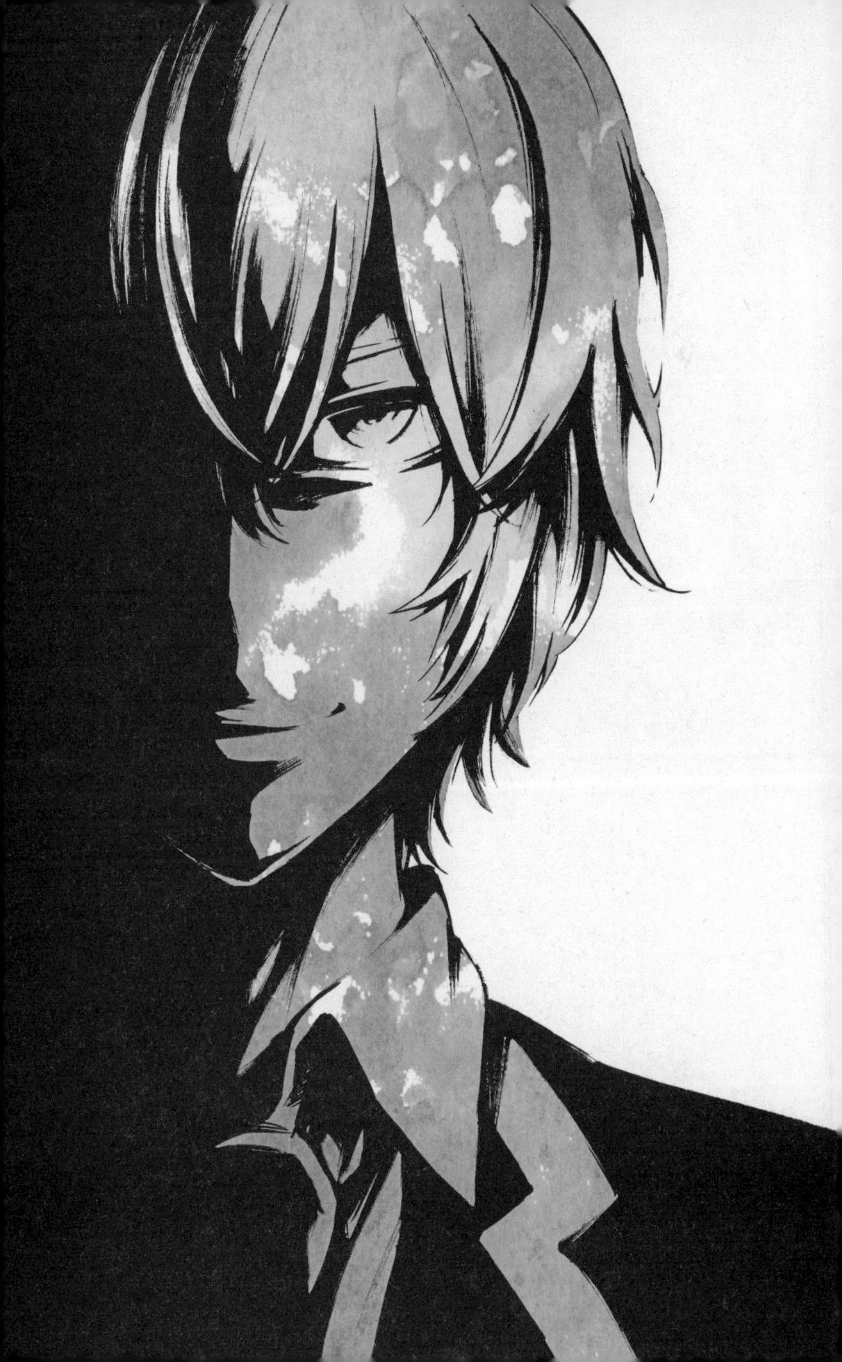

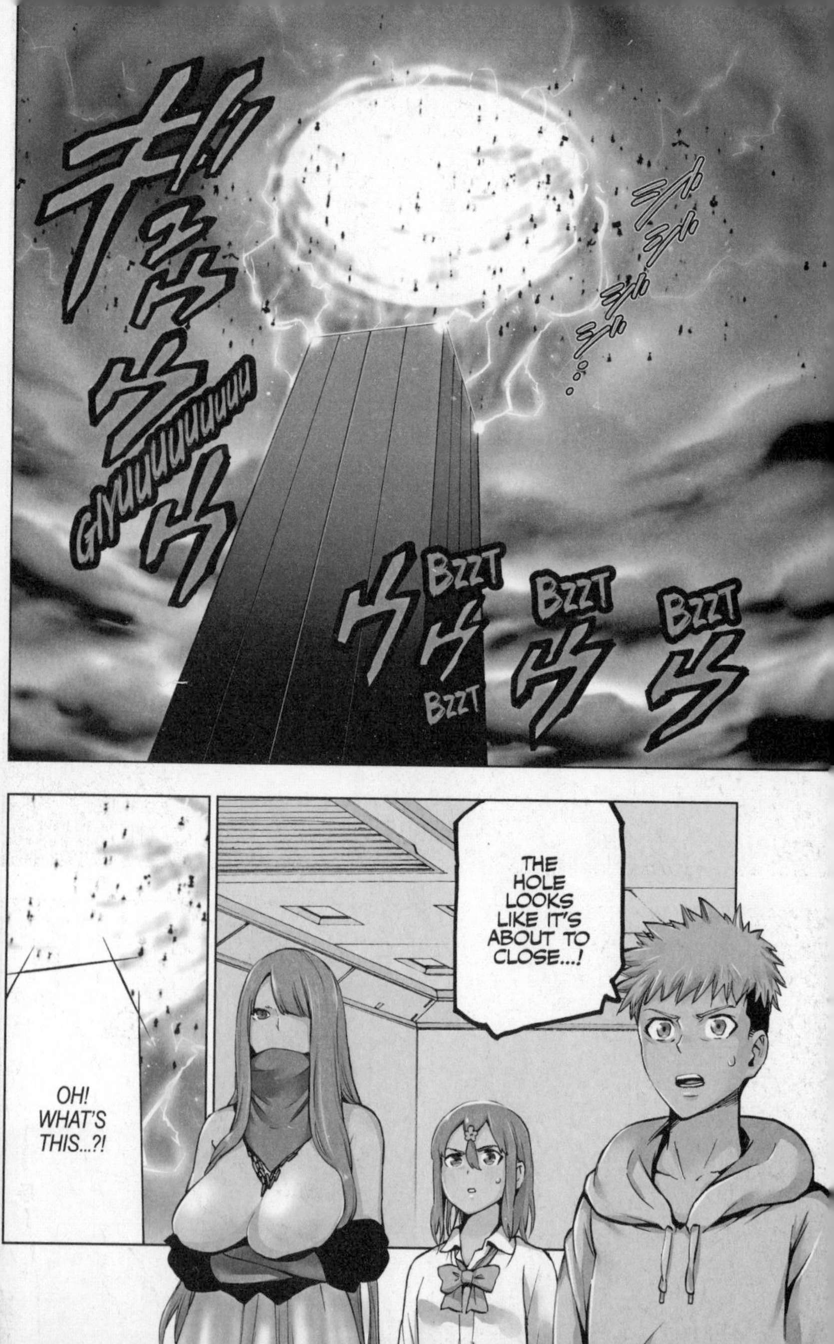
GIYUUUUUUUU
BZZT
BZZT
BZZT
BZZT
THE HOLE LOOKS LIKE IT'S ABOUT TO CLOSE...!
OH! WHAT'S THIS...?!

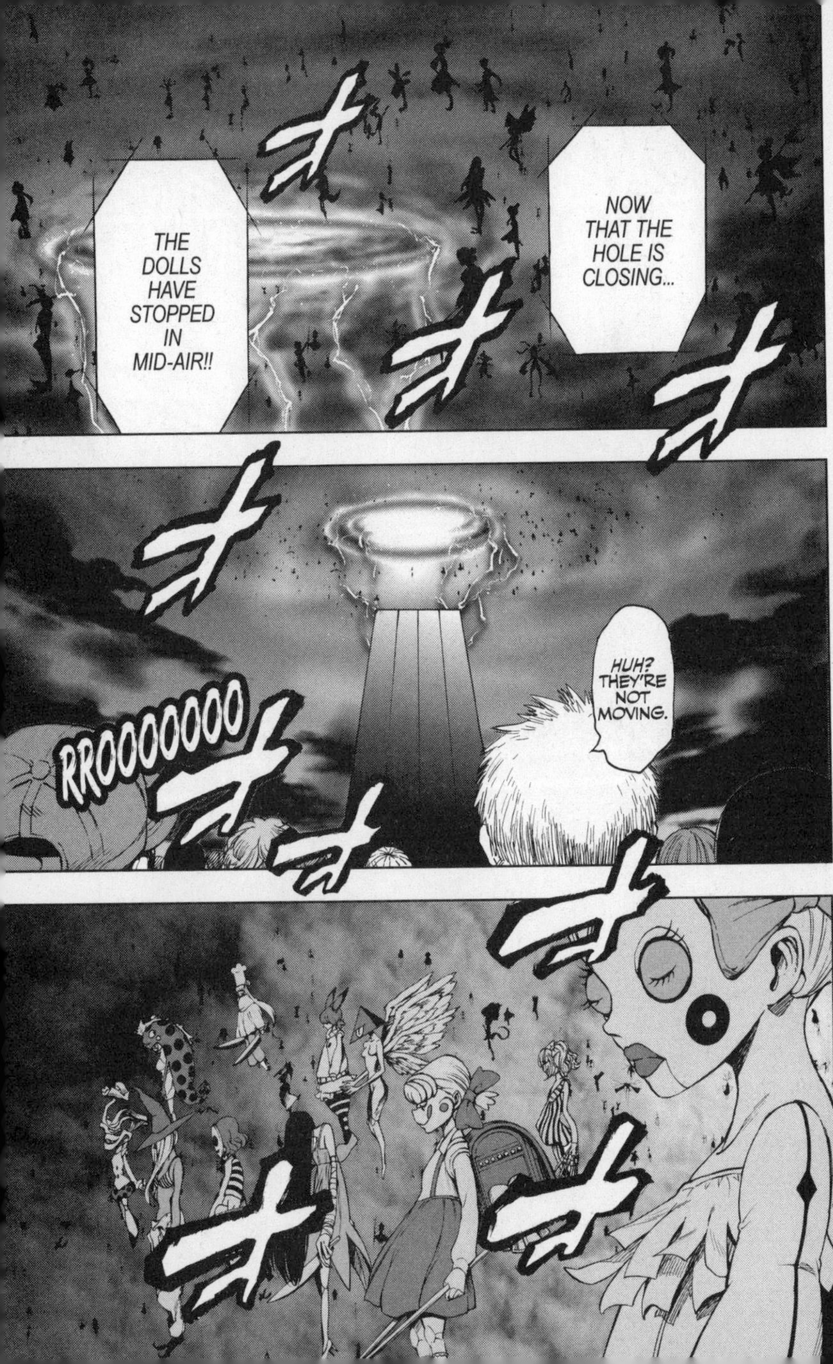
NOW THAT THE HOLE IS CLOSING...
THE DOLLS HAVE STOPPED IN MID-AIR!!
HUH? THEY'RE NOT MOVING.
RROOOOOOO

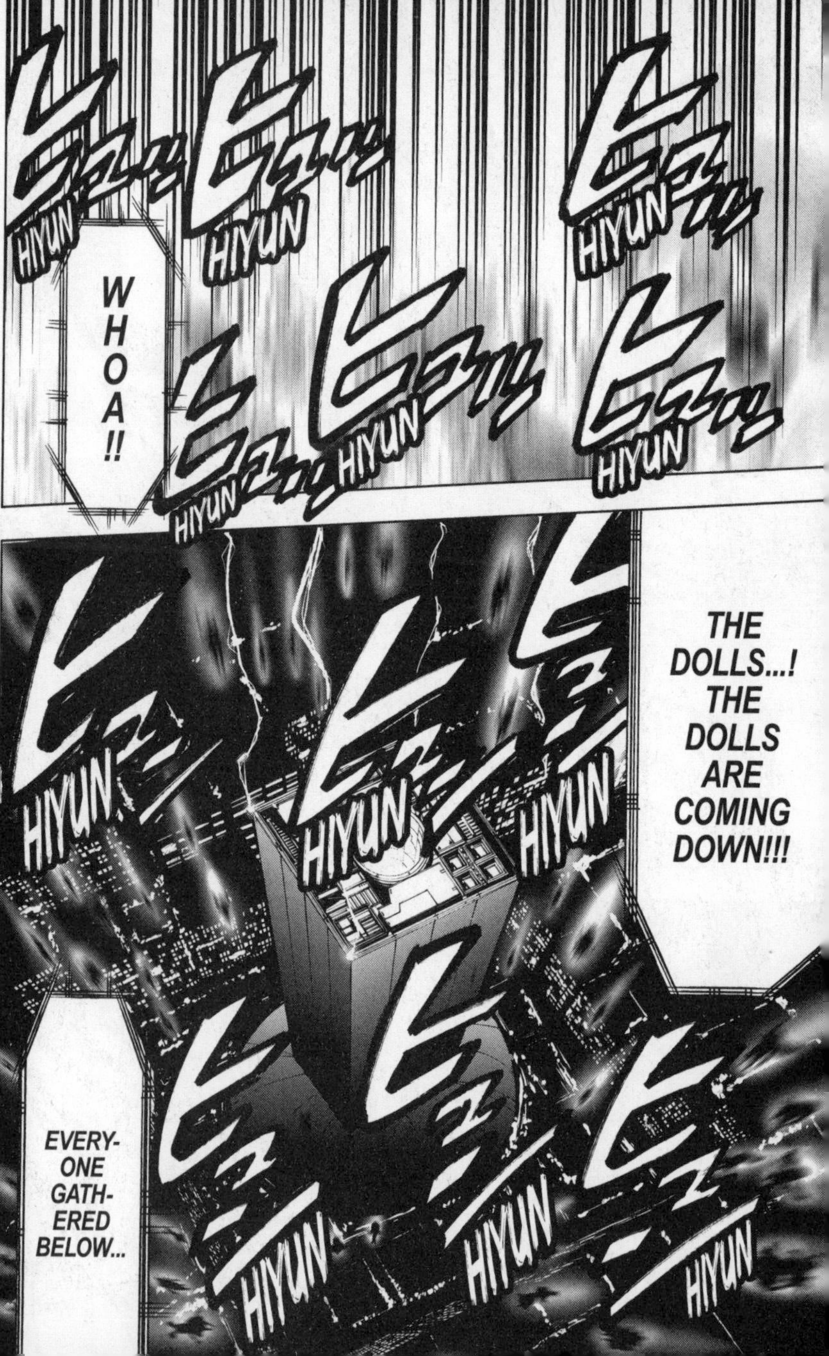
HIYUN
HIYUN
HIYUN
WHOA!!
HIYUN
HIYUN
HIYUN
THE DOLLS...! THE DOLLS ARE COMING DOWN!!!
HIYUN
HIYUN
HIYUN
HIYUN
HIYUN
HIYUN
EVERY-ONE GATH-ERED BELOW...

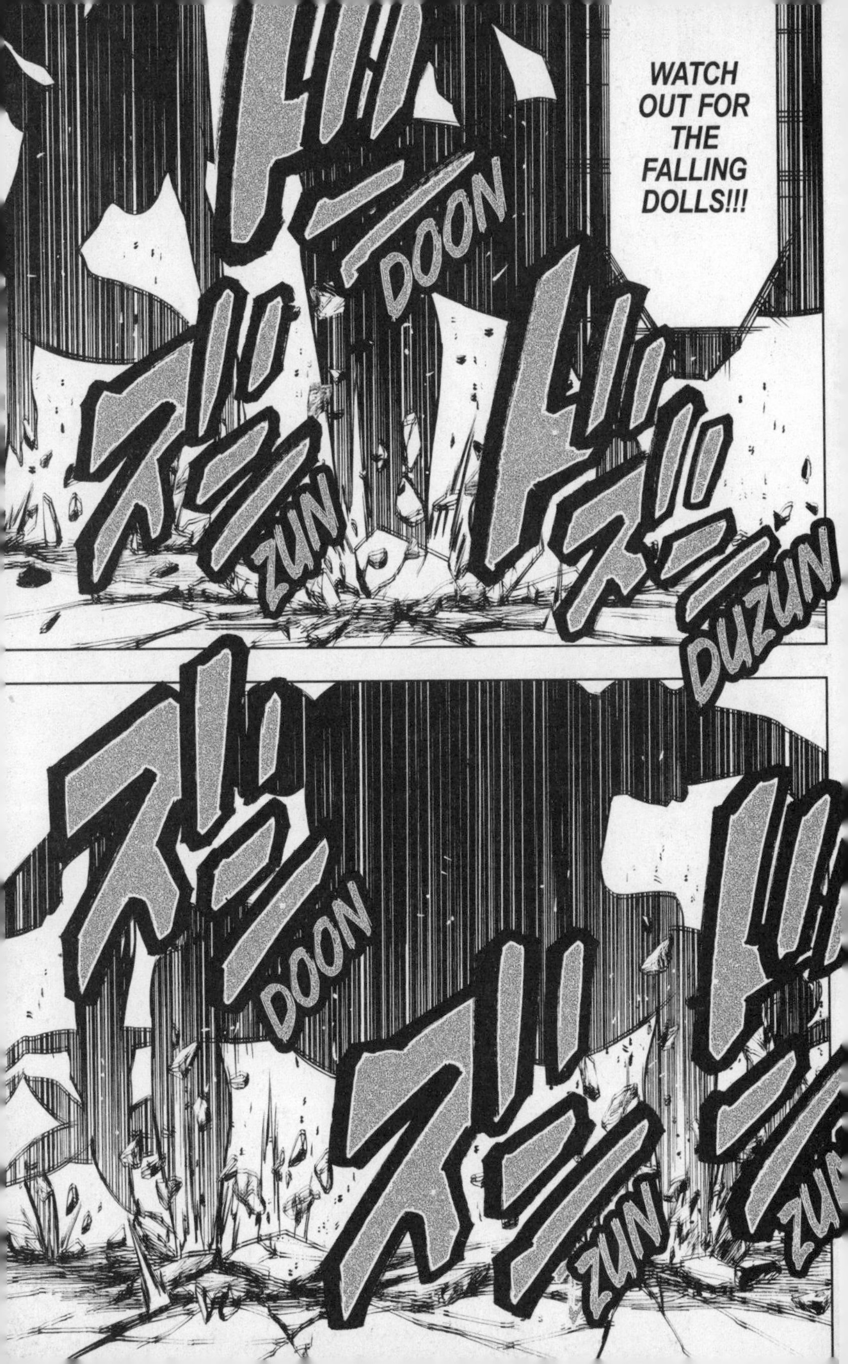
WATCH OUT FOR THE FALLING DOLLS!!!
DOON
DUZUN
ZUN
DOON
ZUN

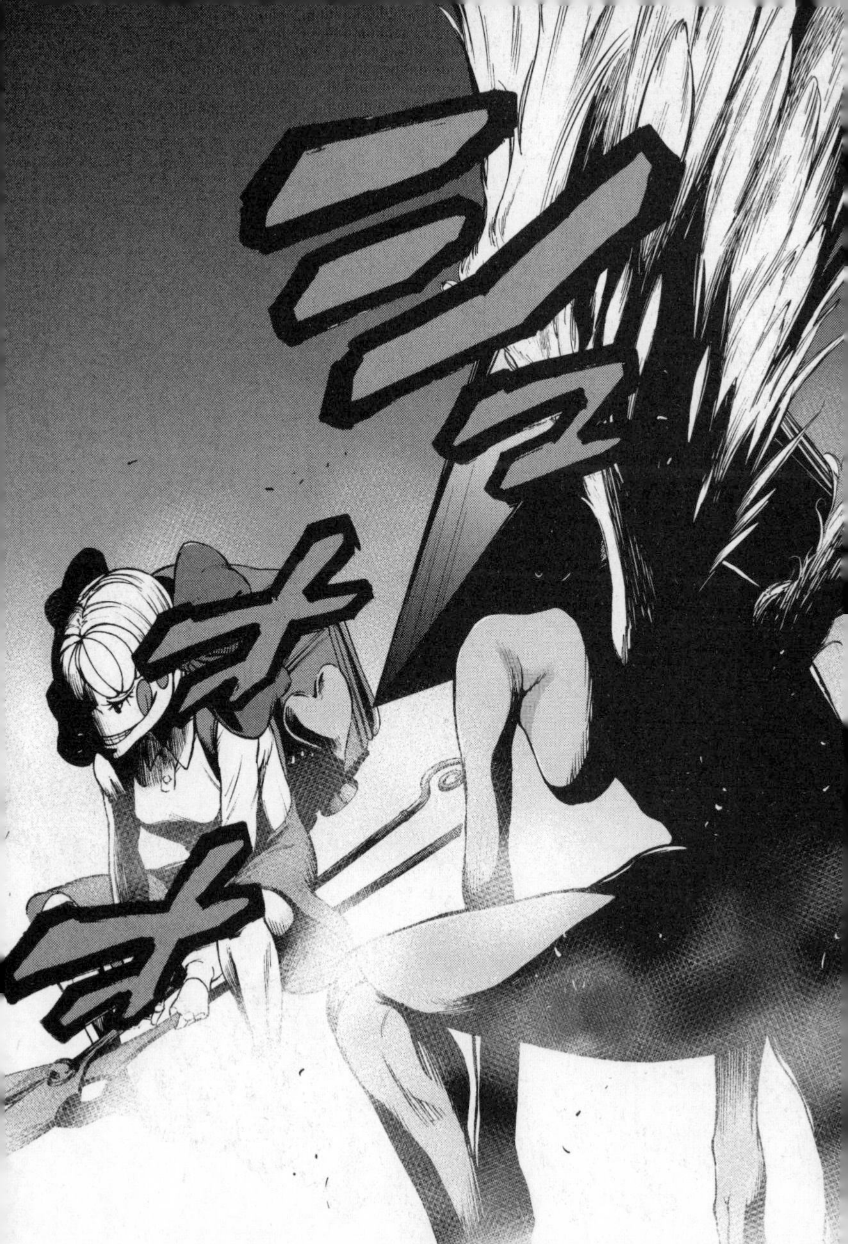

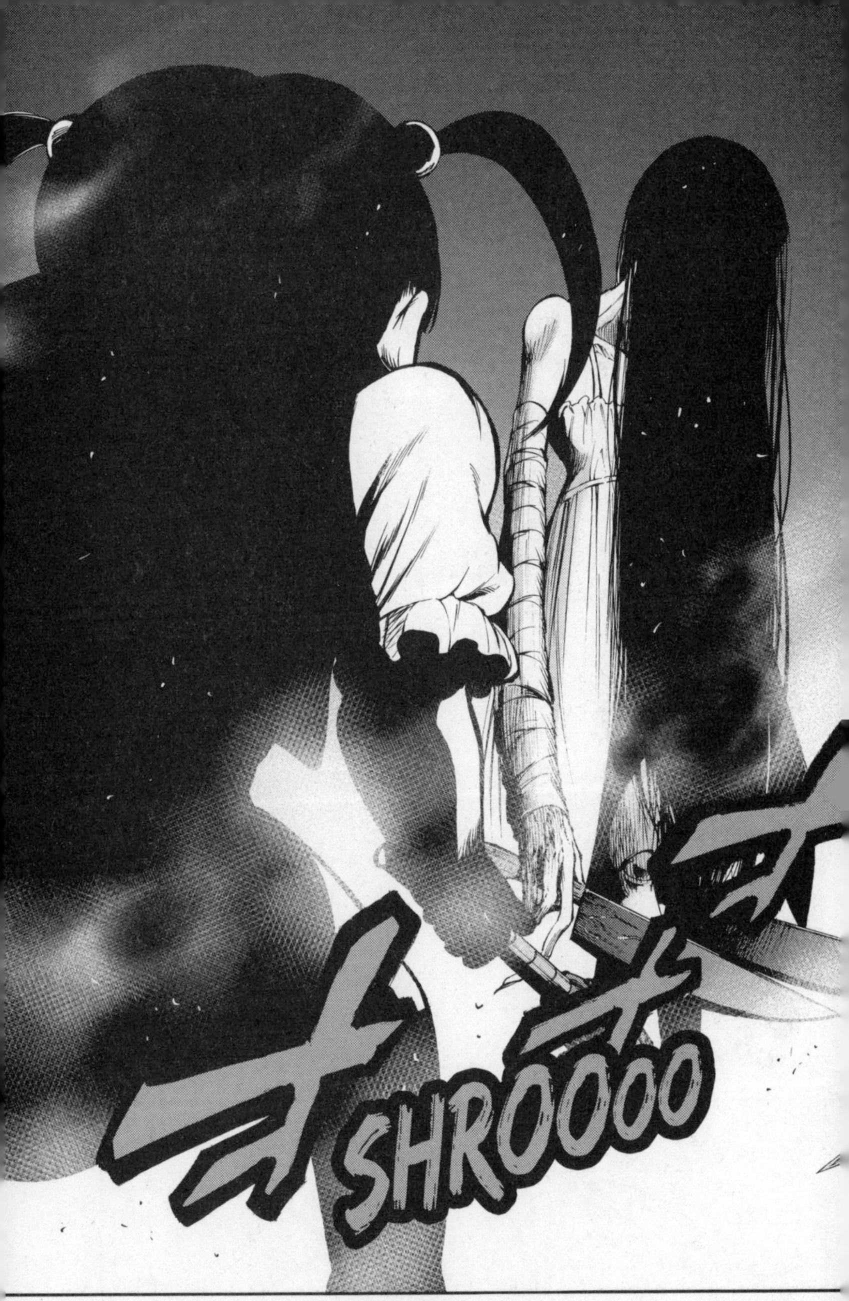
SHROOOO

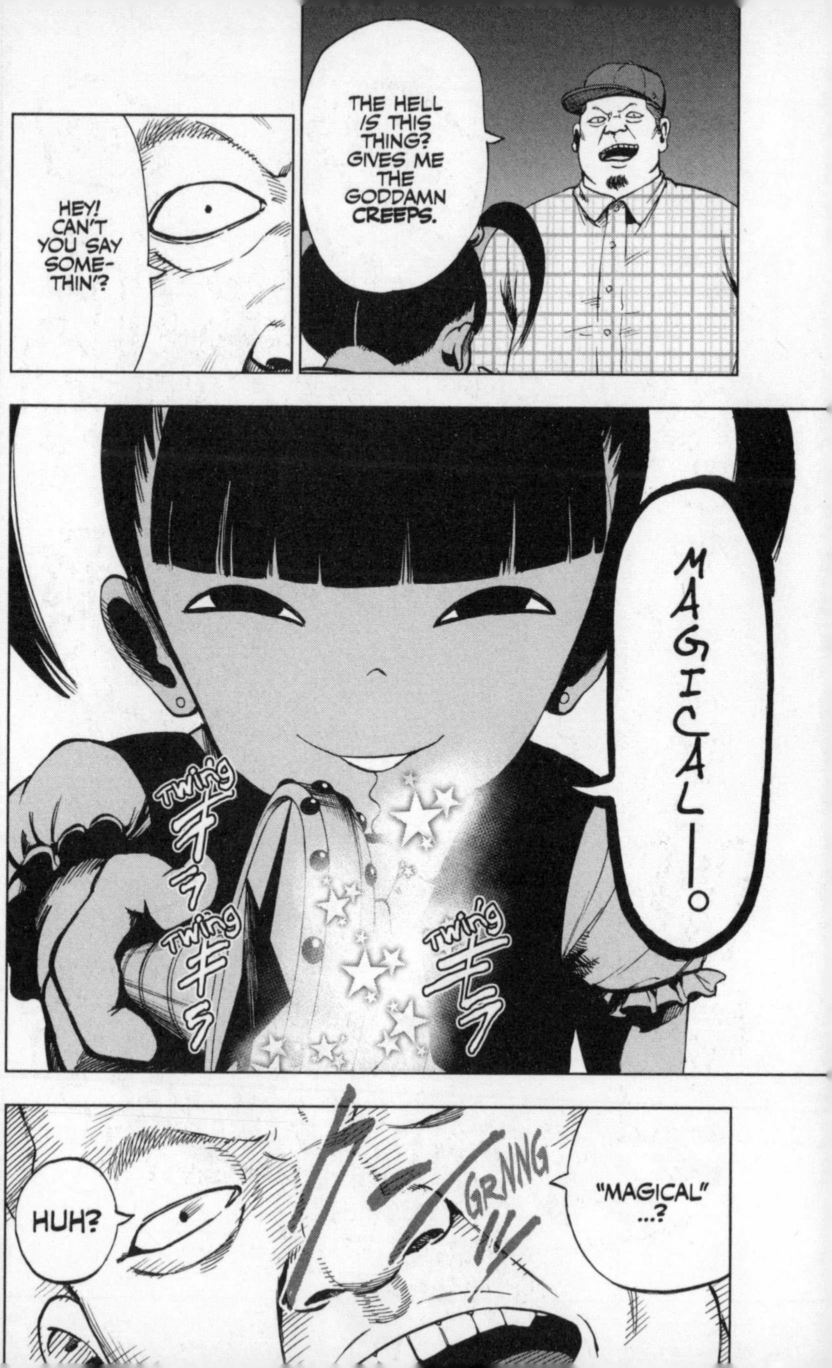
THE HELL IS THIS THING? GIVES ME THE GODDAMN CREEPS.
HEY! CAN'T YOU SAY SOME-THIN'?
MAGICAL!
TWING
TWING
TWING
"MAGICAL" ...?
GRNNG
HUH?

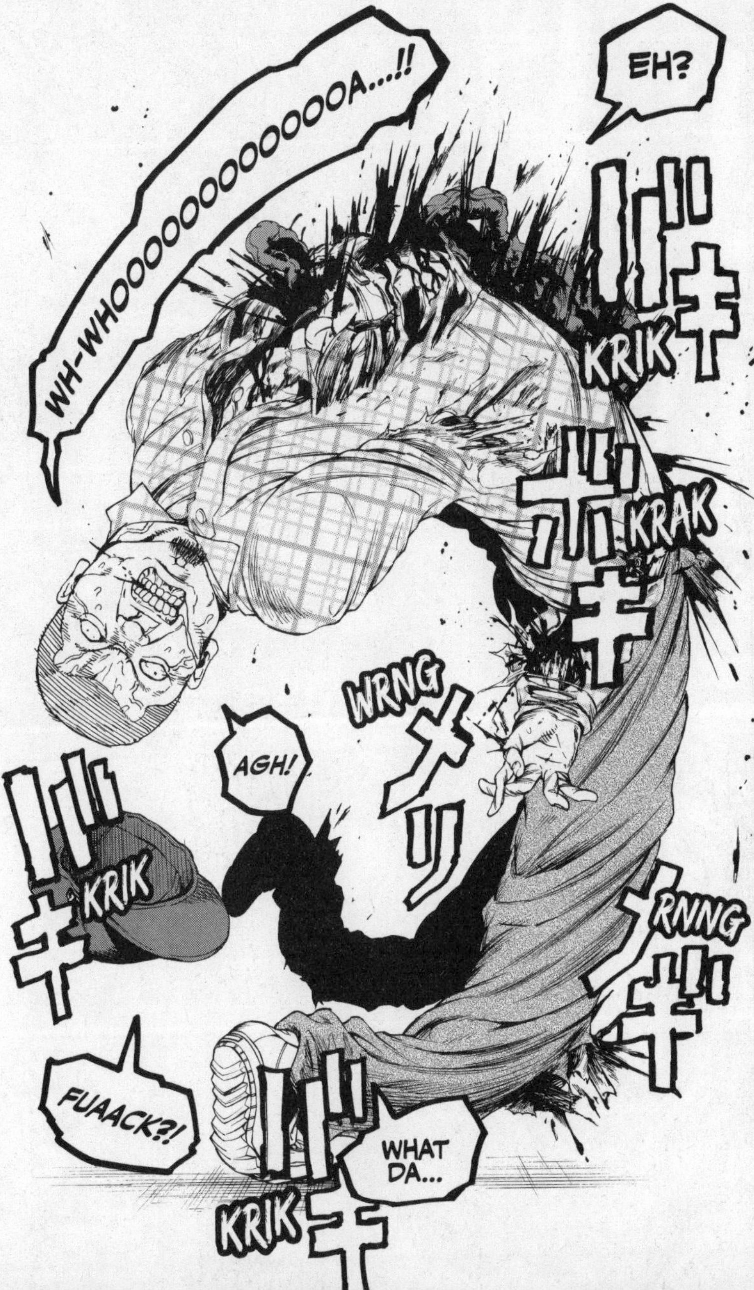
EH?
WH-WHOOOOOOOOOOOOOOOA....!!
KRIK
KRAK
WRNG
AGH!
RNNG
KRIK
FUAACK?!
WHAT DA...
KRIK

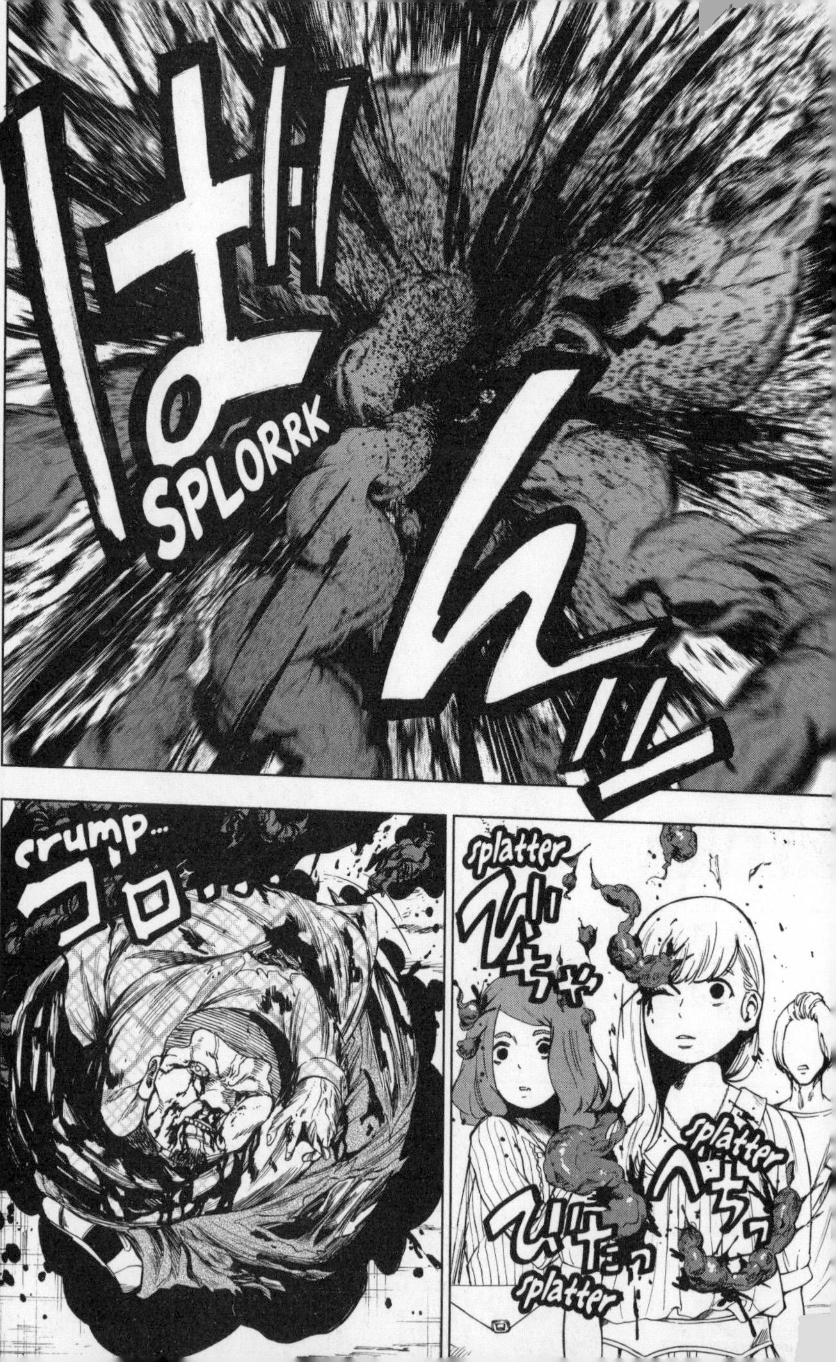
SPLORRK
splatter
splatter
splatter
crump...
コロ...

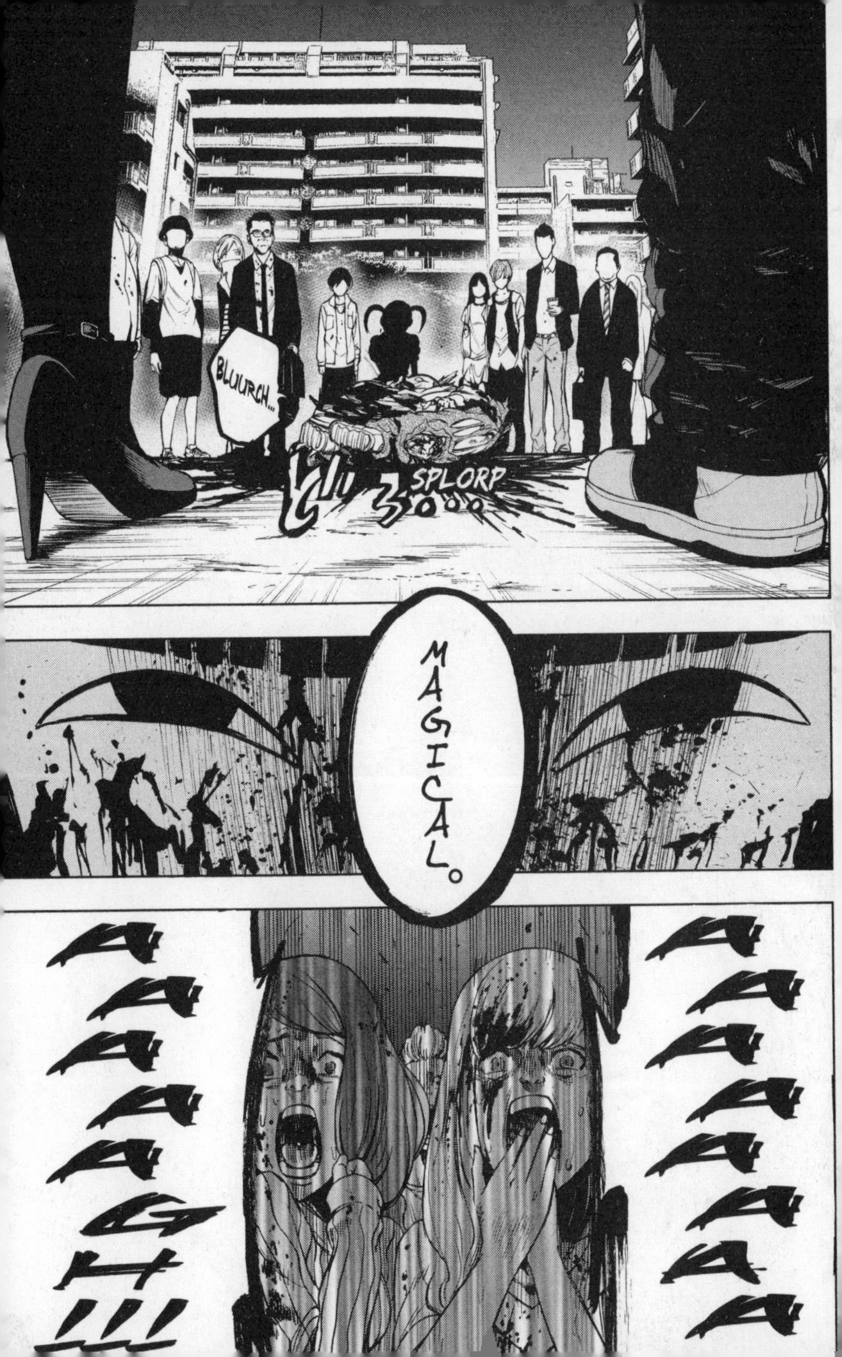
BLUURCH...
SPLORP
MAGICAL.
AAAAAAAA
AAAAAGH!!!

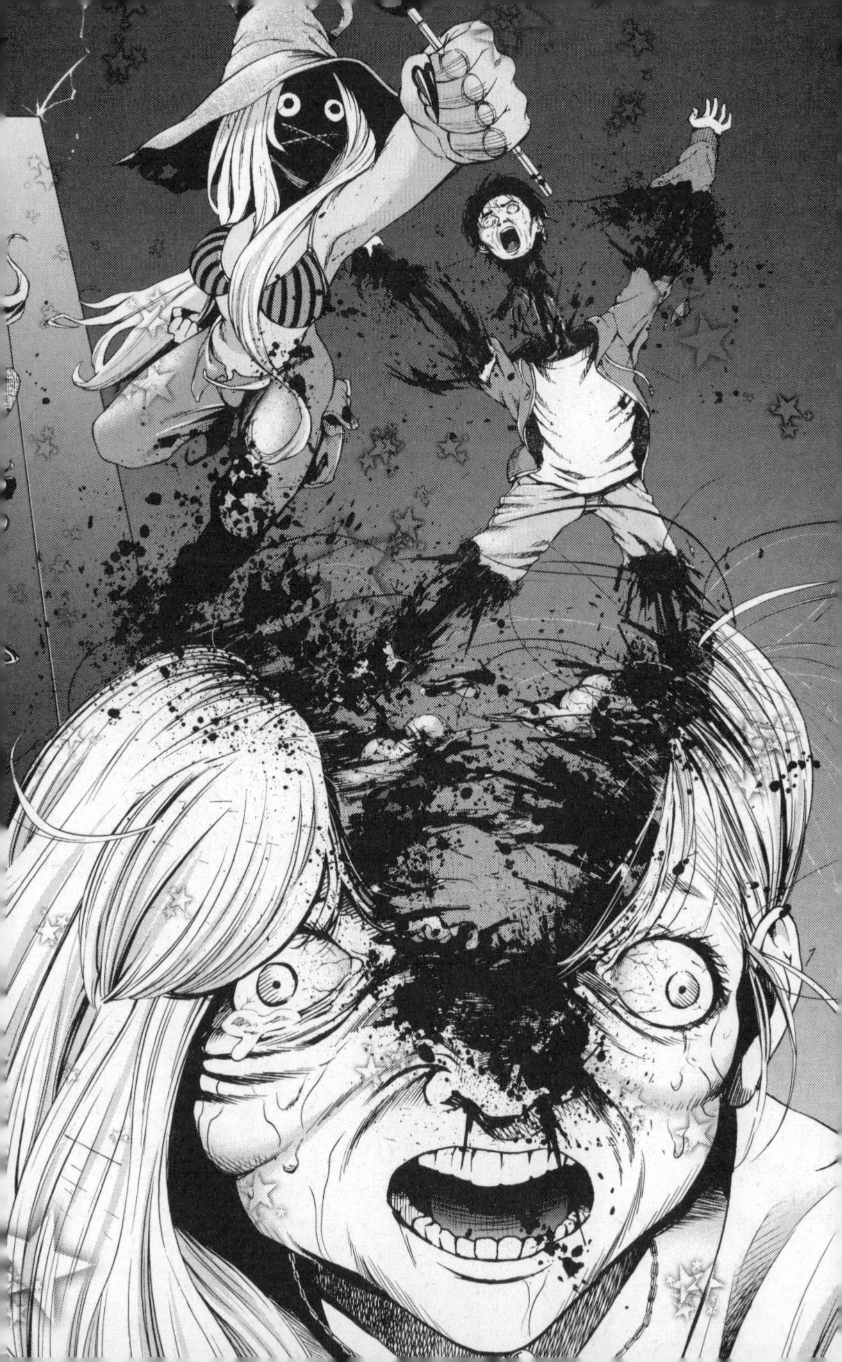

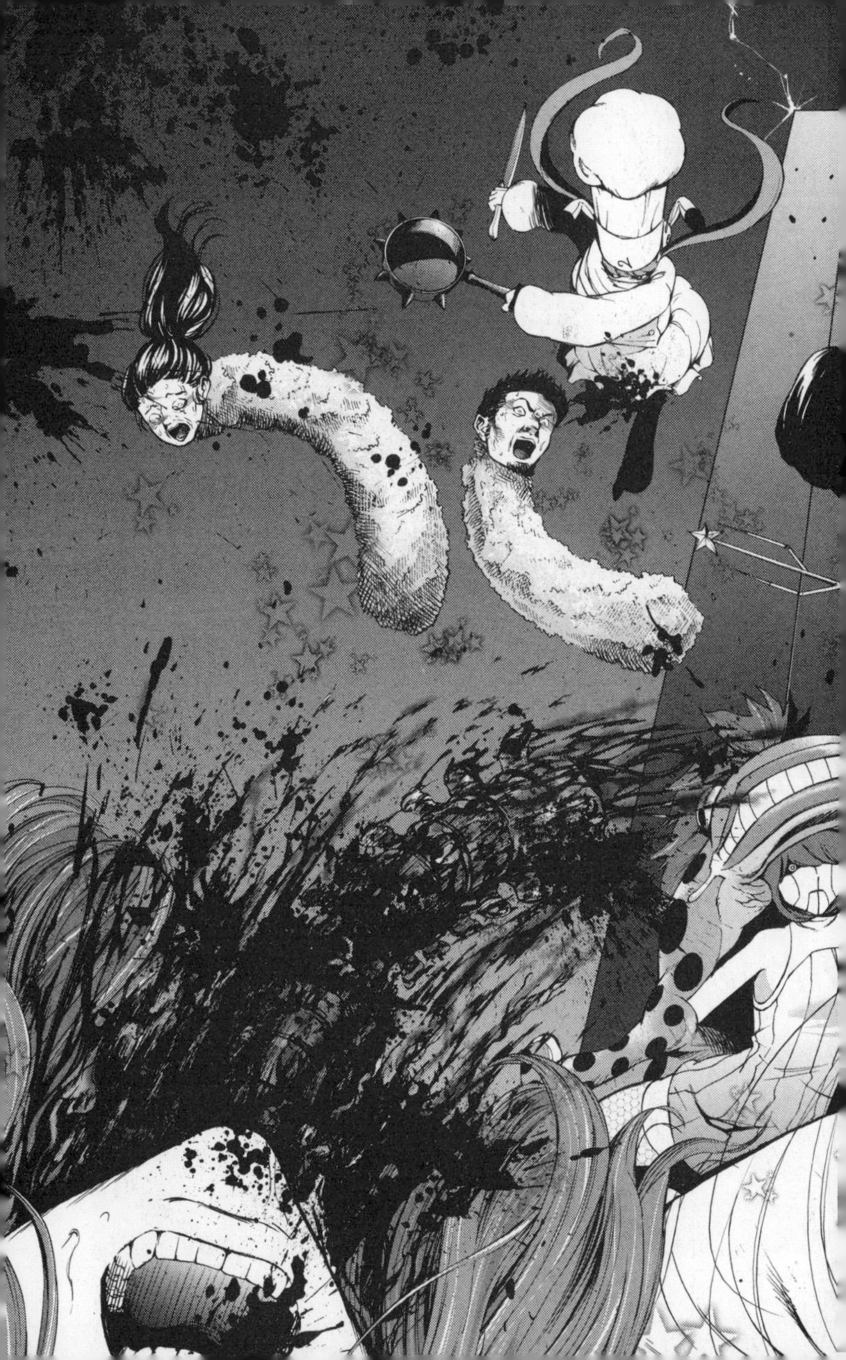

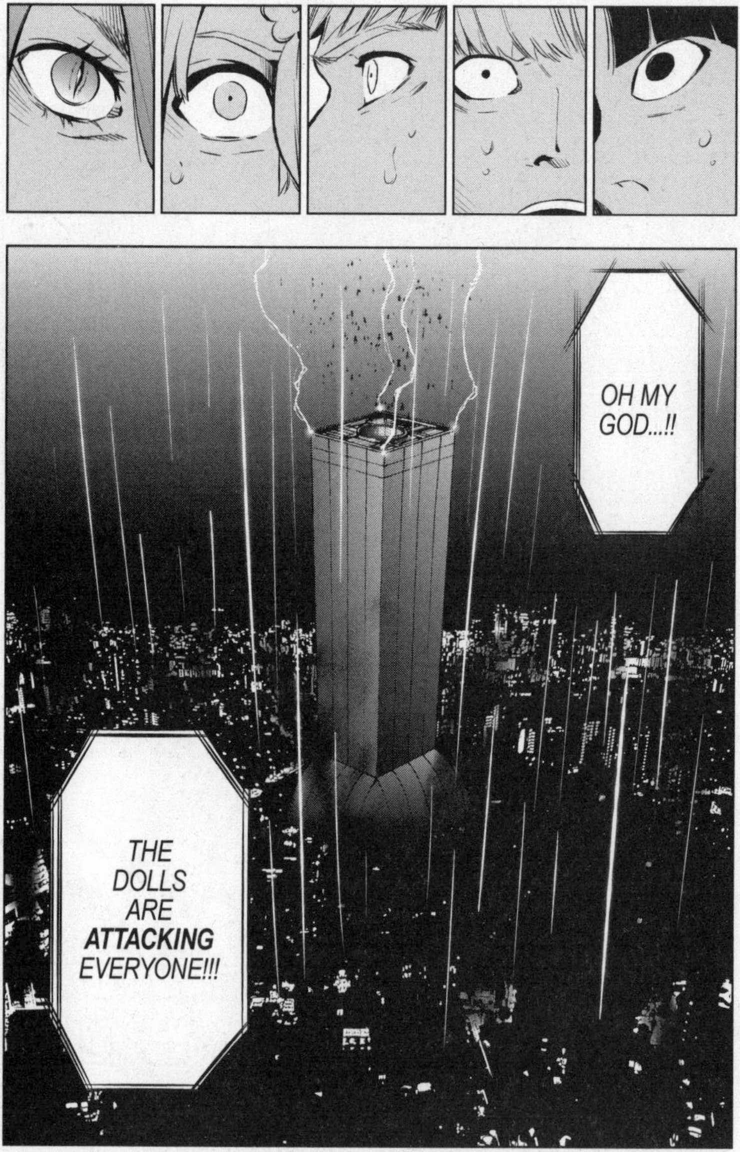
OH MY GOD...!!
THE DOLLS ARE **ATTACKING** EVERYONE!!!

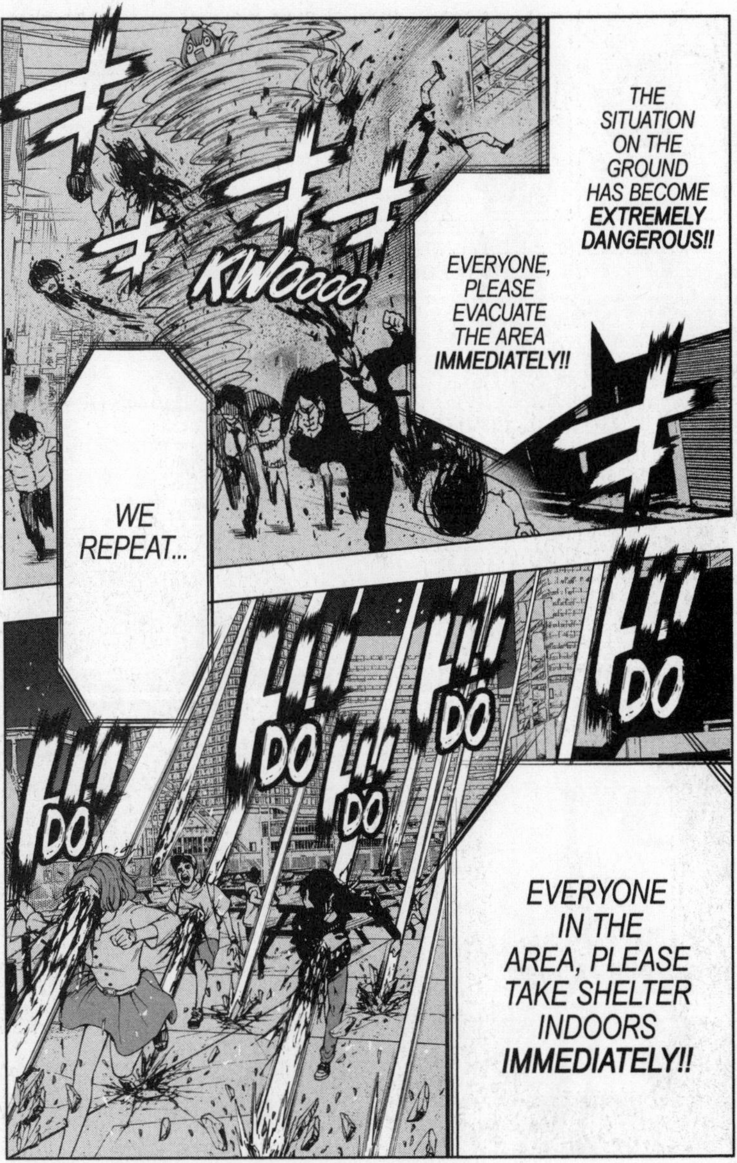
THE SITUATION ON THE GROUND HAS BECOME EXTREMELY DANGEROUS!!
EVERYONE, PLEASE EVACUATE THE AREA IMMEDIATELY!!
KWOOOOO
WE REPEAT...
DO
DO
DO
DO
DO
EVERYONE IN THE AREA, PLEASE TAKE SHELTER INDOORS IMMEDIATELY!!

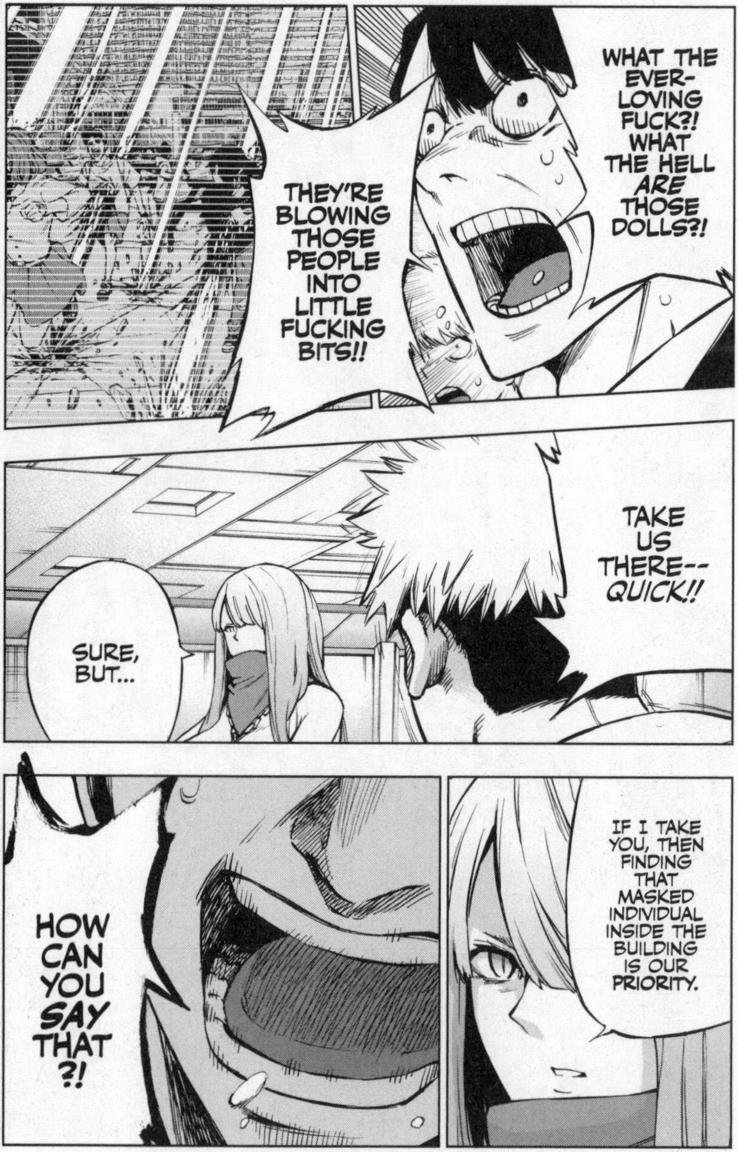
WHAT THE EVER-LOVING FUCK?! WHAT THE HELL ARE THOSE DOLLS?!
THEY'RE BLOWING THOSE PEOPLE INTO LITTLE FUCKING BITS!!
TAKE US THERE-- QUICK!!
SURE, BUT...
IF I TAKE YOU, THEN FINDING THAT MASKED INDIVIDUAL INSIDE THE BUILDING IS OUR PRIORITY.
HOW CAN YOU SAY THAT?!

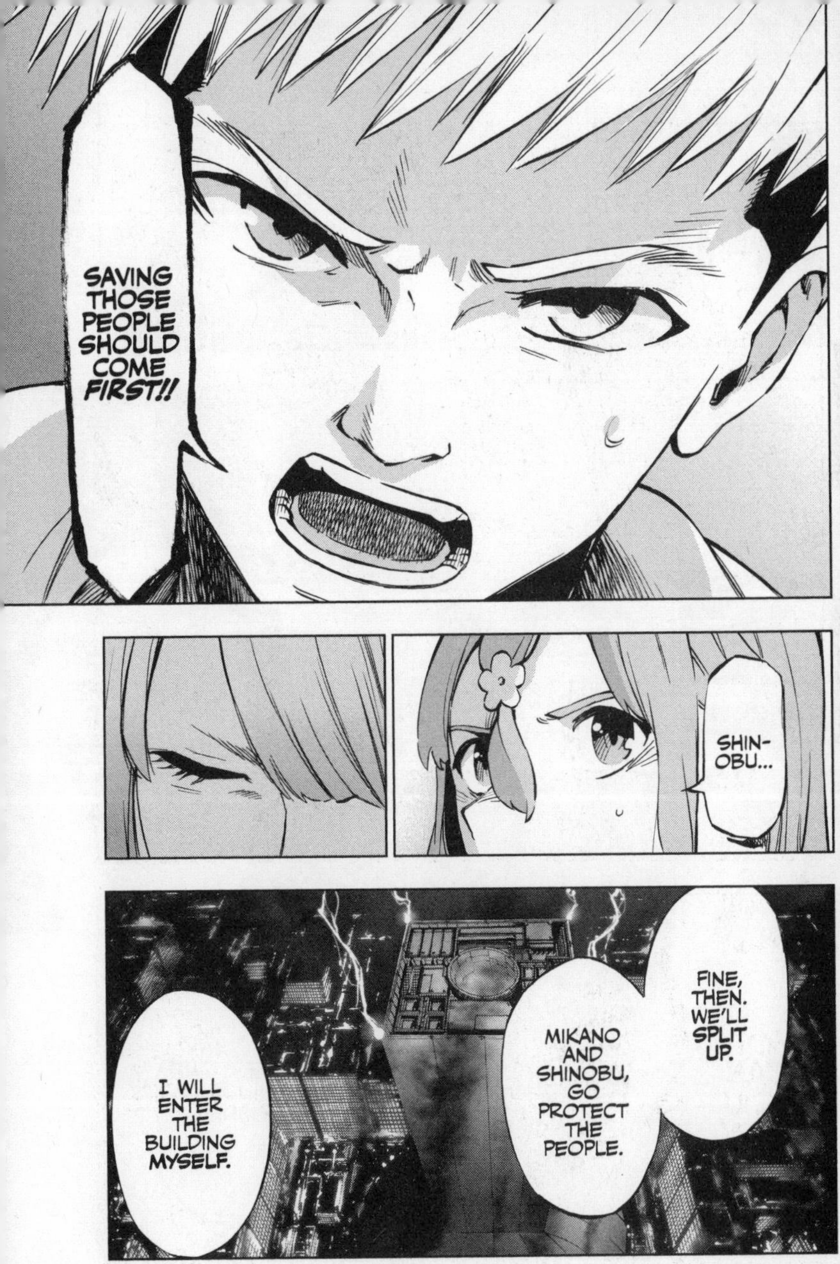
SAVING THOSE PEOPLE SHOULD COME FIRST!!
SHIN-OBU...
FINE, THEN. WE'LL SPLIT UP.
MIKANO AND SHINOBU, GO PROTECT THE PEOPLE.
I WILL ENTER THE BUILDING MYSELF.

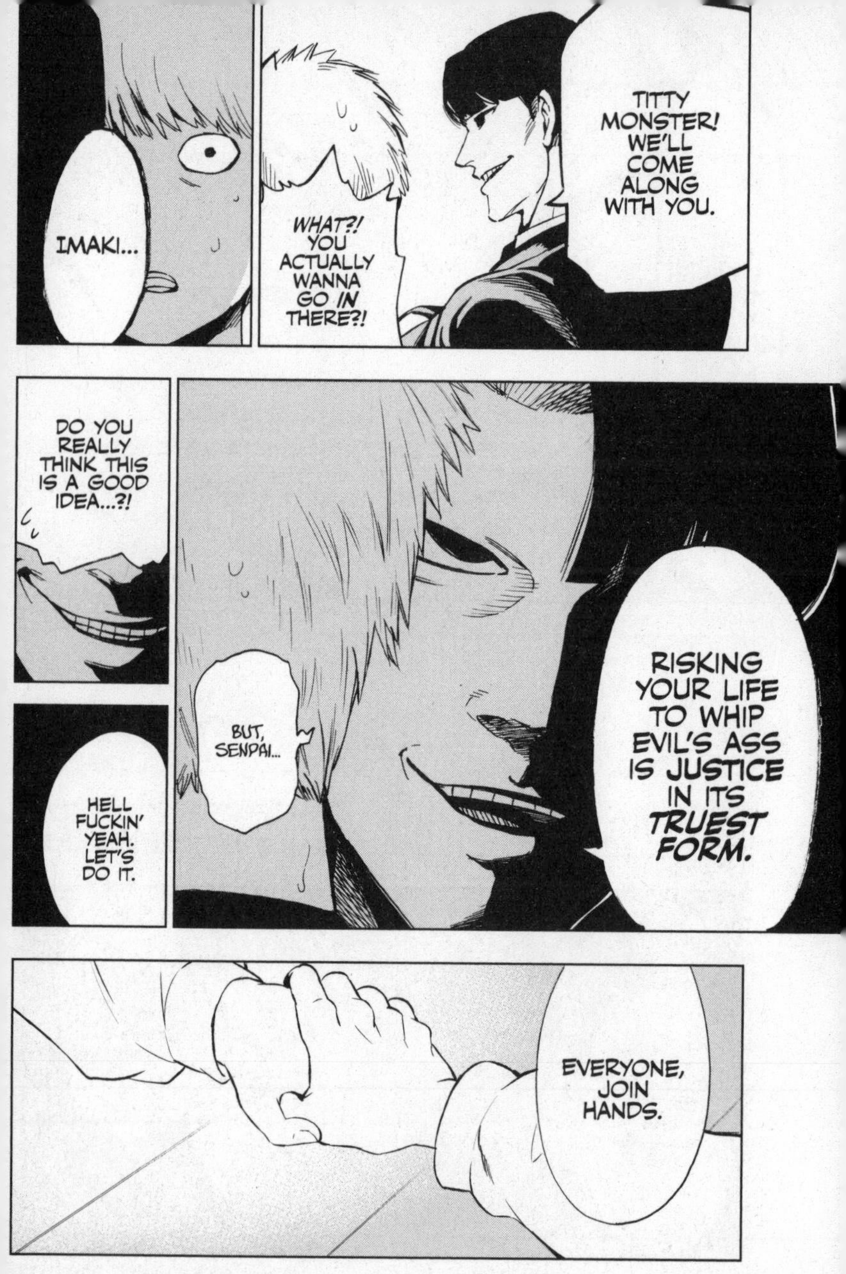
TITTY MONSTER! WE'LL COME ALONG WITH YOU.
WHAT?! YOU ACTUALLY WANNA GO IN THERE?!
IMAKI...
RISKING YOUR LIFE TO WHIP EVIL'S ASS IS JUSTICE IN ITS TRUEST FORM.
BUT, SENPAI...
DO YOU REALLY THINK THIS IS A GOOD IDEA...?!
HELL FUCKIN' YEAH. LET'S DO IT.
EVERYONE, JOIN HANDS.

SHVUFF...
CRACKLE...
GWOOOOO
BZZT
BZZT
ZZRT
ZRT...

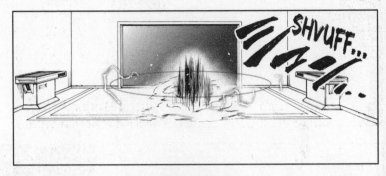

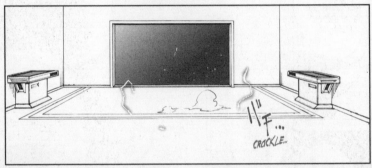

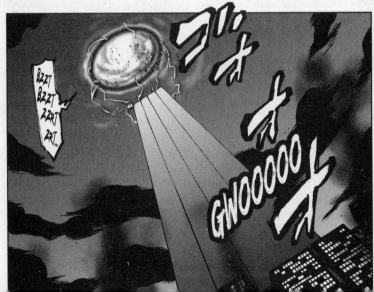

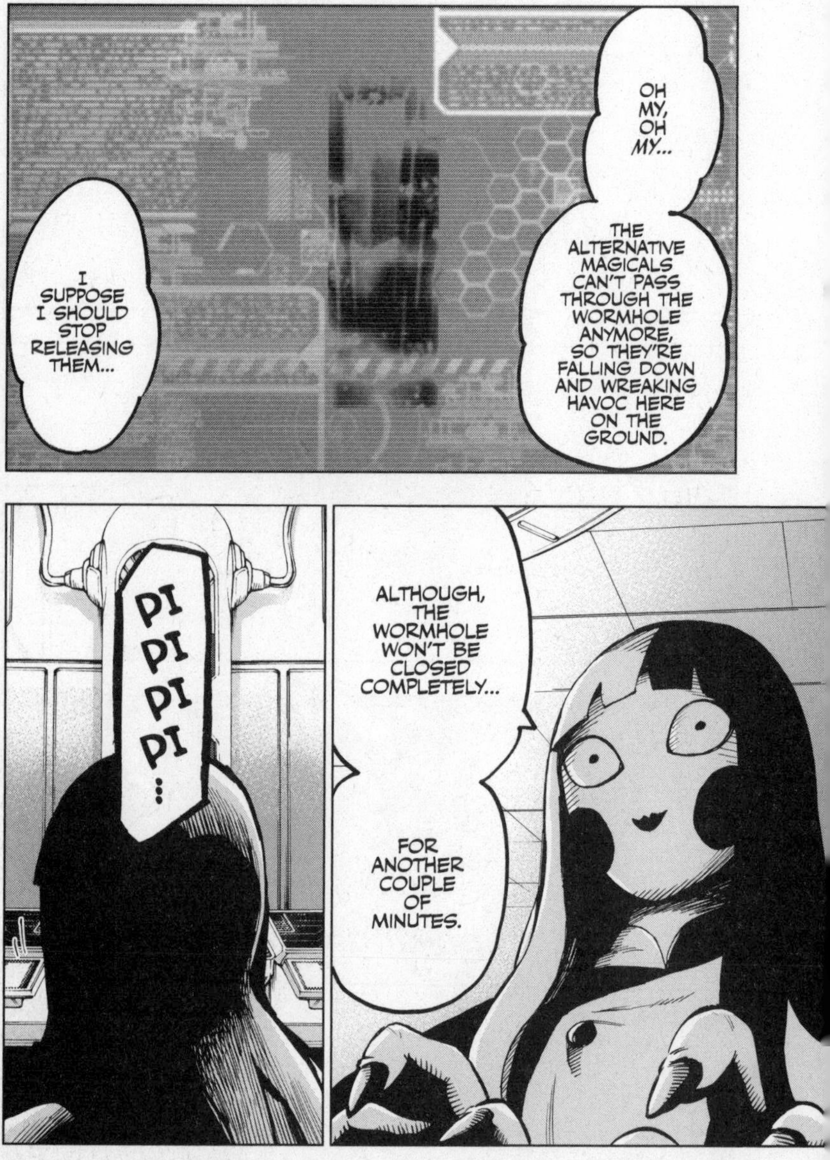
OH MY, OH MY...
THE ALTERNATIVE MAGICALS CAN'T PASS THROUGH THE WORMHOLE ANYMORE, SO THEY'RE FALLING DOWN AND WREAKING HAVOC HERE ON THE GROUND.
I SUPPOSE I SHOULD STOP RELEASING THEM...
ALTHOUGH, THE WORMHOLE WON'T BE CLOSED COMPLETELY...
FOR ANOTHER COUPLE OF MINUTES.
PI PI PI PI...

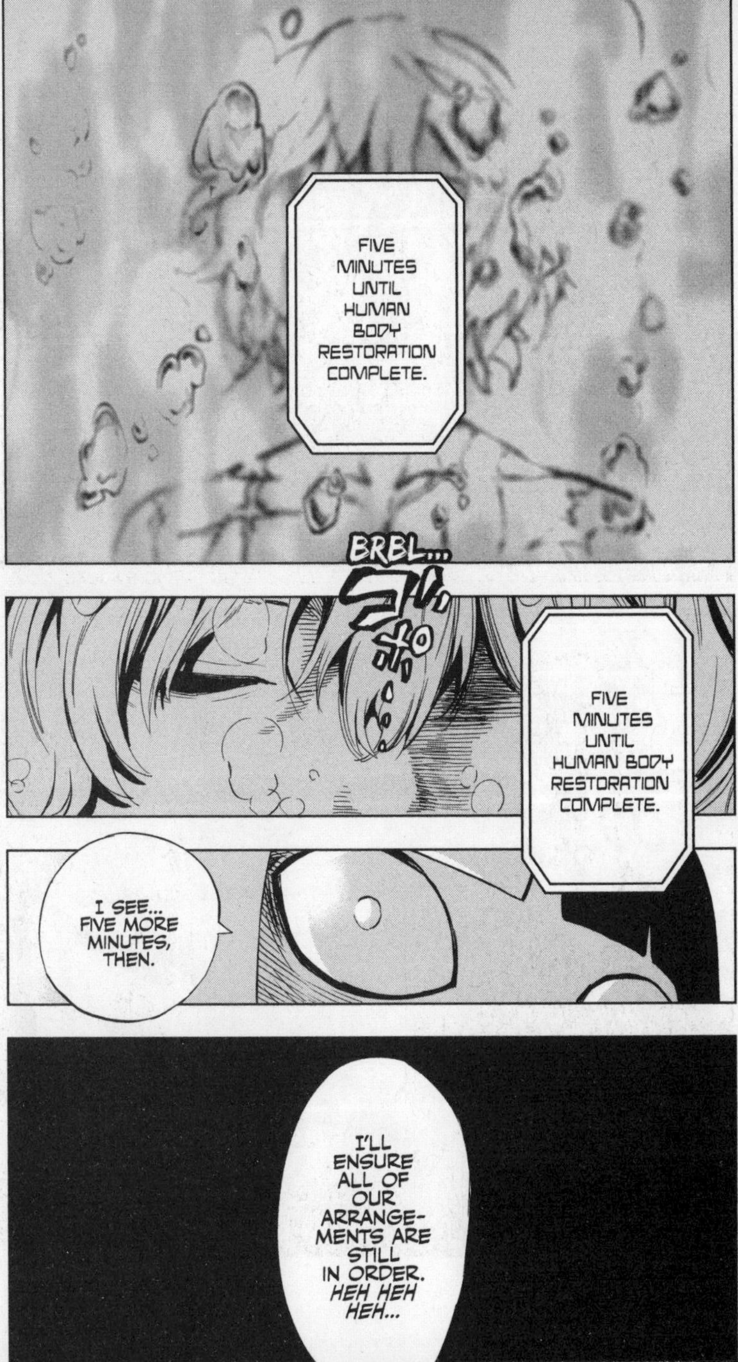
FIVE MINUTES UNTIL HUMAN BODY RESTORATION COMPLETE.
BRBL...
FIVE MINUTES UNTIL HUMAN BODY RESTORATION COMPLETE.
I SEE... FIVE MORE MINUTES, THEN.
I'LL ENSURE ALL OF OUR ARRANGE-MENTS ARE STILL IN ORDER. *HEH HEH HEH...*

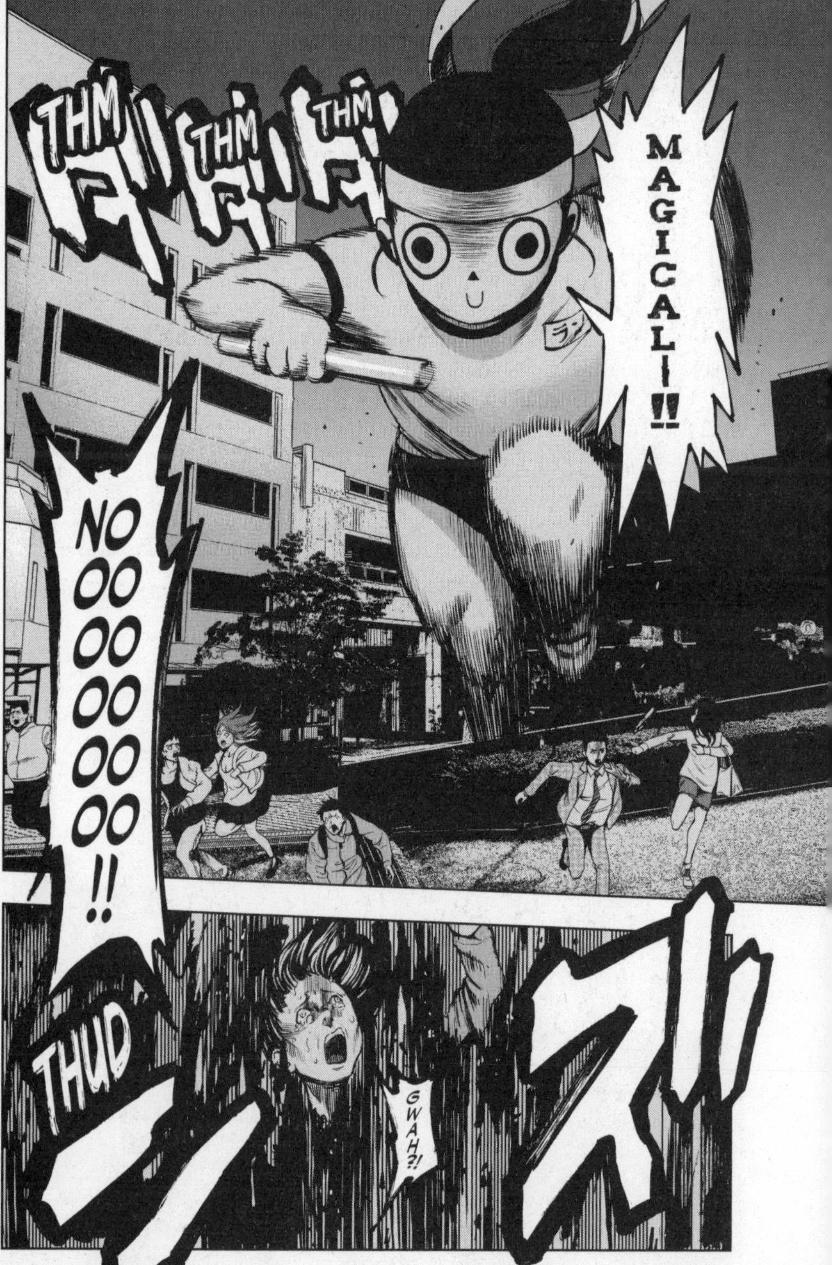
MAGICAL!!
THM THM THM
NOOOOOOOOOOOOOOO!!
GWAH?!
THUD

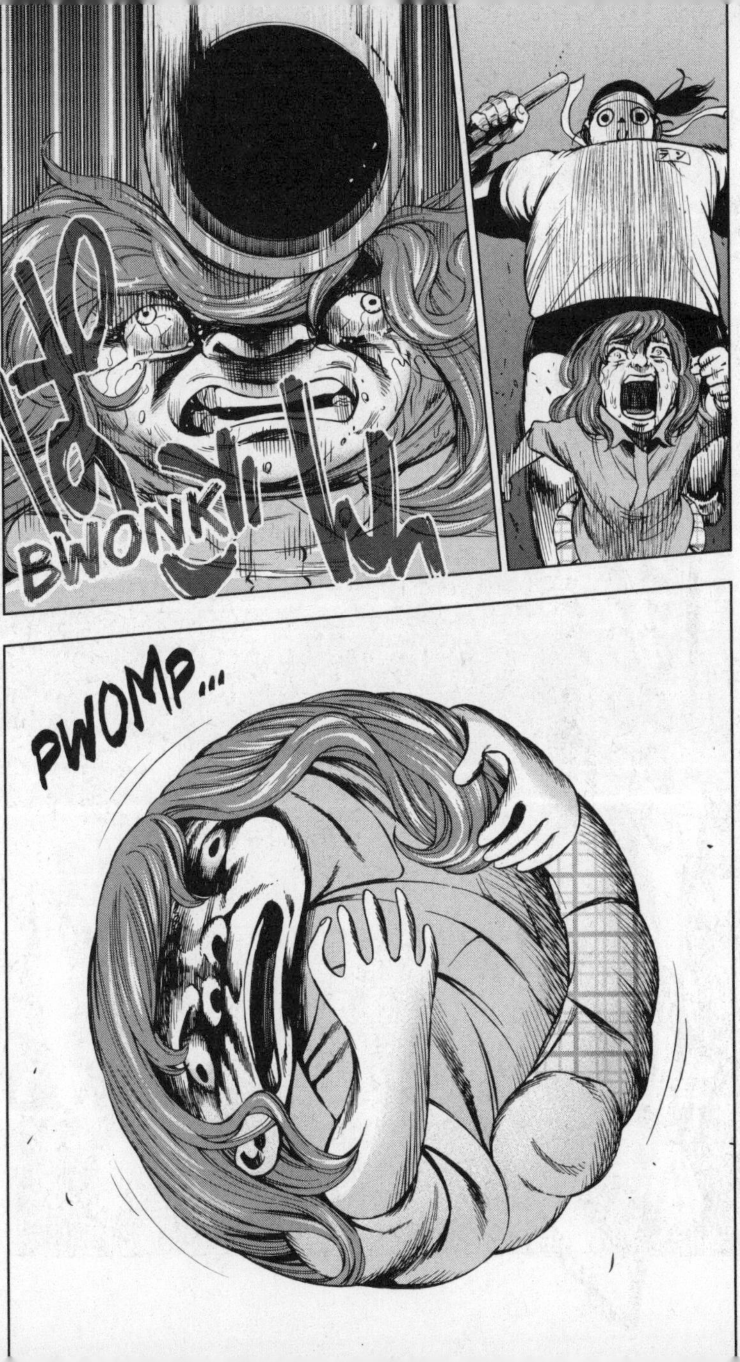
BWONK!!
PWOMP...

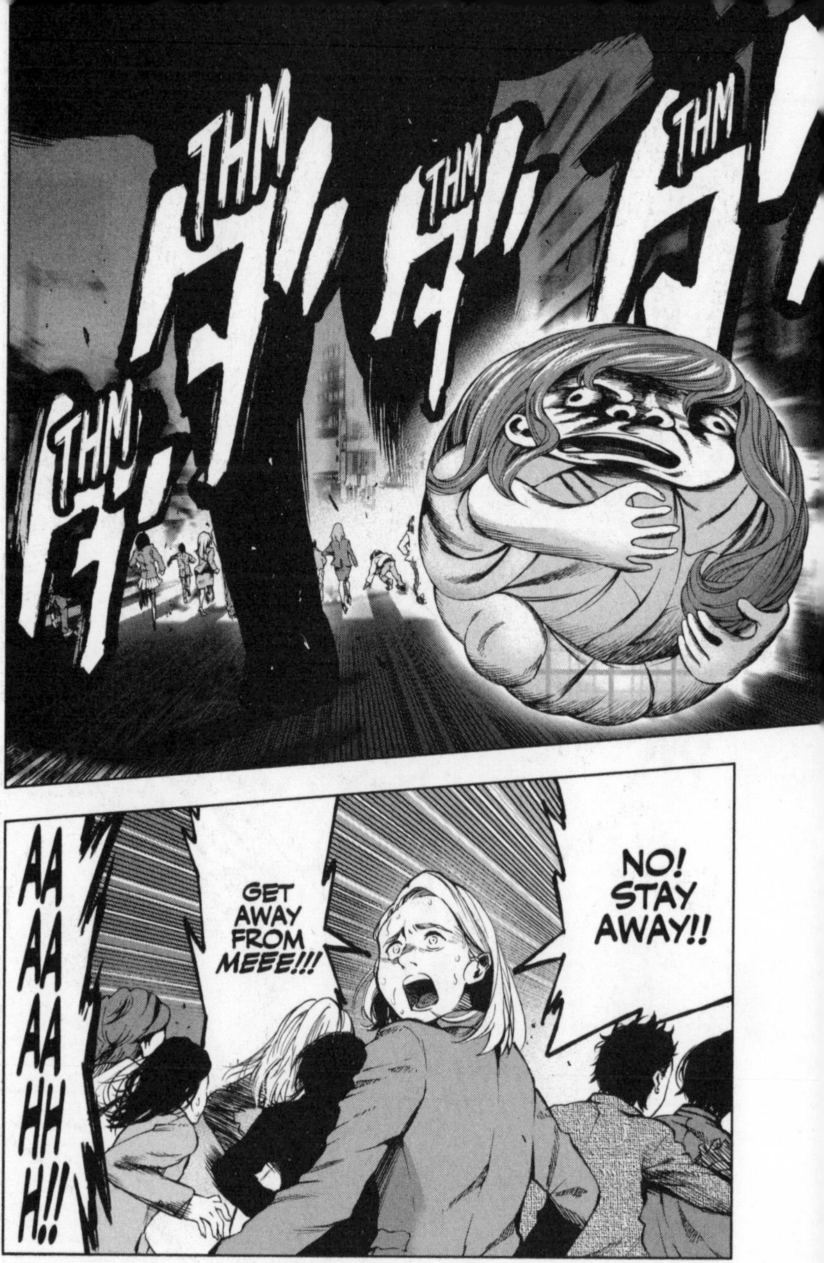
THM
THM
THM
THM
NO! STAY AWAY!!
GET AWAY FROM MEEE!!!
AAAAAAAAAAHHHHH!!

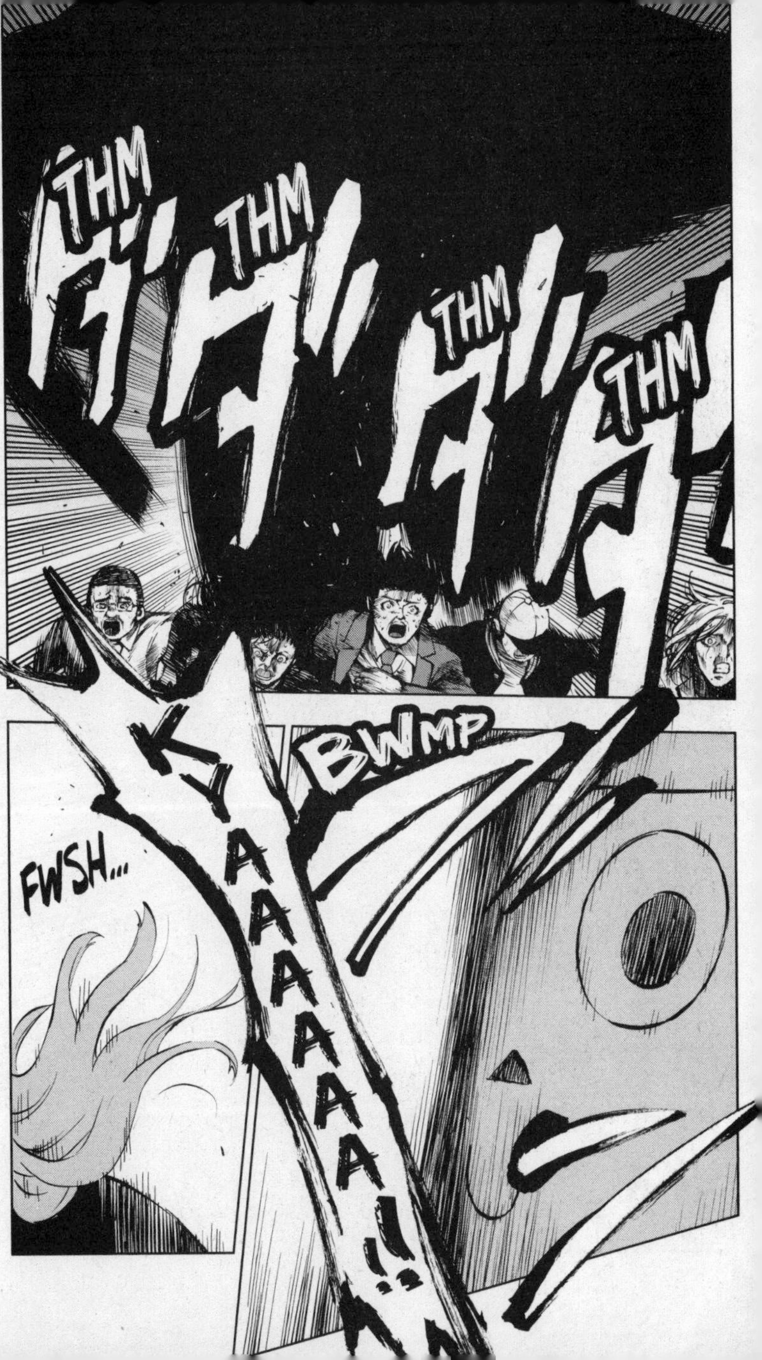
THM
THM
THM
THM
KYAAAAAAA!!
BWMP
FWSH...

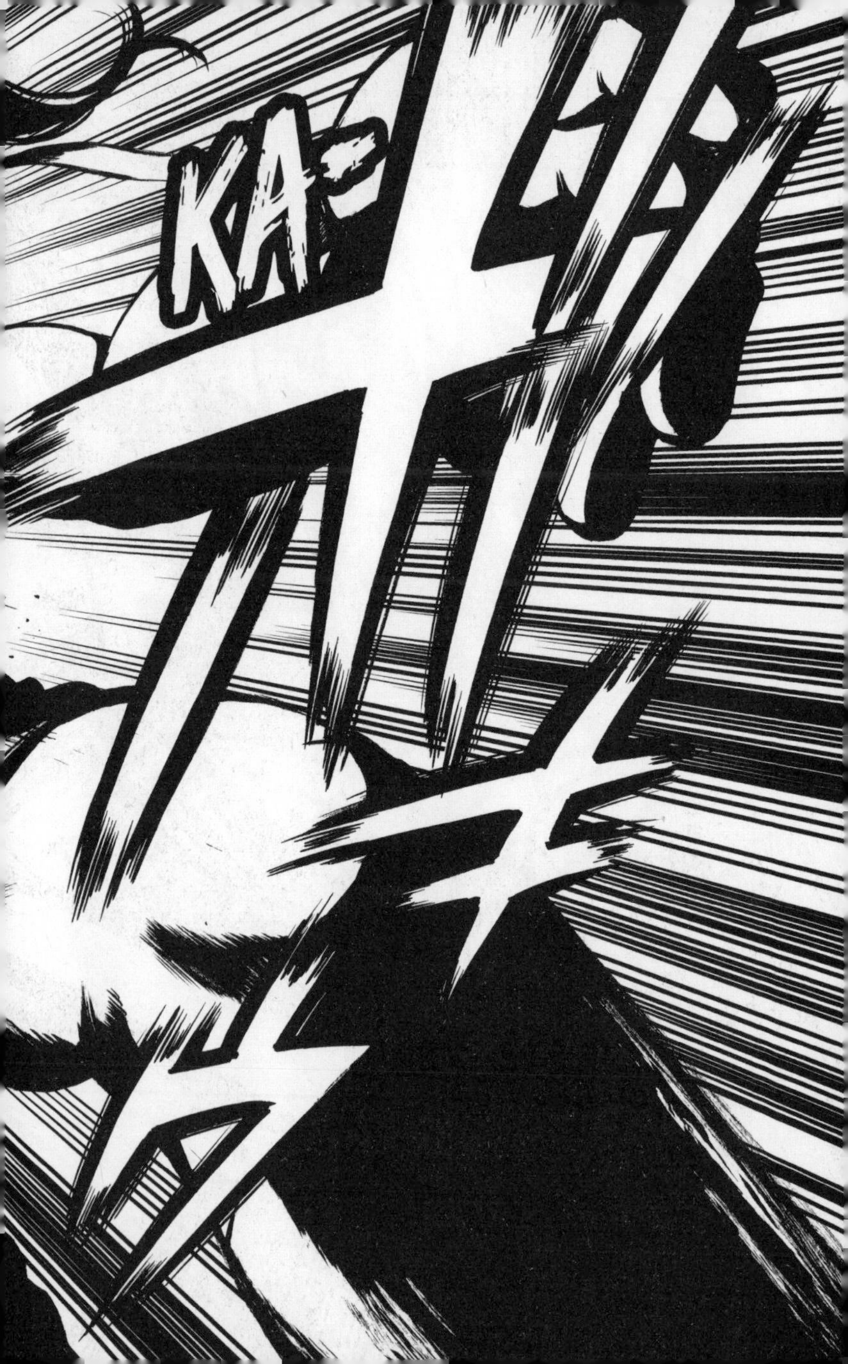
KA-CHAK

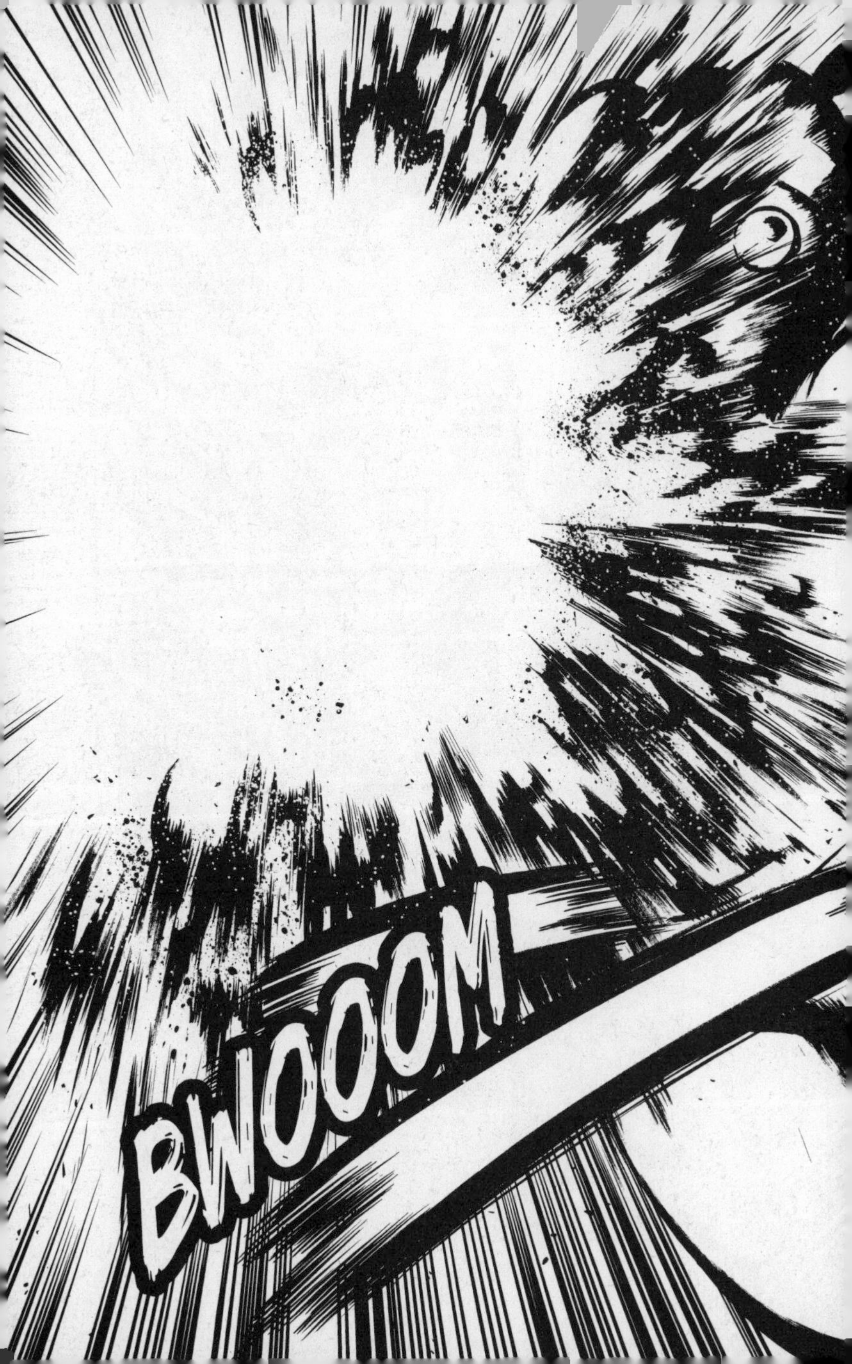
BWOOOM

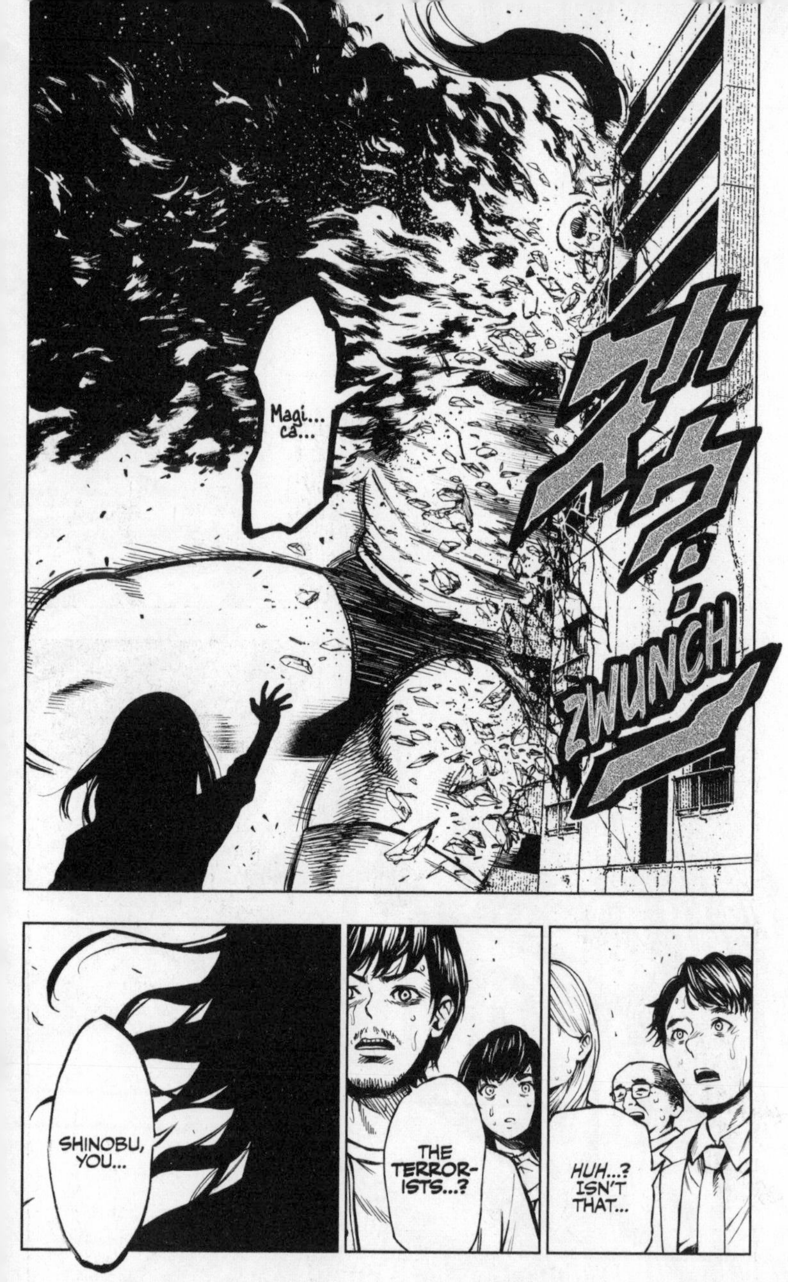
Magi... ca...
ZWUNCH
HUH...? ISN'T THAT...
THE TERROR-ISTS...?
SHINOBU, YOU...

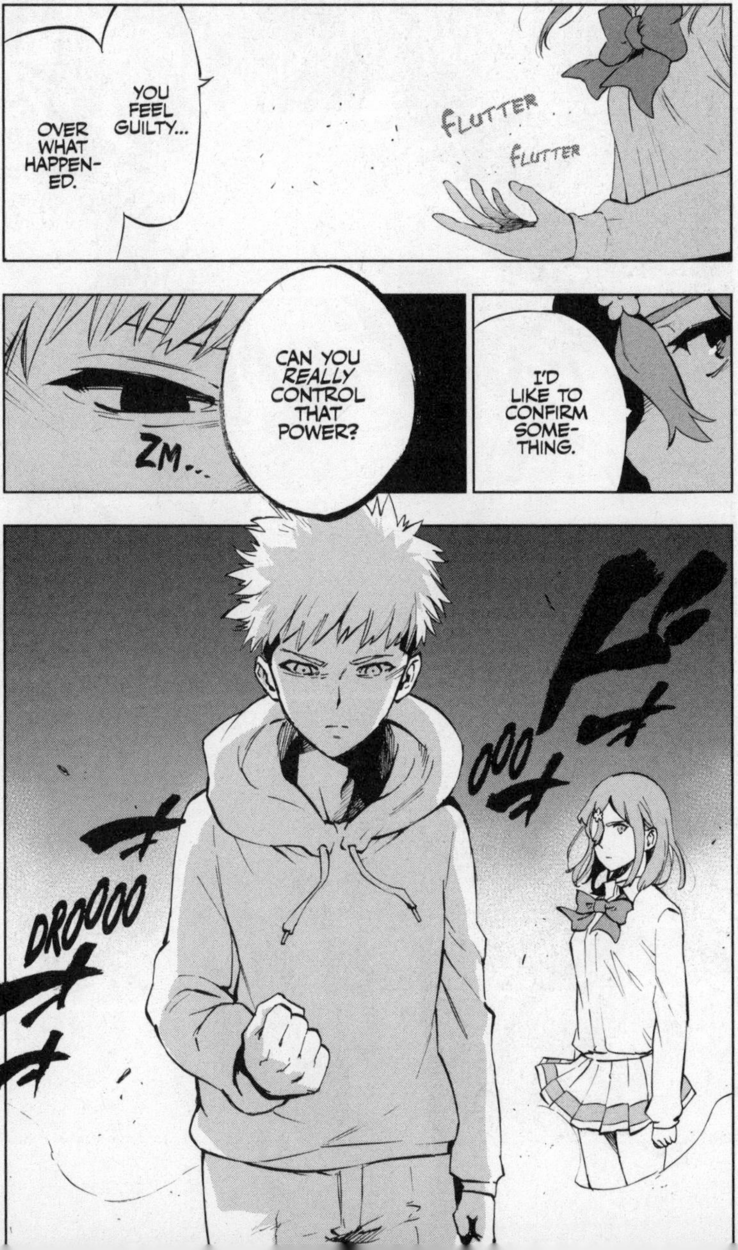
FLUTTER
FLUTTER
YOU FEEL GUILTY...
OVER WHAT HAPPEN-ED.
I'D LIKE TO CONFIRM SOME-THING.
CAN YOU *REALLY* CONTROL THAT POWER?
ZM...
OOO
DROOOO

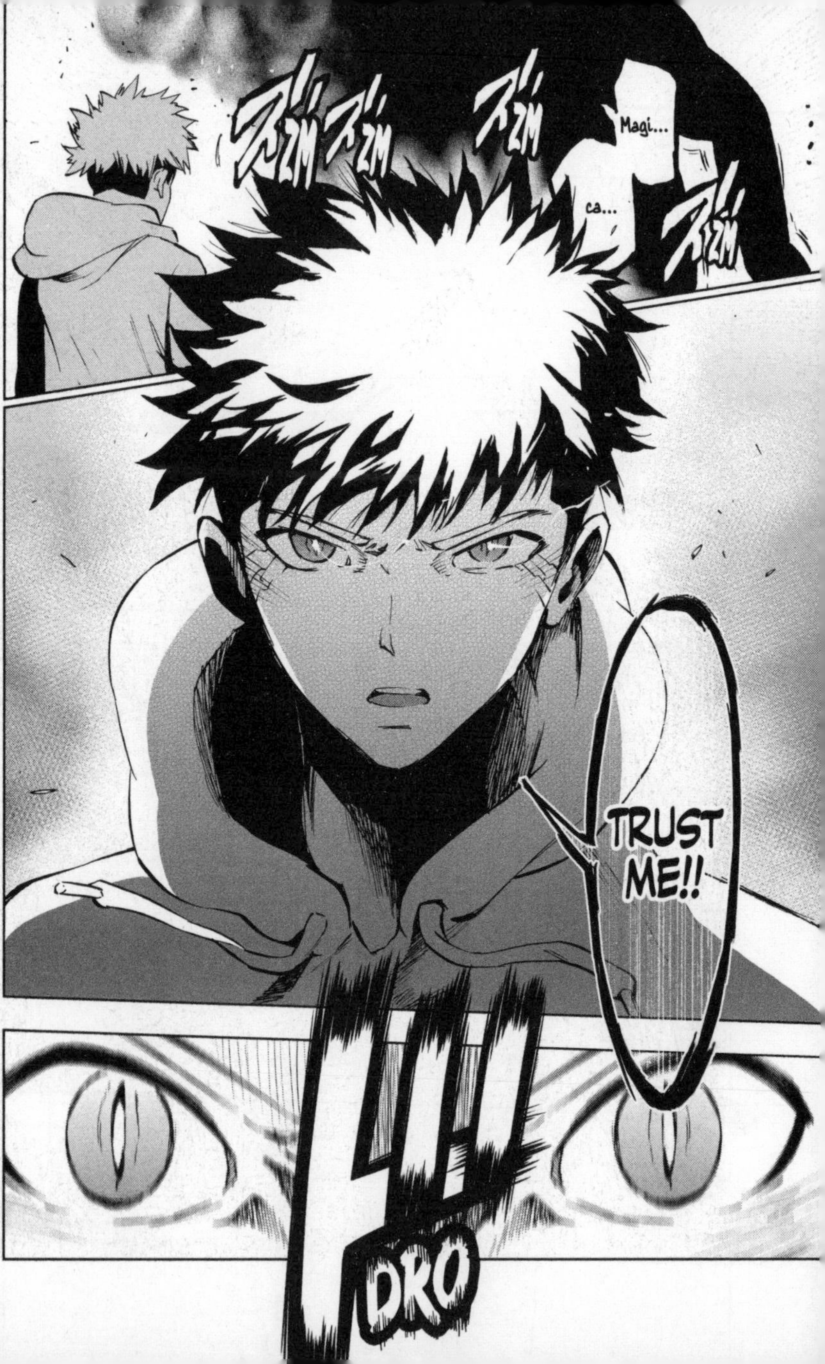
Magi...
ca...
ズZM
ズZM
ズZM
ズZM
TRUST ME!!
DRO

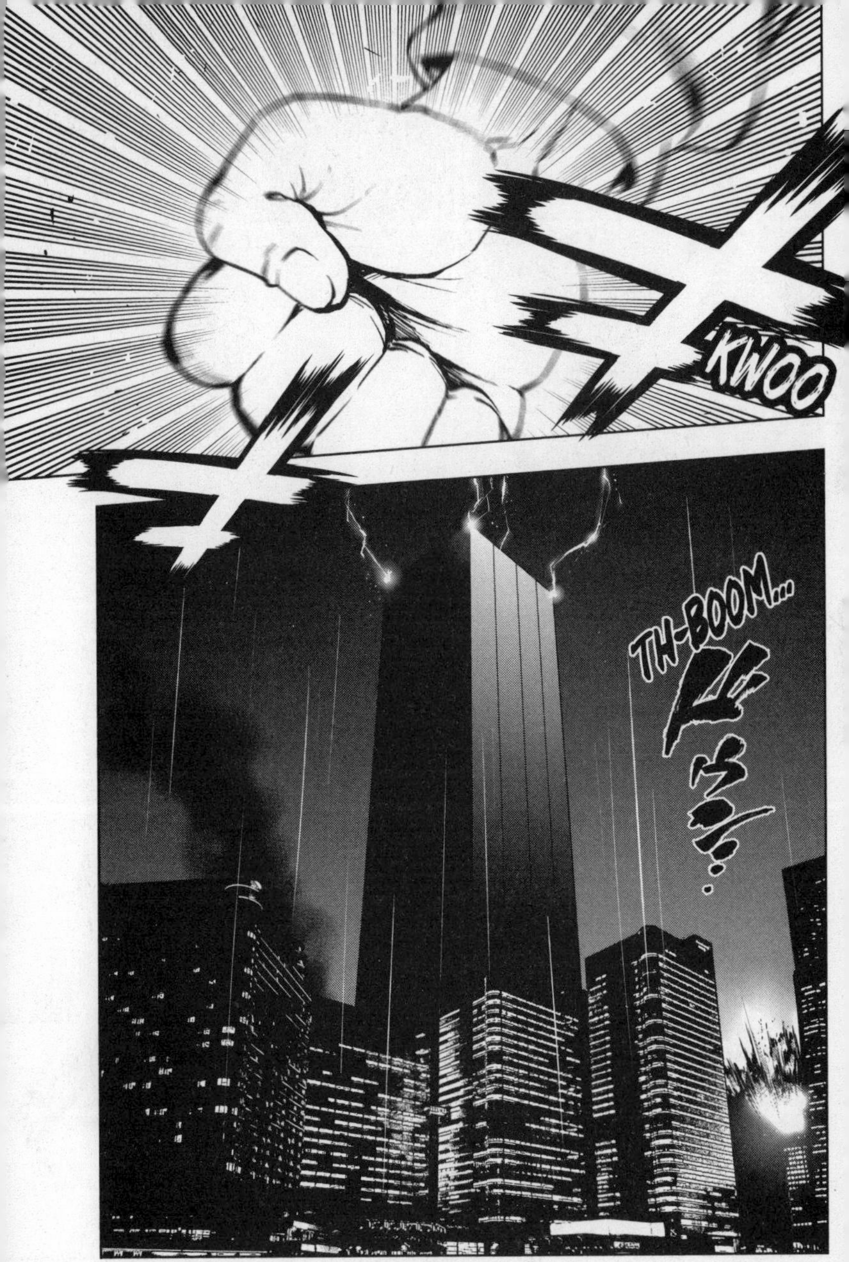
KWOO
TH-BOOM...

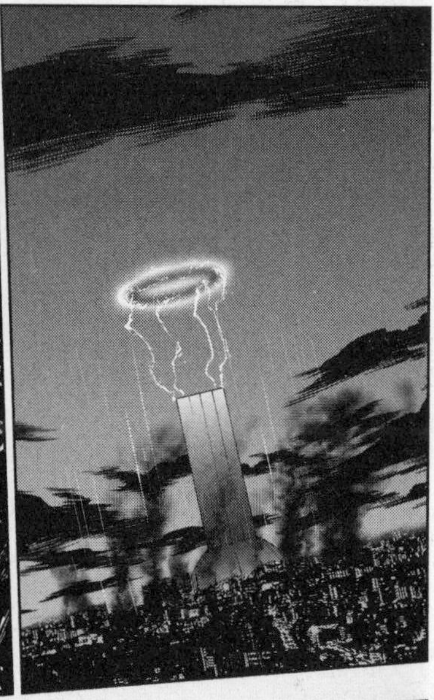

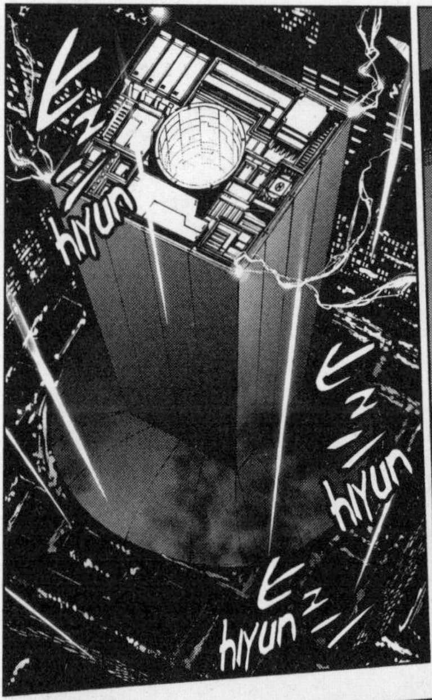
hiyun
hiyun
hiyun

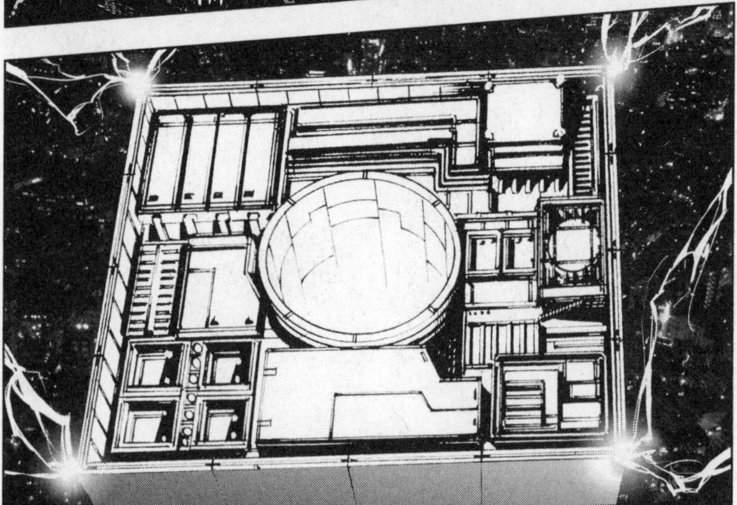

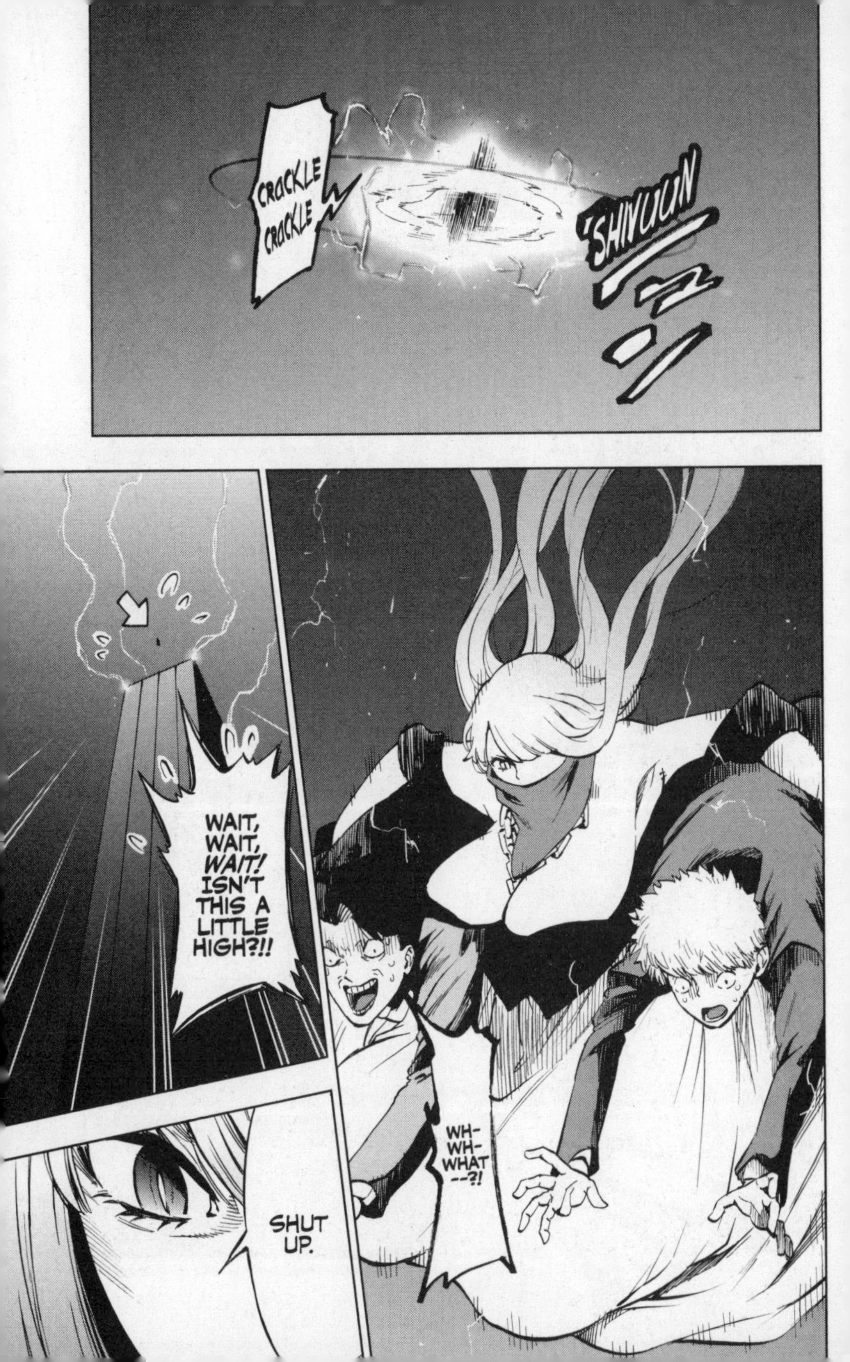
SHIVUUN
CRACKLE CRACKLE
WH-WH-WHAT--?!
WAIT, WAIT, WAIT! ISN'T THIS A LITTLE HIGH?!!
SHUT UP.

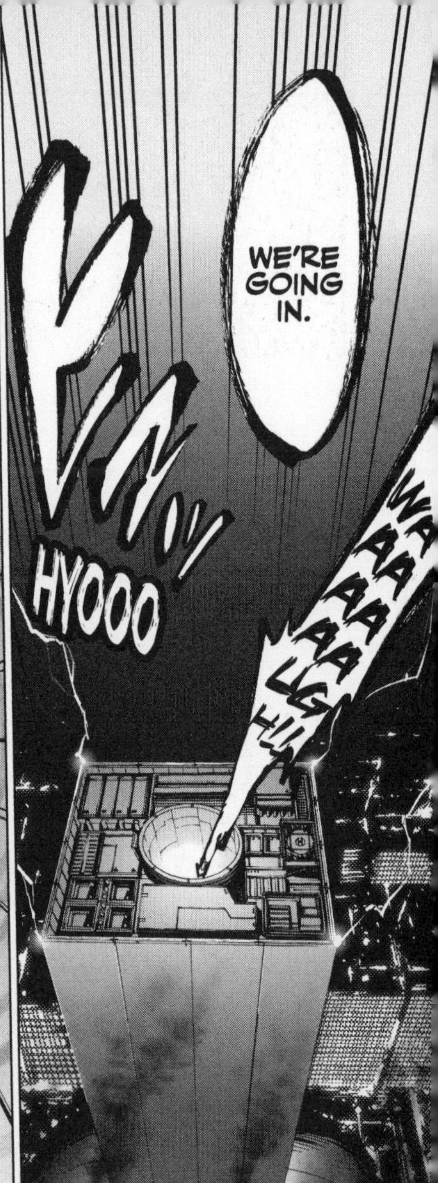
WE'RE GOING IN.
HYOOO
WAAAAAAAAAUGH!!
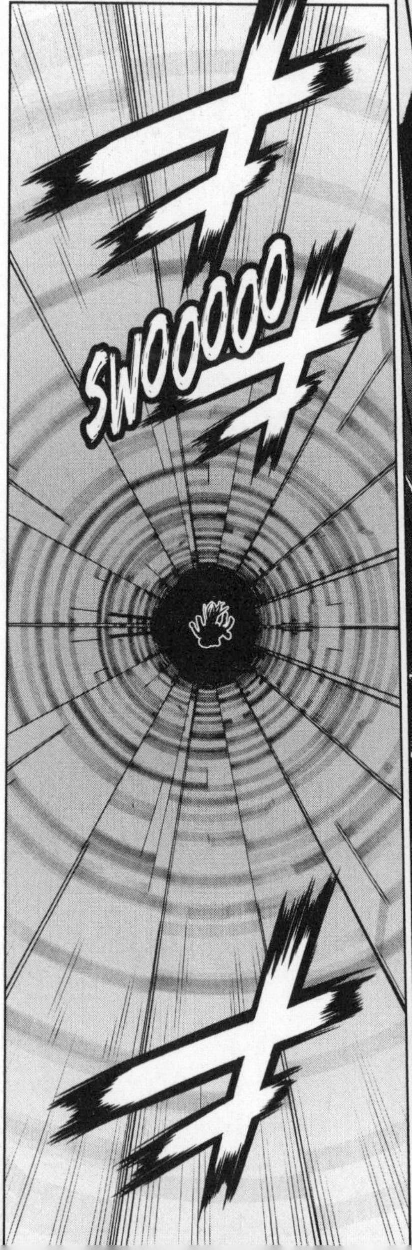
SWOOOOO

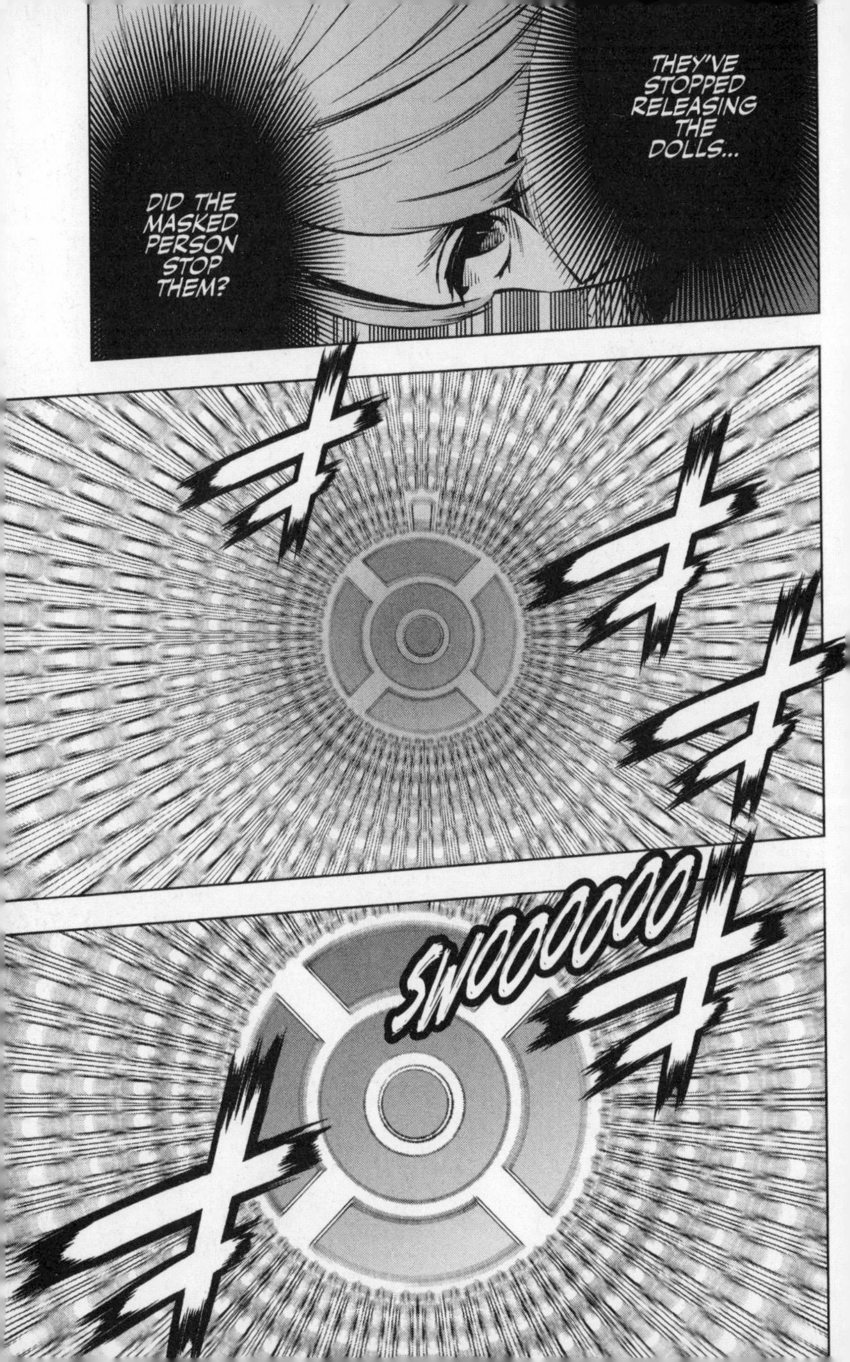
THEY'VE STOPPED RELEASING THE DOLLS...
DID THE MASKED PERSON STOP THEM?
SWOOOOOOO

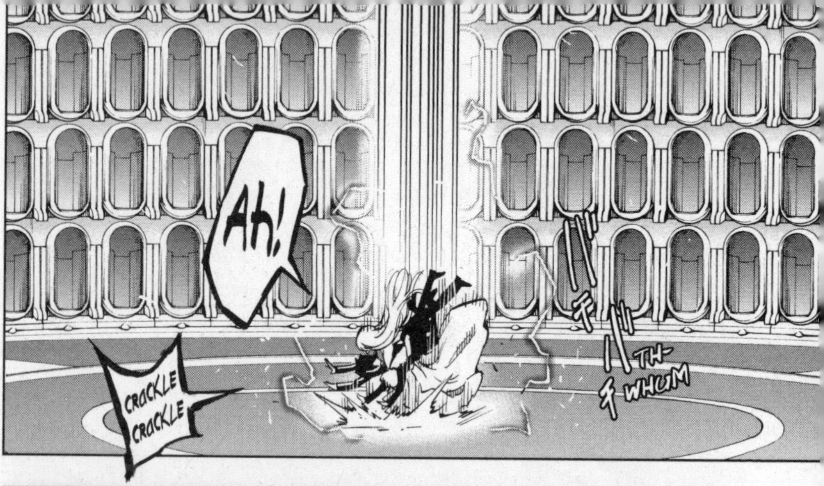
Ah!
TH-WHUM
CRACKLE CRACKLE
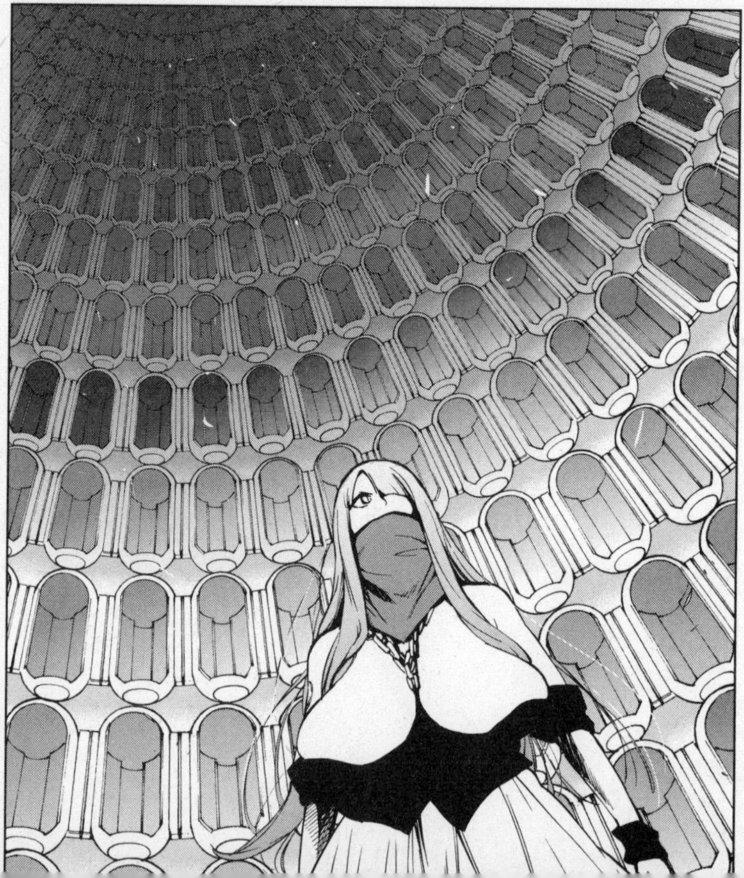

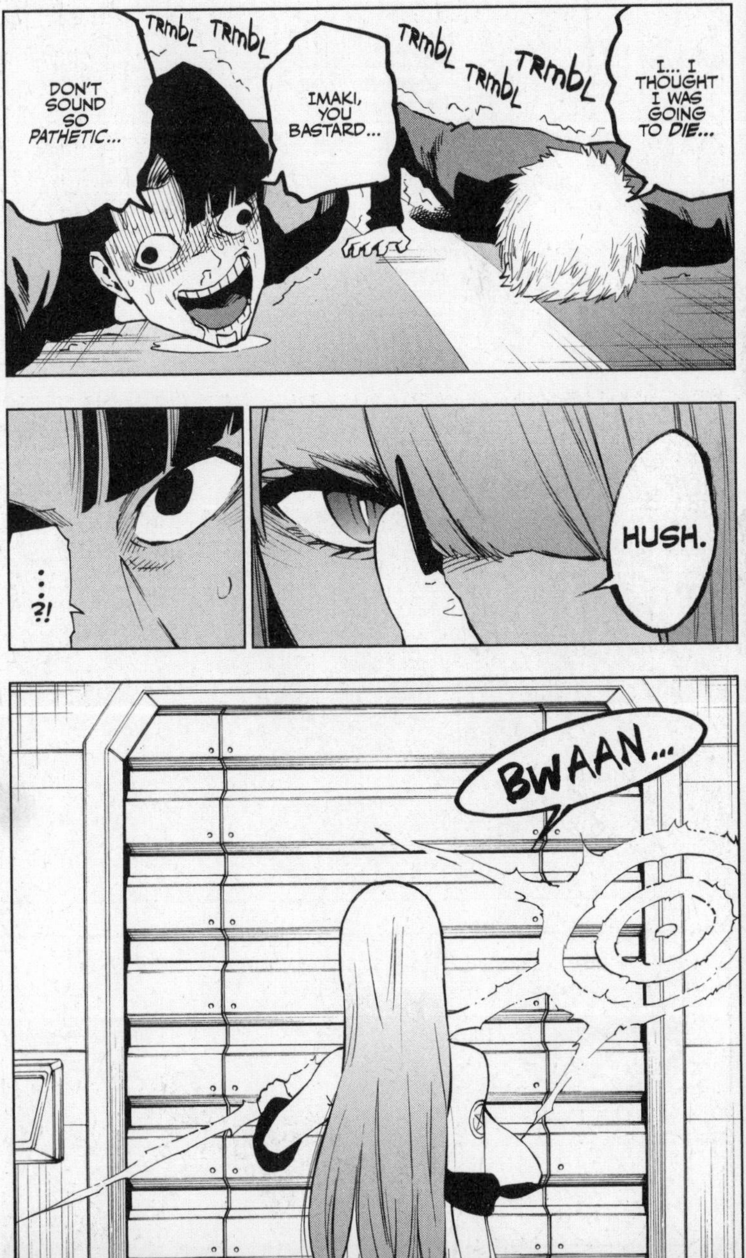
I... I THOUGHT I WAS GOING TO *DIE*...
TRMBL
TRMBL
TRMBL
IMAKI, YOU BASTARD...
TRMBL
TRMBL
DON'T SOUND SO *PATHETIC*...
HUSH.
...?!
BWAAN...

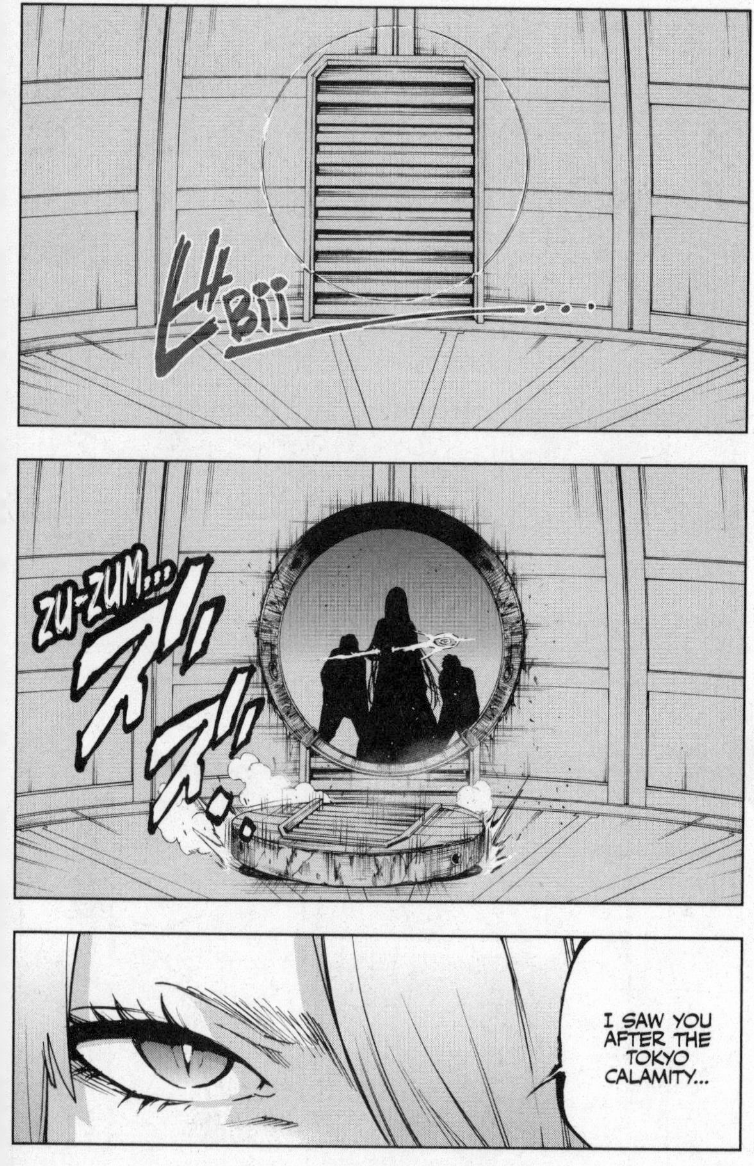
Bii
ZU-ZUM...
I SAW YOU AFTER THE TOKYO CALAMITY...

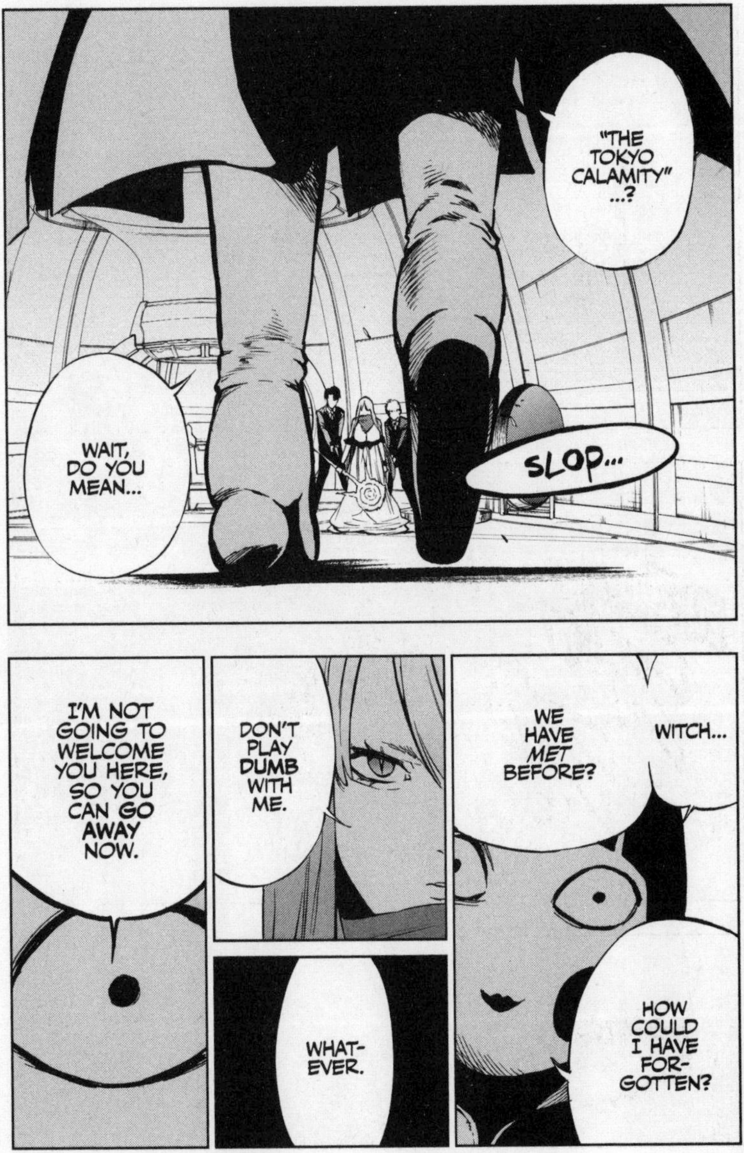
"THE TOKYO CALAMITY" ...?
SLOP...
WAIT, DO YOU MEAN...
WITCH...
WE HAVE *MET* BEFORE?
HOW COULD I HAVE FOR-GOTTEN?
DON'T PLAY DUMB WITH ME.
WHAT-EVER.
I'M NOT GOING TO WELCOME YOU HERE, SO YOU CAN GO AWAY NOW.

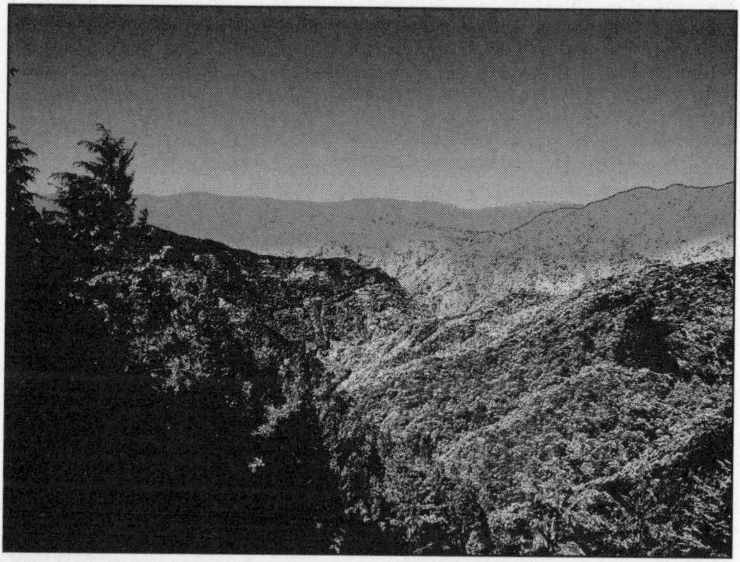

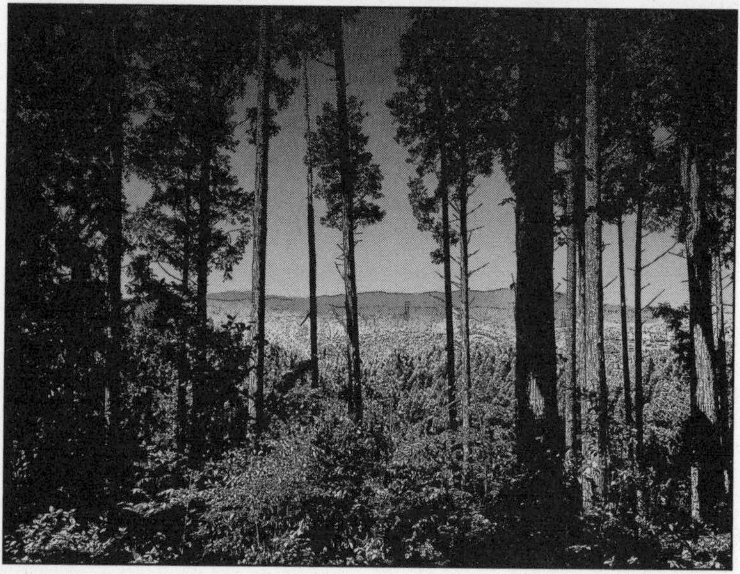

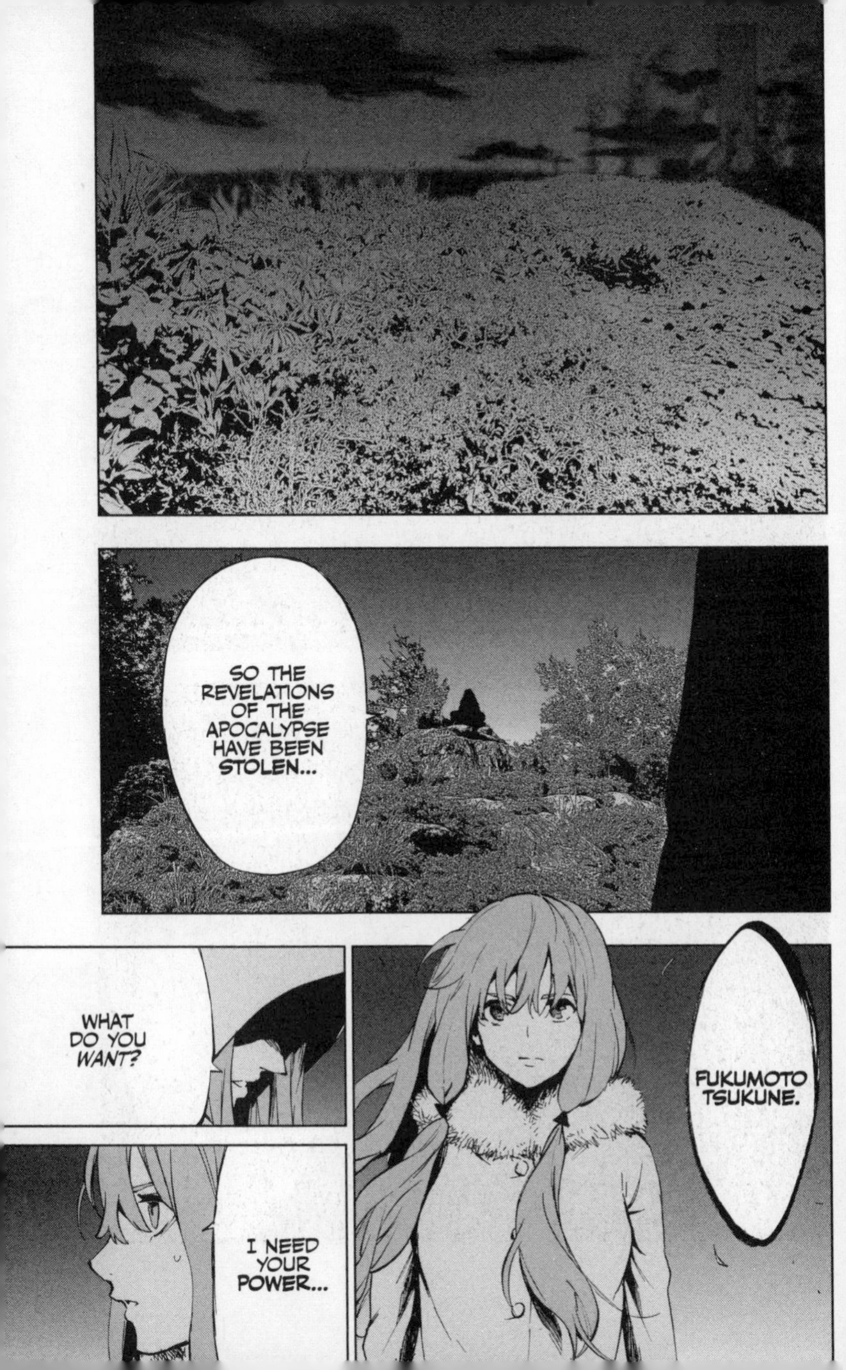
SO THE REVELATIONS OF THE APOCALYPSE HAVE BEEN STOLEN...
FUKUMOTO TSUKUNE.
WHAT DO YOU WANT?
I NEED YOUR POWER...

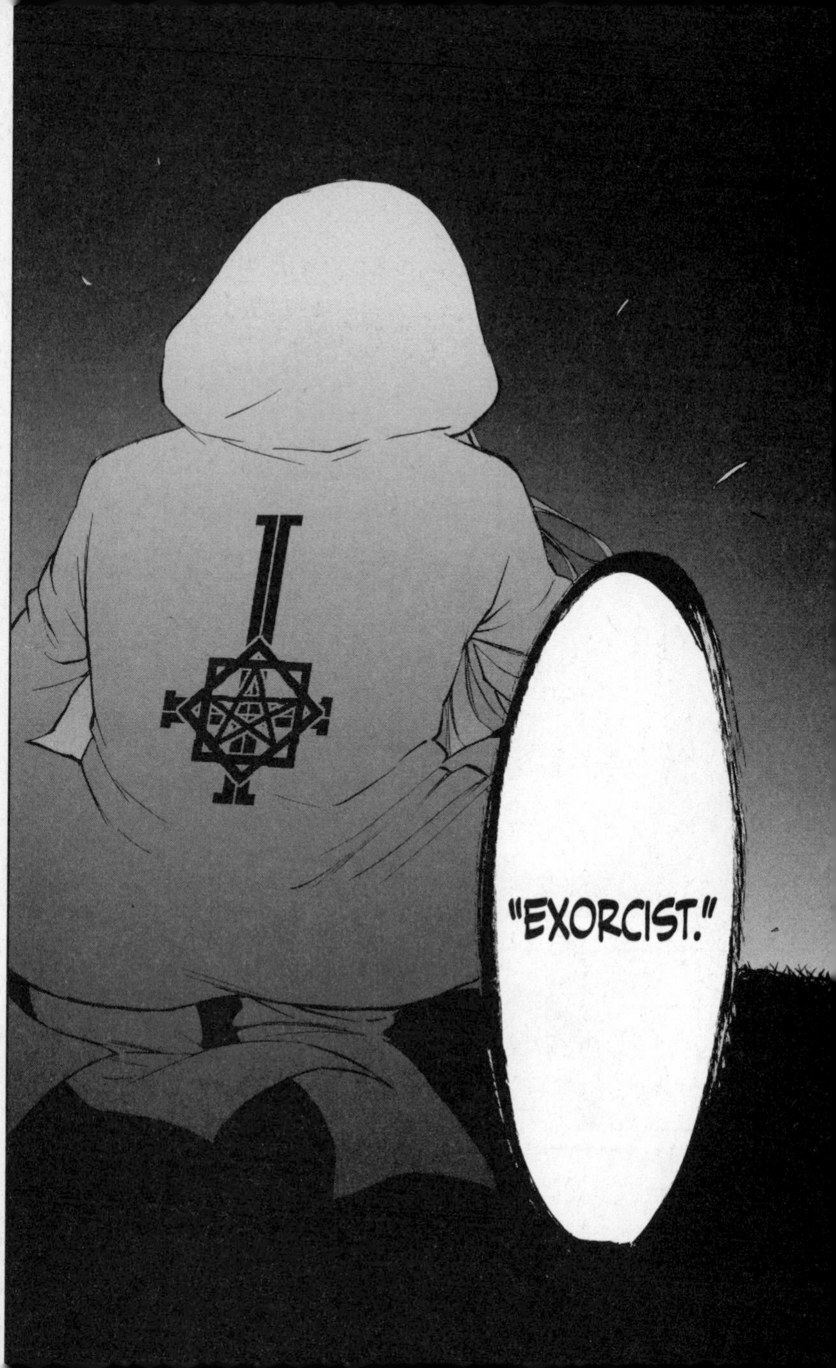
"EXORCIST."

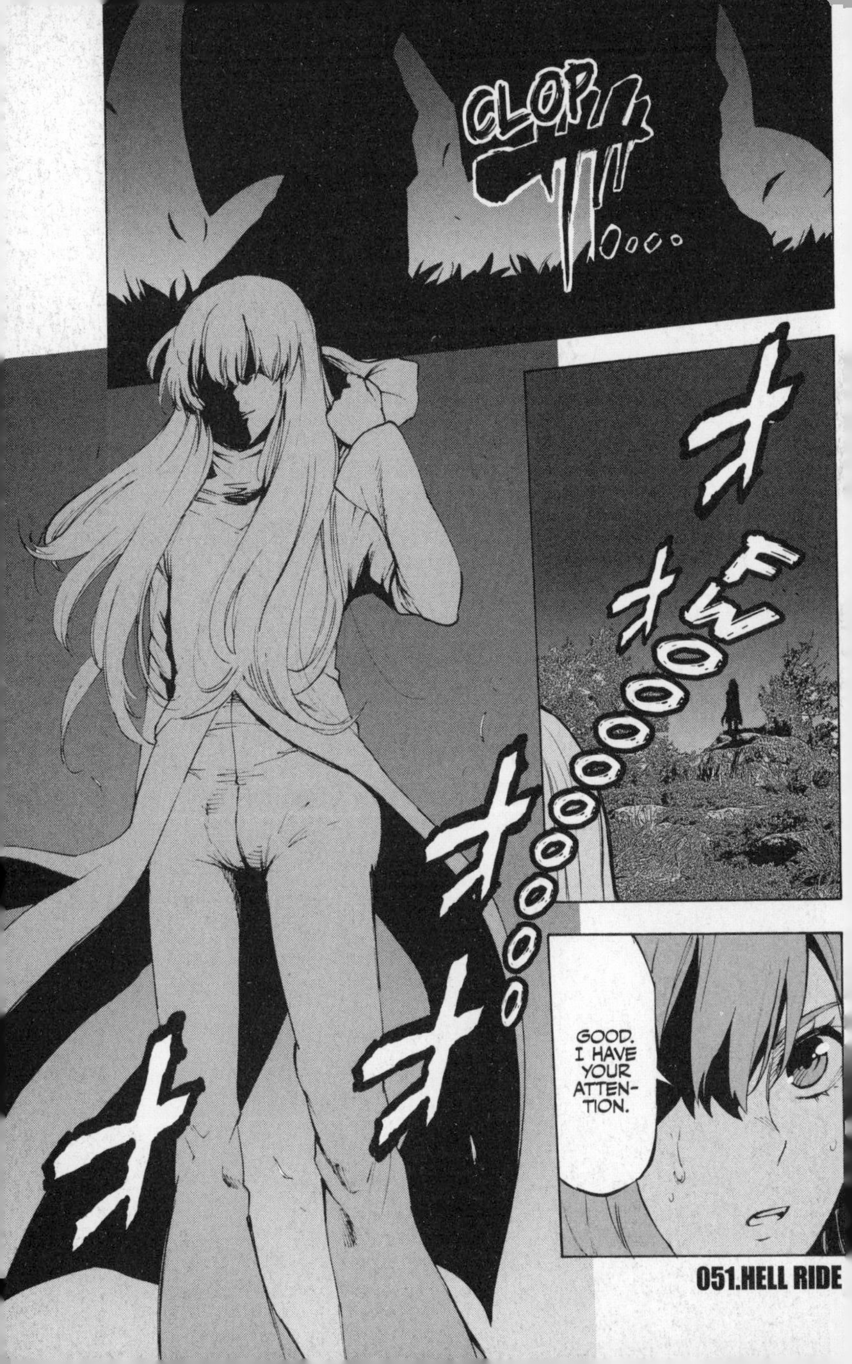
CLOP
FWOOOOOOOOOO
GOOD. I HAVE YOUR ATTENTION.

051.HELL RIDE

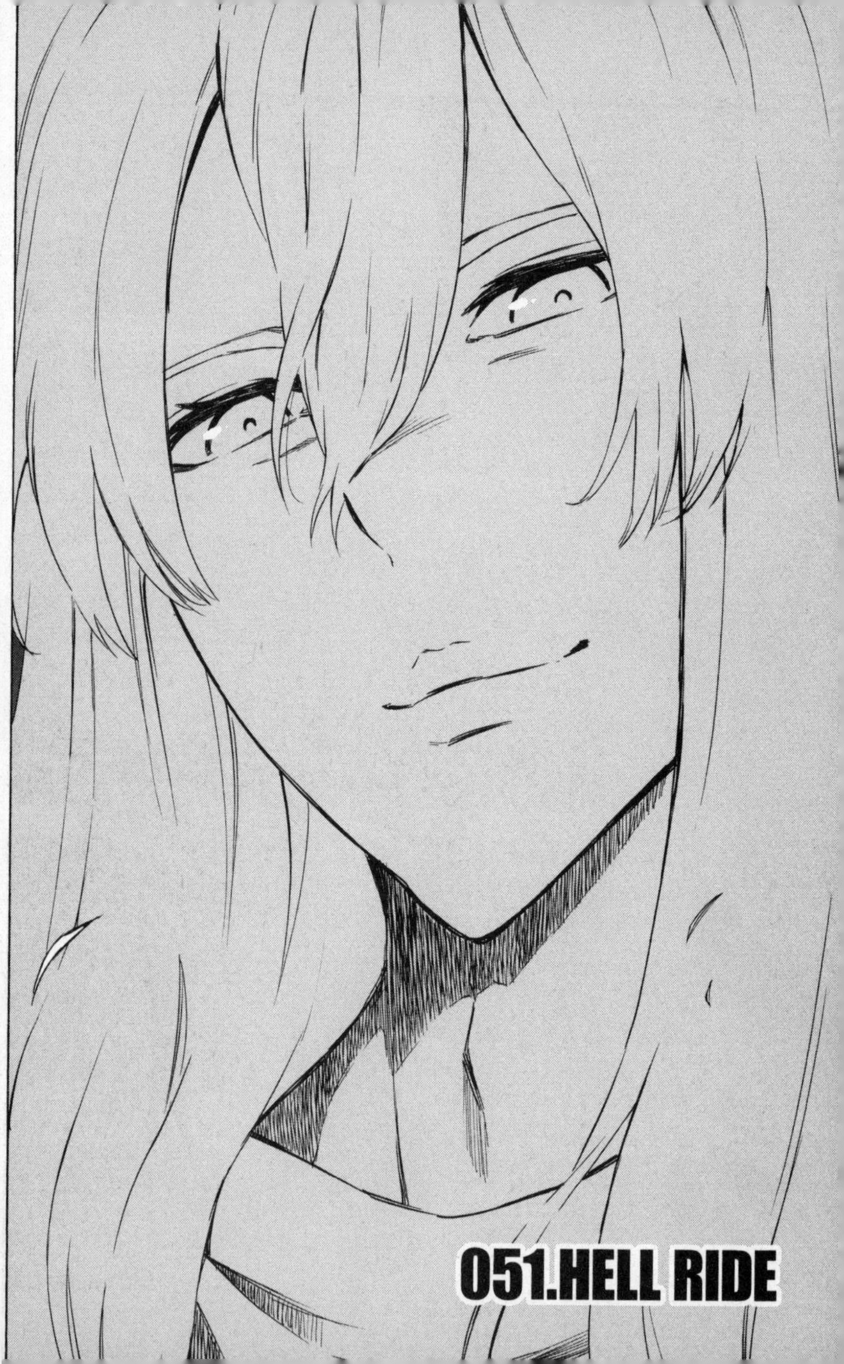
051.HELL RIDE

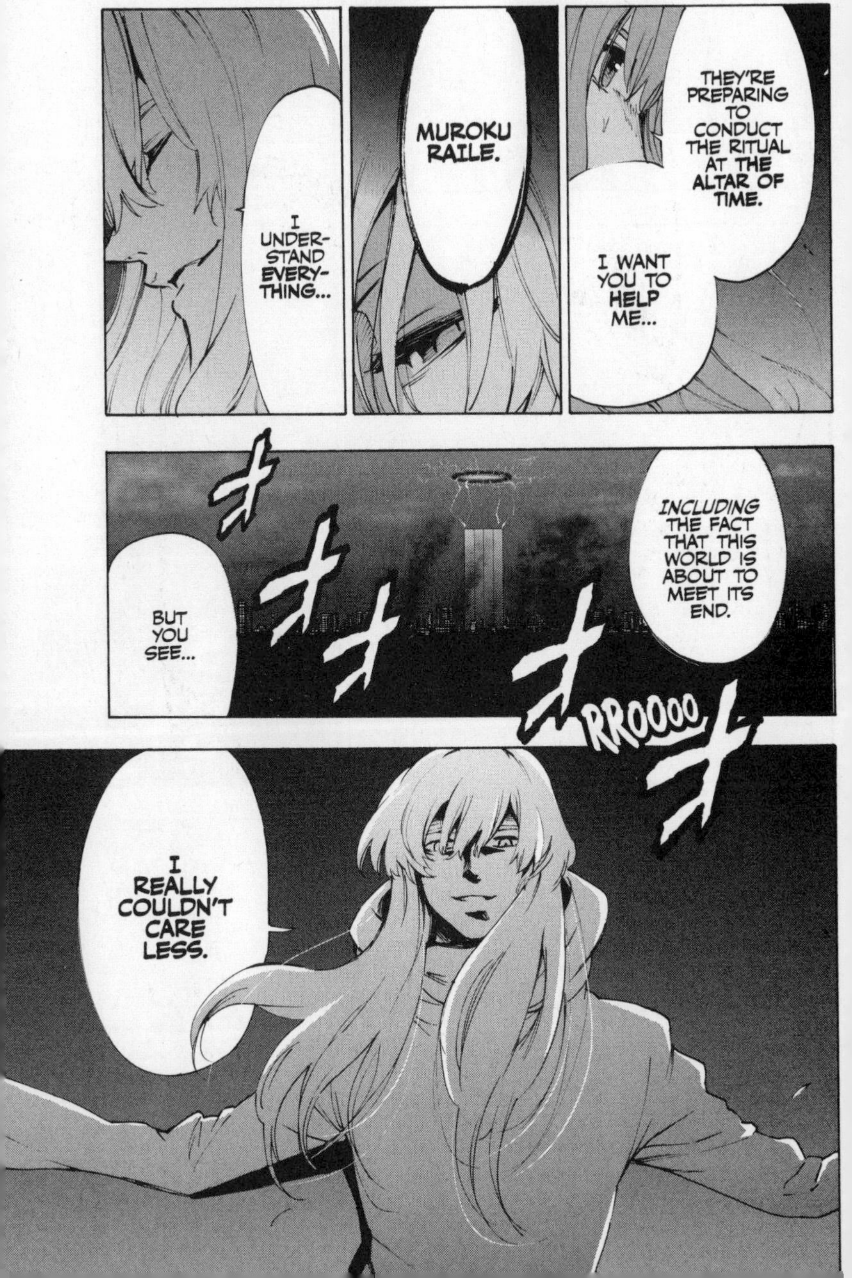
THEY'RE PREPARING TO CONDUCT THE RITUAL AT THE ALTAR OF TIME.
I WANT YOU TO HELP ME...
MUROKU RAILE.
I UNDER-STAND EVERY-THING...
INCLUDING THE FACT THAT THIS WORLD IS ABOUT TO MEET ITS END.
BUT YOU SEE...
RROOOO
I REALLY COULDN'T CARE LESS.

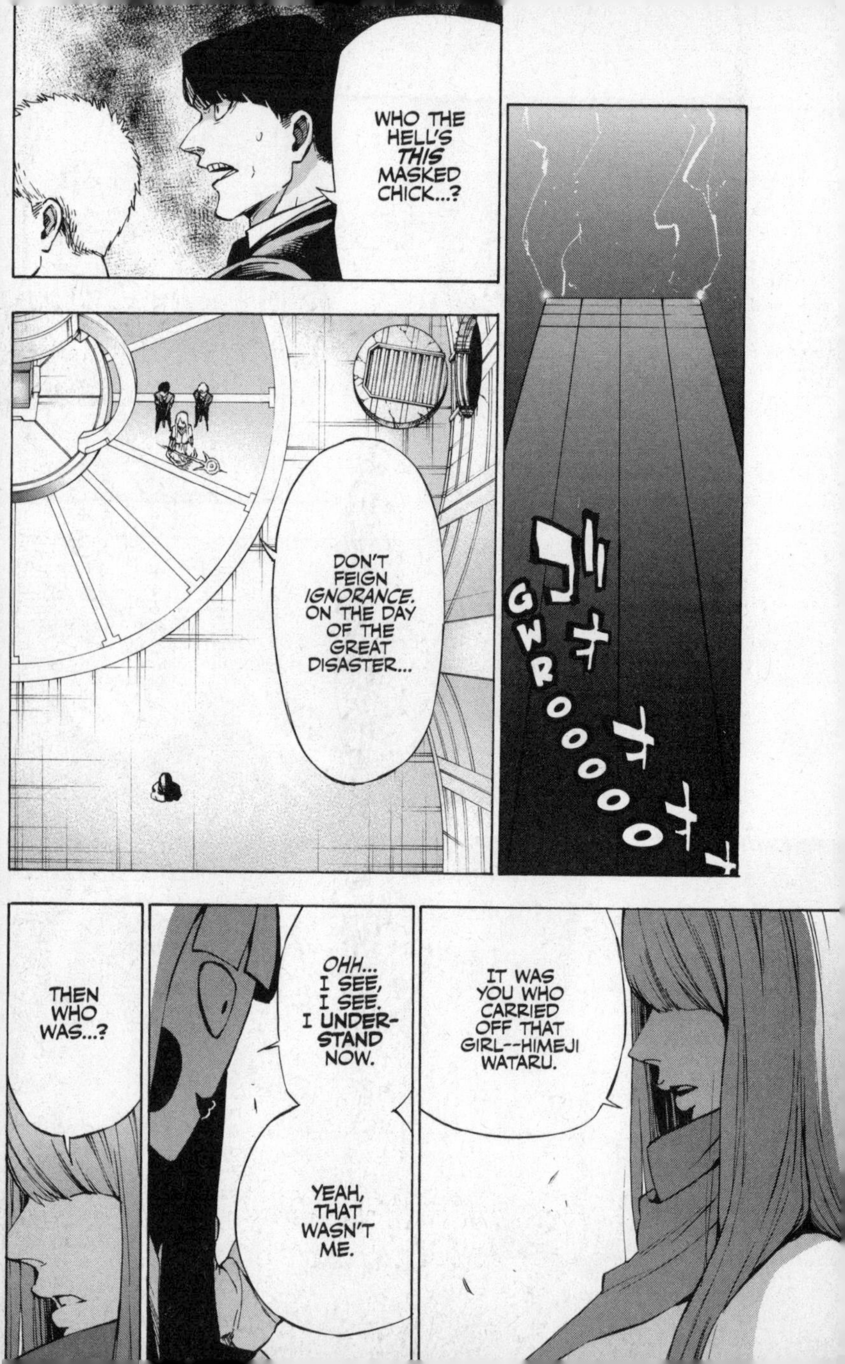
GWROOOOOO
WHO THE HELL'S *THIS* MASKED CHICK...?
DON'T FEIGN *IGNORANCE.* ON THE DAY OF THE GREAT DISASTER...
IT WAS YOU WHO CARRIED OFF THAT GIRL--HIMEJI WATARU.
OHH... I SEE, I SEE. I UNDERSTAND NOW.
YEAH, THAT WASN'T ME.
THEN WHO WAS...?

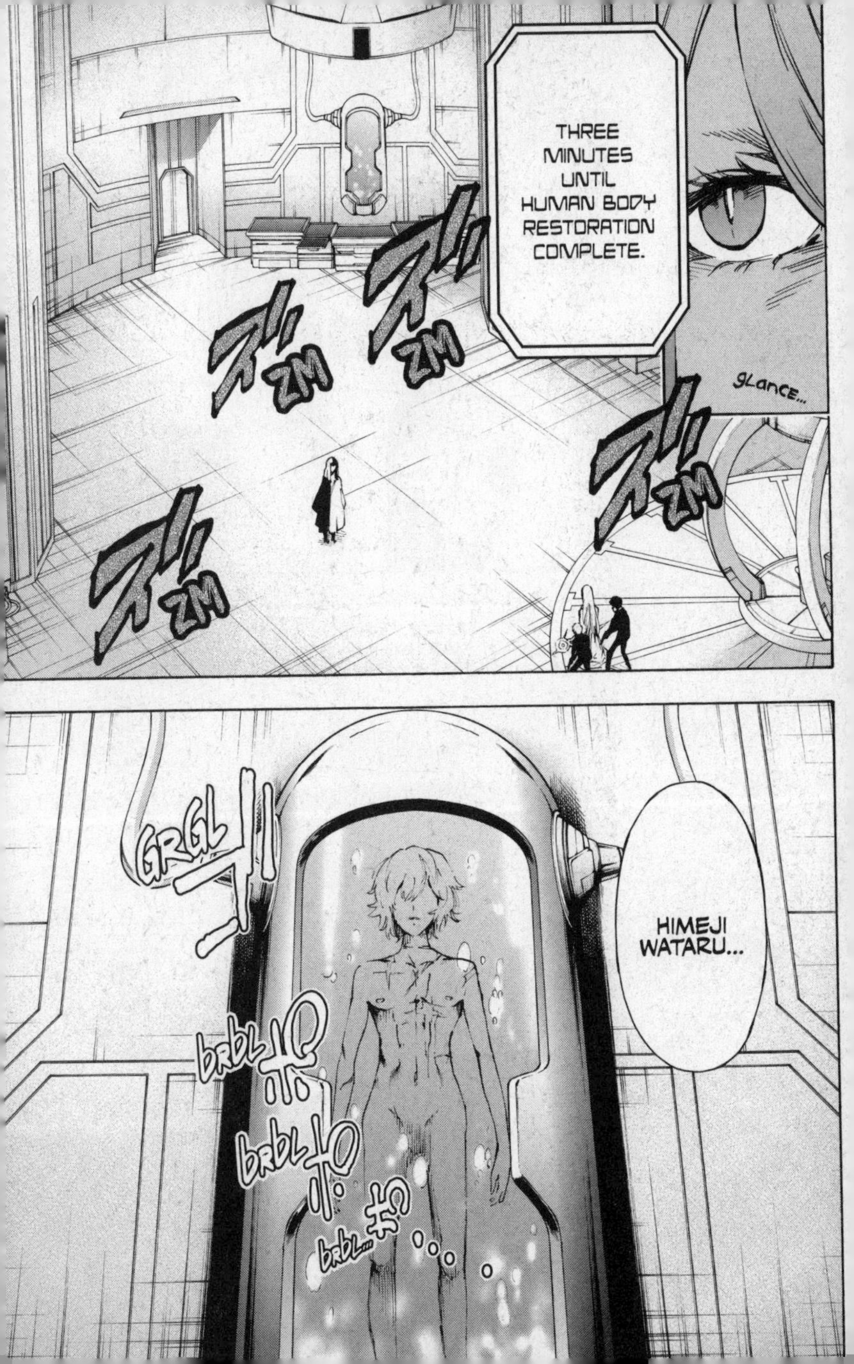
THREE MINUTES UNTIL HUMAN BODY RESTORATION COMPLETE.
GLANCE...
ZM
ZM
ZM
ZM
ZM
HIMEJI WATARU...
GRGL
brbl
brbl
brbl...

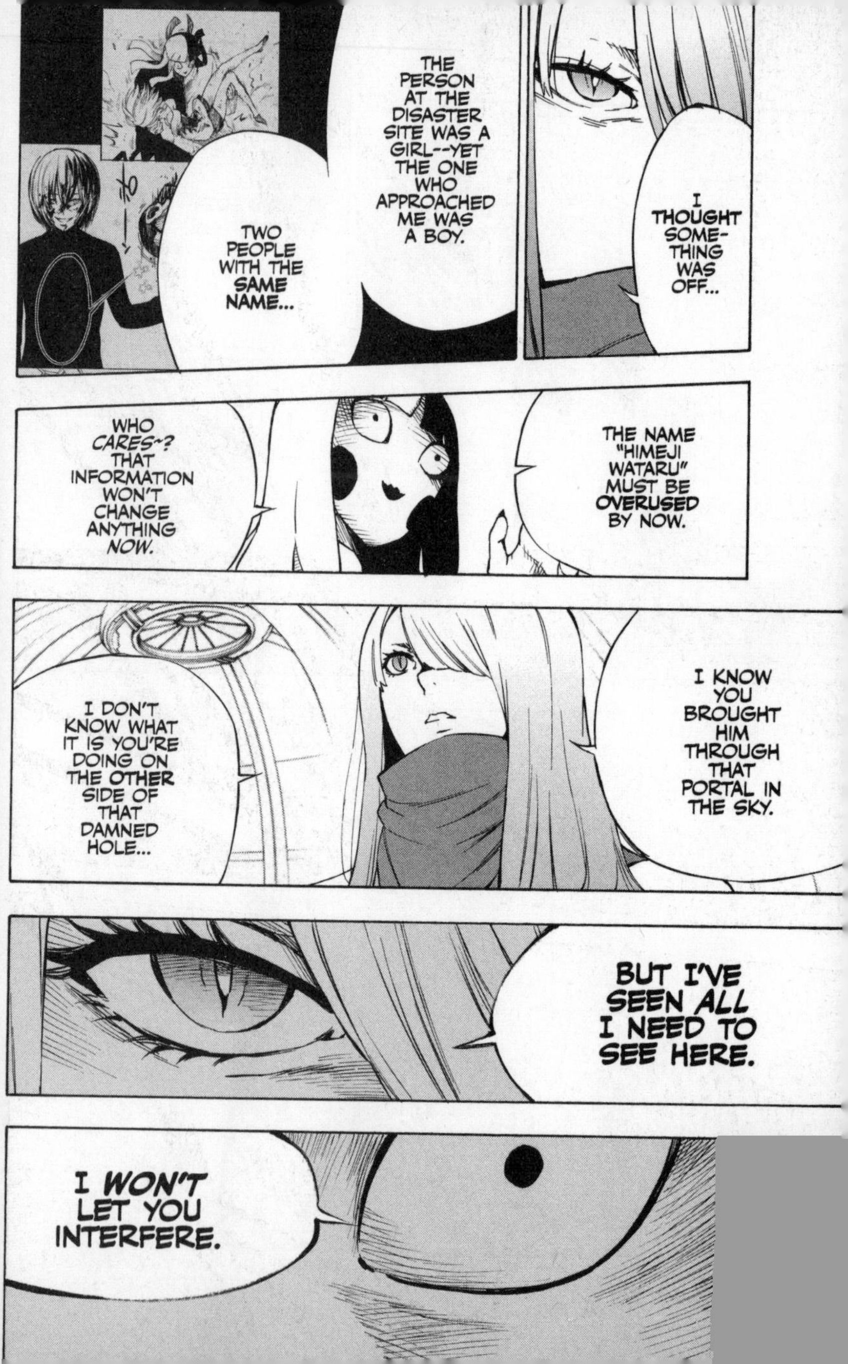
I THOUGHT SOMETHING WAS OFF...
THE PERSON AT THE DISASTER SITE WAS A GIRL--YET THE ONE WHO APPROACHED ME WAS A BOY.
TWO PEOPLE WITH THE SAME NAME...
THE NAME "HIMEJI WATARU" MUST BE OVERUSED BY NOW.
WHO *CARES~?* THAT INFORMATION WON'T CHANGE ANYTHING *NOW.*
I KNOW YOU BROUGHT HIM THROUGH THAT PORTAL IN THE SKY.
I DON'T KNOW WHAT IT IS YOU'RE DOING ON THE OTHER SIDE OF THAT DAMNED HOLE...
BUT I'VE SEEN *ALL* I NEED TO SEE HERE.
I *WON'T* LET YOU INTERFERE.

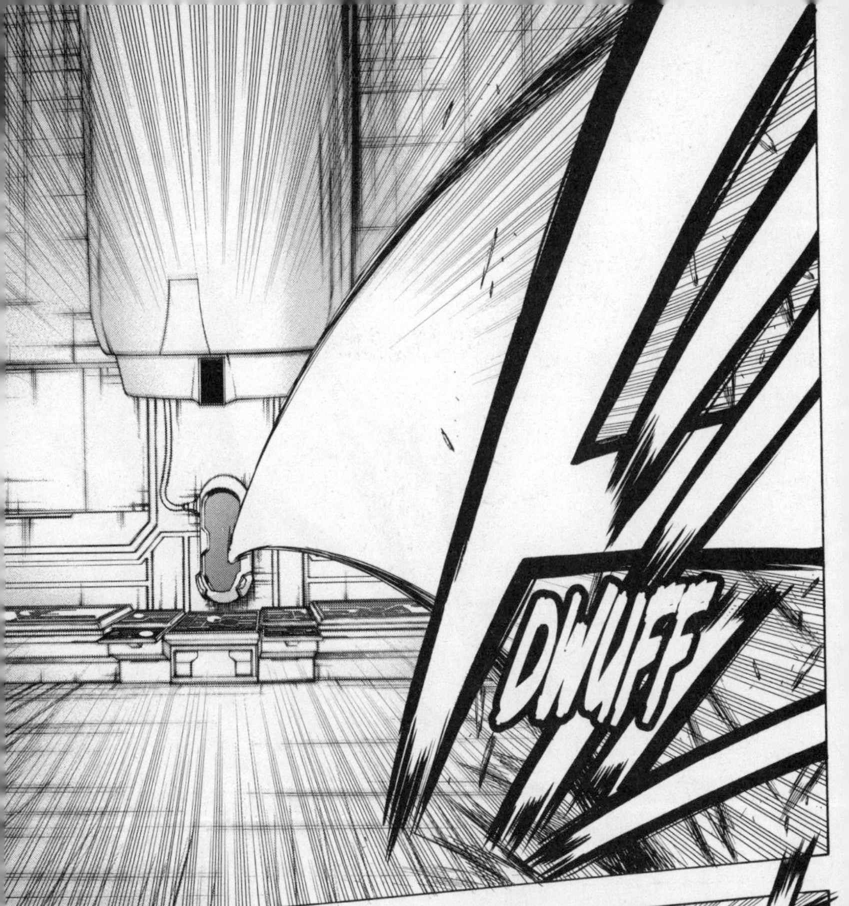
DWUFF
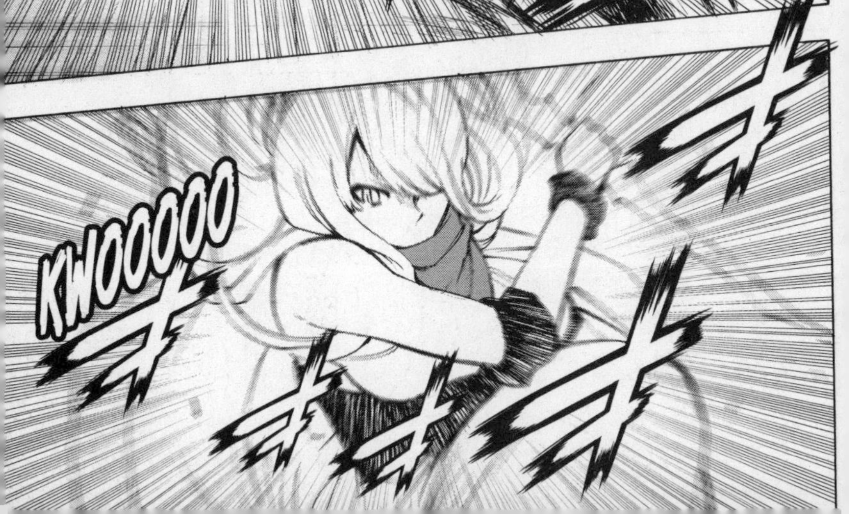
KWOOOOO

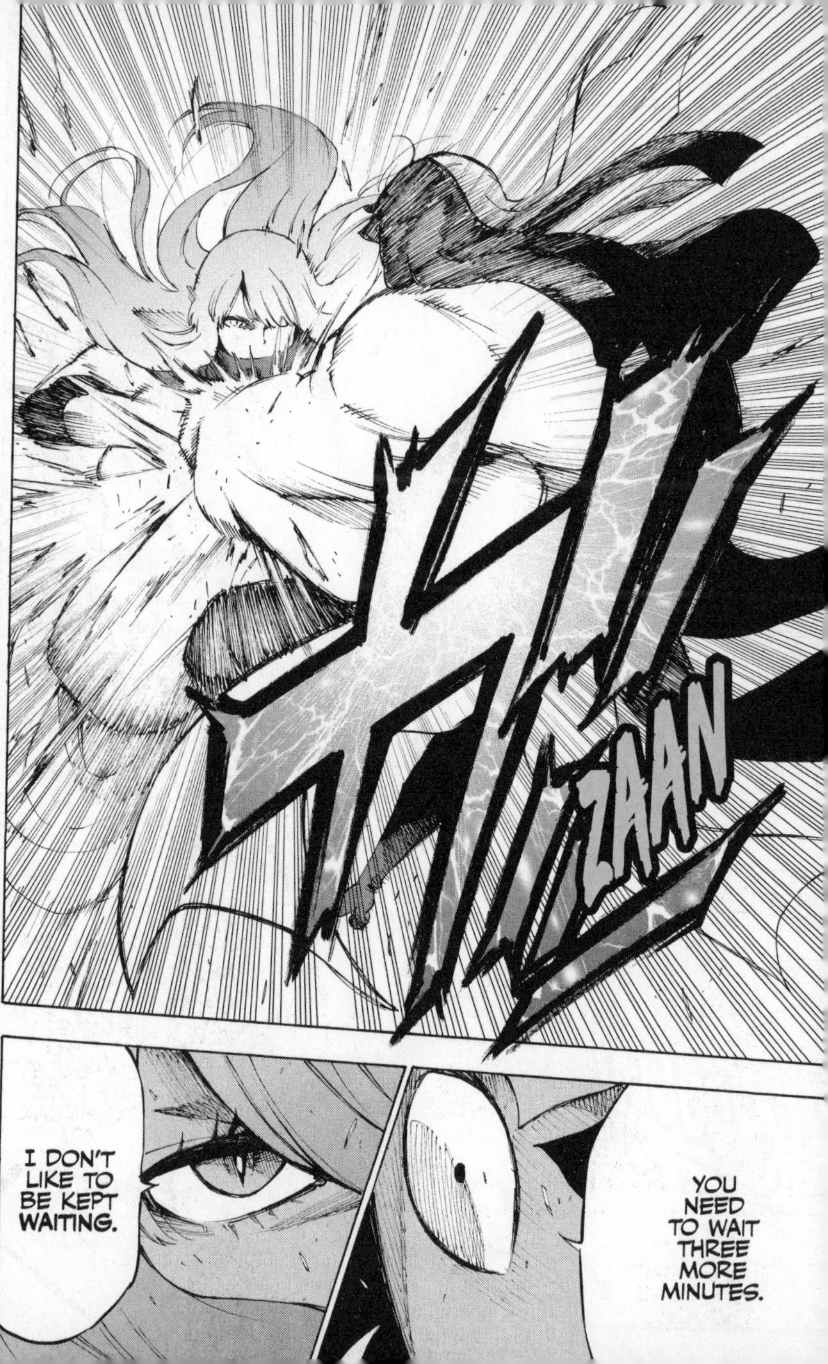
ZAAN
YOU NEED TO WAIT THREE MORE MINUTES.
I DON'T LIKE TO BE KEPT WAITING.

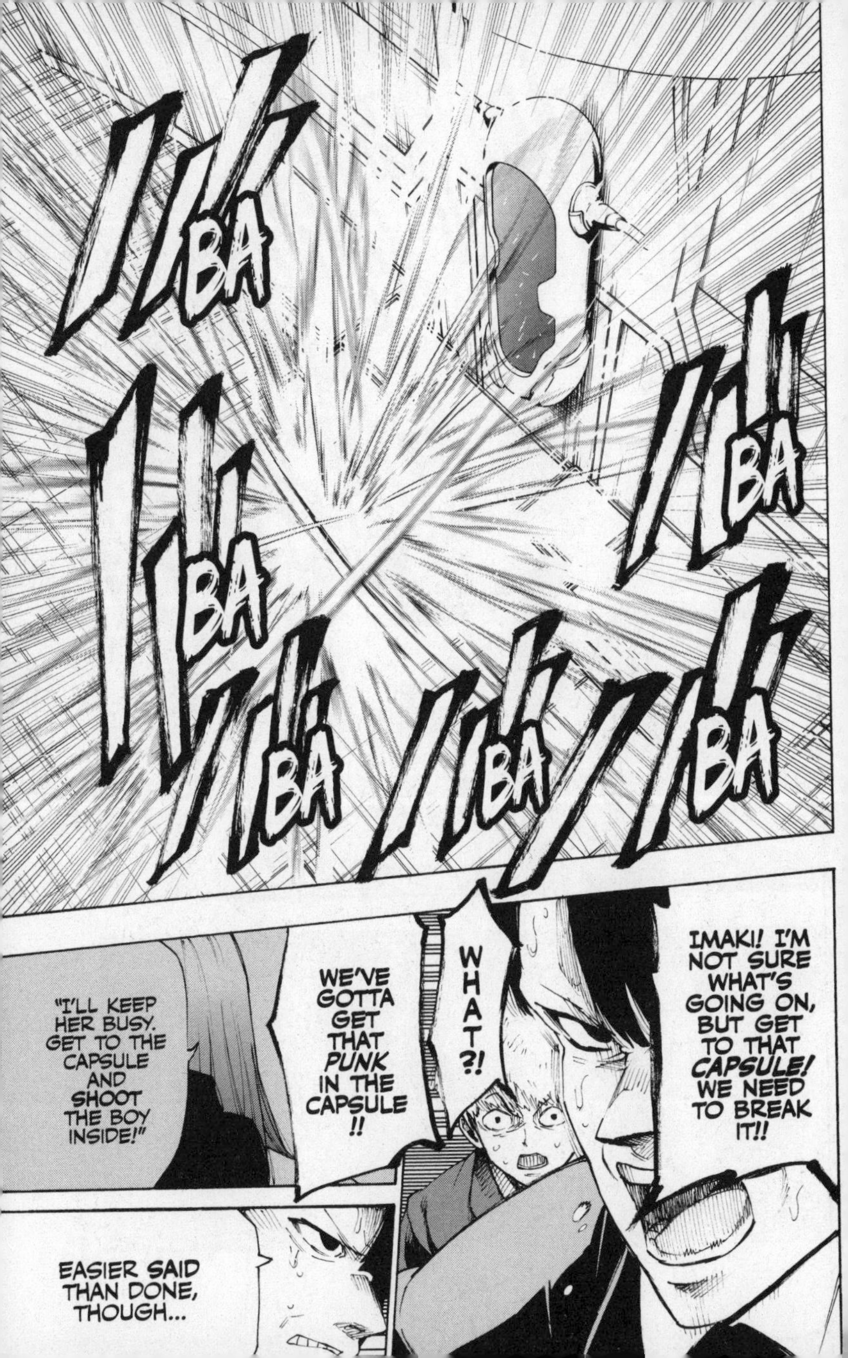
BA
BA
BA
BA
BA
BA
IMAKI! I'M NOT SURE WHAT'S GOING ON, BUT GET TO THAT *CAPSULE!* WE NEED TO BREAK IT!!
WHAT?!
WE'VE GOTTA GET THAT *PUNK* IN THE CAPSULE !!
"I'LL KEEP HER BUSY. GET TO THE CAPSULE AND SHOOT THE BOY INSIDE!"
EASIER SAID THAN DONE, THOUGH...

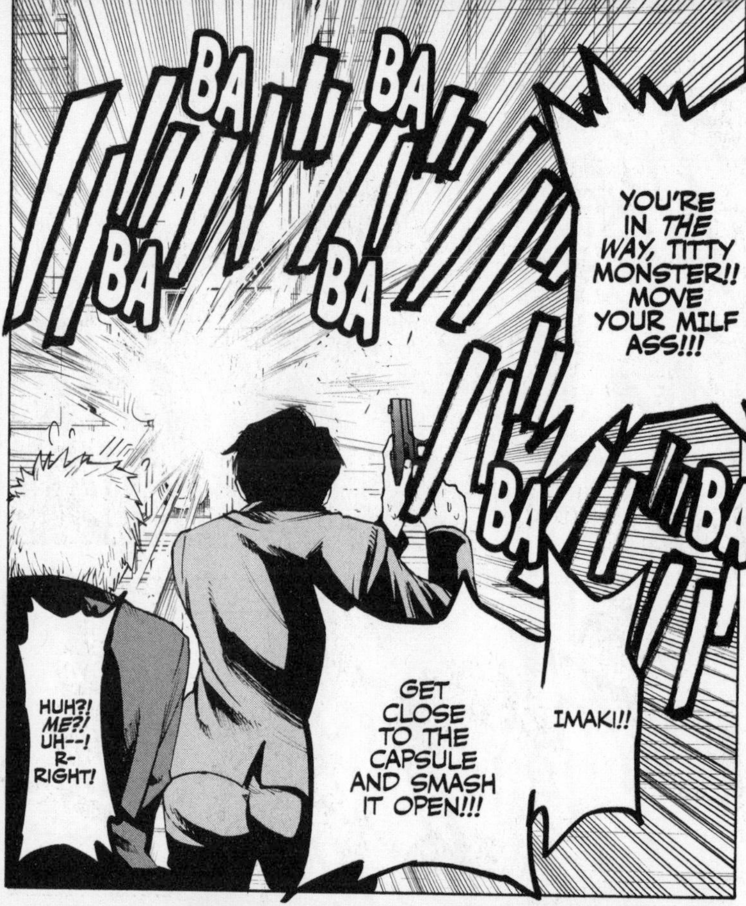
YOU'RE IN THE WAY, TITTY MONSTER!! MOVE YOUR MILF ASS!!!
BA BA
BA BA
BA BA
IMAKI!!
GET CLOSE TO THE CAPSULE AND SMASH IT OPEN!!!
HUH?! ME?! UH--! R-RIGHT!

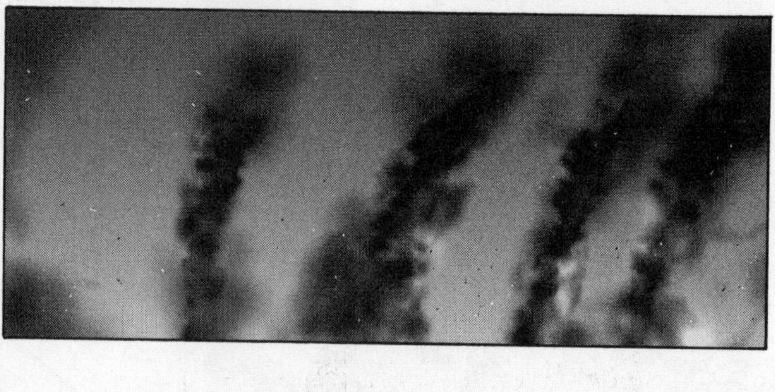

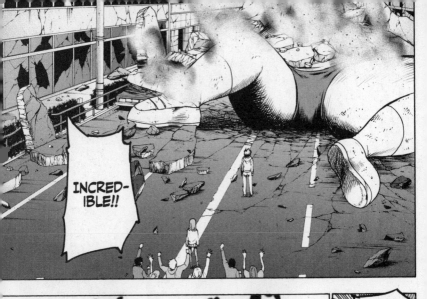

INCRED-IBLE!!

HE TOOK DOWN THAT THING IN ONE HIT!!!

SHIN-OBU! ABOVE YOU!!

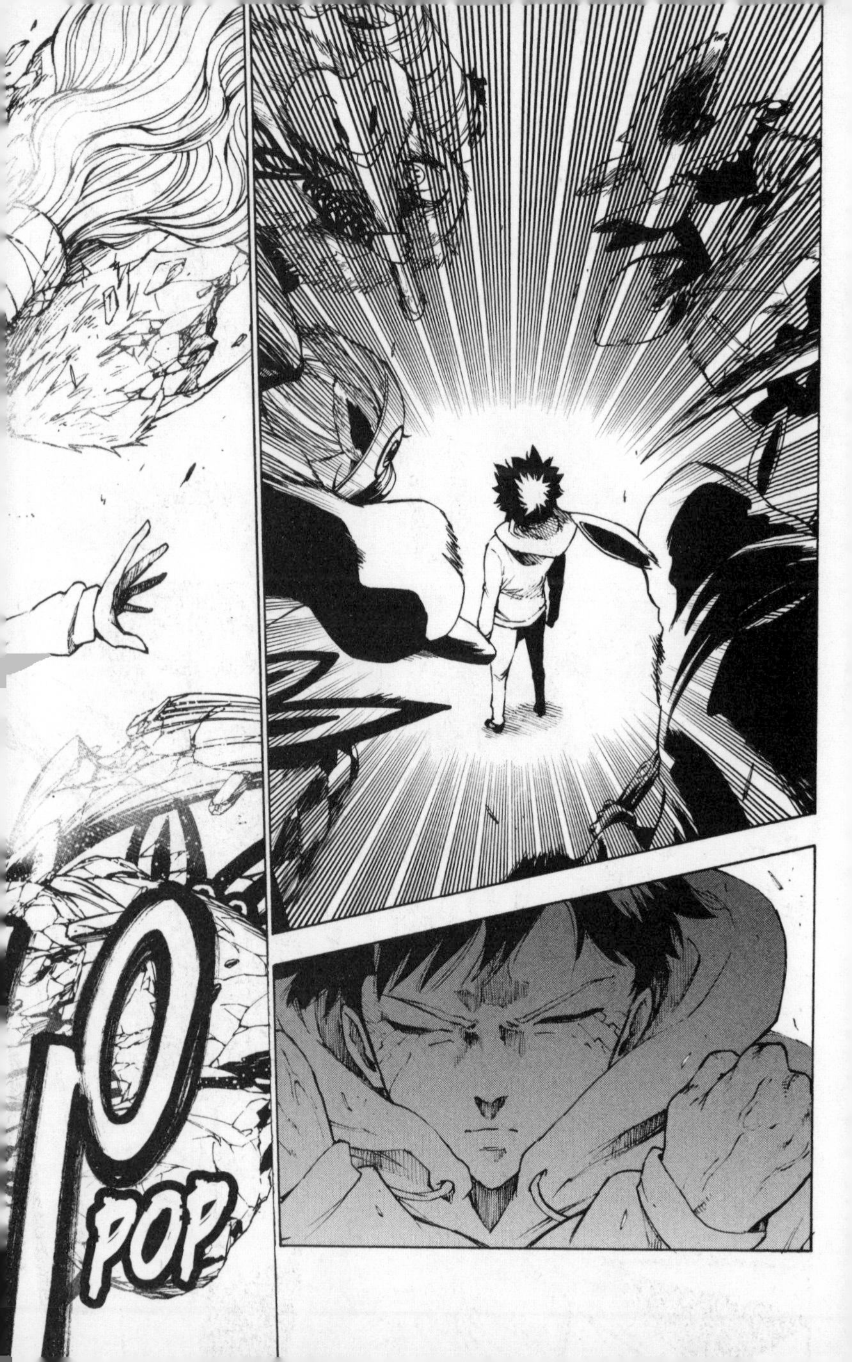
POP

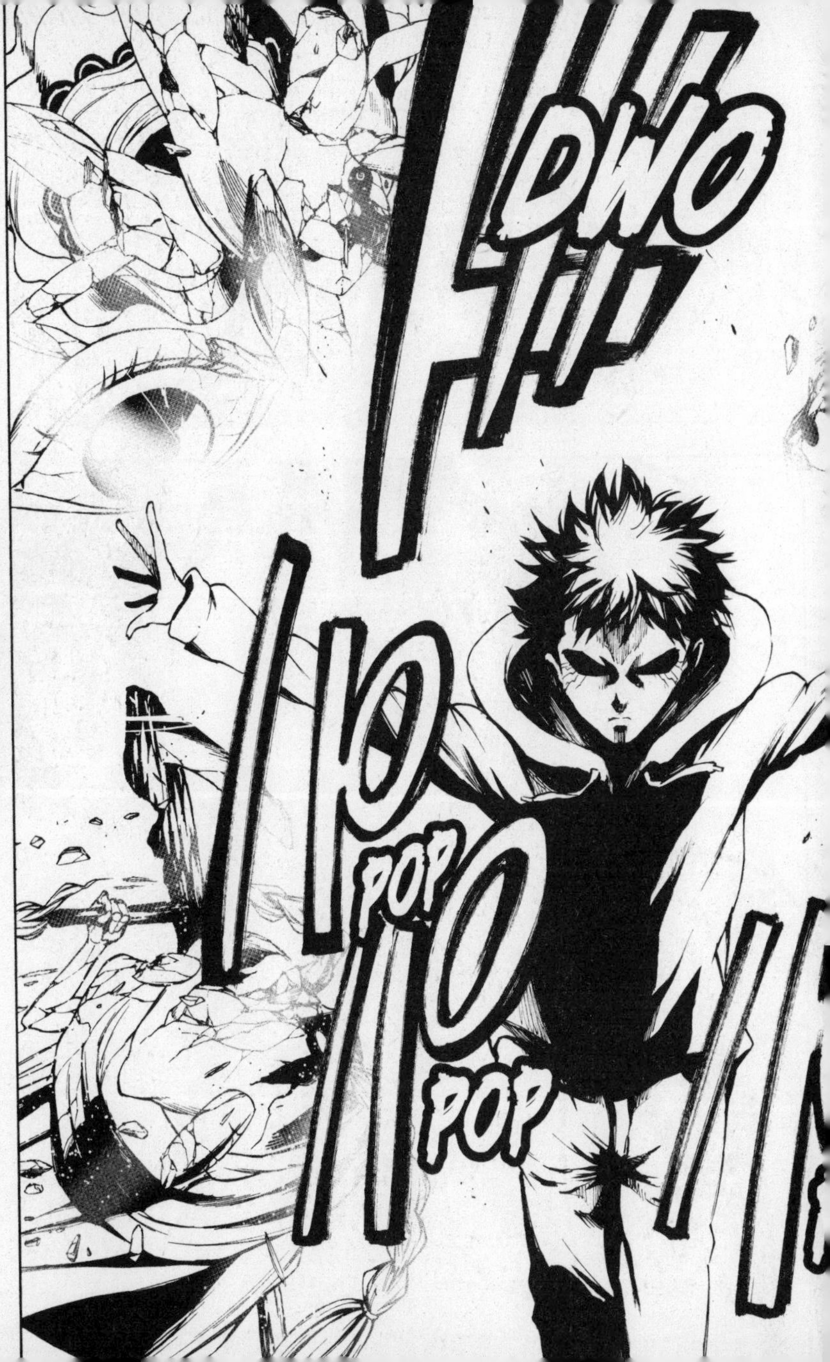
POP
POP

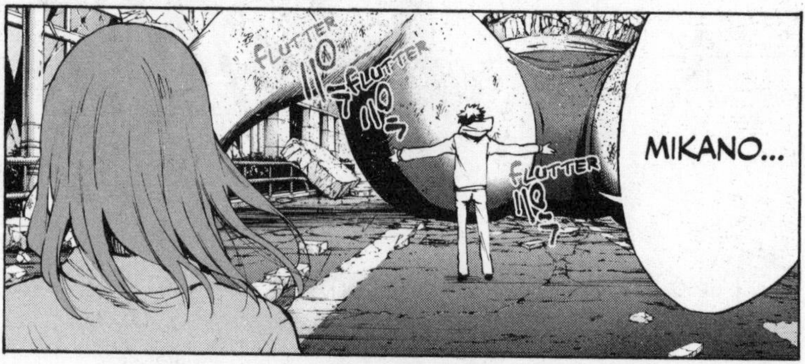
MIKANO...
FLUTTER
FLUTTER
FLUTTER

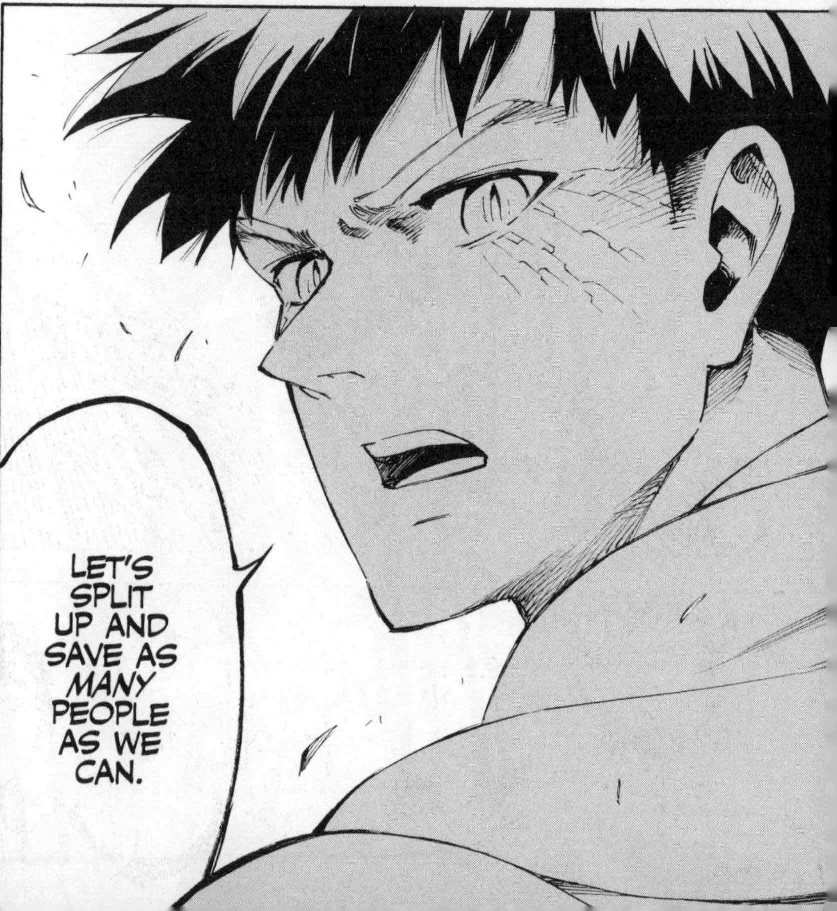
LET'S SPLIT UP AND SAVE AS *MANY* PEOPLE AS WE CAN.

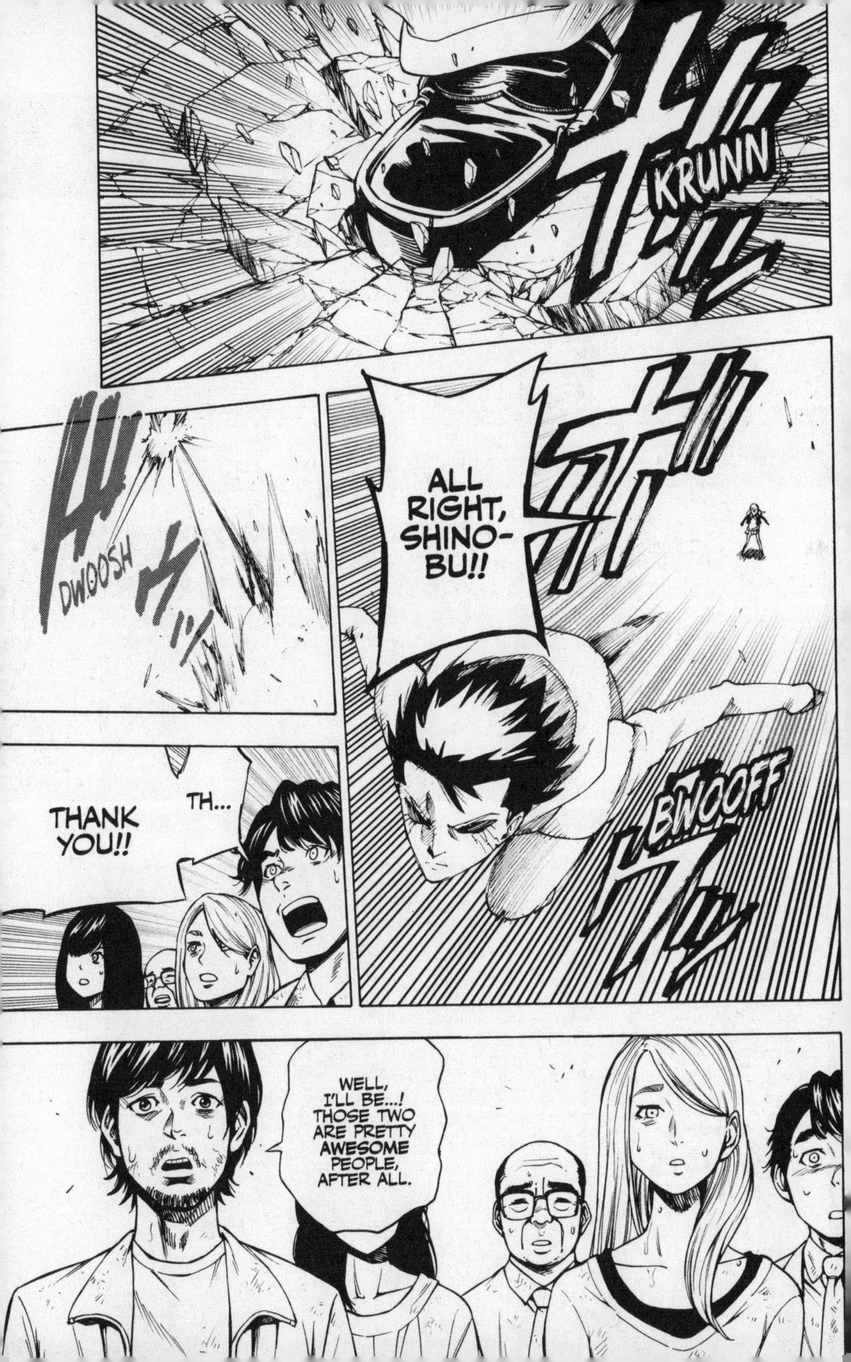
KRUNN
ALL RIGHT, SHINOBU!!
BWOOFF
DWOOSH
TH...
THANK YOU!!
WELL, I'LL BE...! THOSE TWO ARE PRETTY AWESOME PEOPLE, AFTER ALL.

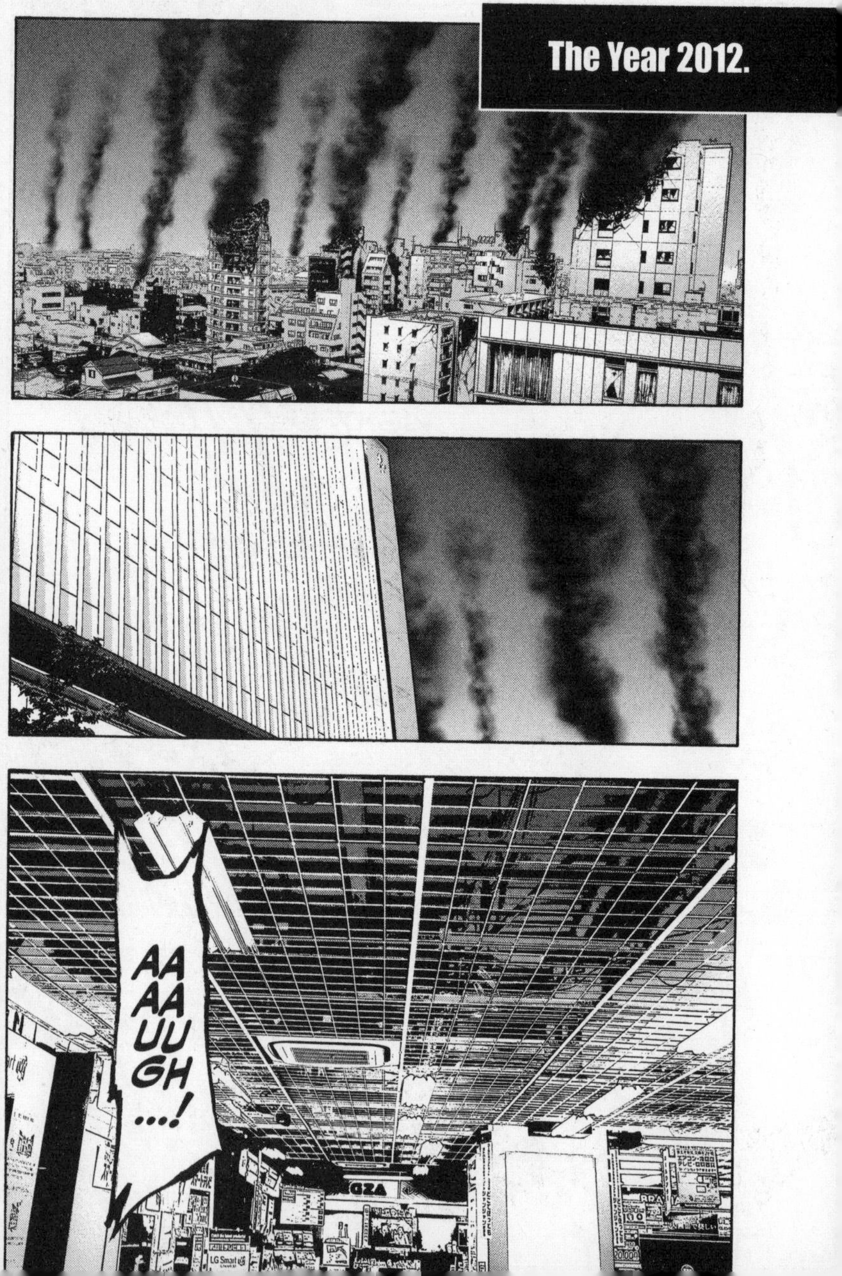
The Year 2012.
AAAAUUGH...!

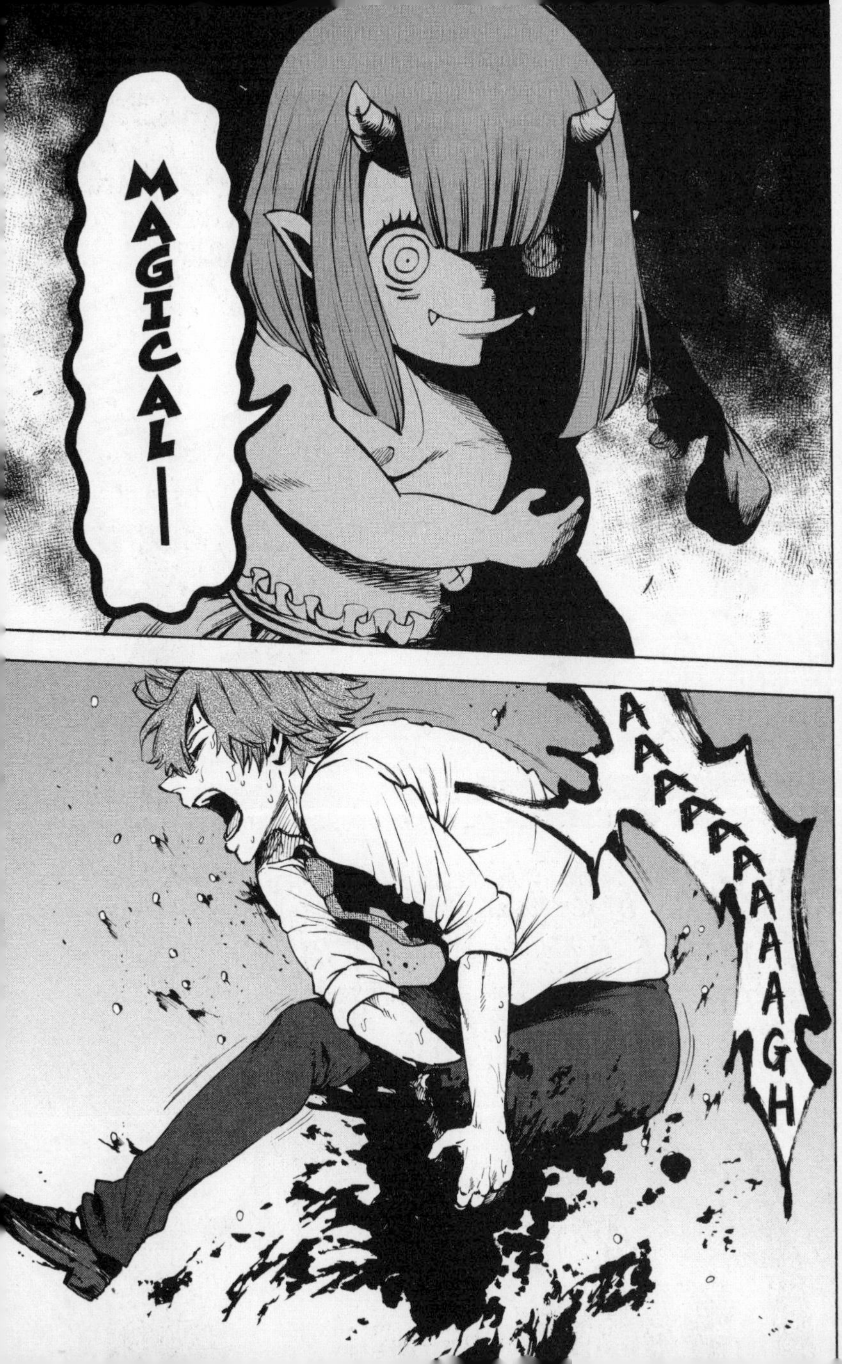
MAGICAL!
AAAAAAAAAAAGH

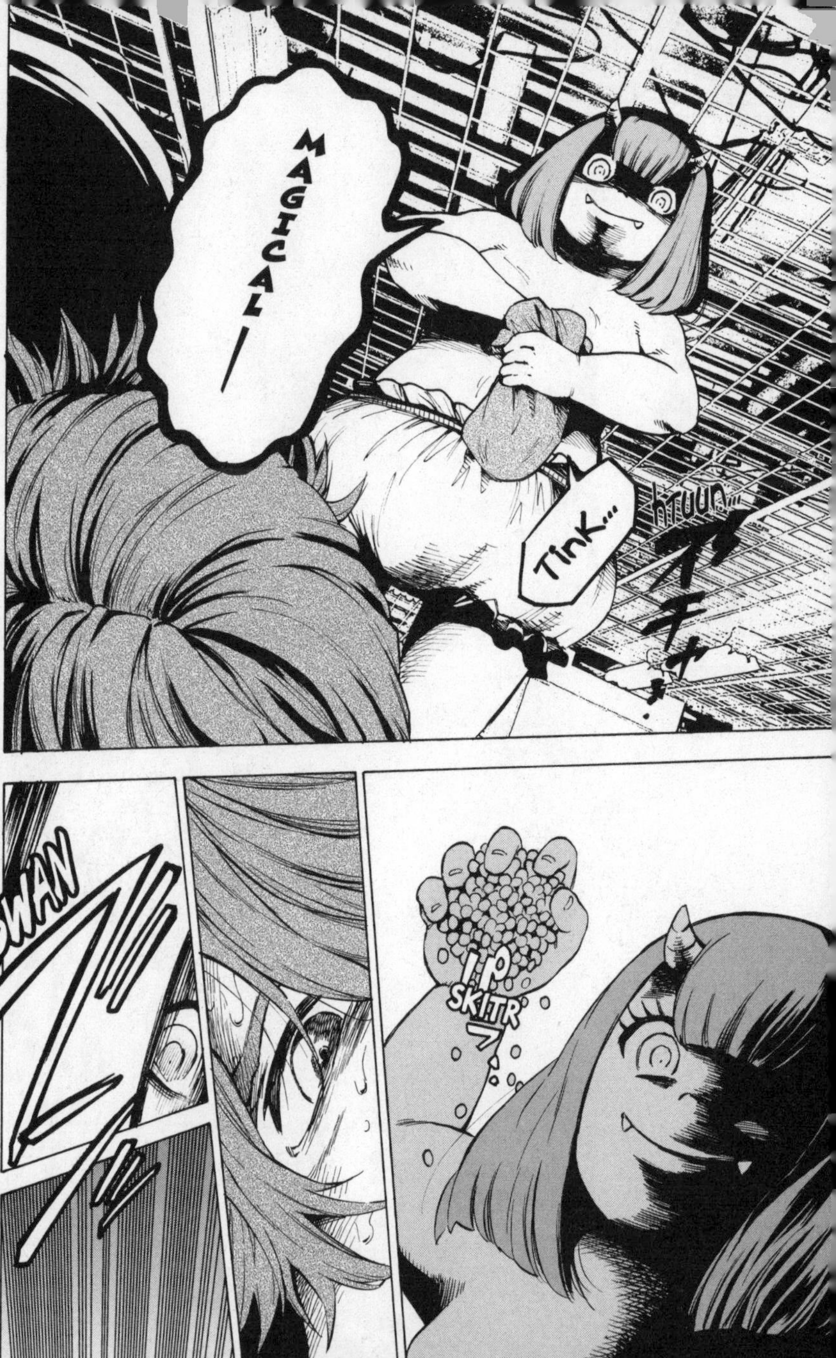
MAGICAL—
Tink...
htuun...
SKITR
BWAN

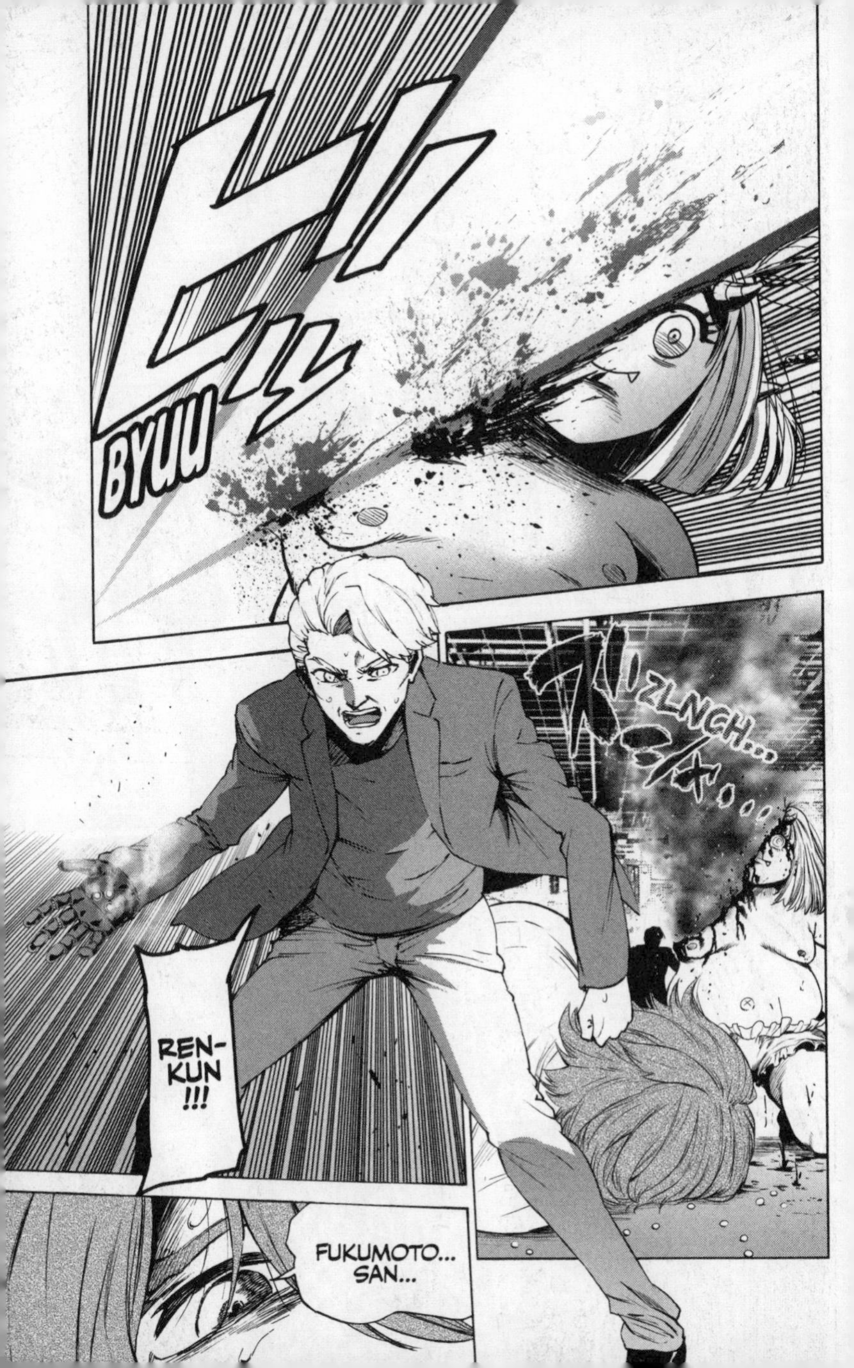
BYUU
ZLNCH...
REN-KUN!!!
FUKUMOTO... SAN...

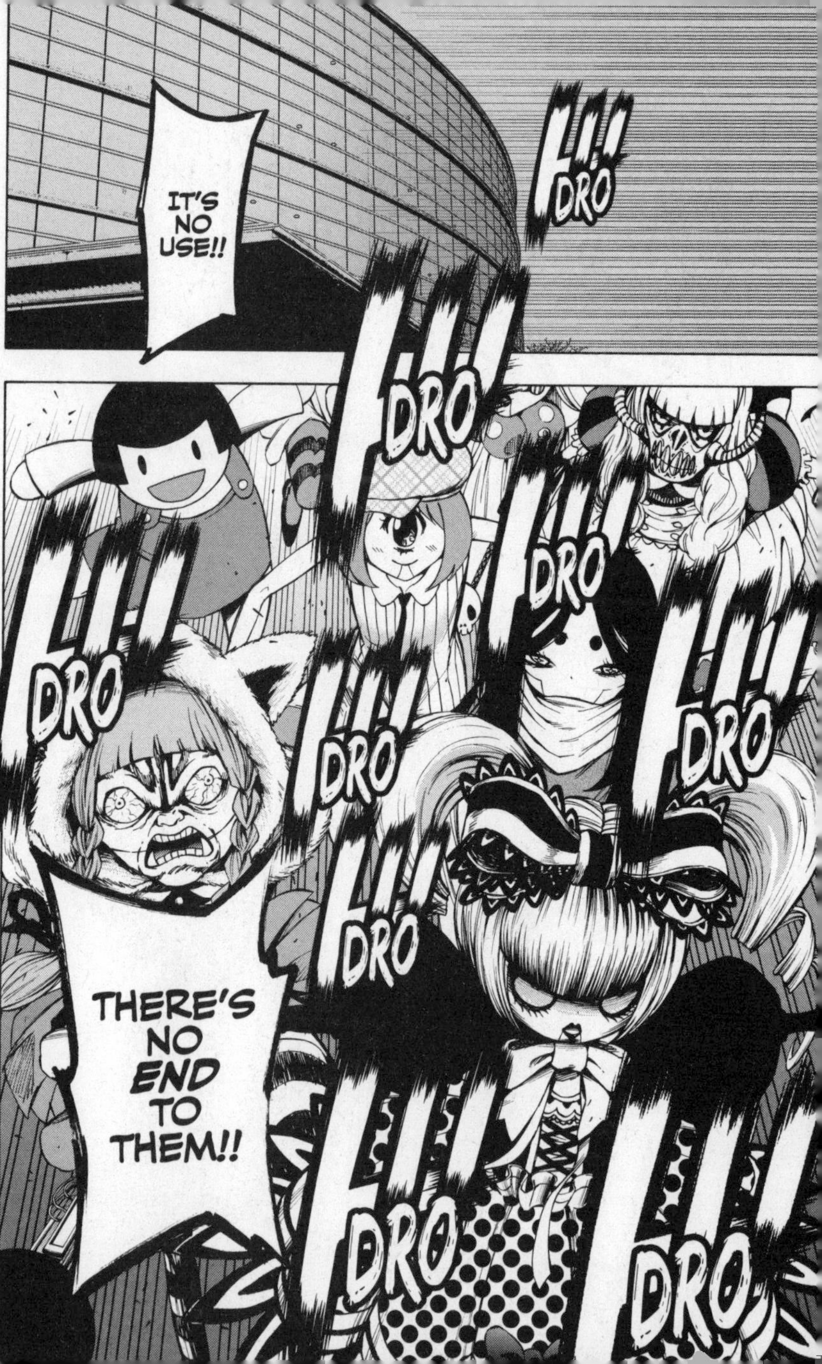
DRO
IT'S NO USE!!
DRO
DRO
DRO
DRO
DRO
THERE'S NO END TO THEM!!
DRO
DRO
DRO

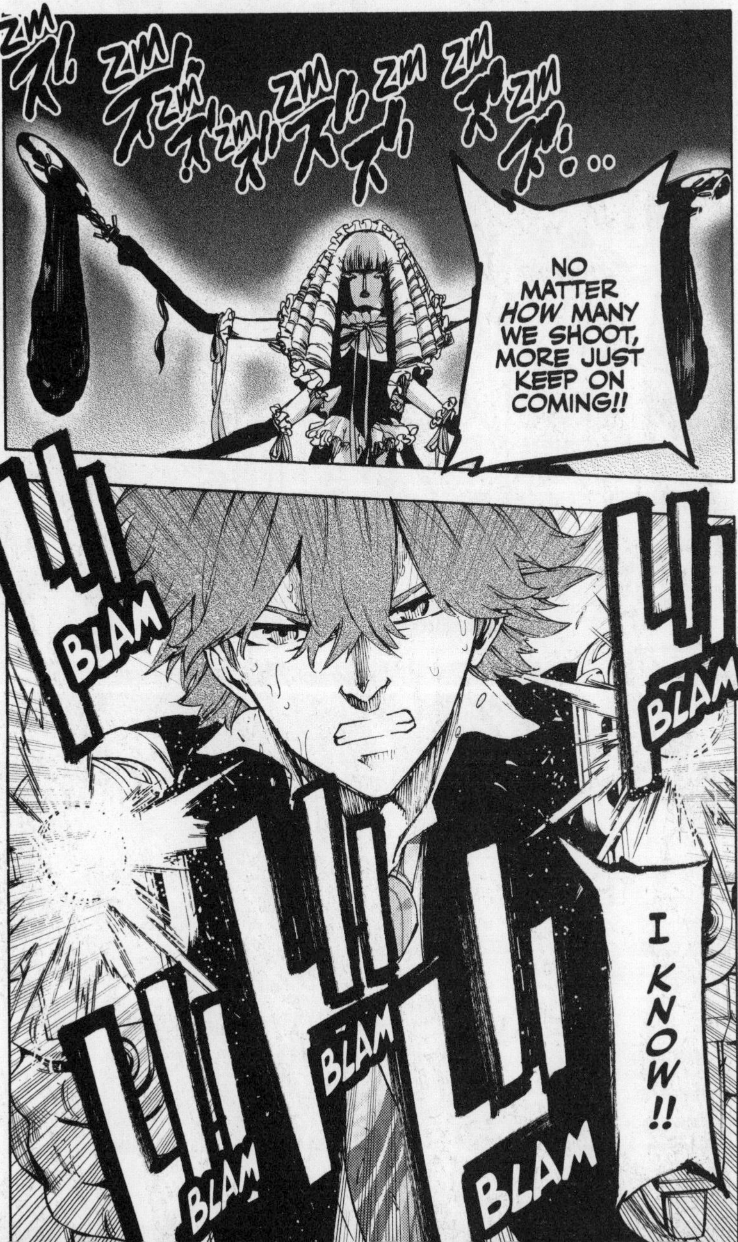
ZWM ZWM ZWM ZWM ZWM ZWM ZWM ZWM...
NO MATTER HOW MANY WE SHOOT, MORE JUST KEEP ON COMING!!
BLAM
BLAM
I KNOW!!
BLAM
BLAM
BLAM

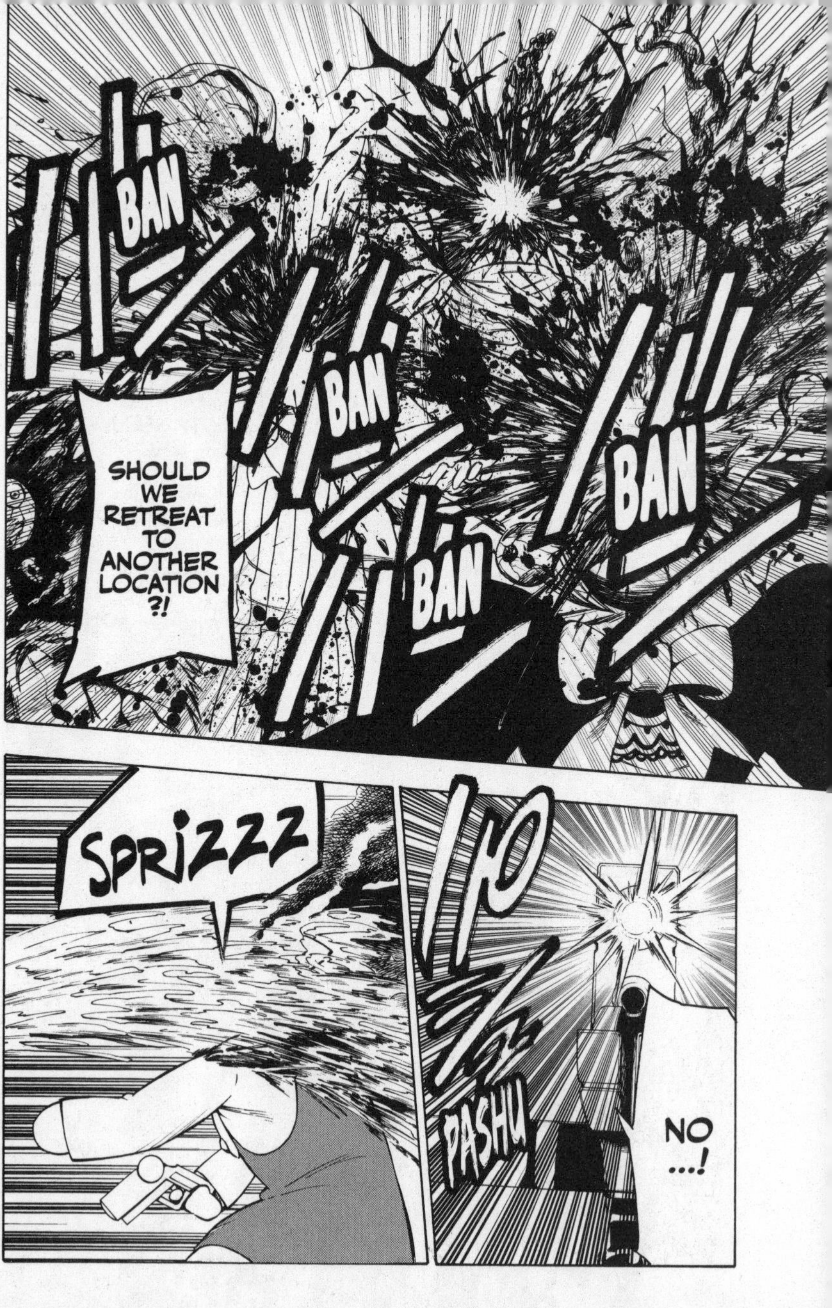
BAN
BAN
BAN
BAN
SHOULD WE RETREAT TO ANOTHER LOCATION?!
BAN
PASHU
NO...!
SPRIZZZ

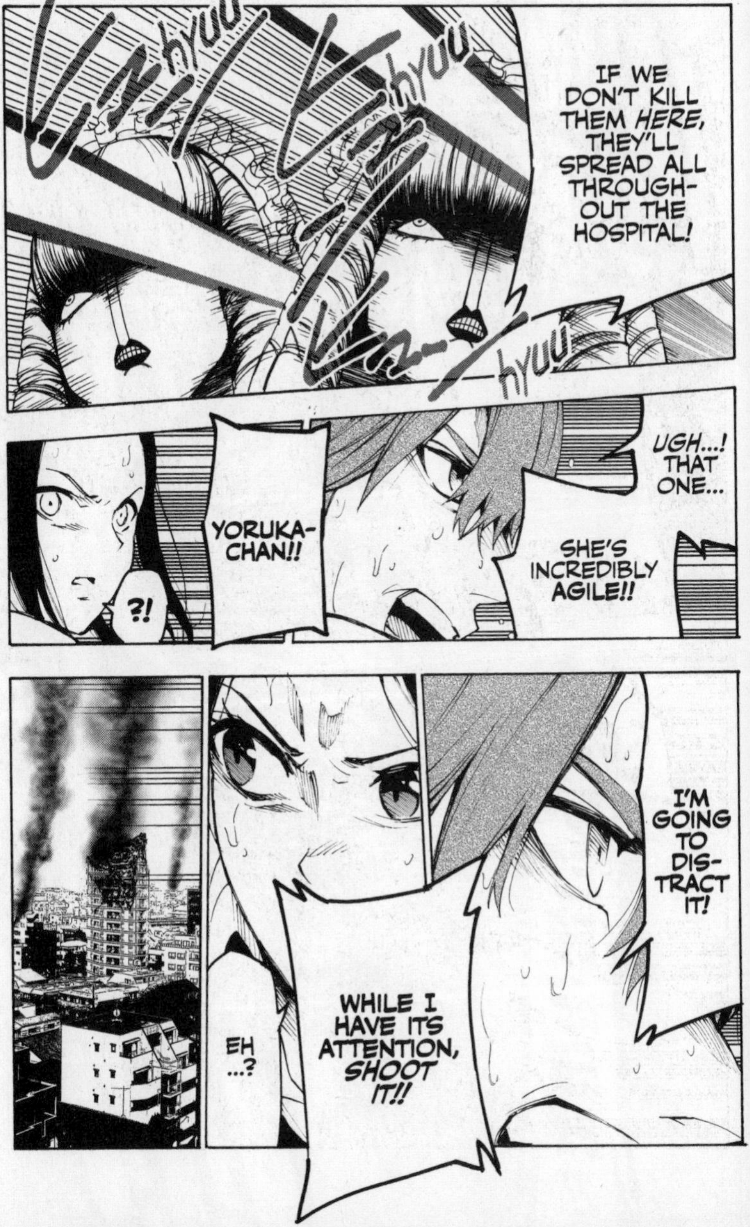
IF WE DON'T KILL THEM *HERE*, THEY'LL SPREAD ALL THROUGH-OUT THE HOSPITAL!
hyuu
hyuu
hyuu
UGH...! THAT ONE...
SHE'S INCREDIBLY AGILE!!
YORUKA-CHAN!!
?!
I'M GOING TO DIS-TRACT IT!
WHILE I HAVE ITS ATTENTION, *SHOOT IT!!*
EH ...?

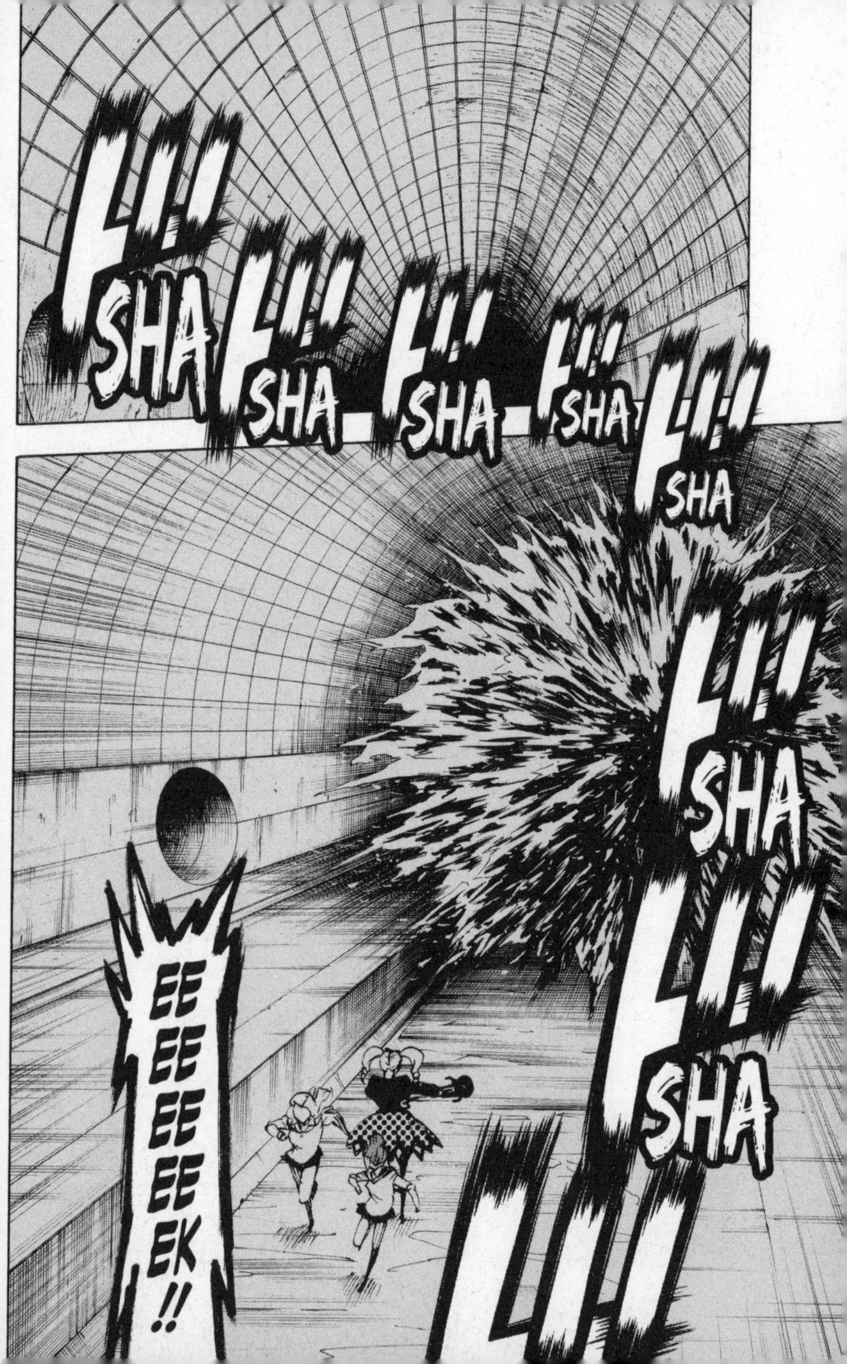
SHA
SHA
SHA
SHA
SHA
SHA
SHA
EEEEEEEEEEEK!!

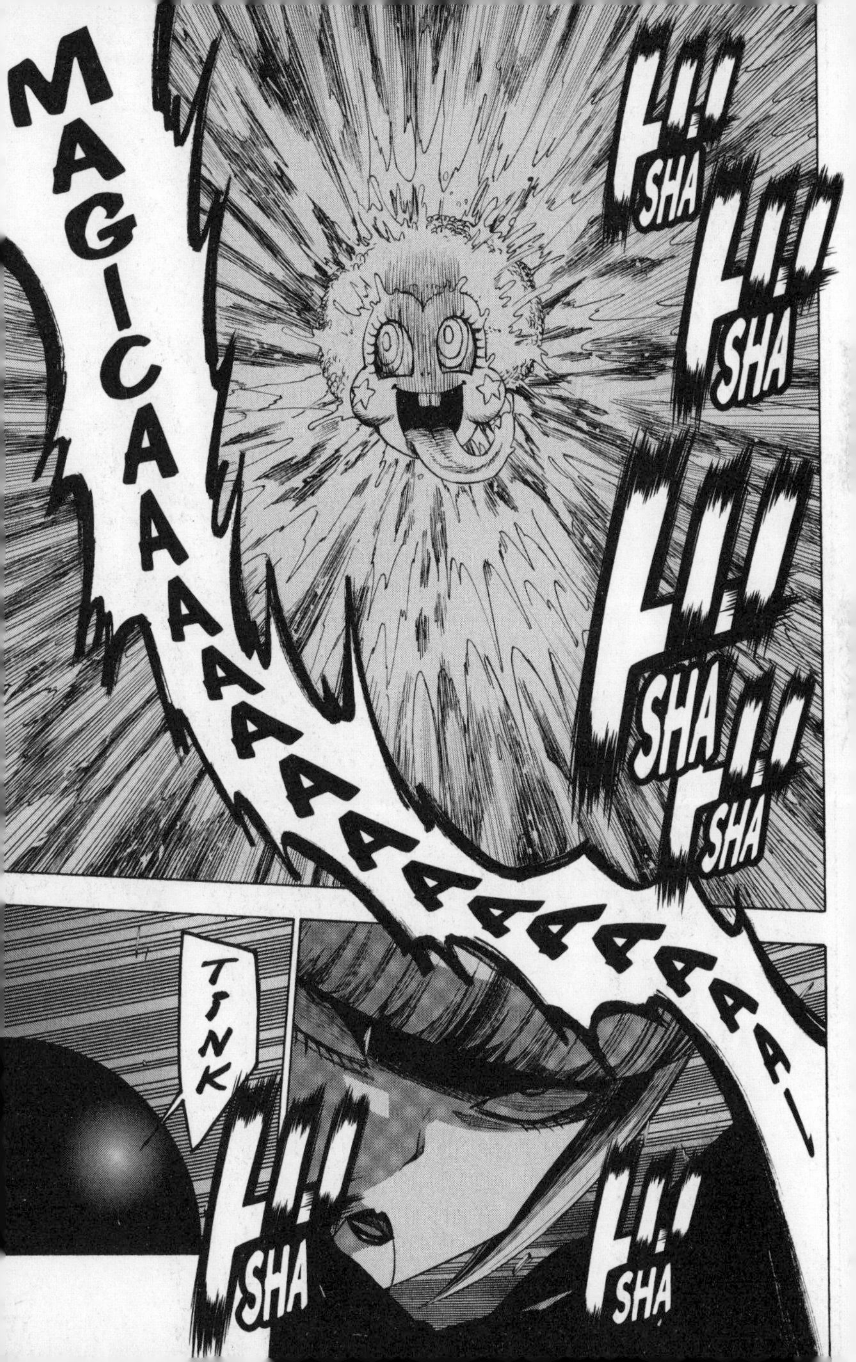
SHA
SHA
SHA
SHA
MAGICAAAAAAAAAAAAAAAA—
TINK
SHA
SHA

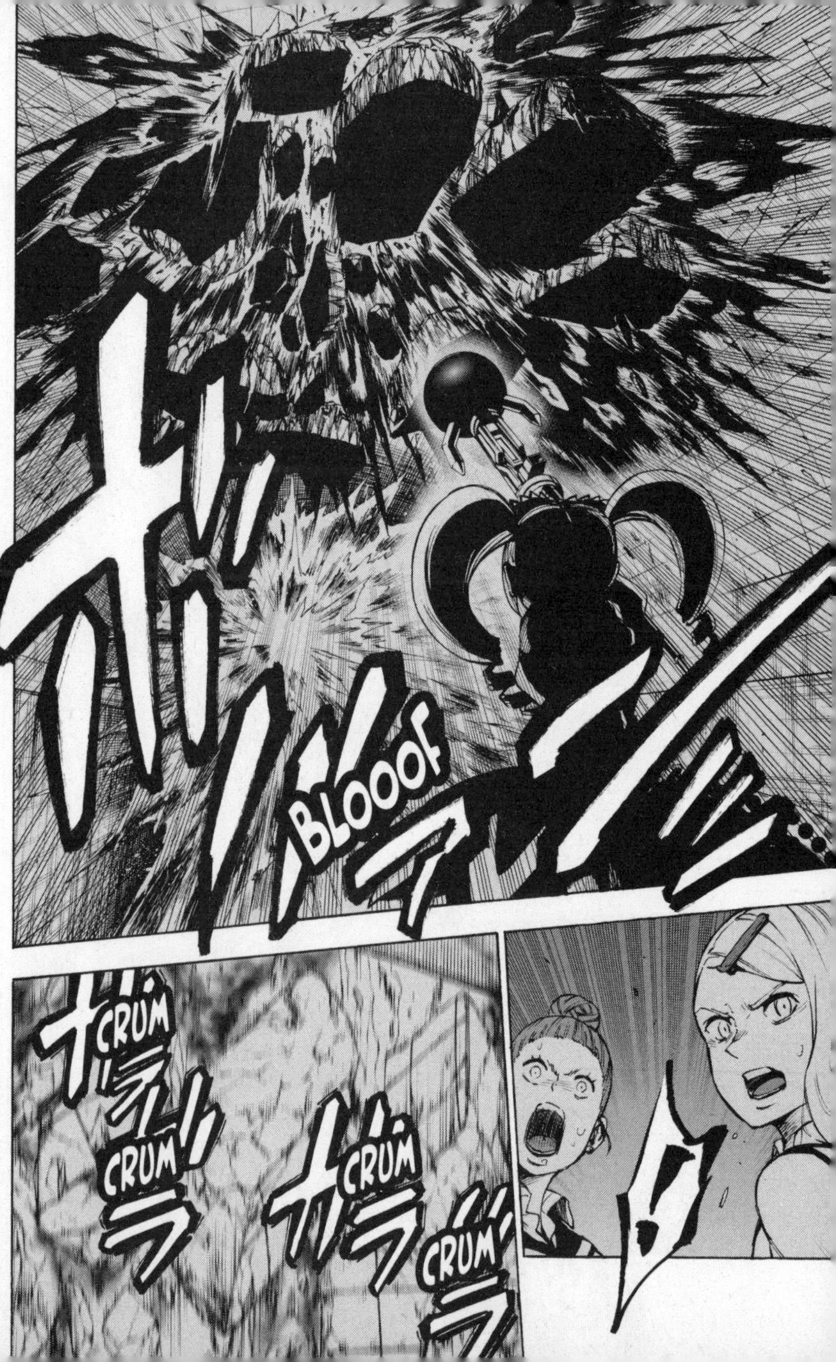
BLOOOF
!
CRUM
CRUM
CRUM
CRUM

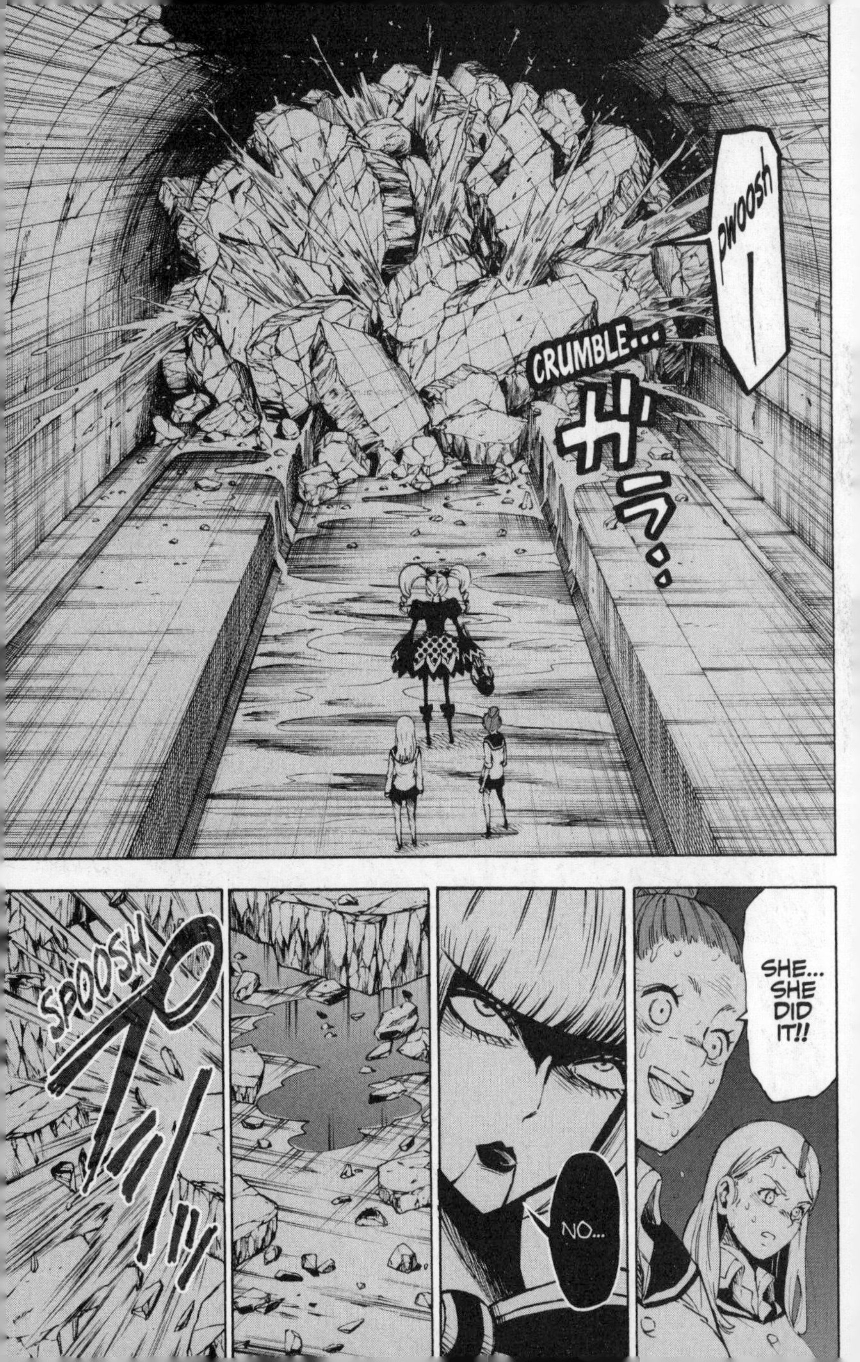
pwoosh
CRUMBLE...
ガラ。。
SHE... SHE DID IT!!
NO...
SPOOSH

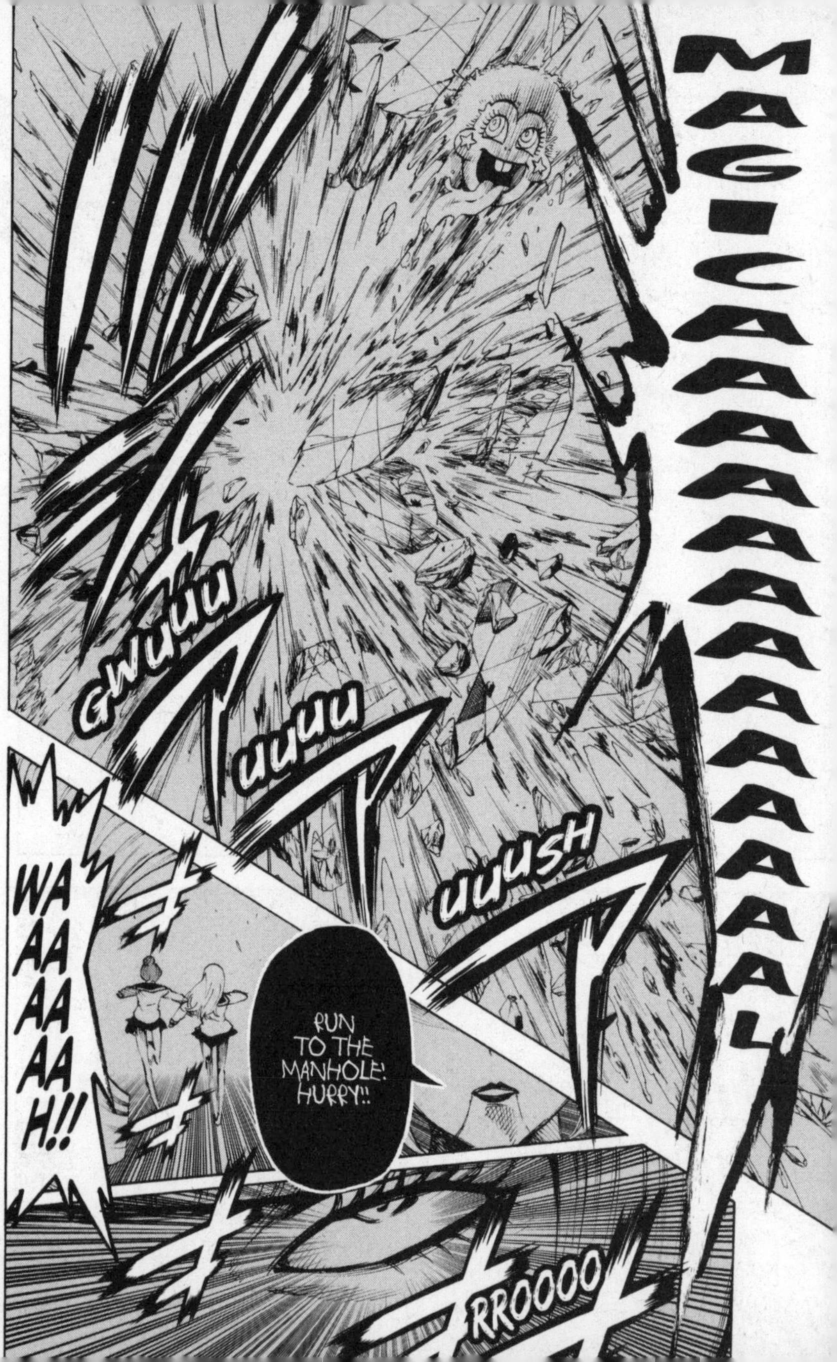
MAGICAAAAAAAAAAAAAAL
GWUUUU
UUUUU
UUUSH
RUN TO THE MANHOLE! HURRY!!
WAAAAAAAAAH!!
RROOOO

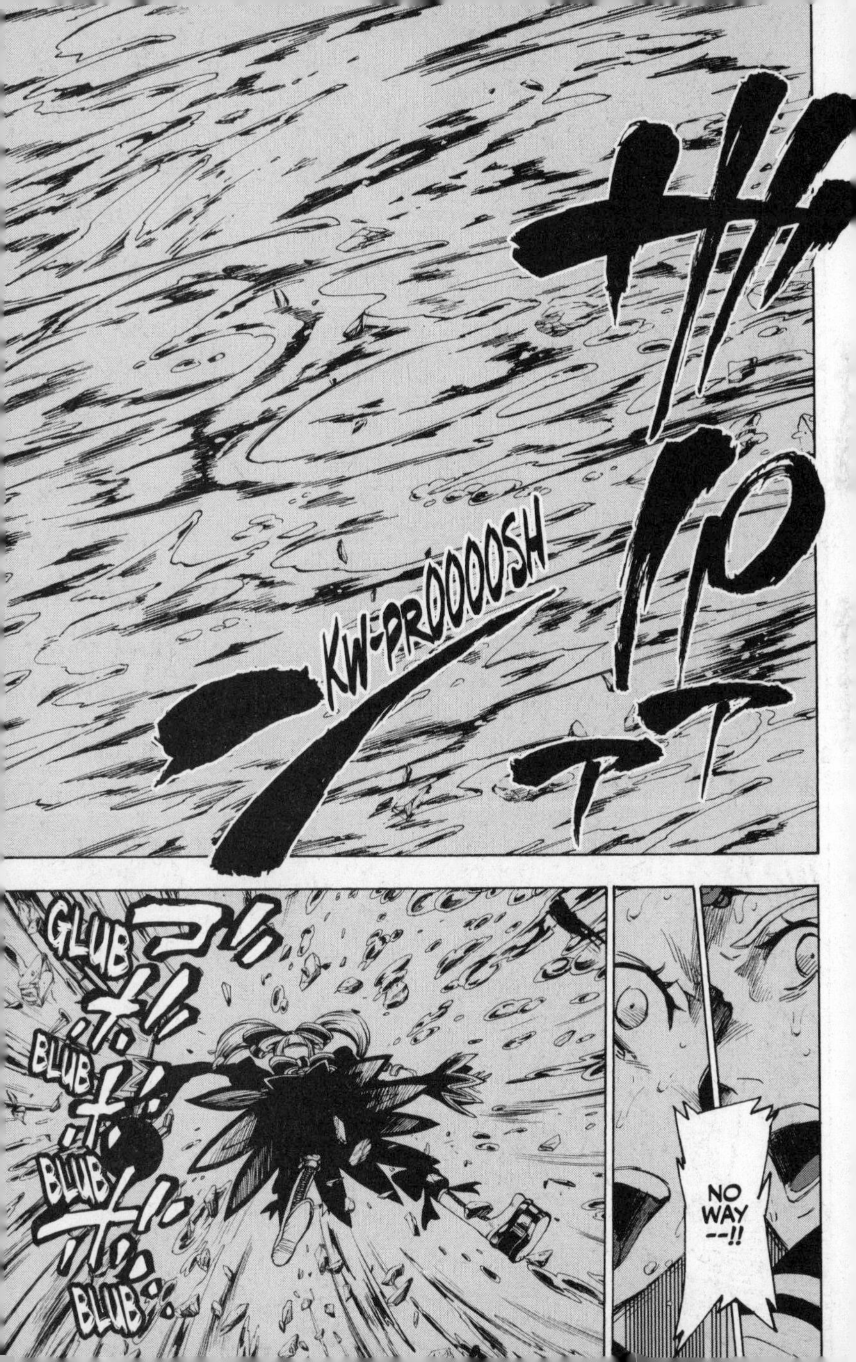
KW-PROOOSH
NO WAY --!!
GLUB
BLUB
BLUB
BLUB

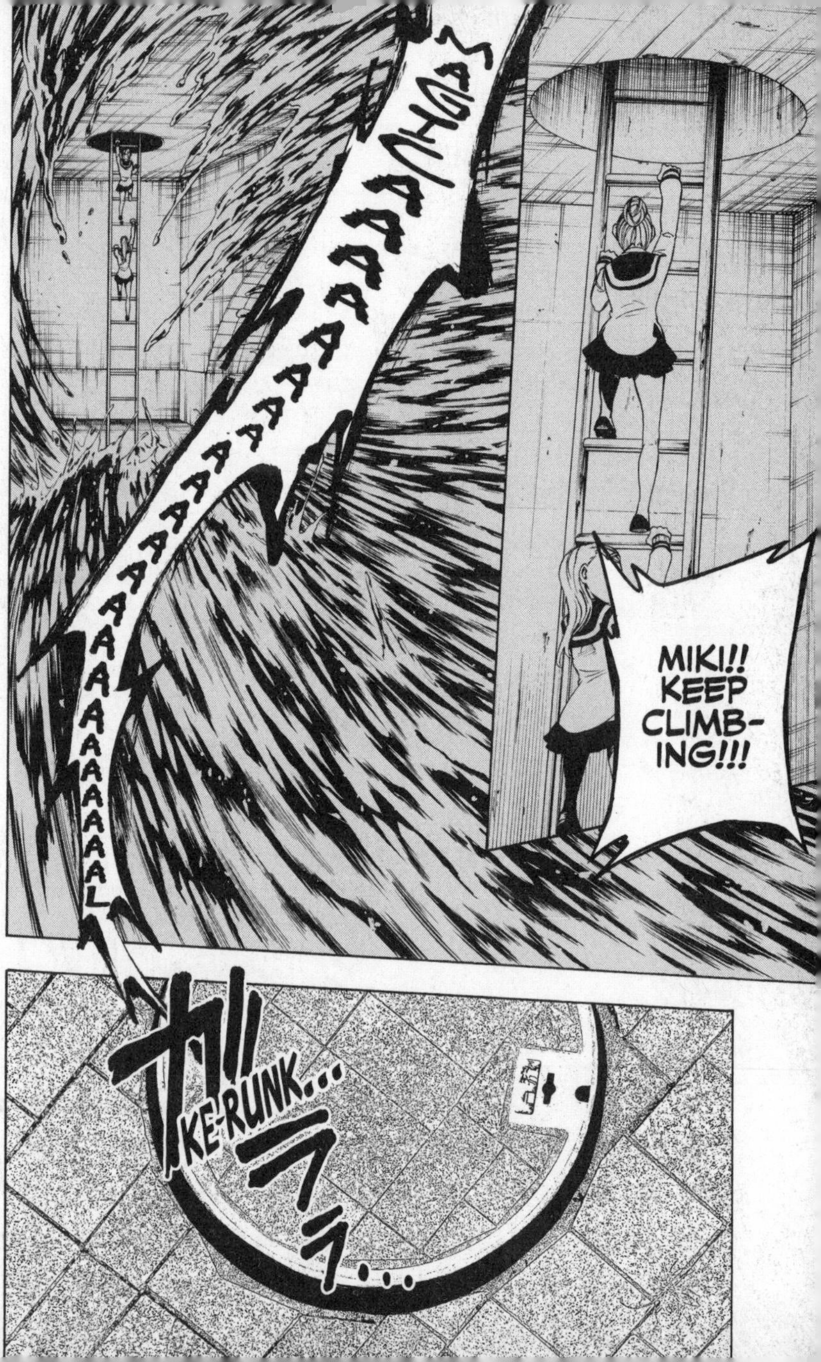
MAGICAAAAAAAAAAAAAAAAAAAAAAAAAAAAAL
MIKI!! KEEP CLIMB-ING!!!
KE-RUNK...

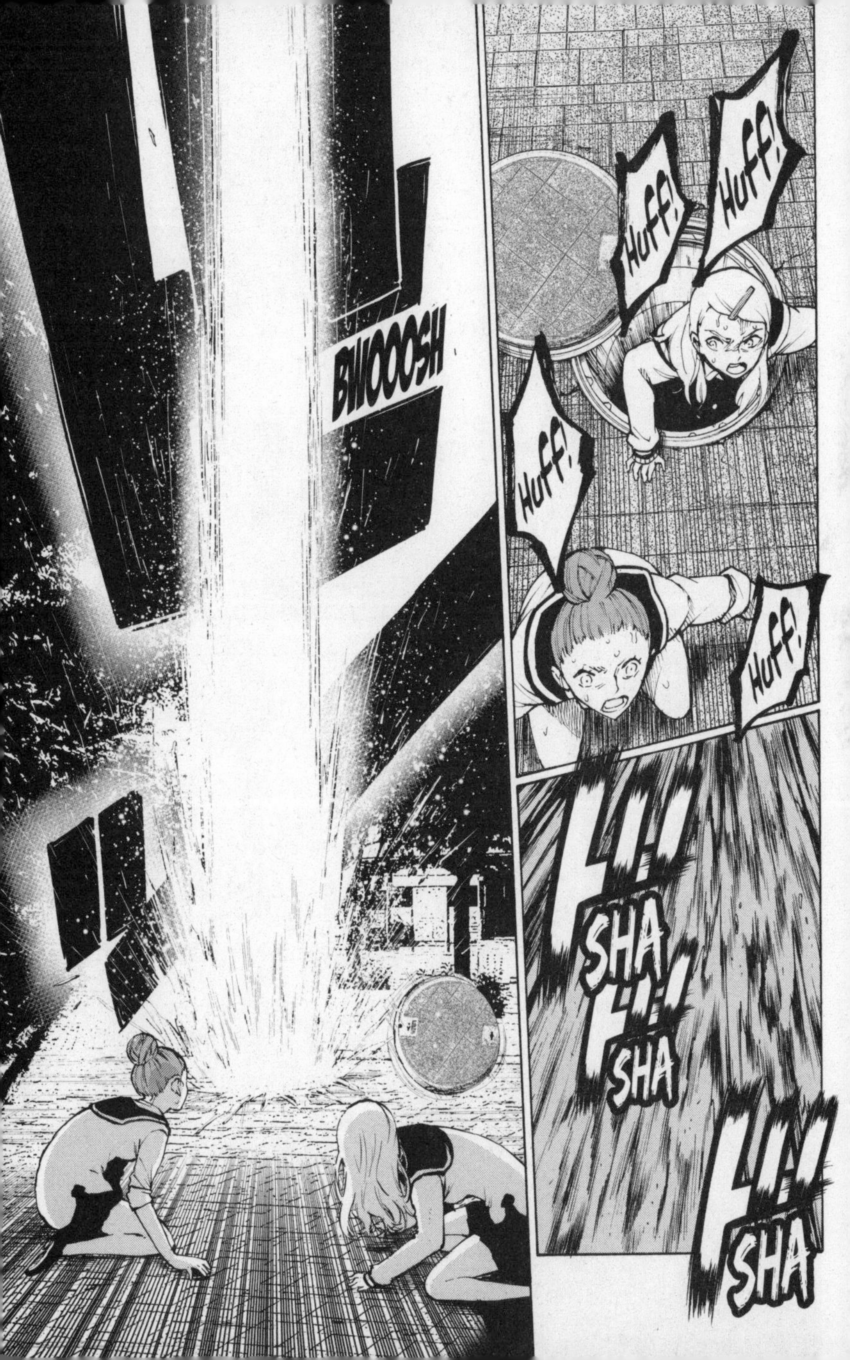
Huff!
Huff!
Huff!
Huff!
SHA
SHA
SHA
BWOOOSH

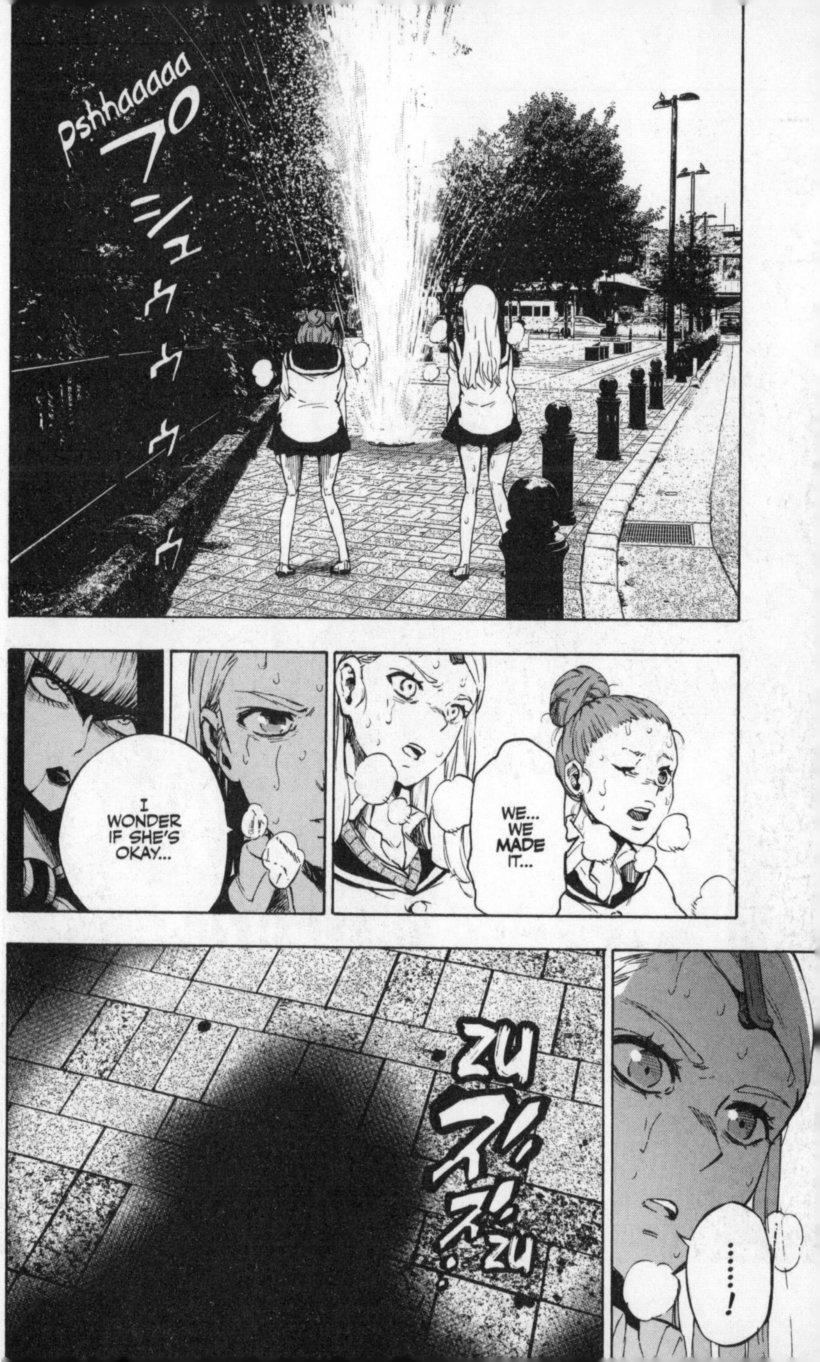
pshhaaaaa
プシュウウウウ
WE... WE MADE IT...
I WONDER IF SHE'S OKAY...
......!
zu
ズズ
zu

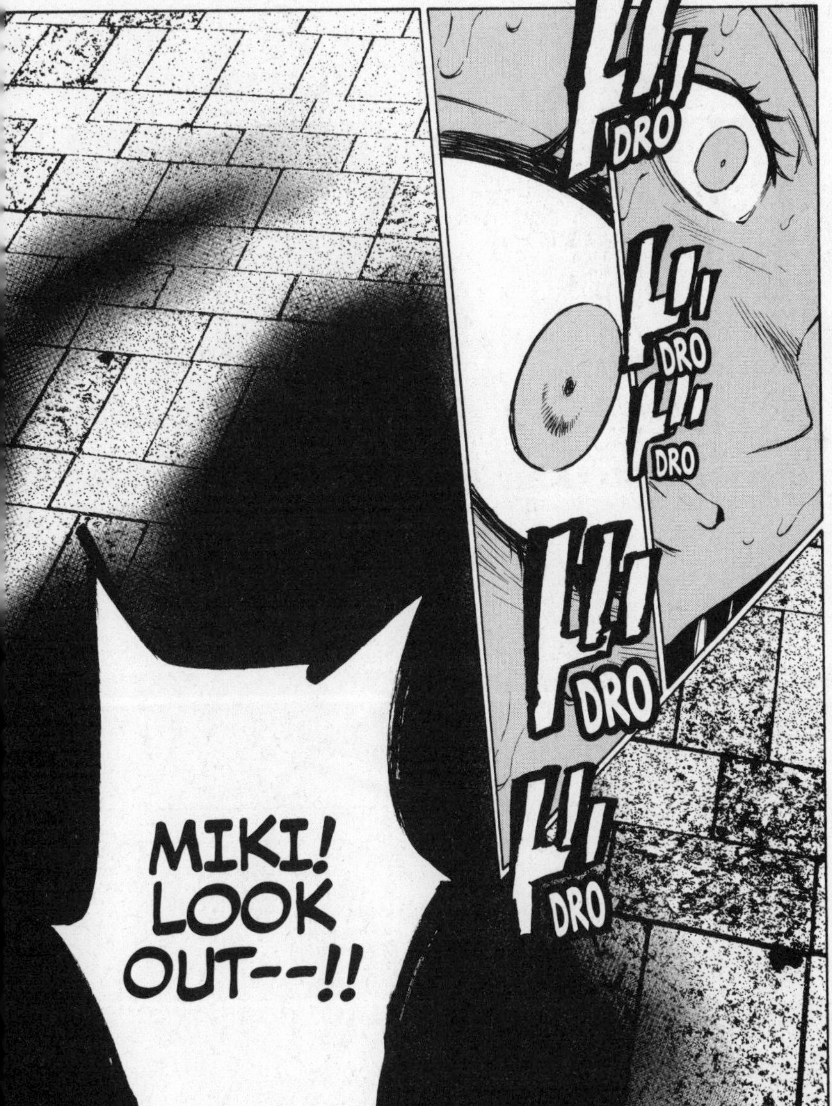
DRO
DRO
DRO
DRO
DRO
MIKI! LOOK OUT--!!

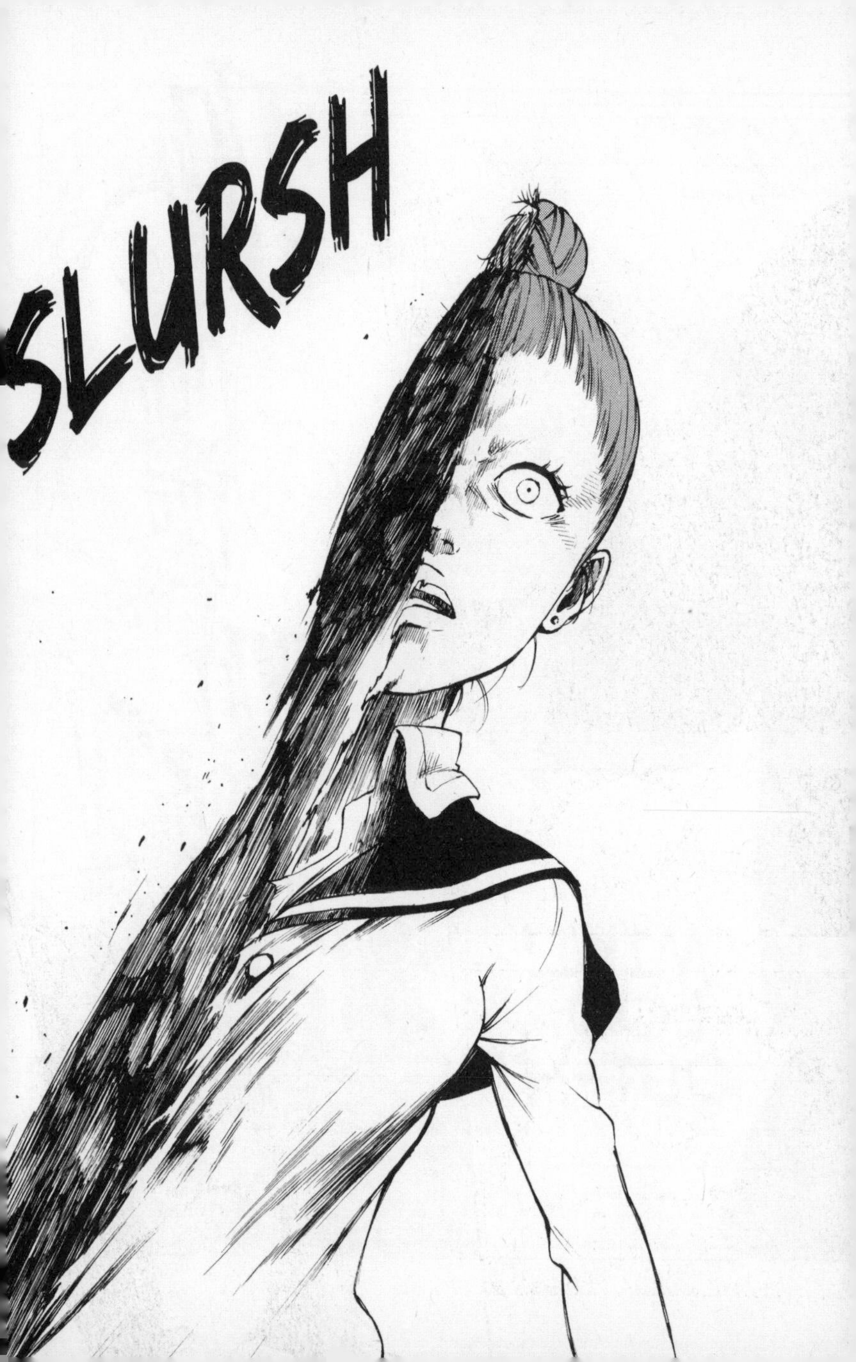
SLURSH

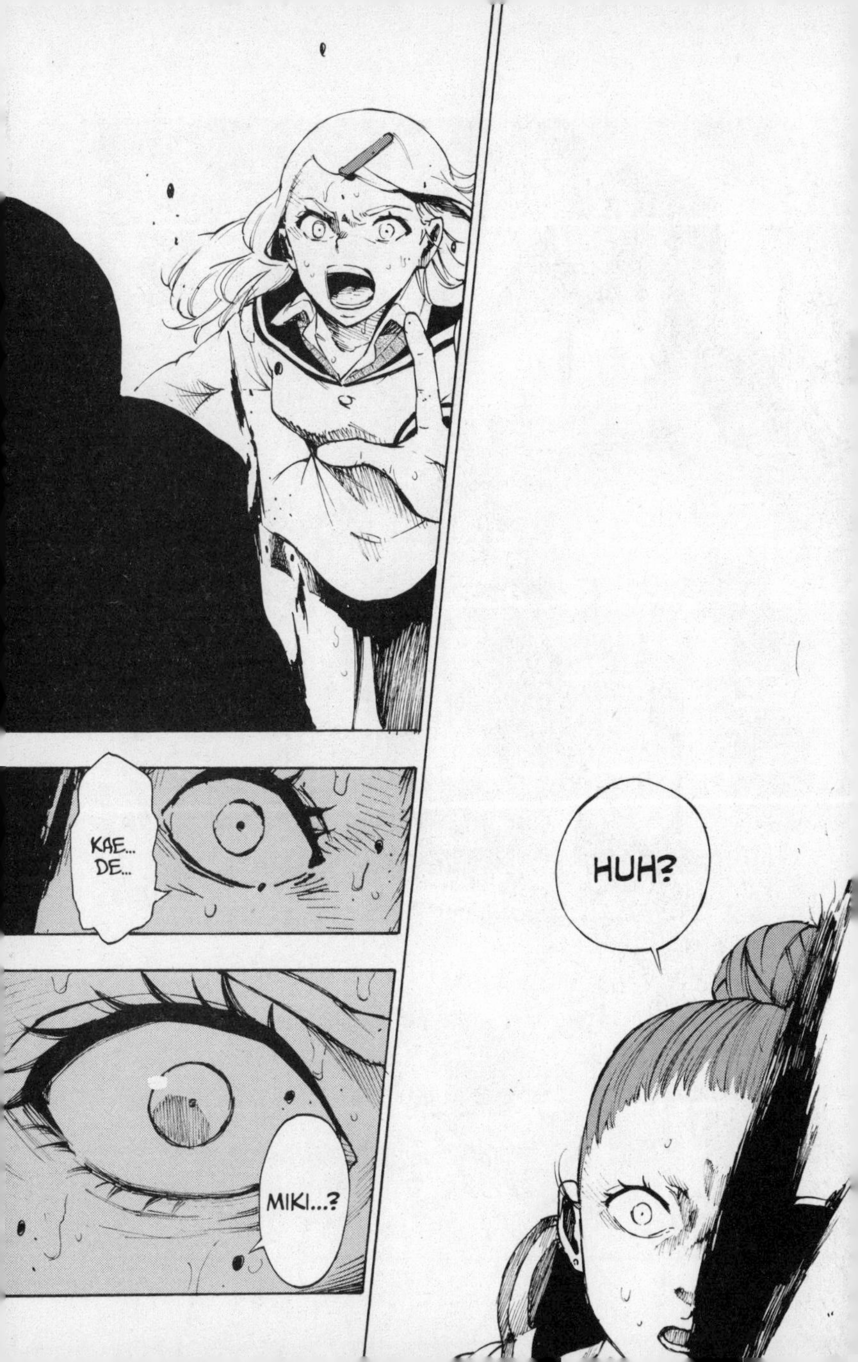
HUH?
KAE... DE...
MIKI...?

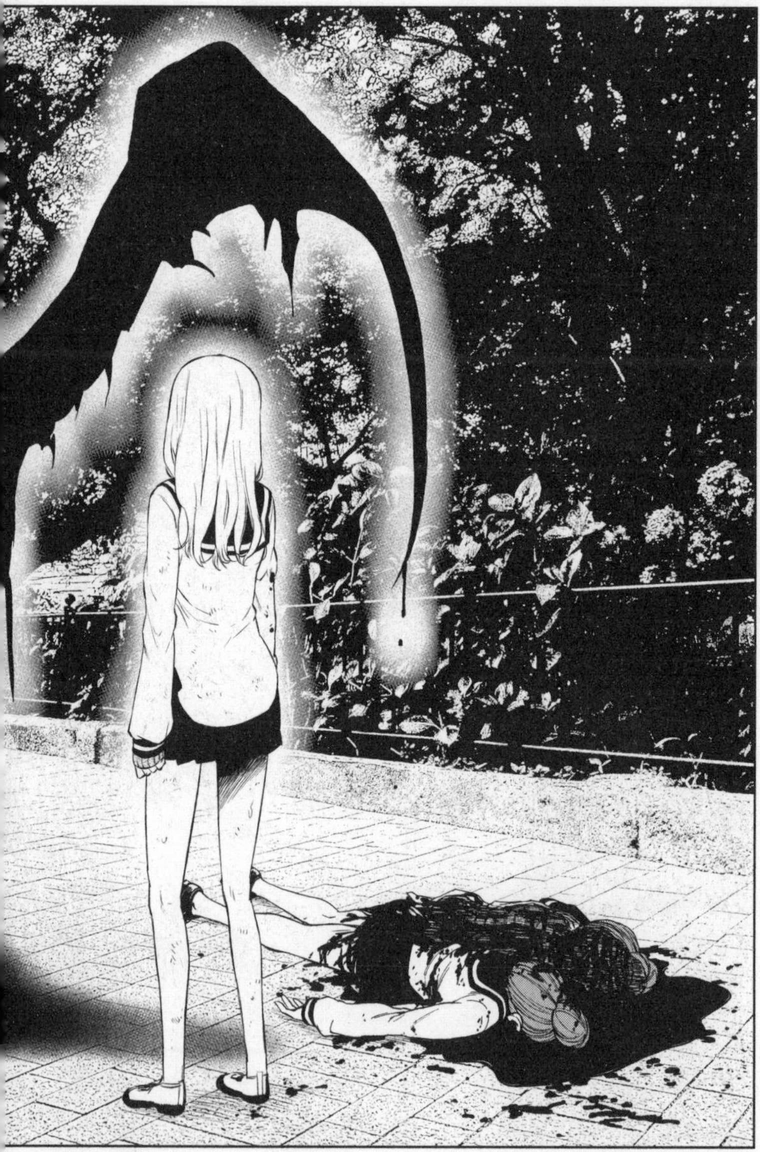

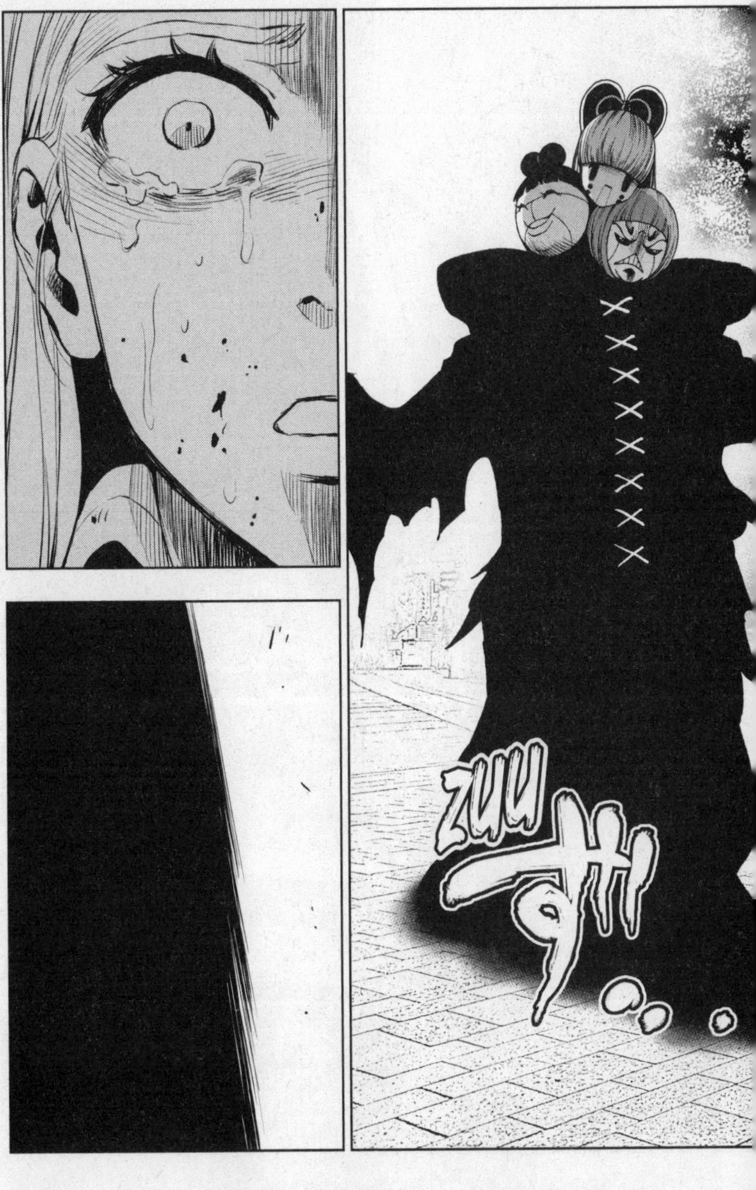
ZUU
ズ...

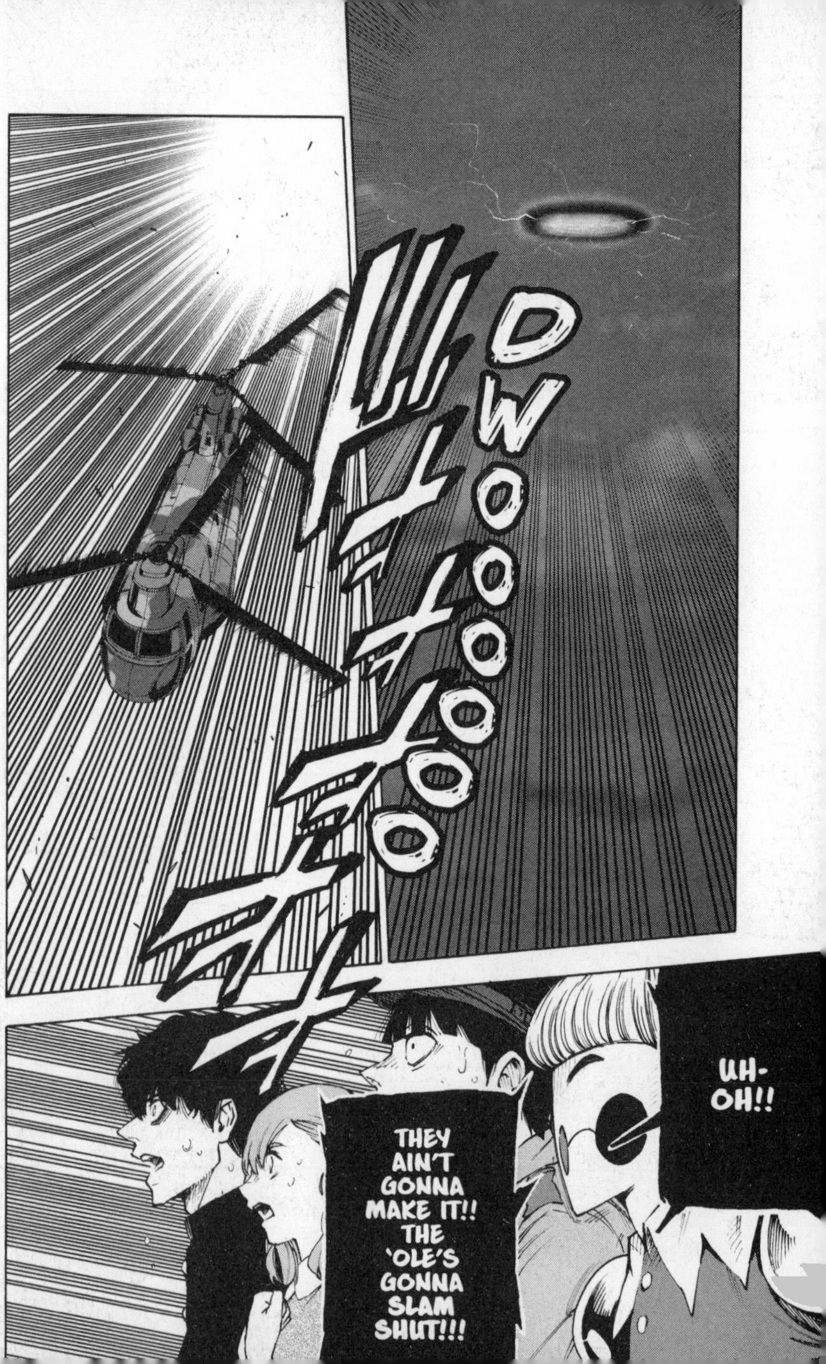
DWOOOOOO
UH-OH!!
THEY AIN'T GONNA MAKE IT!! THE 'OLE'S GONNA SLAM SHUT!!!

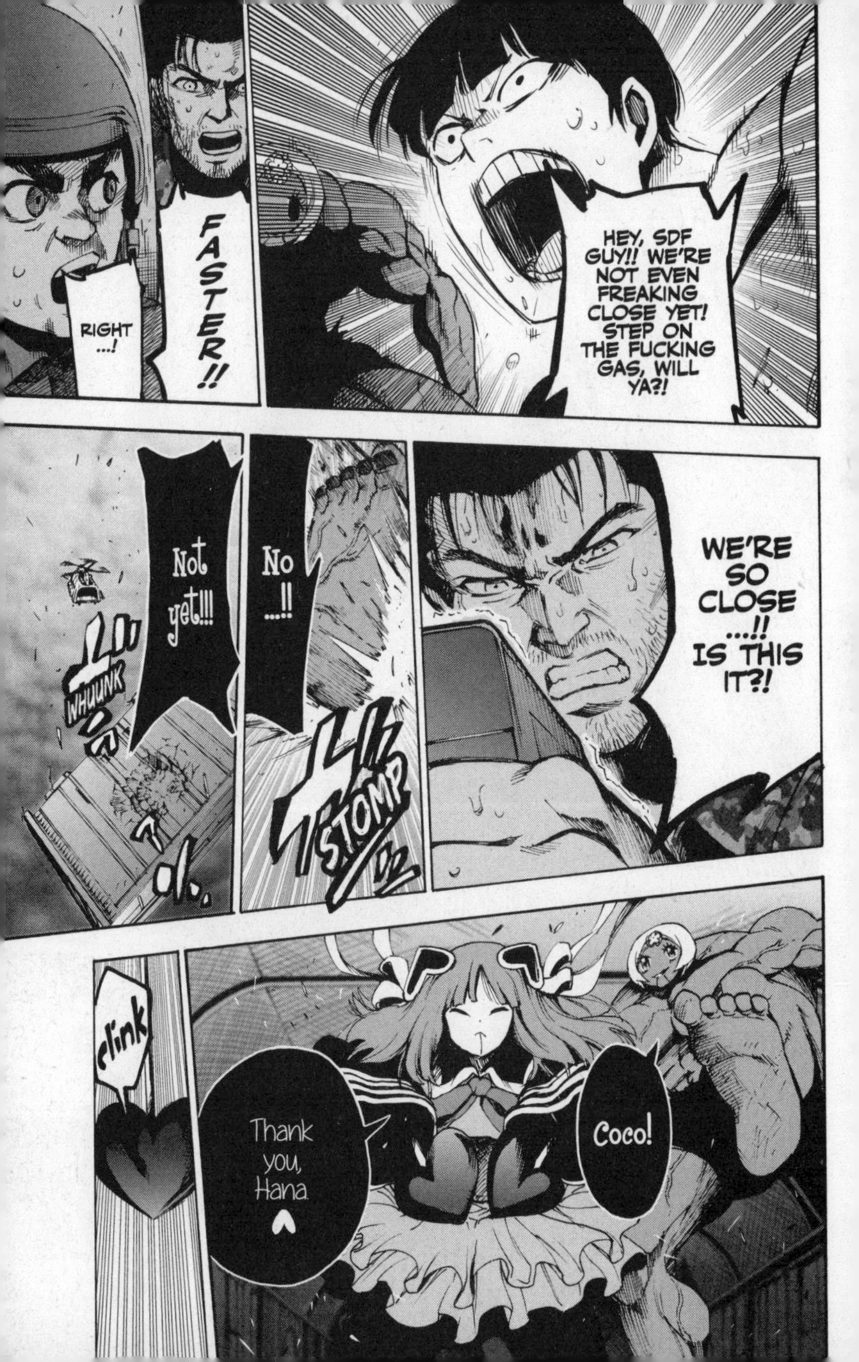
HEY, SDF GUY!! WE'RE NOT EVEN FREAKING CLOSE YET! STEP ON THE FUCKING GAS, WILL YA?!
FASTER!!
RIGHT ...!
WE'RE SO CLOSE ...!! IS THIS IT?!
No ...!!
STOMP
Not yet!!!
WHUUNK
Coco!
Thank you, Hana.
clink

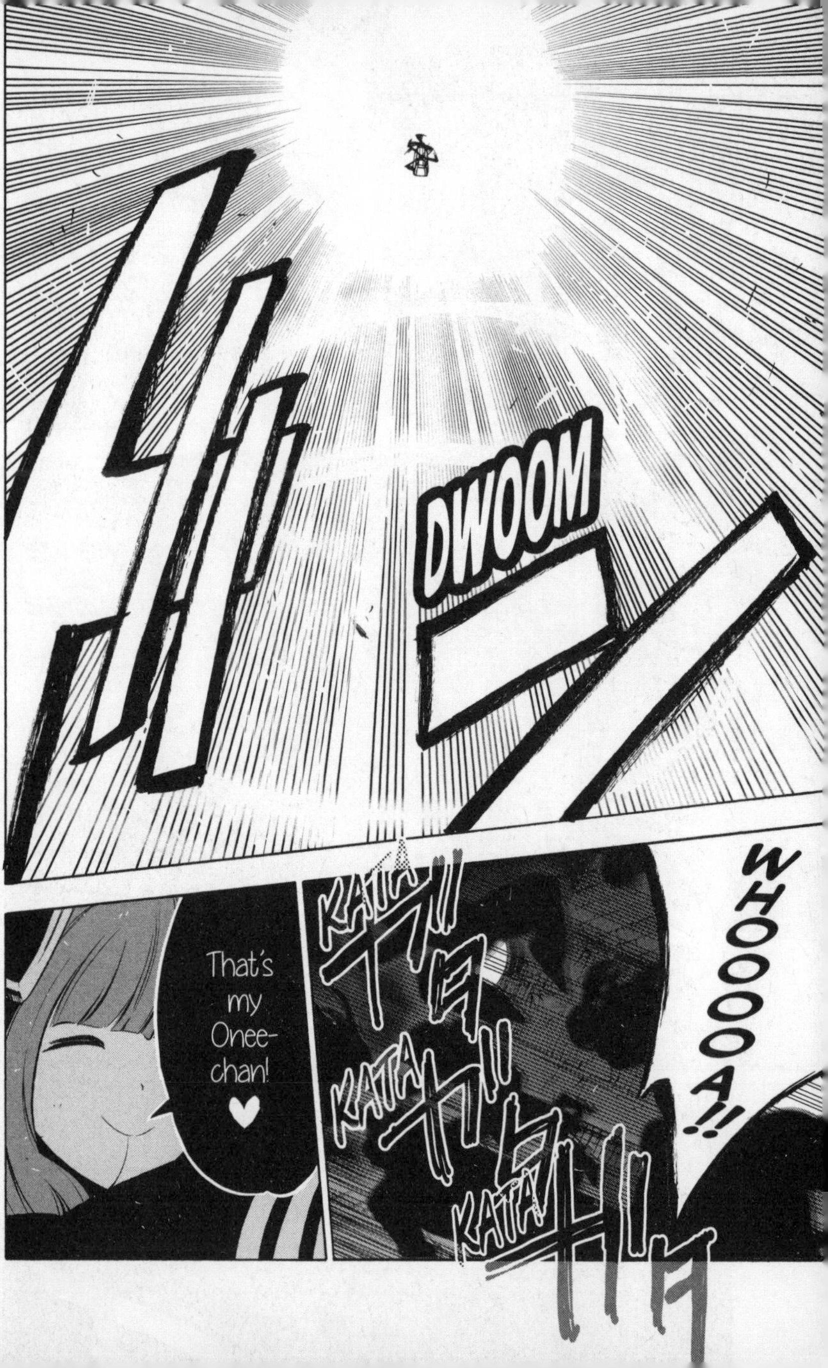
DWOOM
WHOOOOA!!
KATA
KATA
KATA
That's my Onee-chan! ♥

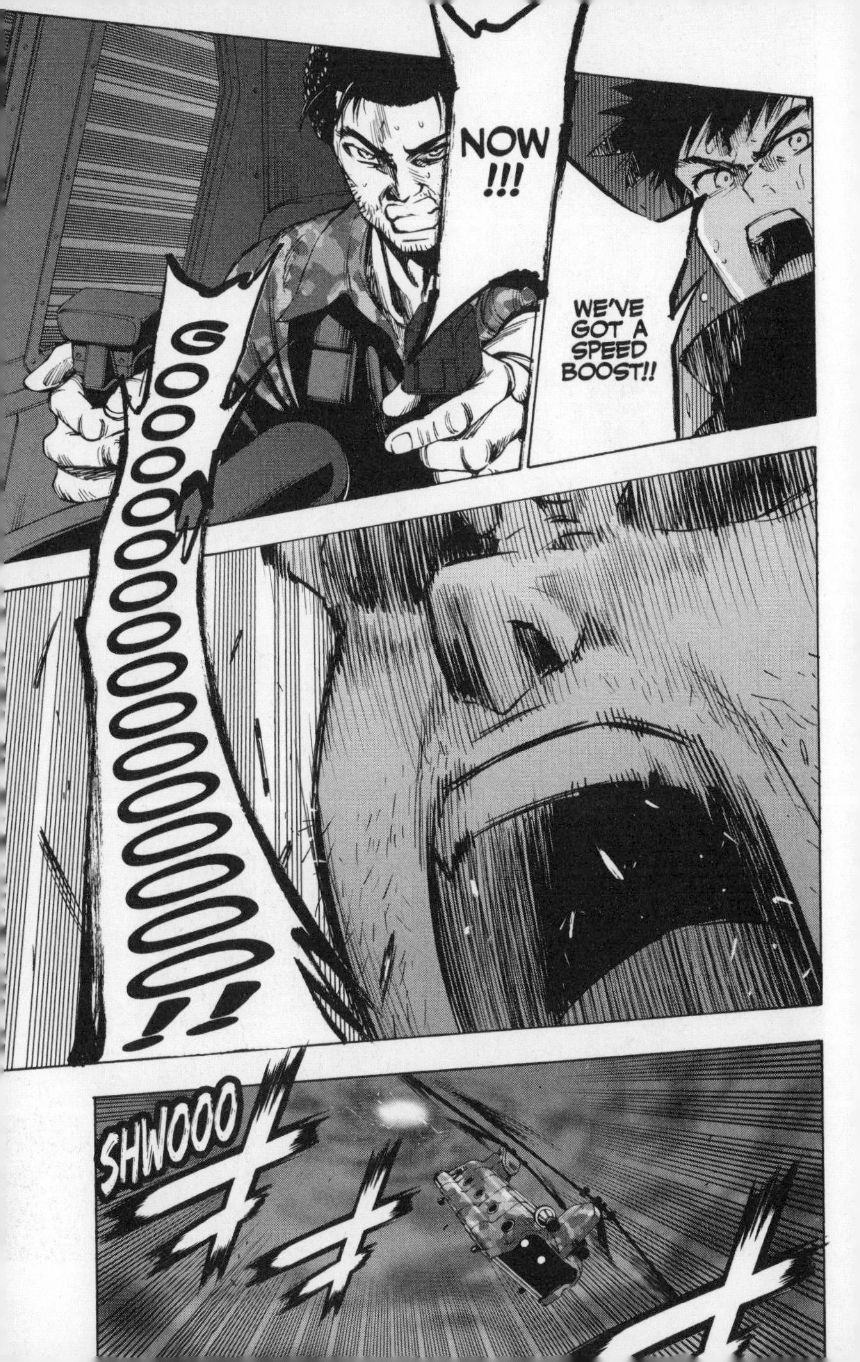
WE'VE GOT A SPEED BOOST!!
NOW !!!
GOOOOOOOOOOOOOOOOOO!!
SHWOOO

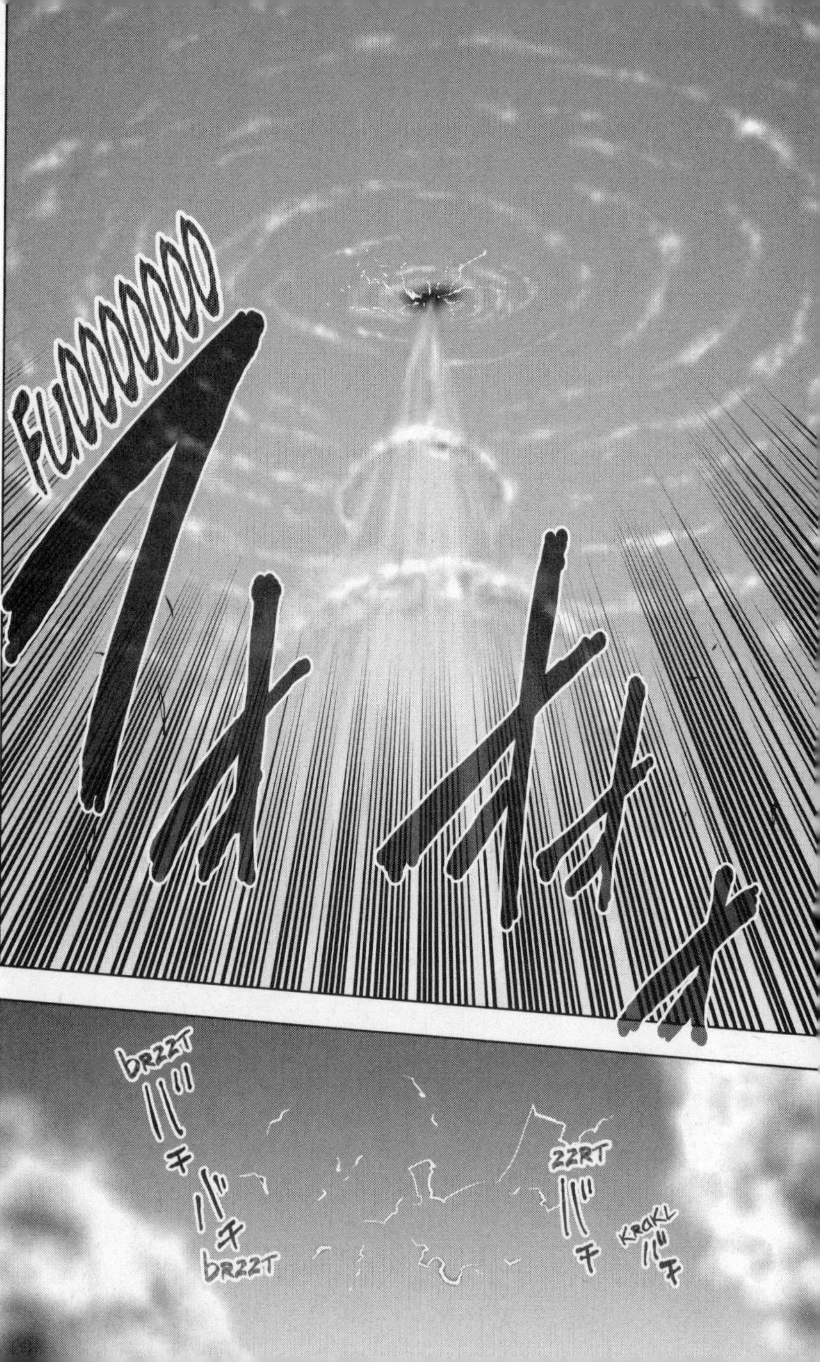
FUOOOOOO
フォォォォォ
ZZRT
バチ
KRAKL
バチ
bRZZT
バチバチ
bRZZT

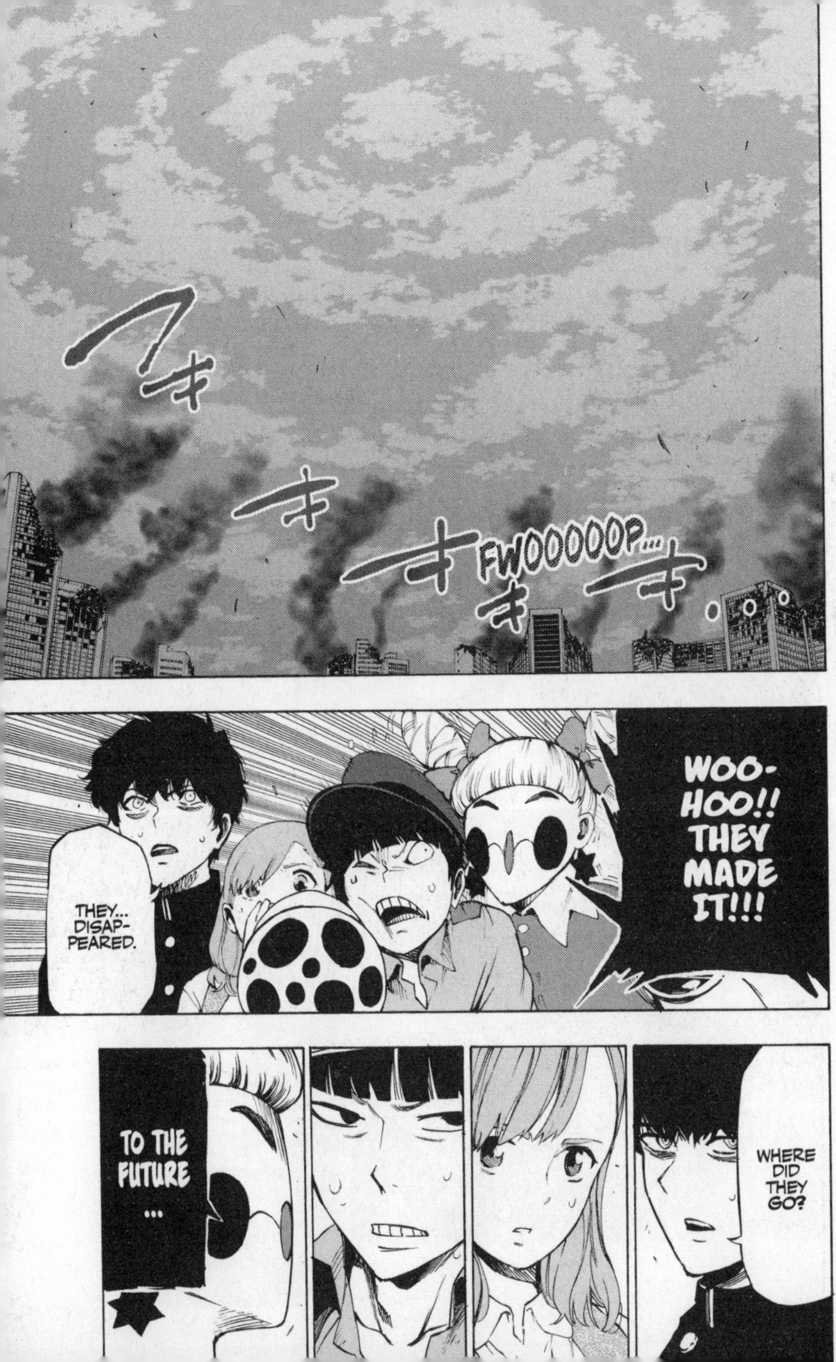
FWOOOOOP...
WOO-HOO!! THEY MADE IT!!!
THEY... DISAP-PEARED.
WHERE DID THEY GO?
TO THE FUTURE ...

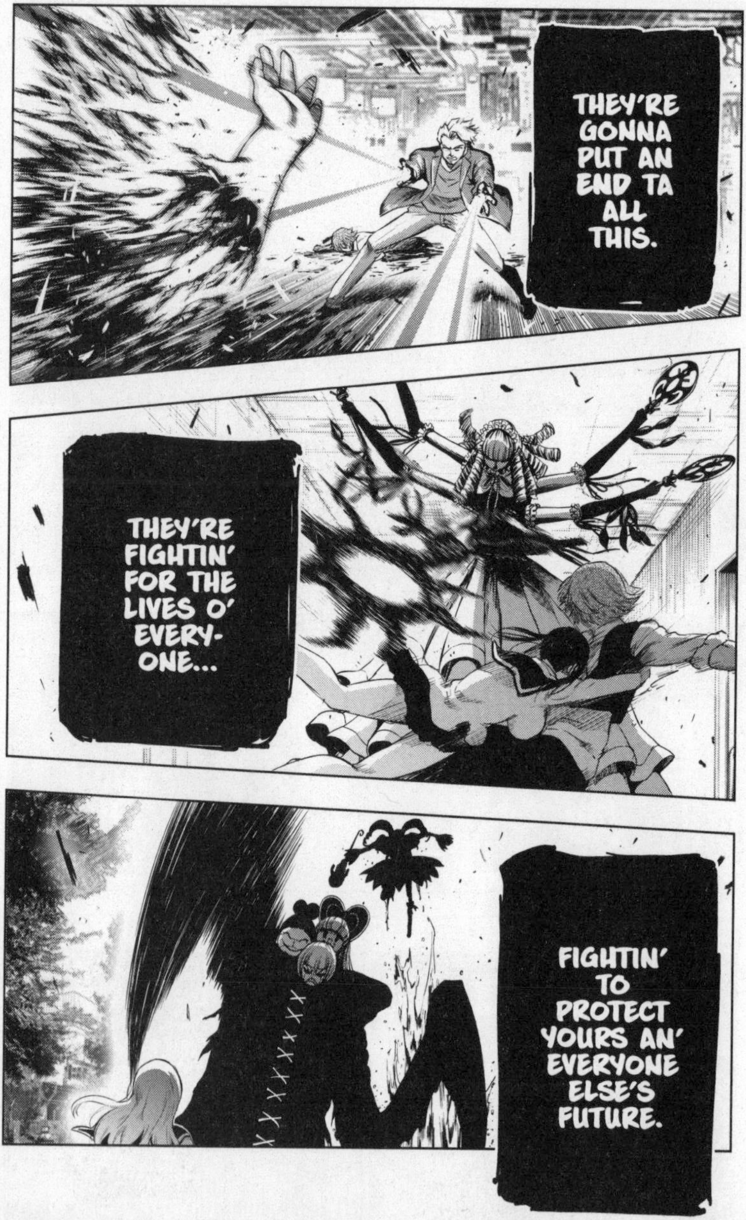
THEY'RE GONNA PUT AN END TA ALL THIS.
THEY'RE FIGHTIN' FOR THE LIVES O' EVERY-ONE...
FIGHTIN' TO PROTECT YOURS AN' EVERYONE ELSE'S FUTURE.

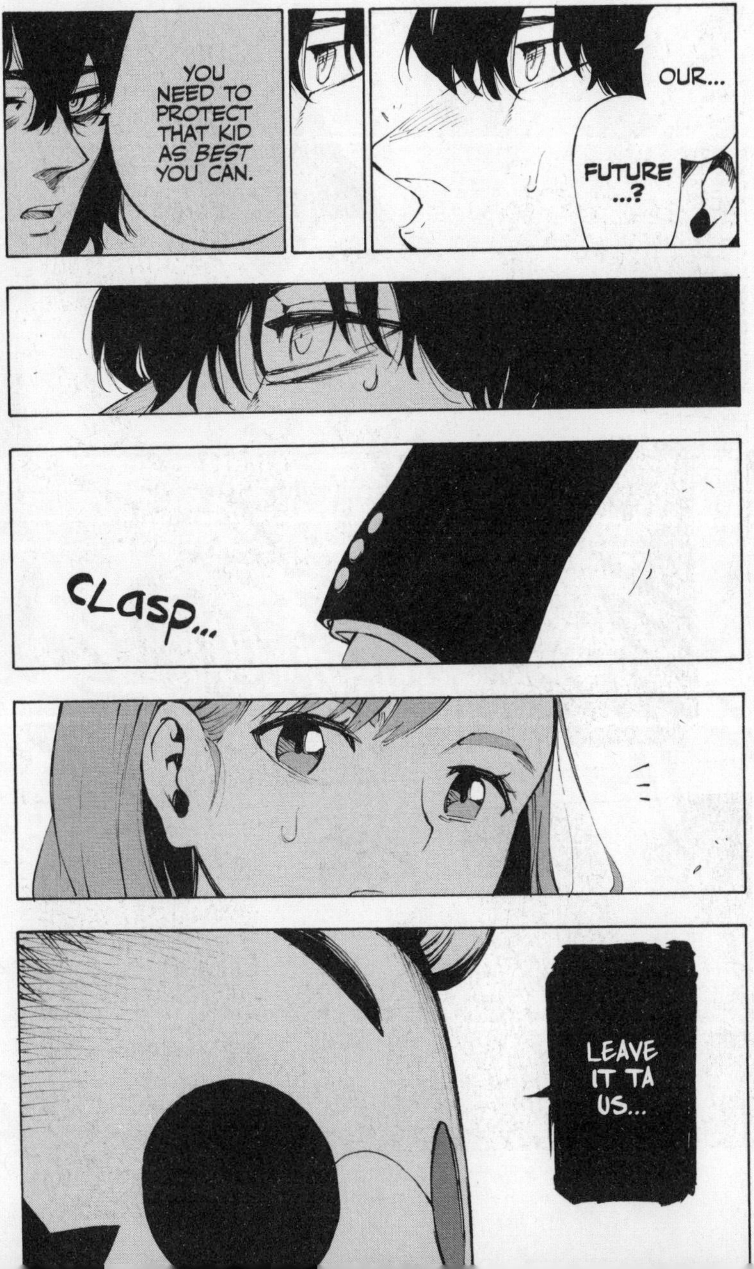
OUR...
FUTURE ...?
YOU NEED TO PROTECT THAT KID AS *BEST* YOU CAN.
CLASP...
LEAVE IT TA US...

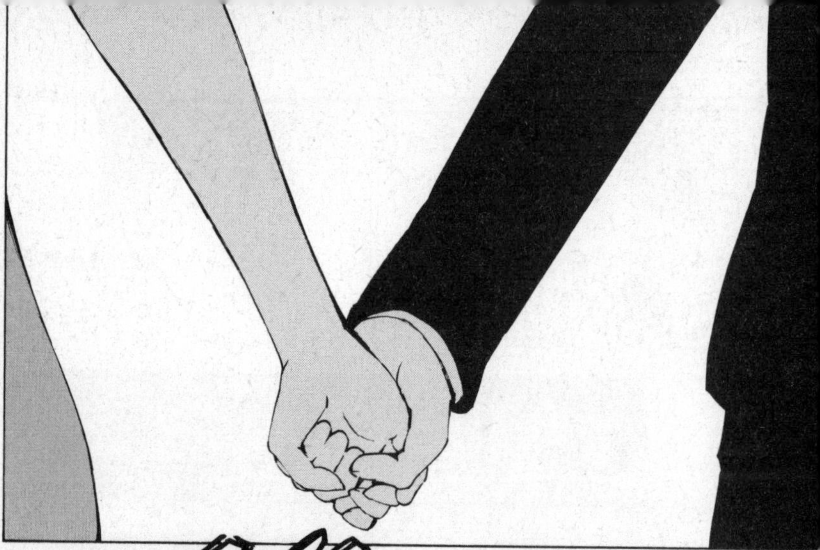
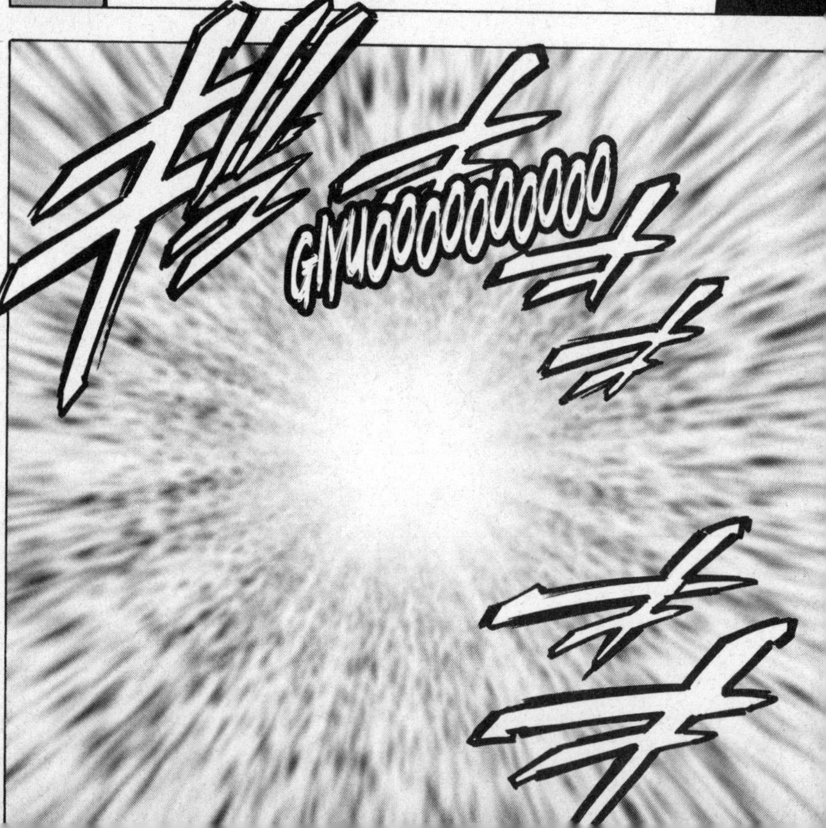
GIYUOOOOOOOOO

to be continued…

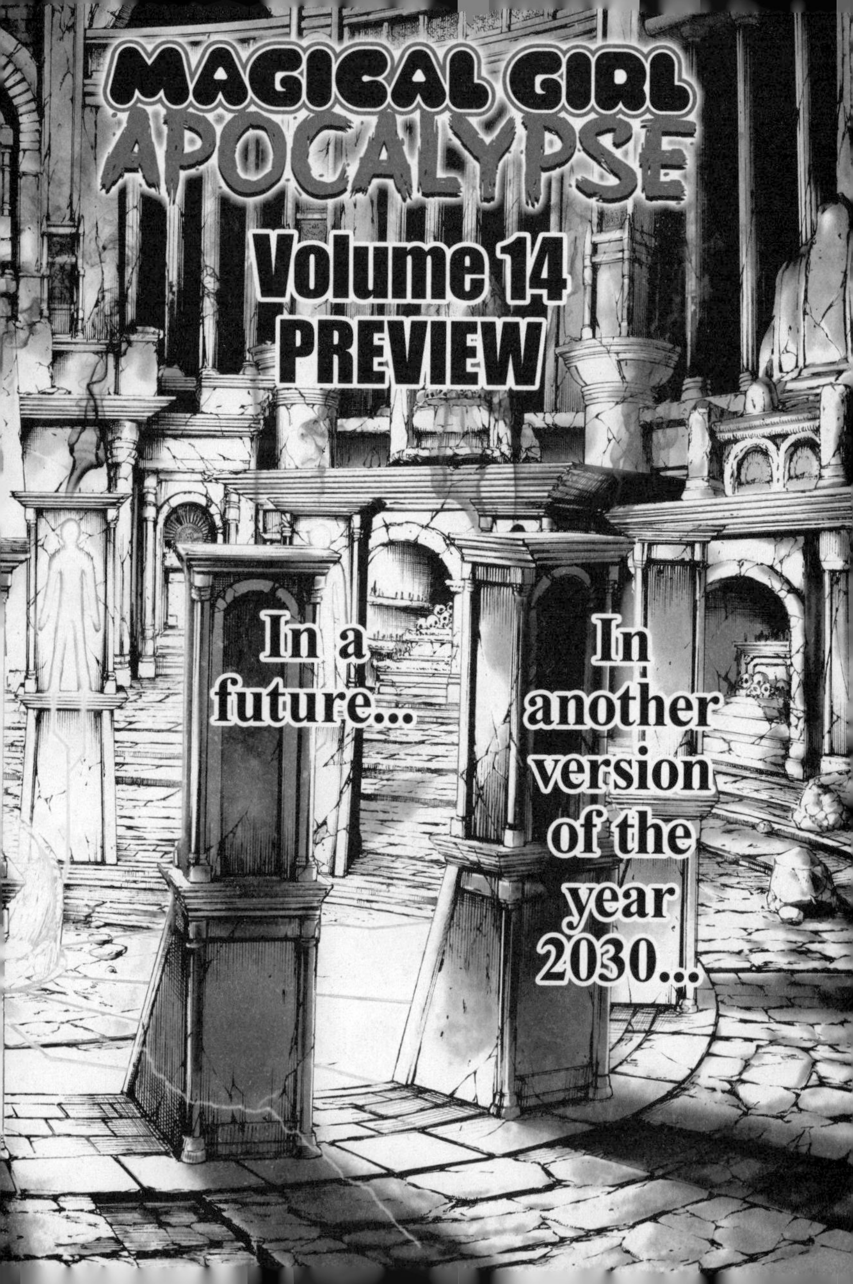
MAGICAL GIRL APOCALYPSE
Volume 14
PREVIEW
In a future...
In another version of the year 2030...

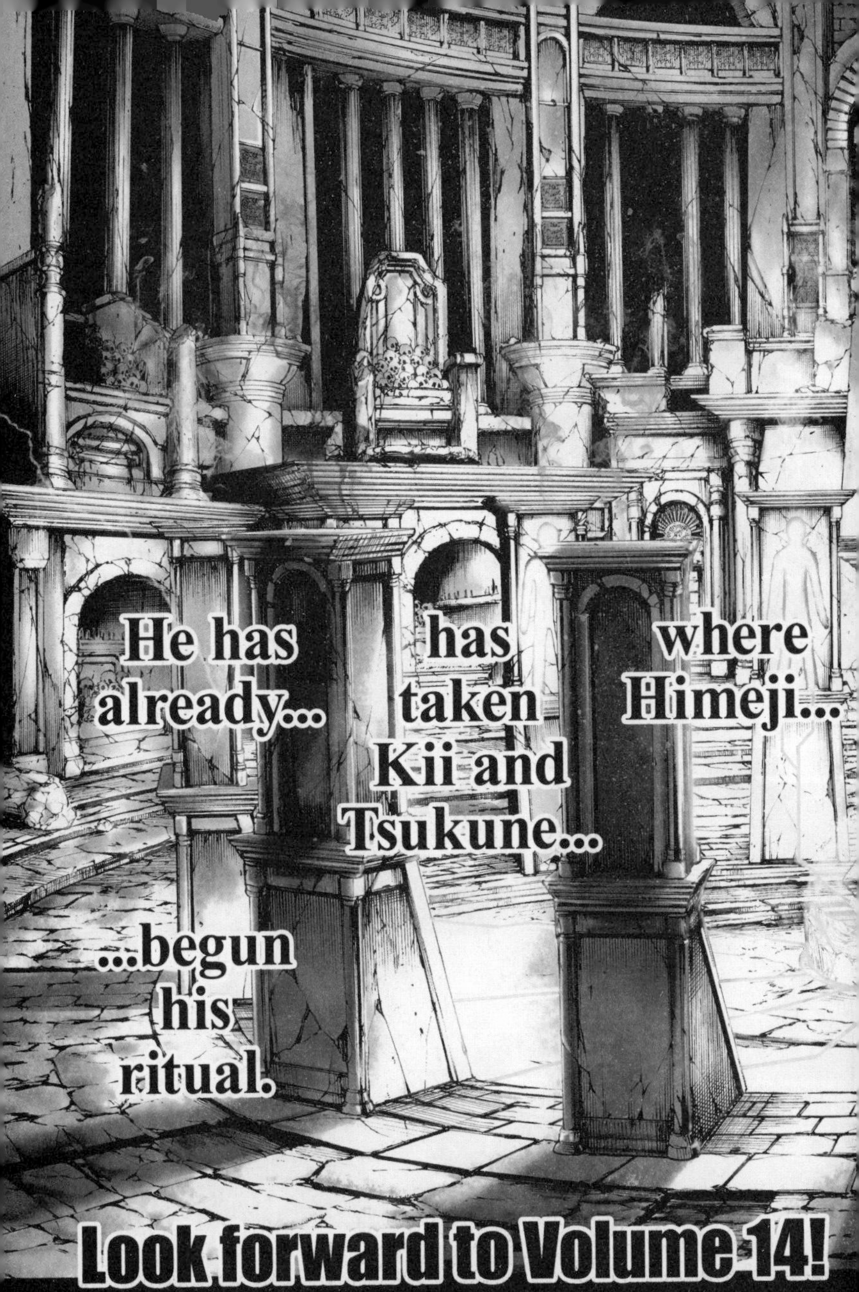
where Himeji...
has taken Kii and Tsukune...
He has already...
...begun his ritual.
Look forward to Volume 14!